D0294266

Human Biology

for A2

Mary Jones, Geoff Jones

CAMBRIDGE
UNIVERSITY PRESS

CAMBRIDGE UNIVERSITY PRESS

Cambridge, New York, Melbourne, Madrid, Cape Town, Singapore, São Paulo

Cambridge University Press

The Edinburgh Building, Cambridge CB2 2RU, UK

www.cambridge.org

Information on this title: www.cambridge.org/9780521548922

© Cambridge University Press 2005

This book is in copyright. Subject to statutory exception
and to the provisions of relevant collective licensing agreements,
no reproduction of any part may take place without
the written permission of Cambridge University Press.

First published 2005

Printed in the United Kingdom at the University Press, Cambridge

A catalogue record for this publication is available from the British Library

ISBN-13   978-0-521-54892-2 paperback
ISBN-10   0-521-54892-6 paperback

Produced by Geoff Jones

Front cover photograph: child scuba diver; copyright Alexis Rosenfeld/Science Photo Library

COLEG LLANDRILLO
LIBRARY RESOURCE CENTRE
CANOLFAN ADNODDAU LLYFRGELL

GENERAL   9/07

087435   LRC   611 JON

Contents

Acknowledgements

We are grateful to the following for permission to reproduce photographs:

John Adds 3, 79, 104, 111, 113, 120, 228, 242t, 242b; Alamy 23 (f1 online), 36 (Photofusion Picture Library), 49 (Brian Atkinson), 122 (Tim Graham), 123 (Iain Masterton), 142 (Goodshoot), 159r (Agripicture Images), 185 (MedioImages Fresca Collection), 194 (Image Source), 224 (Ian M. Butterfield); Mark Colyer 144m, 144b, 145; Corbis 1 (Bettmann), 22 (Helen Atkinson), 28l (Paul Morris), 28r (Don Mason Photography), 41 (Bettmann), 43 (Nancy Cohn), 62 (Gideon Mendel), 71 (Kennan Ward), 83 (Reuters), 94 (Ed Kashi), 135 (Reuters), 140 (Patrick Bennett), 148l (Hulton-Deutsch Collection), 148r (Ray Bird/Frank Lane Picture Agency), 156 (Roger Ressmeyer), 165 (Bettman), 168 (Mike Buxton/Papilio), 207 (Bettmann), 214 (George B. Diebold), 227 (Reuters), 251 (Pascal Parrot), 259 (Darren Modricker); Getty Images 77 (John Gichigi/Allsport); Eleanor Jones 70t, 70b, 210l; Geoff Jones 144t, 146, 150 all, 154, 159l; Kospictures.com 18 (Charles Hood); Vanessa Miles 171; Nature Picture Library 151 (Chris Gomersall), 210r (Doug Wechser); Rosenbach Museum and Library, Philadelphia 245; Science Photo Library 10 (BSIP/Chassenet), 24 (Michael Donne), 48 (Mauro Fermariello), 81 (Geoff Tompkinson), 84 (Zephyr), 90 (Colin Cuthbert), 91 (John Greim), 101 (VVG), 118 (Andy Walker/ Midland Fertility Services), 126 (Garry Watson), 131 (Mauro Fermariello), 134 (CC Studio), 172 (Hattie Young), 201 (National Library of Medicine), 203 (Dr Yorgos Nikas), 211tl (Tom McHugh/Field Museum, Chicago), 211tr (Volker Steger/Nordstar – 4 Million Years of Man), 211ml (Christian Jegou/Publiphoto Diffusion), 233 (Saturn Stills), 235 (Ian Boddy), 238 (VVG), 254t (Susumu Nishinaga), 254b (Prof. P. Motta/Dept of Anatomy, University 'La Sapienza', Rome), 255 (Sheila Terry), 261 (Simon Fraser), 264 (Dr P. Marazzi), 265 (Sinclair Stammers), 266 (Will & Deni McIntyre); University of Liverpool 32 (Geoffrey Williams); University of Wisconsin-Madison 86 (Jeff Miller); Wellcome Photo Library 8 (University of Edinburgh), 15 (Dr David Furness), 125 (Wellcome Photo Library).

Picture research: Vanessa Miles

Introduction

This book has been endorsed by OCR as providing complete coverage of Unit 2866 and Unit 2867 of the OCR Human Biology Advanced GCE (A2) specification. Chapters 1 to 7 cover Unit 2866, *Energy, Control and Reproduction*, while chapters 8 to 12 cover Unit 2867, *Genetics, Homeostasis and Ageing*.

The material in this book builds on that covered in the AS course. In the examination papers for both Unit 2866 and Unit 2867, there will be synoptic questions that require you to draw together knowledge and concepts from your AS course and your A2 course. As you read through this A2 book, you will find regular references back to the AS text book, and you will probably find it helpful to follow up these cross references if you are uncertain that you have remembered all the relevant facts.

As in the AS book, the text generally follows the sequence of learning outcomes in the specification. One major exception comes right at the beginning of the book, where chapter 1 starts off with muscle structure and physiology, which is from the second section of this Unit, 5.3.1.2. The first section of the specification, 5.3.1.1, is covered later in the chapter.

Some chapters contain Activities and Procedures, which are boxed and contain text printed in black. You should try to carry out most of the Activities yourself. Most of the Procedures, however, cover techniques carried out in hospitals or by paramedics, and you are not expected to do these yourself – although in some cases you may be able to. You need to learn these Procedures, as they are all listed in the specification and may be tested in your examination papers.

Self-assessment questions, SAQs, appear in every chapter. These are designed to help you to think about and to use the information within the chapter. Many of these questions involve handling and interpretation of data. You should try to do all of the SAQs, and check your answers against those given on pages 270 to 283.

As in the AS text book, each chapter begins with a Case Study, and there are usually other Case Studies within the chapter. The Case Studies are boxed and printed in blue. There are also boxes containing material that takes the subject a little further, sometimes by delving deeper into a particular concept, and sometimes by looking at a wider field of interest related to the specification. These are also printed in blue. So anything printed in blue will probably make interesting reading for you, but you do not need to learn it. These Case Studies and Just for Interest boxes may provide you with ideas for Unit 2868, the Extended Investigation.

Just as for the AS text book, *Human Biology for A2* contains a large vocabulary of technical

terms. You need to be able to use these terms
confidently and appropriately when you write
answers in your examinations. Each new term is
explained as you meet it in the text. The
Glossary on pages 284 to 294 provides
definitions or explanations of most of these
terms. Remember that you will also need to use
the terms that you learnt in your AS course,
which are found in the Glossary in *Human
Biology for AS*.

Energy and respiration

In 1988, the final of the 100 metres at the Seoul Olympics provided one of the closest finishes ever. Four of the runners broke the 10-second barrier. The fastest of these was Ben Johnson of Canada. He not only crossed the line first, but he also broke the world record – though only by one hundredth of a second. He was the fastest human ever.

But Johnson's gold medal was taken away from him only 62 hours after the race. He had tested positive for a drug called stanozolol. He was banned from competing for two years. The runner who came second in the race, Carl Lewis of the USA, was awarded the gold medal.

Stanozolol is listed in the World Anti-Doping Code as an 'anabolic steroid'. A steroid is a type of hormone made from cholesterol (see pages 46–47) and an anabolic steroid is one that stimulates the body to produce more muscle. Ben Johnson had been taking anabolic steroids, given to him by his coach and team doctor, for six years before the 1988 race. The drugs had helped Johnson to build muscle size and strength. After his two-year ban he tried to get back into his sport, but he tested positive for steroids again in 1993, after which he was banned from competing for life in world competition. Following an appeal in 1999, he was allowed to compete in Canada, where he failed yet another drugs test later that year.

Now athletes are tested much more regularly for drugs, and at any time, not just at times when they are competing. But it seems that a few athletes do keep trying to find a way round the regulations. New tests are always being developed, trying to keep one step ahead of some athletes and their trainers who are prepared to use drugs to enhance performance.

ATP and muscle contraction

The temptation to take anabolic steroids was clearly too much for Ben Johnson. The extra abilities they gave him, by increasing his muscle bulk and strength, allowed him to reach the very top in his sport.

Anabolic steroids activate receptor molecules in muscle cells, which causes the genes that code for the synthesis of muscle-building proteins to be switched on. In this chapter, we will look at what these proteins are, how they are involved in muscle contraction, and how they get the energy they need to do this.

ATP

All cells use a substance called **adenosine triphosphate**, usually abbreviated to **ATP**, as their source of energy. Fig 1.1 shows the structure of an ATP molecule. ATP is a **phosphorylated nucleotide**. It is similar to the nucleotides that make up DNA and RNA.

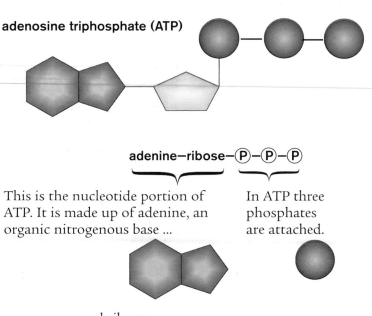

adenosine triphosphate (ATP)

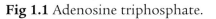

adenine—ribose—(P)—(P)—(P)

This is the nucleotide portion of ATP. It is made up of adenine, an organic nitrogenous base ...

In ATP three phosphates are attached.

... and ribose, a pentose sugar.

Fig 1.1 Adenosine triphosphate.

SAQ

1.1a What are the similarities between an ATP molecule and a nucleotide in a DNA molecule?

 b What are the differences between them?

ATP molecules contain energy. When one phosphate group is removed from each molecule in 1 mole of ATP, 30.5 kJ of energy are released. This is a hydrolysis reaction, and it is catalysed by enzymes called ATPases. The products of this reaction are ADP (adenosine diphosphate) and a phosphate group (P_i) (Fig 1.2).

$$ATP + H_2O \rightleftharpoons ADP + P_i \qquad 30.5 \text{ kJ released}$$

More energy can be obtained if a second phosphate group is removed. AMP stands for adenosine monophosphate.

$$ADP + H_2O \rightleftharpoons AMP + P_i \qquad 30.5 \text{ kJ released}$$

The each-way arrows in these equations mean that the reaction can go either way. ATPases may catalyse the synthesis of ATP, or its break-down.

ATP is used for almost every energy-demanding activity in the body. Table 1.1 lists some of these.

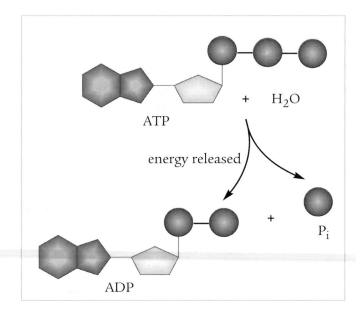

Fig 1.2 Energy is released when ATP is hydrolysed to ADP and P_i.

Table 1.1 The uses of ATP in the body.

Use	Examples
movement	Muscles use energy from the breakdown of ATP to enable them to contract. This causes movement of parts of the body such as the legs, tongue, alimentary canal and heart. Cilia use ATP to move. This moves fluid over them – for example, moving mucus up the passageways to the lungs. Chromosomes are moved around the cell during mitosis by spindle fibres, controlled by the centrioles; this requires ATP.
active transport	Cells use ATP to move substances across cell membranes up their concentration gradient. The protein transporters in the cell membrane use ATP to do this. The sodium-potassium pump is one example of active transport.
anabolic reactions	An anabolic reaction is one where small molecules are linked together to form large ones. This requires energy from ATP. Examples include the replication of DNA, transcription, the synthesis of proteins from amino acids on ribosomes, and the formation of glycogen from glucose molecules in a liver or muscle cell.
maintaining body temperature	The human core (internal) body temperature is maintained at around 37°C. This is usually higher than the surroundings, so heat is constantly lost to the air. To stop core temperature falling, cells use energy from ATP to fuel heat-generating actions – for example, rapid contraction and relaxation of muscles (shivering).

SAQ

1.2 The bar chart shows the relative rate of ATP use by a cell for its various energy–requiring activities.

a Explain why the sodium–potassium pump requires an input of energy.

b Explain why the synthesis of proteins, DNA and RNA requires energy.

c Suggest what the 'other uses of ATP' could be.

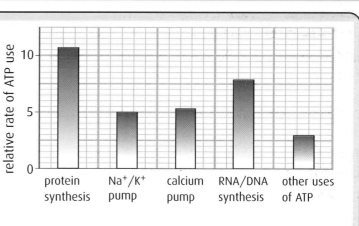

The structure of muscle

One of the major users of ATP in the body is muscle. Muscles use ATP all the time, even when you may think they are resting, but once they begin working their rate of use increases up to 150 times. Before we look at how and why muscles use all this ATP, you need to know something about their structure.

Figs 1.3–1.6 show **striated muscle**. The muscles attached to your skeleton, known as **skeletal muscles**, are made of striated muscle.

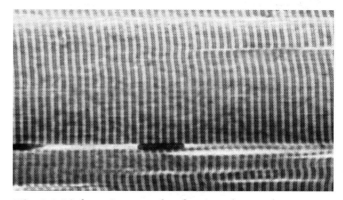

Fig 1.3 Light micrograph of striated muscle, stained to show the banding in muscle fibres.

3

Histology of muscle

Striated muscle is made up of many 'cells' of a similar type, all working together to perform a particular function. So muscle is a kind of **tissue**. The study of tissues is called **histology**.

A skeletal muscle in your body – for example, the biceps muscle in the upper arm – is made up of many **muscle fibres** (Fig 1.4), each about 80 μm in diameter and perhaps several centimetres long. If you look at a stained preparation of muscle fibres using a light microscope, it is possible to see that each fibre is stripey. The stripes make a particular pattern – dark bands alternating with light bands, with another narrow dark stripe down the middle of the light band. 'Striated' means 'striped'.

Each muscle fibre is a very specialised 'cell'. In fact, some biologists consider that it is not a 'cell' at all, because it contains many nuclei. A name for this type of structure is a **syncitium**.

We have two slightly different types of skeletal muscle fibres in our bodies, called fast-twitch and slow-twitch fibres. You can read about these on page 28 (in Chapter 2). Fast-twitch fibres are good for short bursts of intense activity, while slow-twitch fibres are better for activity sustained over a longer period of time. Ben Johnson's muscles, like those of all top-rank sprinters, must contain a large proportion of fast-twitch fibres.

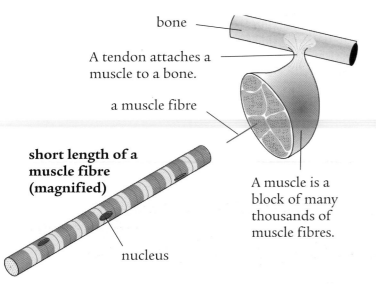

bone

A tendon attaches a muscle to a bone.

a muscle fibre

short length of a muscle fibre (magnified)

nucleus

A muscle is a block of many thousands of muscle fibres.

Fig 1.4 The structure of skeletal muscle.

SAQ

1.3 How does the size of a muscle fibre compare with that of a more 'typical' human cell, such as a lymphocyte? Suggest how this might account for the fact that muscle fibres are syncitial.

Ultrastructure of a muscle fibre

Each muscle fibre is surrounded by a cell surface membrane, often known as the **sarcolemma**. ('Sarco' means 'muscle'. Another term for 'muscle' is 'myo', and you will see that many of the structures in muscle have one of these two words in their names.) The membrane has deep infoldings into the interior of the fibre, called **T-tubules** (Fig 1.5). These run close to the endoplasmic reticulum, which again is often given a special name, **sarcoplasmic reticulum**. The cytoplasm (**sarcoplasm**) contains a large quantity of mitochondria, often packed in as closely as they could possibly be. These carry out aerobic respiration, supplying the ATP that is required for muscle contraction.

But the most striking thing about a muscle fibre is its stripes. These are produced by the arrangement of many small fibrils, called **myofibrils**, in its sarcoplasm. Each myofibril is striped in exactly the same way, and is lined up against the next one, so producing the pattern shown in the whole fibre.

This is as much as we can see using a light microscope, but with an electron microscope it can be seen that each myofibril is itself made up of yet smaller components, called **filaments**. Parallel groups of thick filaments lie between groups of thin ones.

Both thick and thin filaments are made up of protein. The thick filaments are made of **myosin**, whilst the thin ones are made of **actin**. Now at last the reason for the stripes can be seen. The darker parts of the stripes, the **A bands**, are where the myosin filaments are. The lighter parts, the **I bands**, are where the actin filaments are (Fig 1.6). The very darkest parts of the A band are produced by the overlap of the

short length of a muscle fibre

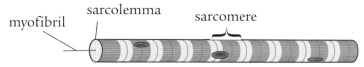

highly magnified edge of a muscle fibre

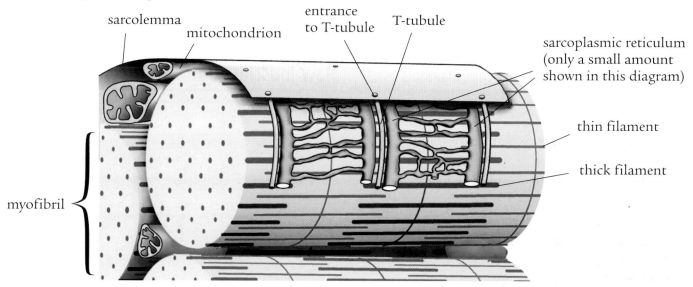

Fig 1.5 Ultrastructure of a muscle fibre.

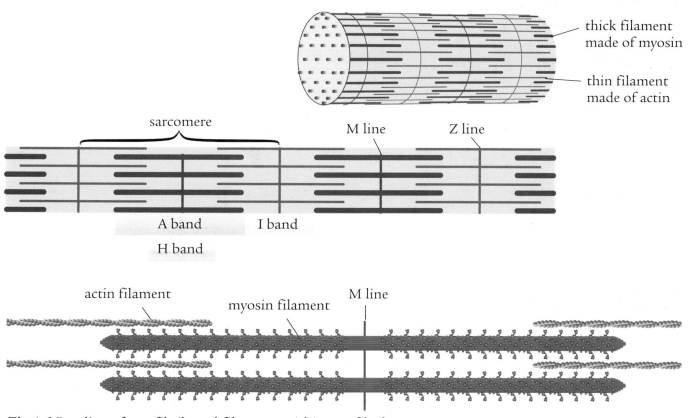

Fig 1.6 Banding of myofibrils and filaments within myofibrils.

myosin and actin filaments, while the lighter area within the A band, known as the **H band**, represents the parts where only myosin is present. A line known as the **Z line** provides an attachment for the actin filaments, while the **M line** does the same for the myosin filaments. The part of a myofibril between two Z lines is called a **sarcomere**.

The structure of the thick and thin filaments

Myosin is a fibrous protein. Each myosin molecule has a tail (attached to the M line) and a head. Several myosin molecules all lie in a bundle together, heads all pointing away from the M line, forming a myosin filament.

Actin is a globular protein, but many actin molecules link together in a long chain. Two of these chains twist together to form an actin filament.

Also twisted around these chains is a fibrous protein called **tropomyosin**. And a fourth protein, called **troponin**, is attached to the actin chain at regular intervals (Fig 1.7).

How muscles contract

Muscles cause movement by contracting. The sarcomeres in each myofibril get shorter as their Z lines are pulled closer together. Fig 1.7 shows how this happens. It is known as the **sliding filament theory** of muscle contraction.

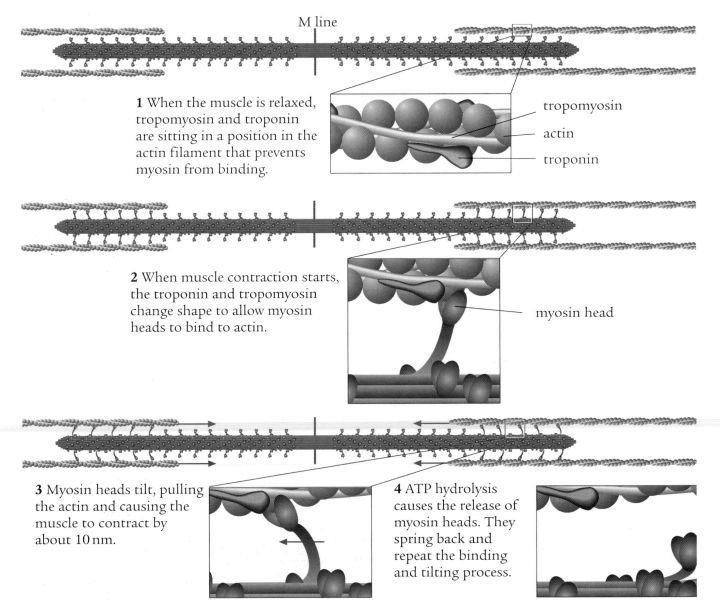

M line

1 When the muscle is relaxed, tropomyosin and troponin are sitting in a position in the actin filament that prevents myosin from binding.

tropomyosin

actin

troponin

2 When muscle contraction starts, the troponin and tropomyosin change shape to allow myosin heads to bind to actin.

myosin head

3 Myosin heads tilt, pulling the actin and causing the muscle to contract by about 10 nm.

4 ATP hydrolysis causes the release of myosin heads. They spring back and repeat the binding and tilting process.

Fig 1.7 Muscle contraction.

The energy for the movement comes from ATP molecules that are attached to the myosin heads. Each myosin head acts as an **ATPase**.

When a muscle contracts, the troponin and tropomyosin molecules change shape. They move to a different position on the actin filaments, and this exposes parts of the actin molecules which act as binding sites for myosin. The myosin heads bind with these sites, forming cross-bridges between the two types of filaments.

Next, the myosin heads tilt, pulling the actin filaments along towards the centre of the sarcomere. The heads then hydrolyse ATP molecules, which provides enough energy to force the heads to let go of the actin. They tip back to their previous positions and bind again to the exposed sites on the actin. But, of course, the actin has moved along by now, so the heads are now binding to a different part of the actin filaments. They tilt again, pulling the actin filaments even further along, then hydrolyse more ATP molecules so that they can let go again. This goes on and on, so long as the troponin and tropomyosin molecules aren't blocking the binding sites, and so long as the muscle has a supply of ATP.

Stimulating muscle to contract

Now you have seen what happens when muscle contracts, but what makes it do it?

Skeletal muscle contracts when it receives an impulse from a nerve cell (see page 65). As you will see in Chapter 4, nerve cells carry impulses in the form of **action potentials**, which are brief changes in the balance of plus and minus charges on either side of their cell surface membranes. An action potential sweeps along a nerve cell and then along the sarcolemma (cell surface membrane) of a muscle fibre, before plunging down into its centre along the membranes of the T-tubules (Fig 1.8).

The impulse is picked up by the membranes of the sarcoplasmic reticulum. Here, in the cisternae of the reticulum, calcium ions have been collecting up, pumped in by active transport. The arrival of the impulse causes this active transport to stop, and calcium channels in the membranes open. The calcium ions flood out, down their concentration gradients, into the sarcoplasm.

The calcium ions rapidly bind with the troponin molecules that are attached to the actin filaments. This changes the shape of the troponin molecules, which causes the troponin and tropomyosin to move away and expose the binding sites for the myosin heads. These attach, and the process of muscle contraction begins.

1 Nerve impulses (action potentials) $\longrightarrow$ run along the muscle fibre membrane (sarcolemma).

2 The sarcolemma is folded into the fibre along the T-tubules. The tubules take the impulses right into the fibre and along the membrane of the sarcoplasmic reticulum.

sarcolemma

T-tubule

sarcoplasmic reticulum

actin filament

3 When the impulses arrive at the sarcoplasmic reticulum calcium ions are released. $\longrightarrow$ They bind to the troponin of the actin filaments and muscle contraction starts.

Fig 1.8 How a nerve impulse makes a muscle contract.

1.4 The electronmicrograph shows some sarcomeres in part of a muscle that has contracted.

  a Name the parts labelled A to D.

  b Describe how you can tell that this electronmicrograph is from contracted muscle and not relaxed muscle.

  c The electronmicrograph is magnified 27 000 times. Calculate the length of the sarcomere labelled S. Give your answer in µm.

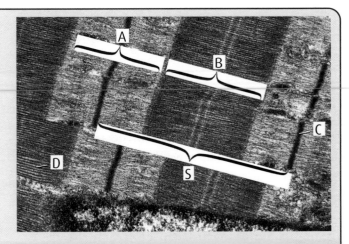

1.5 The diagrams show a sarcomere in four different states of contraction.

  a Name the parts labelled P to R.

  b Explain why there are no actin–myosin cross-bridges visible in diagram A.

  c Muscle fibres are able to contract with more force in some states of contraction than others. Suggest which of the diagrams shows the state that can develop the greatest force, and explain the reasons for your answer.

  d Explain why the muscle shown in diagram D would not be able to contract any further.

  e Muscle can contract with force, but it is not able to pull itself back to its original relaxed length.

  i With reference to the mechanism of muscle contraction, explain why this is so.

  ii Suggest how the muscle in diagram D could be returned to the state shown in diagram A.

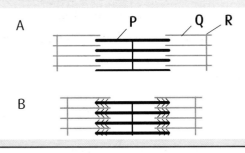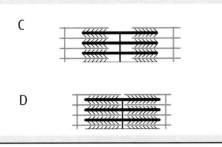

JUST FOR INTEREST

Duchenne muscular dystrophy

This genetic disease, seen only in boys, is caused by a faulty version of a large protein called dystrophin. This protein makes up part of the Z lines, and anchors the actin filaments in the muscle to the sarcolemma. With the faulty protein the muscles do not develop as they should. The first signs of the illness are seen when the boy is two or three years old. He will begin to have difficulties with walking, getting up from lying on the floor or a bed, and with walking upstairs. He is likely to be in a wheelchair by the age of 8 to 11. As the condition also affects heart muscle, he may not live beyond his early 20s.

There is no effective treatment for Duchenne muscular dystrophy, but there is research into a gene therapy solution to the disease. There is also a stem cell therapy being investigated. Trials in mice have shown some success, and clinical trials are now being carried out with human patients.

Summary

1 ATP, adenosine triphosphate, is the energy currency of every cell. It is needed for all energy-using activities, such as muscle contraction, active transport, anabolic reactions and maintenance of body temperature.

2 Energy is released from ATP when it is converted to ADP and P_i. This reaction, and the reverse reaction in which ATP is synthesised from ADP and P_i, is catalysed by ATPase.

3 Skeletal muscle is made of long fibres, each of which contains many nuclei and is known as a syncitium. Each fibre is surrounded by a cell surface membrane or sarcolemma, which dips deeply into the fibre at intervals to form T-tubules. The cytoplasm, or sarcoplasm, contains many mitochondria.

4 Skeletal muscle fibres look striped because of the regular arrangement of myofibrils inside. A myofibril contains thick filaments made of the protein myosin, and thin filaments mainly made of actin with smaller amounts of two other proteins, troponin and tropomyosin.

5 The tails of the actin filaments are attached to a Z line. The part of a myofibril between two Z lines is known as a sarcomere.

6 When an action potential (nerve impulse) arrives at a muscle fibre, it is carried deep into the sarcoplasm along the T-tubules. This causes the release of calcium ions from the cisternae of the sarcoplasmic reticulum, into the sarcoplasm.

7 The calcium ions bind with troponin, which moves the troponin and tropomyosin molecules and exposes binding sites for myosin on the actin filaments.

8 The heads of the myosin molecules bind with the actin filaments. The heads tilt, sliding the actin filaments towards the centre of the sarcomere. ATP is then hydrolysed by the myosin heads, providing the energy required for the heads to detach and reset to their original position. They then rebind and the process repeats itself.

Rigor mortis

Rigor mortis means 'rigidity of death'. After death, muscles become rigid. The time it takes for it to develop and then fade away can be used to determine the time of death.

In resting muscle, most myosin heads are not attached to actin filaments. Transporter proteins pump calcium ions into the cisternae of the sarcoplasmic reticulum, so troponin and tropomyosin cover the attachment sites.

When an animal or person dies, respiration in the muscles stops and ATP production ceases.

Calcium ions are no longer pumped into the cisternae of the sarcoplasmic reticulum, so myosin heads bind to the actin filaments. Because there is no ATP left, they stay attached and muscle is held rigidly.

Rigor mortis lasts for around 1 to 3 days. By this time, enzymes leaking out of lysosomes will have partially destroyed the cells, and the actin–myosin bridges will have broken apart. The times at which the various stages of rigor mortis occur are affected by a number of factors, of which temperature is the most important.

JUST FOR INTEREST

Aerobic respiration

Andrea is 17. Ever since she was small, she has not been strong, and she has found it very tiring and difficult to do any exercise that makes her the least bit out of breath. It has been getting worse lately and she has decided that there really must be something wrong, and that she wants to know what it is.

Her GP, too, has always been rather concerned about her, but she has never been dangerously ill and he has never pushed her parents to take her to a consultant for diagnosis. Now he does so. The consultant asks Andrea how she feels, and she describes the muscle cramps she gets whenever she tries to run or do any strenuous exercise. But she can walk all day with no problems.

Andrea has a blood test. The results take a long while to come back, because the consultant was not sure what he was looking for and therefore many different tests had to be done before they found a clue. Andrea has a faulty version of a gene coding for an enzyme called phosphofructokinase that should be present in her muscles. This enzyme catalyses one of the steps by which glucose is broken down in respiration, to produce the ATP her muscles need. This step is part of the first stage of respiration, called glycolysis. Andrea does have some working enzyme, but nowhere near enough. If her muscles are not working too hard, then enough ATP can be made to keep them going. There is no cure for her, but she should be able to lead a fairly normal life, so long as she avoids strenuous exercise.

The faulty enzyme that Andrea has catalyses a crucial step in a chain of reactions – or **metabolic pathway** – that gradually breaks down glucose, releasing some of the energy from the glucose which is used to synthesise ATP. This pathway is called **glycolysis**. 'Glyco' means 'sugar' and 'lysis' means 'breaking down'.

Every cell needs energy, so every cell needs ATP. We have seen how muscle cells use ATP. Other cells with different functions may not need quite so much ATP as muscles do, but they all need some. ATP is the 'energy currency' of a cell. ATP cannot be transported from one cell to another, so each cell has to make its own ATP. The reactions by which this happens are called **respiration**. In respiration, glucose or another substrate is oxidised, in a series of small steps, and some of the energy from the substrate is incorporated into ATP molecules.

The reactions of **aerobic respiration** take place in four stages – glycolysis, the link reaction, the Krebs cycle and oxidative phosphorylation.

Glycolysis

Glycolysis is a metabolic pathway that takes place in the cytoplasm of many of our body cells. Each step of the pathway is catalysed by a specific enzyme. Fig 1.9 shows this pathway.

Phosphorylation

The first step of glycolysis involves adding a phosphate group to the glucose molecule. This step actually *uses* ATP rather than making it. However, it is necessary in order to give the glucose molecule enough energy to react in the next step. The adding of phosphate is called **phosphorylation**.

Next, the glucose phosphate is changed to **fructose phosphate**. This does not add or take away anything, but simply reorganises the atoms in the glucose into fructose. Then another ATP is added, producing **fructose bisphosphate**. (This is the step catalysed by the enzyme phosphofructokinase, the enzyme that did not work correctly in Andrea's muscles.)

Fructose, like glucose, has six carbon atoms in each molecule. Now the fructose bisphosphate splits apart to form two molecules of **triose phosphate**, each with three carbon atoms.

Oxidation

Both of the triose phosphate molecules are now gradually converted to another 3-carbon molecule, **pyruvate**, in a series of small steps. These steps involve the removal of hydrogen, so they are oxidation reactions (Fig 1.10). The enzymes that catalyse this reaction are known as **dehydrogenases**. The general term for enzymes that bring about reactions involving **oxidation** and **reduction** is **oxidoreductases**.

The hydrogen is taken up by a substance called **NAD**, which is therefore reduced to $NADH + H^+$ (reduced NAD). The reaction won't happen unless oxidised NAD is there to pick up the hydrogen, so NAD is said to be a **coenzyme**. It is essential for it to be present before the enzyme that catalyses this reaction can operate.

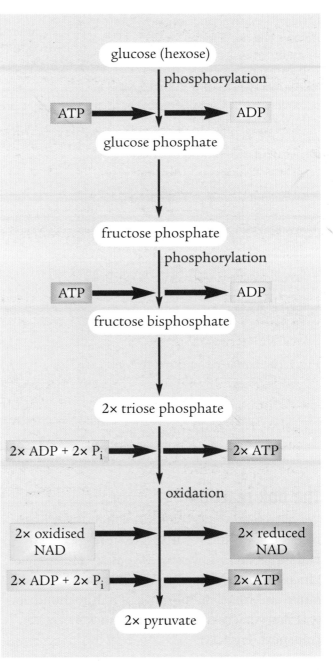

Fig 1.9 Glycolysis.

We will come back later to look more closely at what happens to the reduced NAD after this process.

SAQ

1.6   When one substance is reduced, another is usually oxidised. When NAD is reduced to $NADH + H^+$ in glycolysis, what substance is oxidised?

Oxidation and reduction can involve the movement of an atom of hydrogen from one substance to another. The substance losing the hydrogen is oxidised and the substance gaining it is reduced.

Other oxidation and reduction reactions are listed in this table.

Oxidation	Reduction
loss of hydrogen atoms	gain of hydrogen atoms
loss of electrons	gain of electrons
gain of oxygen atoms	loss of oxygen atoms

Fig 1.10 Oxidation and reduction.

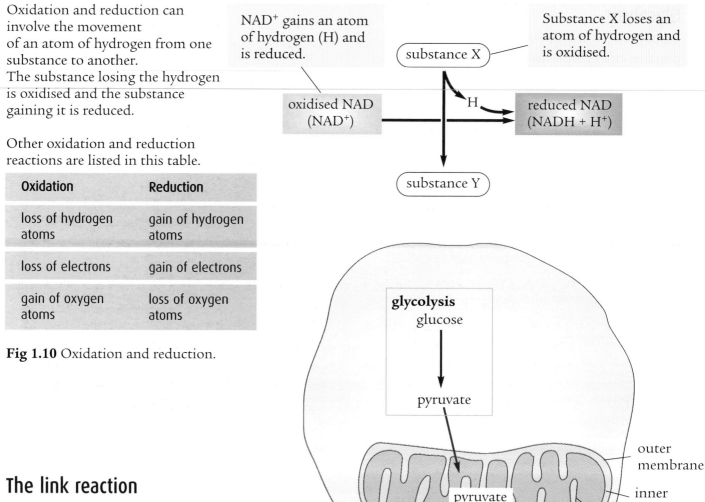

NAD$^+$ gains an atom of hydrogen (H) and is reduced.

Substance X loses an atom of hydrogen and is oxidised.

substance X

oxidised NAD (NAD$^+$)

H

reduced NAD (NADH + H$^+$)

substance Y

glycolysis
glucose

pyruvate

outer membrane

inner membrane

pyruvate

crista

matrix

Fig 1.11 Pyruvate is moved into the mitochondrial matrix, where the link reaction, Krebs cycle and oxidative phosphorylation occur.

The link reaction

We have seen that glycolysis, which takes place in the cytoplasm, results in the production of two molecules of pyruvate for every molecule of glucose. The pyruvate now passes through the outer and inner membranes of a mitochondrion. It is moved across these membranes by active transport (Fig 1.11).

In the matrix of the mitochondrion, carbon dioxide is removed from the pyruvate (Fig 1.12). This is called **decarboxylation**. The carbon dioxide diffuses out of the mitochondrion, then out of the cell. As pyruvate is a 3-carbon (3-C) compound, the loss of one of its carbon atoms when carbon dioxide is removed converts it to a 2-C compound.

At the same time, hydrogen is removed, which – just as in glycolysis – is picked up by NAD. The rest of the pyruvate combines with **coenzyme A** (CoA) to produce **acetyl coenzyme A** (acetyl CoA).

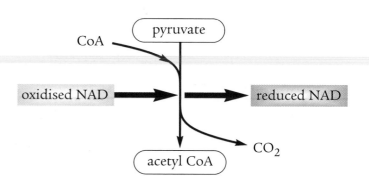

CoA

pyruvate

oxidised NAD

reduced NAD

acetyl CoA

CO$_2$

Fig 1.12 The link reaction.

SAQ

1.7   Describe what happens to the carbon dioxide that is made in the link reaction, once it has diffused out of the cell.

Krebs cycle

The acetyl CoA, still in the matrix of the mitochondrion, now becomes a substrate in a cycle of metabolic reactions called the **Krebs cycle**. Fig 1.13 shows some of the main steps in this cycle.

The acetyl CoA first combines with a 4-carbon compound called **oxaloacetate**. (You can see that the coenzyme A part is given off at this point, ready to combine with more pyruvate.) This produces a 6-carbon compound called **citrate**. In a series of small steps, the citrate is converted back to oxaloacetate. As this happens, more

carbon dioxide is released and more NAD is reduced as it accepts hydrogen. In one stage, a different coenzyme, called **FAD**, accepts hydrogen. And at one point in the cycle, a molecule of ATP is made.

Each of the steps in the Krebs cycle is catalysed by a specific enzyme. These enzymes are all present in the matrix of the mitochondrion. Those which cause oxidation are oxidoreductases (or dehydrogenases). Those which remove carbon dioxide are decarboxylases.

Remember that respiration produces ATP for the cell to use as an energy source. At first sight it looks as though the contribution of the Krebs cycle to this is not very large, because only one ATP molecule is produced during one 'turn' of the cycle. However, as you will see, all those reduced NADs and FADs are used to generate a very significant amount of ATP – much more than can be done from glycolysis.

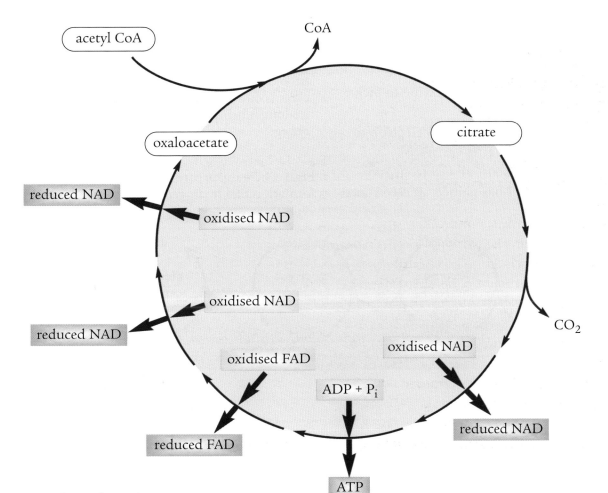

Fig 1.13 The Krebs cycle.

Oxidative phosphorylation

The last stages of aerobic respiration involve the use of oxygen to produce ATP from ADP and P_i.

$$ADP + P_i \longrightarrow ATP$$

This process is called 'phosphorylation' because it adds phosphate to ADP. It is said to be 'oxidative' because, as you will see, it uses oxygen.

The electron transfer chain

Fixed into the inner membrane of the mitochondrion is a series of molecules called **electron carriers**. They make up the **electron transfer chain**.

Each reduced NAD molecule releases its hydrogens. Each hydrogen atom splits into a hydrogen ion, H^+, and an electron, e^- (Fig 1.14). The electrons are picked up by the first of the electron carriers (Fig 1.15).

This electron carrier has now been reduced, because it has gained an electron. The reduced NAD has been oxidised, because it has lost hydrogen. The NAD can now go back to the Krebs cycle and be reused as a coenzyme to pick up hydrogen again.

The first electron carrier passes its electron to the next in the chain. The first carrier is therefore oxidised (it has lost an electron) and the second is reduced (it has gained an electron).

The electron is passed all the way down the chain. As it does so, it releases energy. This energy is used to make ATP, as explained below.

At the end of the electron transfer chain, the electron combines with a hydrogen ion and with oxygen, to form water. This is why we need oxygen. The oxygen acts as the final electron and hydrogen ion acceptor for the electron transport chain.

One of the carriers in the electron transport chain is cytochrome c. Cyanide ions can bind to cytochrome c and completely prevent it from functioning. This is why cyanide is such a powerful poison – it brings the electron transport chain to a complete halt.

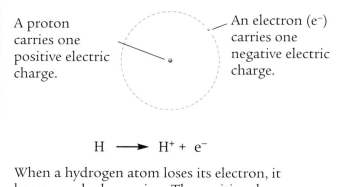

A proton carries one positive electric charge.

An electron (e^-) carries one negative electric charge.

$$H \longrightarrow H^+ + e^-$$

When a hydrogen atom loses its electron, it becomes a hydrogen ion. The positive charge on it is due to the charge on the proton that is no longer being cancelled out by the electron's charge.

Fig 1.14 The structure of a hydrogen atom and the formation of a hydrogen ion.

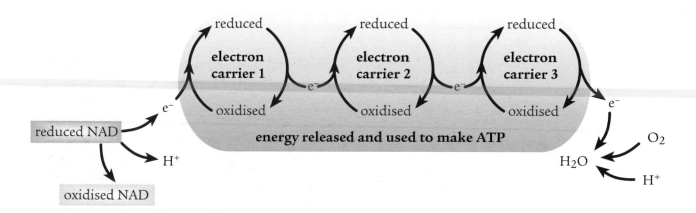

Fig 1.15 The electron transfer chain.

ATP synthesis

We have seen that when the hydrogens were donated to the electron transfer chain by NAD and FAD they split into an electron and a hydrogen ion. These hydrogen ions have an important role to play.

The electrons release energy as they pass along the electron transfer chain. Some of this energy is used to pump hydrogen ions across the inner membrane of the mitochondrion and into the space between the inner and outer membranes (Fig 1.16). This builds up a concentration gradient for hydrogen ions, because there are more of them on one side of the membrane than the other. It is also an electrical gradient, because the hydrogen ions, H^+, have a positive charge; there is now a greater positive charge on one side of the membrane than the other. The hydrogen ions are allowed to diffuse back down this **electro-chemical gradient** through a group of protein molecules that form a special channel for them to travel through. Apart from these channels, the membrane is impermeable to hydrogen ions. The channel protein acts as an ATPase. As the hydrogens pass through, the energy that they gained by being actively transported against their concentration gradient is used to make ATP from ADP and P_i.

The ATPase channels are so large that they can be seen in electronmicrographs as 'stalked particles' (Fig 1.17).

1 The electron transfer chain provides energy to pump hydrogen ions from the matrix into the space between the two mitochondrial membranes.

2 When the hydrogen ions are allowed to diffuse back through ATPase, the transferred energy is used to make ATP from ADP and P_i.

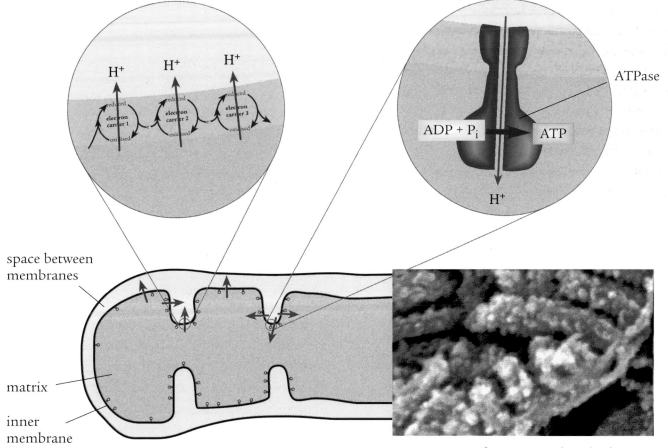

space between membranes

matrix

inner membrane

ATPase

ADP + P_i ATP

H^+

Fig 1.17 EM of inner mitochondrial membrane showing ATPase particles.

Fig 1.16 Oxidative phosphorylation.

For every two hydrogens donated to the electron transfer chain by NAD, three ATP molecules are made. The hydrogens donated by FAD start at a later point in the chain, so only two ATP molecules are formed. However, we also need to remember that some energy has been put in to these processes. In particular, energy is needed to transport ADP from the cytoplasm and into the mitochondrion. (You can't make ATP unless you have ADP and P_i to make it from.) Energy is also needed to transport ATP from the mitochondrion where it was made into the cytoplasm where it will be used. Overall, we can say that the hydrogens from each reduced NAD produce two and a half ATPs, while those from reduced FAD produce about one and a half ATPs.

We can now count up how much ATP is made from the oxidation of one glucose molecule. Table 1.2 shows the balance sheet. If you want to work this out for yourself, remember that each glucose molecule produces two pyruvate molecules, so there are two Krebs cycles for each glucose molecule.

Table 1.2 ATP molecules produced from one glucose molecule.

Process	ATP used	ATP produced
glycolysis		
phosphorylation of glucose	2	
phosphorylation of ADP		4
from reduced NAD		5
link reaction		
from reduced NAD		5
Krebs cycle		
phosphorylation of ADP		2
from reduced NAD		15
from reduced FAD		3
Totals	2	34
Net yield		32

Note These are maximum values and the yield will vary from tissue to tissue.

Proton leak

Going through the ATPases is not the only way that protons (hydrogen ions) can move down the electrochemical gradient from the space between the membranes of the mitochondrion and into its matrix. Some of the protons leak through other parts of the inner membrane.

Proton leak is important in generating heat. In babies, in a special tissue known as brown fat, the mitochondrial membrane contains a transport protein called uncoupling protein, (UCP), which allows protons to leak through the membrane. The energy involved is not linked to the production of ATP (uncoupled). Instead, it is transfered to heat. Brown fat in babies can produce a lot of heat.

Some people's mitochondrial membranes are leakier than others, and it is likely that this difference can at least partly account for people's different metabolic rates.

During the First World War, some women became thin because they were exposed to a chemical called 2,4-dinitrophenol, while making artillery shells. For a short time in the 1930s it was used as a diet pill. It increases the inner mitochondrial membrane's leakiness. But it was soon banned because it increased the likelihood of developing cataracts and damaging the nervous system. Safer drugs are being developed that may help obese people to lose weight by increasing proton leak.

Summary

1. ATP is made by every cell, by a series of metabolic reactions called respiration. Respiration is the gradual oxidation of a substrate, such as glucose, in a series of small steps. Energy released from the substrate during these reactions is used to make ATP.

2. The first stage of respiration is glycolysis, which takes place in the cytoplasm. Glucose (6C) is phosphorylated and converted to fructose bisphosphate. This splits into two triose phosphates, which are each converted to the 3C compound, pyruvate.

3. The conversion of triose phosphate to pyruvate releases sufficient energy to convert two ADP molecules to ATP, by the addition of a phosphate group. This step also releases hydrogens, which are picked up by the coenzyme NAD. Reduced NAD, that is NADH + H^+, is formed.

4. Two ATPs are put in at the beginning of glycolysis, and four are synthesised, so the net production of ATP is two molecules for every glucose molecule used.

5. When oxygen is available, the pyruvate is transferred into a mitochondrion by active transport. The link reaction then takes place in the matrix of the mitochondrion. Carbon dioxide is removed from pyruvate, converting it to a 2C compound. Hydrogen is also removed, and picked up by NAD. The remainder of the molecule combines with coenzyme A to produce acetyl coenzyme A.

6. Acetyl coenzyme A combines with the 4C compound, oxaloacetate, forming the 6C compound citrate. This is reconverted to oxaloacetate by a series of small steps that make up the Krebs cycle. During the Krebs cycle, more hydrogens are released and picked up by NAD or FAD, carbon dioxide is released, and some ATP is produced directly.

7. The reduced NAD and FAD donate their hydrogens to the electron transfer chain which is situated in the inner membrane of the mitochondrion. The hydrogens split into hydrogen ions and electrons. The electrons are passed down the chain, losing energy as they do so. At the end of the chain, electrons, hydrogen ions and oxygen combine to form water.

8. The hydrogen ions are pumped across the inner membrane into the intermembranal space, by active transport. This builds up an electrochemical gradient. The hydrogen ions move down this gradient, passing through a channel in the membrane formed by ATPase and providing enough energy to produce ATP from ADP and P_i.

9. Overall, taking into account the ATP that is used during glycolysis and for the transport of ADP into the mitochondrion and ATP out of it, 32 molecules of ATP are made for every glucose molecule.

Anaerobic respiration

Tanya Streeter grew up as a small child on the island of Grand Cayman in the Caribbean. She spent as much time as she could in the sea. She then went to school in Britain but now is back in the Caribbean doing what she does better than any other woman (and nearly every man) – holding her breath.

Tanya holds numerous records for free diving. She dives with no breathing aids, just her own body. On Monday July 21st 2003, she added another record to her collection as she went down to a depth of 122 m on a 'sledge' and then kicked her way back to the surface. The previous record for this kind of dive was 120 m, held by a man. Tanya's 2003 dive lasted for 3 minutes and 38 seconds.

Part of her training for her dives is to practise holding her breath for as long as she can. She usually does this in a swimming pool, lying face down on the surface while someone at the edge of the pool times her, and is ready to help should she black out – holding your breath for a long period is a very dangerous thing to do. She can hold her breath like this for nearly 6 minutes. This is extremely difficiult, because you have to overcome your body's desperate efforts to take a breath. As carbon dioxide builds up in the blood, the brain's breathing control centre sends ever more urgent messages to the breathing muscles, and overriding this with your own will takes a huge effort.

While she is underwater, Tanya's muscles, brain cells and other parts of her body first use up whatever oxygen is already present in her body, providing the ATP needed to keep her cells alive by aerobic (oxygen-using) respiration. But as the oxygen disappears, they turn more and more to anaerobic respiration. Anaerobic respiration is not very efficient and can produce only a tiny amount of ATP compared with aerobic respiration. It also causes a build-up of lactate in the tissues and the blood. Tanya's training increases the ability of her cells to rely on anaerobic respiration, and to tolerate high concentrations of lactate.

The lactate pathway

We have seen that oxygen is needed to accept the electron at the end of the electron transfer chain. If there is no oxygen present – for example, if a person is holding their breath, or is exercising vigorously so that they're unable to take in oxygen at a fast enough rate to supply their muscles – then there is nowhere for the electron to go. The whole electron transfer chain stops, like a traffic jam forming if there is a broken-down vehicle blocking the road.

The back-up goes further than this. The reduced NADs and FADs can't release their hydrogens, so there are no coenzymes available to pick up hydrogens from the Krebs cycle. So the Krebs cycle stops too. And so does the link reaction. The whole process of respiration backs up all the way from the formation of pyruvate onwards.

But pyruvate does have an alternative, unblocked route to go down. It can be changed into **lactate**. This reaction requires the addition of hydrogen, so this is taken from reduced NADs. The pyruvate is acting as an alternative hydrogen acceptor. These NAD molecules can now accept hydrogen as glycolysis takes place, just as they usually do. So at least some ATP can be made, as glycolysis carries on as usual.

The metabolism of pyruvate by this route can be summarised in this equation:

$$C_2H_3OCOOH + NADH + H^+ \longrightarrow C_2H_5OCOOH + NAD$$
$$\text{pyruvate} \hspace{4.5cm} \text{lactate}$$

The oxidation of glucose by means of glycolysis and the lactate pathway is known as **anaerobic respiration** (Fig 1.18).

We can compare aerobic and anaerobic respiration to see how much energy they can transfer to ATP from glucose. The percentage of the energy in the glucose that is transferred to ATP is the **efficiency** of the process.

If one mole of glucose is hydrolysed to carbon dioxide and water, 2880 kJ of energy is released. If one mole of ATP is hydrolysed, 30.6 kJ of energy are released.

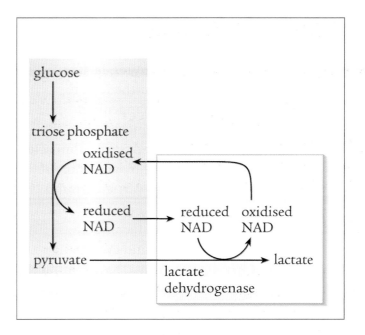

Fig 1.18 Anaerobic respiration. Producing lactate from pyruvate generates oxidised NAD and allows glycolysis to procede.

In aerobic respiration, we have seen that there is a net gain of 32 ATP molecules for every glucose molecule. So the overall efficiency of aerobic respiration is:

$$\frac{32 \times 30.6 \times 100}{2880} = 34\%$$

However, in anaerobic respiration only 2 molecules of ATP are made. So the overall efficiency of anaerobic respiration is:

$$\frac{2 \times 30.6 \times 100}{2880} = 2\%$$

SAQ

1.8   How many more ATPs can be made from one molecule of glucose in aerobic respiration, compared with anaerobic respiration?

Excessive post-exercise oxygen consumption

As anaerobic respiration continues, lactate builds up. This could stop even the lactate pathway and glycolysis from happening. However, the lactate can be removed from the cells where it is being produced, such as muscle.

The lactate diffuses into the blood, where it dissolves in the plasma and is carried around the body. A high concentration of lactate often makes a person feel disorientated and nauseous, as it affects cells in the brain and eventually stops muscles from contracting. The 400 m race is notorious for producing high concentrations of lactate in a runner's blood, and some 400 m runners actually vomit after running this race.

When the lactate reaches the liver, the liver cells absorb it and use it. They convert it back to pyruvate. Later, when oxygen becomes available again, the liver cells will oxidise the pyruvate using the link reaction and Krebs cycle. They also convert some of it to glycogen, which they store as an energy reserve.

This removal of lactate by the liver cells requires oxygen. Imagine that a runner has just run a 400 m race. During most of the race, his muscles will have been using oxygen at a faster rate than it can be supplied to them. The difference between the oxygen demand of the muscles and the oxygen they receive is known as the **oxygen deficit** (Fig 1.19). They will have to switch over to anaerobic respiration, so lactate is produced. At the end of the race, the runner will have to breathe faster and deeper in order to get extra oxygen into his body, because this is needed by the liver cells so that they can remove lactate.

It is as though the muscles have been working on 'borrowed' oxygen. They have kept respiring and producing ATP, even though they can only get a very little ATP out of each glucose molecule. After the race has ended, extra oxygen is needed to get rid of the lactate, paying back the 'borrowed' oxygen. This is known as **excessive post-exercise oxygen consumption**, or

EPOC. EPOC can be defined as the total oxygen consumed after exercise in excess of the pre-exercise level.

Lactate threshold

Muscles are most likely to respire anaerobically during a relatively short, fast period of exercise – for example, running a 400 m race. Arterioles carrying oxygen to the muscles dilate and heart rate is increased, the extra oxygen keeping them respiring aerobically for a while.

Training programmes improve blood supply to muscles, so they can work longer and harder before they have to switch to anaerobic respiration. Long, steady runs help, because they improve cardiac output and the rate of oxygen absorption in the lungs. They also encourage more capillaries to grow in the muscles.

A sprinter will push their muscles to the very limit in training. If they have trained well, the supply of oxygen to their muscles will be much better than that of most people. Nevertheless, they will reach a point where oxygen begins to run out and anaerobic respiration takes over. This is called the **lactate threshold**, because anaerobic respiration produces lactate.

Training aims to increase the lactate threshold and also the body's tolerance to the build-up of lactate. Training continuously at around 85–90% of maximum heart rate for about 20 minutes, even only once a week, helps to achieve this.

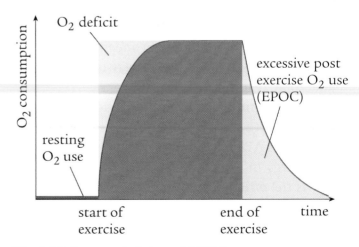

Fig 1.19 Oxygen deficit and EPOC.

Summary

1. When the demand for oxygen from respiring cells exceeds the supply, the electron transfer chain and Krebs cycle stop.

2. In these conditions, glycolysis continues as usual and forms pyruvate. The pyruvate is converted to lactate. Hydrogen is taken from reduced NAD. There is therefore a continuous supply of NAD which can act as a coenzyme in the glycolysis pathway.

3. Glycolysis and the lactate pathway are the only method of making ATP when no oxygen is present. This is known as anaerobic respiration. It produces only 2 molecules of ATP per glucose, whereas aerobic respiration produces 32. The efficiency of anaerobic respiration is 2%, whereas for aerobic respiration it is 34%.

4. The difference between the amount of oxygen required by the muscles for aerobic respiration and the oxygen that is available to them is the oxygen deficit.

5. Lactate diffuses into the blood and is carried to the liver, where it is metabolised when oxygen becomes available to produce pyruvate. This can then enter the link reaction in the usual way.

6. The removal of lactate by the liver after exercise requires extra oxygen. Heart rate and breathing rate therefore continue at a high level after exercise has ended, to supply this oxygen to the liver. The extra oxygen required is known as the excessive post-exercise consumption (EPOC).

7. Training programmes aim to improve the blood supply to muscles, by improving cardiac output and the efficiency of oxygen uptake by the lungs. They may also cause more capillaries to grow in the muscles. This all helps to get more oxygen to the muscles, so anaerobic respiration does not have to take place so early. Long, steady runs help to achieve this.

8. Training also aims to increase an athlete's tolerance to the build-up of lactate in the tissues.

CHAPTER 2

Improving athletic performance

The London Marathon, a gruelling race of 26.2 miles, was a triumph for Britain's Paula Radcliffe in 2003. She came home in the fastest time ever for a woman, beating her own previous world record to set a new one of 2 hours 15 minutes. It was Paula's day – a world record in her own country, in perhaps the most famous marathon event in the world.

But behind Paula, in amongst the other 30 000 men and women in the race, was a Sikh runner from Ilford. Fauja Singh took almost three times longer than Paula to finish the race. Still, that is quite a feat for a 92 year old.

Fauja Singh was brought up in a village in India. After his wife died, when he was 81, he moved to England to be near to his son's family. He found life very boring, and had no desire at all to spend his life watching television or playing cards at the community centre. So he took up running.

He entered his first 26 mile race in 2000, aged 89, running the London Marathon in 6 hours and 54 minutes. The next year he ran in the same time, which set a world record for 90 year olds. By the time he raced in the 2003 London Marathon he was so much fitter that he beat his own record, finishing in 6 hours 11 minutes, ahead of 10 000 younger men and women. Later that same year, aged 92, he ran the Toronto marathon in 5 hours 40 minutes, smashing his own world record by almost half an hour.

In 2004, Fauja Singh signed a contract with a major sportswear manufacturer; in return for a sizeable payment, he will wear their clothes, shoes and logo whenever he races. He trains regularly, jogging or walking between 8 and 10 miles each day. He is a vegetarian, and his diet includes nuts, yoghurt, curries and chapattis. His ambition is to be the oldest person ever to run a marathon. To do that, he will need to keep running until he is 98.

Aerobic exercise

Muscles need oxygen and an energy source such as glucose to provide them with the ATP they need for contraction. The oxygen is used to allow aerobic respiration to take place. If oxygen is not supplied to the muscles fast enough, they can get by on anaerobic respiration for a while. But this produces lactate, and as this builds up the muscles stop working.

An endurance athlete is therefore limited in his or her performance by the rate at which oxygen can be supplied to the muscles. The harder the muscles are working, the faster the rate at which they use energy, and therefore the faster the rate that oxygen must be supplied to them. Marathon runners will try to run at the maximum speed that they can keep up for several hours. Their training increases the ability of the heart and lungs to get oxygen to the muscles as fast as possible over a long period of time.

Even if you have no intention of becoming a marathon runner, your fitness and general health will almost certainly benefit from regular **aerobic exercise** – that is, exercise in which the muscles get most of their energy from aerobic respiration. It can take almost any form you like to mention, so long as it is done at a rate that you can keep up for a reasonable amount of time. Walking, swimming, dancing and cycling, as well as long-distance running, are all forms of aerobic exercise (Fig 2.1).

Short-term effects of aerobic exercise

Effects on the circulatory system

These are outlined in Table 2.1.

When you are about to start exercising, your brain sends nerve impulses along a sympathetic nerve (see page 76) to the sino-atrial node (SAN) – the heart's pacemaker – stimulating it to contract at a faster rate. So your heart starts beating faster even before you have begun the exercise. You might also begin to secrete more of the hormone **adrenaline** into the blood, which has the same effect on the heart as the sympathetic nerve.

Once exercise begins, and the muscles are respiring at a faster rate, cardiac output is further increased. This is brought about by **nitric oxide**, a gas which acts as a hormone. When muscles are using up oxygen quickly, the concentration of oxygen in the blood vessels in the muscles falls, and the cells in the blood vessel walls respond to the lowered oxygen concentration by secreting nitric oxide. The nitric oxide makes the muscles in the walls of arterioles relax, which widens the lumen of the arterioles (vasodilation) and allows more blood to flow through and more quickly. This in turn increases the rate at which blood flows back to the heart in the veins.

Table 2.1 Short-term effects of exercise on circulation.

More nerve impulses to the heart pacemaker, increasing heart rate.
More adrenaline secretion, increasing heart rate.
Nitric oxide secretion, dilating arterioles, which increases blood flow back to heart and increases cardiac output.
Diversion of blood to muscles by changes in dilation of arterioles.
Dilation of arterioles supplying skin capillaries, increasing heat loss from the skin.

Fig 2.1 Aerobic exercise need not be a competitive sport; it could be exercise in a gymnasium.

The heart is designed so that it pumps out blood at the same rate that blood flows into it. (You can imagine what might happen if it did not do this.) So extra blood flowing in, stretching the muscles in the heart wall, causes the heart to contract more forcefully. This increases the stroke volume. The stretching also stimulates the SAN, increasing the rate at which it fires off nerve impulses.

The blood vessels in various parts of the body also respond to the increased demand for oxygen and glucose by the muscles. We have seen that arterioles in the muscles widen (dilate). At the same time, arterioles supplying blood to other parts of the body whose needs are less urgent, such as the digestive system, contract and reduce blood flow. This allows more blood to flow to the muscles. At rest, the percentage of the blood flowing through the muscles is around 20%, but during strenuous exercise it can be over 80%.

All this muscular activity generates a lot of heat in the body. It is important that it can escape, and this is speeded up by dilation of the arterioles supplying blood to the skin surface. This increases the rate at which heat is lost by radiation.

Effects on the gas exchange system

These are outlined in Table 2.2.

Just as heart rate increases during exercise, so does ventilation rate. Breathing becomes faster and deeper, increasing the rate at which oxygen diffuses into the blood in the lungs, and carbon dioxide diffuses out (Fig 2.2).

Fig 2.2 The rate and depth of breathing rises during exercise.

The increased rate of respiration in the muscles causes an increased quantity of carbon dioxide to diffuse from them into the blood. **Chemoreceptors** in the medulla of the brain (see page 81) and in the walls of the carotid arteries detect this by monitoring the pH of the blood. A high concentration of carbon dioxide lowers the pH, making the blood more acidic.

If a low pH is detected, nerve impulses will be sent from the respiratory centre in the medulla to the intercostal muscles and the diaphragm muscles, making them contract harder and more quickly. This increases the rate at which new air is brought into the lungs and stale air removed, which in turn maintains a large concentration gradient between the alveoli and the capillaries. At rest, ventilation rate may be about $10 \, dm^3 \, min^{-1}$. During intense exercise, values of well over $100 \, dm^3 \, min^{-1}$ are achieved.

Table 2.2 Short-term effects of exercise on gas exchange.

Breathing rate increases.
Tidal volume increases.
Increases in the acidity of the blood are detected by chemoreceptors; information is then sent to the brain, which then increases rate and extent of diaphragm and intercostal muscle contractions.

SAQ

2.1   For each of the effects shown in Tables 2.1 and 2.2, explain how it helps the body to cope with aerobic exercise.

Long-term effects of aerobic exercise

Taking regular aerobic exercise over a long period of time can cause major changes to take place in the muscles, circulatory system and gas exchange systems. The magnitude of these changes is, in general, proportional to the amount and intensity of training that is done. However, different people can respond very differently to identical training, and there seems to be a strong genetic component to this.

Changes in the muscles

These are outlined in Table 2.3.

Table 2.3 Long-term effects of exercise on muscles.

Increased muscle size.
Increased cross-sectional area of slow-twitch muscle fibres.
Increased number of capillaries in muscles.
Increased concentration of muscle myoglobin.
More and bigger mitochondria in muscle fibres.
An increase in respiratory enzymes inside the mitochondria.
Increased glycogen stores.

Many changes take place in the muscles that are used in training. These changes are specific – they do not affect other muscles. They include:

- an increase in the cross-sectional area of slow-twitch muscle fibres. These muscle fibres rely largely on aerobic respiration for their ATP production (see page 28). This increases the mass of muscle that can be used during aerobic exercise, as well as increasing the overall size of the muscles.
- an increase in the number of capillaries in the muscle, and also in the ratio of capillaries to muscle fibres. This increases the volume of blood in the muscle, improving oxygen supply.
- an increase in the concentration of myoglobin in the muscle. Myoglobin (see page 40) is a respiratory pigment that stores oxygen, so this increases the amount of oxygen stored within the muscle.
- an increase in the number and size of mitochondria in the muscle fibres and therefore an increase in respiratory enzymes. Mitochondria are the sites where the Krebs cycle and oxidative phosphorylation occur, so this increases the rate at which these processes can occur within the muscle.
- an increase in the glycogen stores, which can be rapidly broken down to glucose for use as a respiratory substrate.

Changes in VO_2 max and the circulatory system

These are outlined in Table 2.4.

Table 2.4 Long-term effects of exercise on circulation.

Increased VO_2 max.
Increased number of red cells.
Increased heart muscle.
Increased stroke volume.
Lowered resting heart rate.
Decrease in resting systolic and diastolic pressure.
Shorter recovery time after exercise.

When a person increases the rate at which they are exercising, their rate of oxygen consumption increases too. However, there comes a point where they can no longer get any more oxygen to their muscles, or where their muscles just cannot use oxygen any faster, at which point the muscles have to switch over to anaerobic respiration. The maximum rate at which oxygen is used, before the muscles have to make the switch, is called **VO_2 max**.

VO_2 max increases with training. A trained athlete can have a higher work rate before their muscles switch to the less energy-efficient anaerobic respiration. The changes in the muscles described on the left contribute to this.

Changes in the cardiovascular system also contribute to this improvement, by increasing the rate at which oxygen can be supplied to the muscles. The changes include:

- an increased number of red blood cells. This increases the ability of the blood to carry oxygen.
- an increase in the size of the heart muscle, especially in the walls of the left ventricle. This increases the force with which the muscle can contract and force blood out of the heart.
- an increase in stroke volume – that is, the volume of blood that is forced out of the heart with each beat.

As a result of these changes, the heart rate of the trained person decreases when they are resting, because the greater stroke volume means that the same quantity of blood can be moved around the body using a slower heart rate. However, the maximum possible stroke volume is considerably increased, so the person can exercise harder and still manage to get enough blood into their muscles to supply the oxygen that they need. The heart rate recovery period – that is, the time taken for the heart rate to return to normal after exercise – decreases with training. This is often used as a good measure of how a person's fitness is improving during a training programme.

Changes in the gas exchange system

These are outlined in Table 2.5.

Table 2.5 Long-term effects of exercise on the gas exchange system.

Increased maximum breathing rate.
Increased tidal volume and vital capacity.

Training increases the rate at which oxygen can be brought into the body and carbon dioxide removed. Everyone's breathing rate and depth increase when they exercise, but the degree to which this happens is improved by regular aerobic training. For example, while a 'normal' person might be able to increase their ventilation rate by up to ten times, a really fit endurance athlete may be able to increase theirs by as much as 20 times. Top Olympic-standard rowers may have ventilation rates of $200\,dm^3\,min^{-1}$. Maximum oxygen intake is also achieved more quickly in a trained person.

> **SAQ**
>
> 2.2 Construct a table describing and explaining the long-term changes that occur as a result of regular aerobic exercise.

> **SAQ**
>
> 2.3 A group of untrained people undertook a training programme involving aerobic exercise over a period of 13 weeks. The graph shows the mean VO_2 max of these people during the training period.
>
> a Explain the meaning of the term VO_2 max.
>
> b Describe the changes in VO_2 max during this training programme.
>
> c Suggest reasons for the changes that you describe.

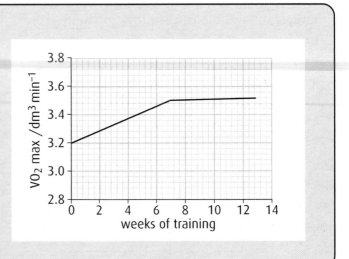

26

2.4 During aerobic exercise, most respiration taking place in the muscles is aerobic. However, even at low rates of exercise some anaerobic respiration also happens.

A person undertook a programme of aerobic training. The graph shows the relationship between the intensity of exercise, measured as power output in watts, and the concentration of lactate in the blood for this person before and after the training programme.

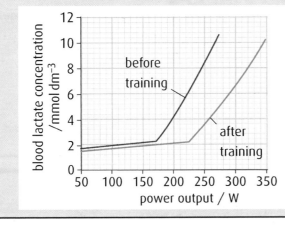

a i Describe the relationship between blood lactate concentration and intensity of exercise, up to a power output of 175 W.

ii Suggest reasons for this relationship.

b The lactate threshold is the point at which more lactate is being produced than can be cleared from the blood.

i Name the organ that is responsible for breaking down lactate.

ii Use the graph to determine the power outputs at which the person reached their lactate threshold before training, and after training.

iii Explain three changes in the body that could contribute to this increase in the lactate threshold after training.

c Explain how an increase in lactate threshold could improve the performance of an endurance athlete such as a rower or marathon runner.

Aerobic training

How much aerobic exercise do you have to do to improve your fitness significantly? There can be considerable differences between different people's response to training. There is also disagreement between 'experts', and the results of new studies into the benefits of exercise are always throwing up fresh ideas.

In general, it seems that to develop and maintain general aerobic fitness, you need to exercise for between 20 and 60 minutes per day. This can be in 10-minute bouts, or in longer periods of continuous exercise.

The form of exercise is very much up to the individual, but it should be aerobic – that is, exercise in which your muscles are respiring aerobically and which you can keep up for a reasonable length of time. It could be walking, jogging, running, cycling, running up and down stairs, swimming, dancing, skiing – almost anything that you choose.

Obviously, if a person has a health problem, then this needs to be taken into account before deciding on an exercise programme. Some people may choose to ask for professional advice about devising an exercise programme. They will be helped to find an intensity of exercise that is high enough to bring about beneficial changes, but not high enough to be unsafe. In general, less fit people should start off with less intensive exercise than a fitter person.

Most people will only want to stay fit enough to feel well and to enjoy an interesting lifestyle. Competitive sportsmen and women, however, will push their abilities to the limit. They will follow an intensive and very focussed exercise regime, tailored to their needs.

Slow-twitch and fast-twitch muscle fibres

There are two different types of muscle fibres in the skeletal muscles in our bodies. They are known as **slow-twitch (type 1)** and **fast-twitch (type 2)** fibres (Fig 2.3).

During aerobic exercise, it is mostly the slow-twitch fibres in your muscles that are working (Fig 2.4). These fibres are adapted for continuous aerobic respiration. They contain a lot of myoglobin, which makes them look dark red, and so are sometimes known as 'red fibres'.

During intensive, short-term exercise, such as sprinting, the fast-twitch fibres are used (Fig 2.5). They are adapted for producing ATP by anaerobic respiration. They therefore do not require stores of oxygen, and do not contain much myoglobin. They are sometimes known as 'white fibres'.

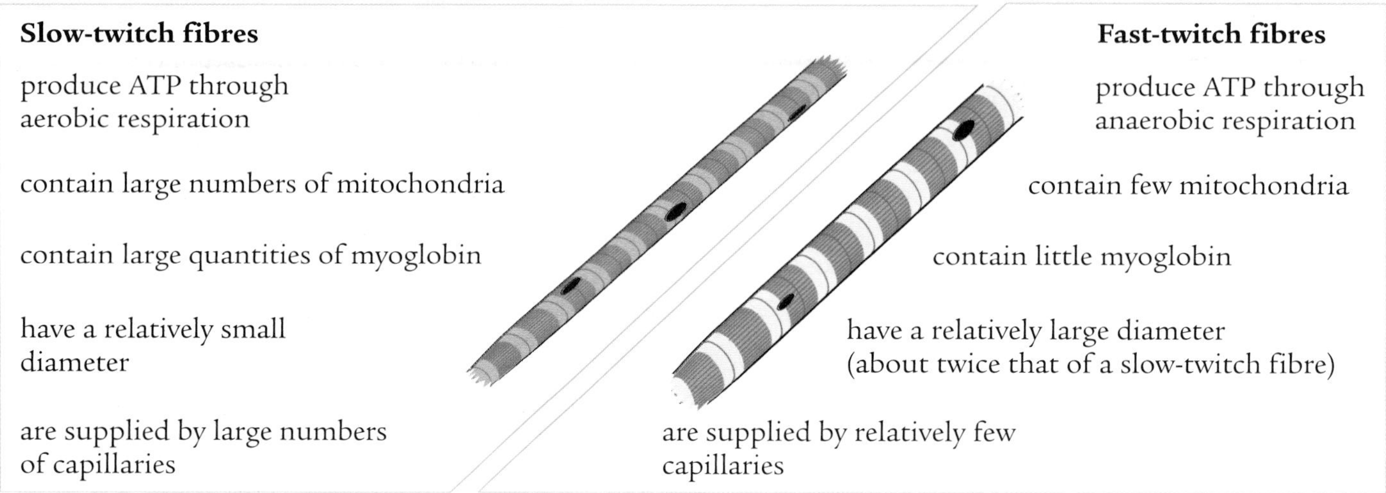

Slow-twitch fibres		Fast-twitch fibres
produce ATP through aerobic respiration		produce ATP through anaerobic respiration
contain large numbers of mitochondria		contain few mitochondria
contain large quantities of myoglobin		contain little myoglobin
have a relatively small diameter		have a relatively large diameter (about twice that of a slow-twitch fibre)
are supplied by large numbers of capillaries		are supplied by relatively few capillaries

Fig 2.3 Slow-twitch and fast-twitch fibres.

Fig 2.4 Slow-twitch muscle fibres are relied on for endurance sporting activities.

Fig 2.5 Fast-twitch muscle fibres are important in both the sprinting and jumping phases of the long jump.

SAQ

2.5 Explain how each of the structural differences between slow-twitch and fast-twitch muscle fibres listed in Fig 2.3 adapts them for their different ways of generating ATP.

Motor units

The two types of muscle fibres also differ in the neurones (nerve cells) that are associated with them.

Muscle fibres contract when an action potential is brought to them by a motor neurone (see pages 7 and 63). A group of muscle fibres and the neurone that supplies them is called a motor unit. Each motor unit contains either all slow-twitch fibres or all fast-twitch ones.

Each motor unit of slow-twitch fibres is innervated by a small motor neurone. These motor units contain between 10 and 100 muscle fibres. In contrast, each motor unit of fast-twitch fibres is innervated by a much larger motor neurone, and contains from several hundred to more than one thousand muscle fibres.

At low rates of exercise, only the motor neurones associated with slow-twitch fibres will bring action potentials to the muscle. As exercise rate increases, more and more fast-twitch motor units are recruited.

It seems that the relative numbers of slow-twitch and fast-twitch motor units in a person's muscles are largely determined by their genes. Sportspeople who are successful in endurance events have relatively more slow-twitch fibres than people who are good at 'explosive' events, such as throwing a javelin, long-jumping or sprinting. However, training does have a large effect on the make-up of a person's muscles. Aerobic training causes the cross-sectional area of slow-twitch fibres to increase by up to 25%. There is also some evidence suggesting that some fast-twitch fibres may change into slow-twitch fibres, but, if this does happen, it is not on a large scale.

Respiratory substrates

In Chapter 1, we saw that the mechanism by which muscles contract involves the activity of the heads of the myosin molecules as ATPases. Muscles must have ATP in order to contract; they cannot use anything else.

There is some ATP in a resting muscle, but not very much. If you run a 100 m sprint, you will use up all the ATP in your leg muscles in the first 2 or 3 seconds. Once this is used up, the muscle must make more ATP if it is to keep working.

Muscle fibres, like all other body cells, produce their ATP through respiration. Respiration needs a source of fuel, such as glucose. However, glucose is not the only fuel that muscles can use.

The substance that is used to produce ATP in a cell by respiration is known as a **respiratory substrate**. Fig 2.6 shows the metabolic pathway by which the respiratory substrate glucose is oxidised and ATP is produced. But you can also see that there are other respiratory substrates that can be oxidised in this series of reactions. **Lipids** can be hydrolysed to glycerol and fatty acids, and then enter glycolysis and the link reaction. **Amino acids**, produced by the hydrolysis of proteins, are fed into the link reaction and the Krebs cycle.

These different respiratory substrates have different energy values. Carbohydrates and protein have very similar energy contents, releasing about $17\,kJ\,g^{-1}$. The values for fats are much higher, around $39\,kJ\,g^{-1}$. The reason for this greater energy content is mainly due to the higher proportion of H atoms to others in the molecules. Most of the energy of respiration is obtained from the electron within each H atom.

Different tissues in the body tend to use different substrates. Red blood cells and brain cells are almost entirely dependent on glucose. Heart muscle gets about 70% of its ATP by using fatty acids as the respiratory substrate. Skeletal muscles readily use fatty acids, as well as carbohydrates.

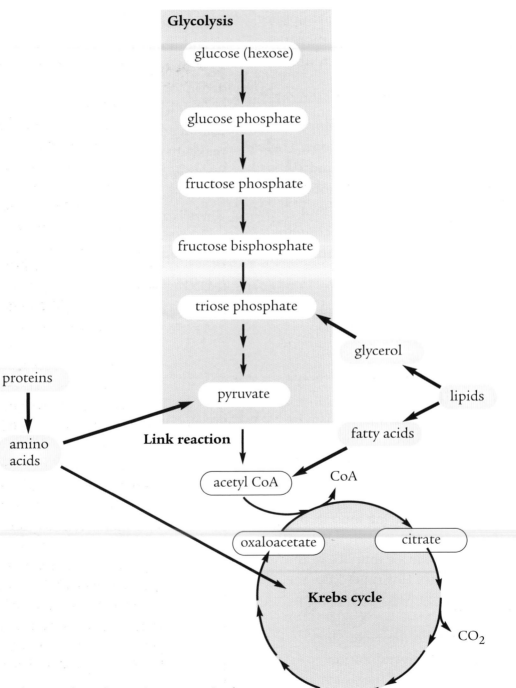

Fig 2.6 How fats, fatty acids and proteins are respired.

2.6   Which respiratory substrates shown in Fig 2.6 can be used only when there is a supply of oxygen? Explain your answer.

2.7   Use the information in Fig 2.6 to explain why Andrea's muscles (in the case study on page 10) could produce enough ATP to keep them going if she did not exercise too vigorously, despite the lack of an enzyme required in glycolysis.

Respiratory quotients

It is possible to find out which kind of respiratory substrate a person's tissues are using by measuring the volume of oxygen they are taking in and the volume of carbon dioxide they are breathing out.

If you divide the volume of carbon dioxide given out over a time period by the volume of oxygen taken in over the same time, you get a value known as the **respiratory quotient**.

$$\text{respiratory quotient} = \frac{\text{volume of } CO_2 \text{ given out}}{\text{volume of } O_2 \text{ taken in}}$$

Respiratory quotient is usually abbreviated to **RQ**. Table 2.6 shows the RQs when the respiratory substrate is carbohydrate (for example, glucose), fat or protein.

Table 2.6 RQs for substrates respired aerobically.

Respiratory substrate	RQ
carbohydrate (glucose)	1.0
fat (lipid)	0.7
protein	0.9

If a mixture of respiratory substrates are being used in the body, then the RQ will lie between the RQs for each substrate alone. For example, if both fat and glucose are being used as respiratory substrates, the RQ will be somewhere between 1.0 and 0.7. For most people RQ is about 0.82 while at rest.

If there is anaerobic respiration beyond the lactate threshold, RQ values will rise above 1.0. If the only respiration that is taking place is anaerobic, $RQ = \infty$.

2.8   A number of obese people were given a very low calorie diet. Their respiratory quotients were measured during the time that they ate this diet. All of the people lost weight during this time.

 The people were followed up over the next two years. Some people put the weight back on and stayed overweight (weight regainers). Others had cycles of dieting to lose weight and then putting it back on (weight cyclers). Some were able to maintain their weight loss over the two-year period (weight losers).

 It was found that weight regainers and weight cyclers had higher RQs while dieting than weight losers.

a   Explain what a high RQ tells us about a person's metabolism.

b   Suggest an explanation for the fact that obese people who had a low RQ were more likely to be able to maintain their weight loss for a longer period of time than those who had a high RQ.

c   It was found that most of the people who showed high RQs during the study had parents who also had high RQs under similar conditions. Similarly, most people with low RQs had parents with low RQs. Suggest explanations for this.

Using a Douglas bag to measure RQ

A Douglas bag is a light, expandable, gas-tight bag that can be carried on the back. It collects expired air. The volume of expired air collected over a particular time period is measured. Its oxygen and carbon dioxide content are also measured. As the oxygen and carbon dioxide content of atmospheric air are already known, this allows the oxygen uptake and carbon dioxide output to be calculated. From these values, RQ can be calculated.

A Douglas bag being used after exercise.

1 Expired air is collected in the bag over a precisely measured time period, such as 3 minutes. The collection of the air must begin at either the start or end of an expiration, and finish at the same point in the breathing cycle. The greater the volume of air collected, the more reliable the results of the investigation, but this will be limited by the capacity of the Douglas bag.

2 The volume of the expired air is measured.

3 The concentrations of oxygen and carbon dioxide in the expired air are measured automatically using instruments such as an oxygen probe and a carbon dioxide analyser. These values can then be used to calculate the volumes of oxygen and carbon dioxide in the expired air that was collected.

4 The volumes of oxygen and carbon dioxide that would be present in the same volume of atmospheric air are also calculated.

5 The results in 3 and 4 are then used to calculate the volume of oxygen used by the subject and the volume of carbon dioxide given out.

6 These values can then be used to calculate the RQ.

7 The procedure is then repeated. A mean RQ can then be calculated.

Example

Expired air

Volume of expired air given out per minute
= 100 dm^3
Concentration of oxygen in this air
= 15.28%
So the rate at which oxygen is given out
= 15.28 dm^3 min^{-1}
Concentration of carbon dioxide in this air
= 4.45%
So the rate at which carbon dioxide is given out
= 4.45 dm^3 min^{-1}

Inspired air

Concentration of oxygen in this air
= 19.78%
So the rate at which oxygen is breathed in
= 19.78 dm^3 min^{-1}
Concentration of carbon dioxide in this air
= 0.04%
So the rate at which carbon dioxide is breathed in
= 0.04 dm^3 min^{-1}

Calculating RQ

The volume of oxygen used in the body
= 19.78 − 15.28 = 4.50 dm^3 min^{-1}
The volume of carbon dioxide produced by the body
= 4.45 − 0.04 = 4.41 dm^3 min^{-1}

$$RQ = \frac{\text{volume of } CO_2 \text{ produced}}{\text{volume of } O_2 \text{ used}}$$

$$= \frac{4.41}{4.50}$$

$$= 0.98$$

This value lies between 1, which would indicate that carbohydrate is being used as the respiratory substrate, and 0.9, which would indicate use of fat or protein.

So we can say that this person is using carbohydrate as their main respiratory substrate, plus a small amount of either fat or protein.

Using a spirometer to measure the rate of oxygen consumption

In your AS work, you will have seen how to use a spirometer to measure tidal volume, inspiratory reserve volume, expiratory reserve volume and vital capacity. To do this, the spirometer chamber can be filled with ordinary atmospheric air. Soda lime is used to absorb all the carbon dioxide from the expired air before it goes back into the chamber.

To measure the rate of oxygen consumption, however, the spirometer is filled with medical-grade oxygen, rather than air. As before, soda lime is used to absorb all the carbon dioxide in the expired air.

Spirometer

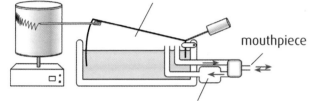

balanced float enclosing medical-grade oxygen

mouthpiece

container into which soda lime is placed to absorb carbon dioxide

Each time the subject takes a breath in, they breathe in pure oxygen from the chamber. Each time they breathe out, they breathe out a mixture of oxygen and carbon dioxide. This carbon dioxide is all absorbed by the soda lime. So the gas that goes back into the chamber is just the oxygen that is breathed out.

If we calculate the difference between the volume of oxygen breathed in and the volume of oxygen breathed out, we know how much oxygen the person used.

Our results are more reliable if we do this calculation over a number of breaths, rather than just one.

Example

This spirometer trace was made while the subject was sitting and relaxing.

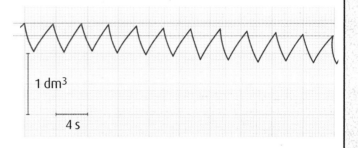

1 dm³

4 s

At rest, between time 0 and 40 s the oxygen used
  = 0.2 dm³
So the rate of oxygen use
  = 0.3 dm³ min⁻¹

Questions

This spirometer trace was made while the same subject was walking on a treadmill.

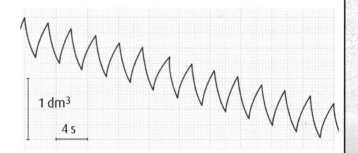

1 dm³

4 s

a Calculate the rate of oxygen use per minute while using the treadmill. Show all of your working.
b Use your answer to a to calculate the increase in the rate of oxygen use while walking compared with relaxing.
c Use your answers to a and b to calculate the percentage increase in the rate of oxygen use while walking compared with relaxing.

Carbohydrate loading

A person who wants to increase their athletic performance will try to maximise the energy stores in their muscle cells. These stores are in the place where they are needed, actually inside the muscle fibres, and they can be used to produce ATP much faster than if the muscles had to rely only on glucose supplied in the blood.

Endurance athletes usually try to increase the glycogen stores in their muscles by **carbohydrate loading**. They eat foods containing a lot of carbohydrate – pasta is a favourite – in the run-up to their event. The carbohydrate is broken down to glucose in the digestive system and absorbed into the blood. Some of this glucose is taken into the muscle fibres and converted to glycogen for storage.

There is some disagreement about the best way of doing this. When this strategy was first introduced in the late 1960s, research suggested that an athlete gains maximum benefit if they undergo three or four really hard training days while eating a low carbohydrate diet, to use up all the glycogen in their muscles. The muscle stores were then recharged by eating a large amount of carbohydrate in the next three to four days, leading up to the race. More recently, it has been found that the long 'depletion phase' is not needed. Instead, many endurance athletes now tend to follow a regime of a few days of hard exercise while eating a high carbohydrate diet. This appears to elevate muscle glycogen levels enough to improve their performance significantly.

It isn't always easy to eat as much extra carbohydrate as is needed. The amount that is recommended to achieve carbohydrate loading of the muscles is between 6 to 10 g of carbohydrate per kilogram of body mass. That means that a 70 kg athlete should be trying to eat between 420 and 700 g of carbohydrate on each of the three days before the race. To do that, you have to eat something that does not look at all like a healthy diet, with lots of sugary foods, soft drinks, honey and so on. This carbohydrate-loading diet will probably cause body mass to increase, perhaps by as much as 2 kg, and some athletes are very uncomfortable with this idea.

It is important to realise what carbohydrate loading can or cannot do. It cannot help your muscles to work harder or faster. What it can do is help them to work for longer. So carbohydrate loading is only of any benefit to endurance athletes. It will not help sprinters or jumpers. It can't help football players, either, because they do not usually have long enough between games to fit in a several-day long carbohydrate loading programme.

ACTIVITY 2.1

Carbohydrate loading

Use the internet to collect information about the use of carbohydrate loading to improve athletic performance. Choose one of the following questions and discuss the differing views that are held. Try to include some data that have been collected through scientific research to support your arguments.

- Does carbohydrate loading help performance in a competitive event?
- When and how should carbohydrate loading happen?
- Does carbohydrate loading work as well for women as for men?
- Are there any dangers associated with carbohydrate loading?

Summary

1. In aerobic exercise, muscles depend largely on aerobic respiration to supply them with ATP. This kind of exercise can be done over a fairly long period of time – for example, walking, jogging or dancing.

2. The short-term effects of aerobic exercise include:
   - an increase in heart rate and stroke volume, therefore increasing cardiac output and speeding up the supply of oxygen to the muscles;
   - dilation of the arterioles supplying blood to the skin, so that more blood passes through the surface capillaries and loses heat by radiation; this helps to lose some of the heat generated by the working muscles;
   - an increase in the rate and depth of breathing, which helps more oxygen to diffuse into the blood and more carbon dioxide to be lost.

3. The long-term effects of regular aerobic exercise include:
   - an increase in the cross-sectional area of the muscle fibres that depend on aerobic respiration, called slow-twitch fibres;
   - an increase in the quantity of the pigment myoglobin in this muscle, and of glycogen;
   - an increase in the number and size of mitochondria, and an increase in respiratory enzymes in this muscle;
   - an increase in VO_2 max, which is reached faster;
   - an increase in the number of red cells;
   - an increase in the size of heart muscle, and in the stroke volume;
   - an increase in the maximum ventilation rate;
   - a decrease in resting systolic and diastolic pressure;
   - shorter recovery time after exercise.

4. To have a significant effect, aerobic training should involve aerobic exercise lasting for a total of about 20 to 60 minutes each day.

5. Muscles contain slow-twitch fibres, which are adapted for aerobic respiration, and fast-twitch fibres, which are adapted for anaerobic respiration. A marathon runner depends largely on his or her slow-twitch fibres, which can go on working for a long time so long as oxygen is supplied to them. A sprinter depends largely on his or her fast-twitch fibres, which can work very hard for a short period of time, without an oxygen supply.

6. A substance that is used as a fuel in respiration is called a respiratory substrate. Cells can use glucose, fatty acids, glycerol or amino acids as respiratory substrates.

7. RQ is the ratio of carbon dioxide breathed out to oxygen breathed in. The RQ value tells you which substrate(s) are being used in the body for respiration.

8. A Douglas bag can be used to collect expired air, which is then analysed to find the difference in concentration of air breathed out and air breathed in. This can be used to calculate RQ.

9. A spirometer can be used to measure the rate of oxygen consumption.

10. Some endurance athletes eat large quantities of carbohydrate a few days or hours before their race, to increase the glycogen stores in their muscle fibres. This is called carbohydrate loading.

Respiratory pigments

Harry was gardening when it happened. Suddenly, out of the blue, he had a searing pain in his chest, and a feeling of faintness. He could not stand up, and sank to the ground, clutching his chest. He shouted for his wife, but she was inside the house and it was a neighbour who got to him first. The neighbour guessed that Harry might be having a heart attack, and called an ambulance.

Harry felt a bit better by the time he was lifted into the ambulance – the pain had subsided and he could sit up. One of the paramedics gave him an aspirin to swallow. He was taken to A and E, where several tests were carried out to find out if he had had a heart attack. Speed is essential in these circumstances, as the faster that clot-busting drugs can be administered, the better the chance of a successful outcome.

He was asked to provide a urine sample, and also had a sample of blood taken from a vein. Both of these were whisked off to the pathology laboratory to be tested for myoglobin. This is a dark red pigment that is found in muscle cells. It should not be present in blood or in urine. However, when muscle is damaged, myoglobin escapes from it into the blood, and is then excreted in urine. A raised level of myoglobin in the blood or urine indicates that the heart muscle may have been damaged, which is evidence that a heart attack may have occurred. There are other reasons for myoglobin appearing in blood or urine – for example, skeletal muscle may have been damaged – but in this case there was no reason to suspect anything other than a heart attack.

Harry's blood and urine myoglobin levels rose rapidly, and quite large amounts were found in both his blood and his urine one hour after he arrived at A and E. This confirmed the diagnosis of a heart attack. He was given clot-busting drugs, and kept in hospital so that his condition could be monitored over the next few days. He had been badly frightened by the attack, and felt sick and generally unwell. The blood and urine myoglobin levels had fallen back to normal within three days, an indication that the heart muscle was mending. All the same, the heart attack was a warning that something was very wrong, and that further treatment would be needed to prevent it happening again.

The myoglobin test is especially useful because the appearance of myoglobin in urine is one of the first indications of a heart attack. The test is done every one or two hours, for up to 36 hours. If myoglobin levels don't rise within 5 hours, then the person probably has not had a heart attack.

Myoglobin is one of our two respiratory pigments. The other is haemoglobin. **Haemoglobin** is found inside red blood cells, and myoglobin inside muscle fibres. They work together to ensure a supply of oxygen to muscle fibres.

The haemoglobin dissociation curve

Haemoglobin, often abbreviated to Hb, is a globular protein, made up of four polypeptide chains which each contain a haem group. The structure of haemoglobin and how to measure its concentration in the blood are described in *Human Biology for AS* on pages 21 to 24. Haemoglobin is contained within the red blood cells.

Each haem group in each haemoglobin molecule is able to combine with an oxygen molecule, O_2. This means that, when fully saturated with oxygen, each Hb molecule carries four oxygen molecules. Haemoglobin that has bound with oxygen is called **oxyhaemoglobin**.

If the red blood cell is in a place where there is a lot of oxygen present, most of the Hb molecules will bind with their full complement of four oxygen molecules. However, in places where oxygen content is low, fewer Hb molecules bind with oxygen. Even those that do pick up some oxygen may only pick up one, two or three oxygen molecules rather than four.

When all the haemoglobin is combined with as much oxygen as it possibly can – four molecules for every Hb molecule – we say that it is 100% saturated. If only half that much oxygen is combined – probably because each Hb molecule is combined with only two oxygen molecules – we say that the Hb is 50% saturated.

Fig 2.7 shows the percentage saturation of haemoglobin at different oxygen concentrations. It is called a **dissociation curve**.

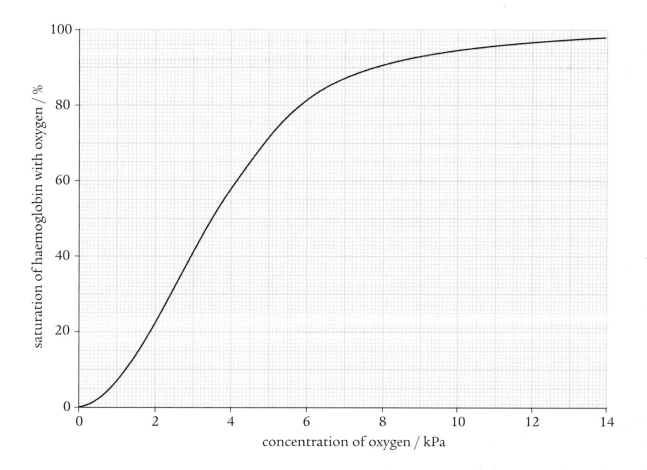

Fig 2.7 The haemoglobin dissociation curve.

2.9   Refer to Fig 2.7 to answer these questions.

a   What is meant by percentage saturation with oxygen?

b   The oxygen concentration in the alveoli of the lungs is about 12 kPa. What is the percentage saturation of the Hb in the lungs?

c   The oxygen concentration in a respiring muscle is about 2 kPa. What is the percentage saturation of the Hb in the muscle?

d   Hb molecules pick up oxygen in the lungs, and unload it in the respiring muscle. Explain how your answers to b and c support this statement.

The S-shaped curve

You would expect the **haemoglobin dissociation curve** in Fig 2.7 to look like an enzyme 'rate against substrate concentration' graph, with a straight line from the origin (Fig 2.8a). But the haemoglobin dissociation curve is S-shaped (Fig 2.8b). This reflects the way in which a haemoglobin molecule binds with its possible four oxygen molecules.

Imagine a Hb molecule with no oxygen bound to it. It is actually quite hard for the first oxygen molecule to bind. You can see from the dissociation curve in Fig 2.7 that in an oxygen concentration of 1 kPa, the Hb molecules are combined with only 7% of their possible full load. You have to increase the concentration to 2.2 kPa before reaching a stage where, on average, each Hb molecule is combined with one oxygen molecule.

However, once this first pair of oxygen atoms has bonded with one of the haem groups in the Hb molecule, the shape of the molecule is slightly changed. This is an example of an **allosteric** effect. (Allosteric means 'different shape'.) This makes it much easier for the next oxygens to bind with it. The dissociation curve is much steeper now (Fig 2.8b).

This ensures that Hb is very good at delivering large amounts of oxygen to the tissues if required. In the lungs, almost all of the Hb is fully saturated with oxygen – it is very good at combining with oxygen. Once it reaches a respiring muscle, where the oxygen concentration is much lower, the Hb readily releases most of its oxygen. It is just as important for a respiratory pigment to release its oxygen as it is for it to bind with it. It is the unexpectedly low **affinity for oxygen** ('affinity' means the ease with which the Hb can pick up oxygen) in the low oxygen conditions next to respiring tissues that causes saturated blood to release most of its oxygen. This effect allows about 15% more oxygen to be released than you would otherwise expect.

a **The 'usual' effect of adding more of one substance that binds to another**

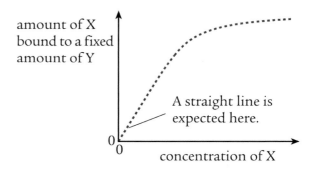

b **The unusual S-shaped curve for oxygen binding to haemoglobin**

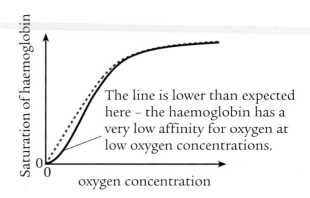

Fig 2.8 The S-shaped curve.

The Bohr effect

The ability of haemoglobin to bind with oxygen is affected not only by the oxygen concentration around it, but also by the carbon dioxide concentration.

In a working muscle, oxygen is being used and carbon dioxide produced. This carbon dioxide diffuses from the muscle fibre into the nearby blood capillaries. Some of it diffuses into the red blood cells.

Red blood cells contain an enzyme called **carbonic anhydrase**. This enzyme catalyses a reaction in which carbon dioxide forms a weak acid called **carbonic acid**:

$$CO_2 + H_2O \rightleftharpoons H_2CO_3$$

Some of the carbonic acid then dissociates (breaks apart) to produce hydrogen ions and hydrogencarbonate ions:

$$H_2CO_3 \rightleftharpoons H^+ + HCO_3^-$$

The hydrogen readily combines with the haemoglobin molecules inside the red blood cells. This forms a compound called **haemoglobinic acid**. However, a haemoglobin molecule that has done this cannot also bind with oxygen. The hydrogen ions make it drop its oxygen.

This effect can be seen on a dissociation curve for haemoglobin in the presence of a high carbon dioxide concentration (Fig 2.9). If you choose a particular value for oxygen concentration, say 4 kPa, you can see that the percentage saturation of Hb is lower when carbon dioxide concentration is high. The curve lies to the right of the curve when the carbon dioxide concentration is low.

This effect of carbon dioxide on the percentage saturation of haemoglobin is known as the **Bohr effect**. We can say that a high carbon dioxide concentration lowers the affinity of haemoglobin for oxygen.

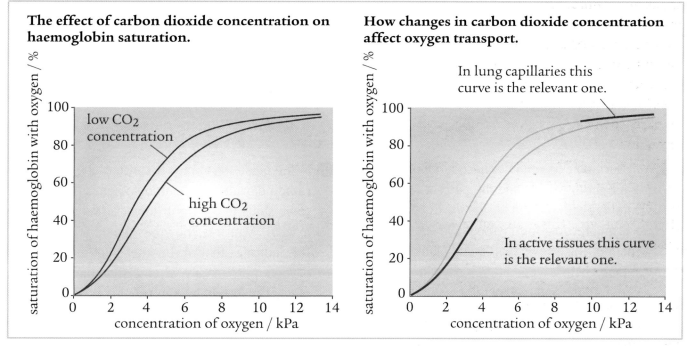

The effect of carbon dioxide concentration on haemoglobin saturation.

How changes in carbon dioxide concentration affect oxygen transport.

Fig 2.9 The Bohr effect.

SAQ

2.10 The carbon dioxide concentration in the lungs is low, whereas the carbon dioxide concentration in a respiring muscle is high. Use the curves in Fig 2.9 to explain how this helps oxygen to be supplied to the muscle.

Myoglobin

We have seen (see page 36) that myoglobin is found in muscle. Like haemoglobin, myoglobin contains haem groups and looks red. It is myoglobin that gives meat its colour.

However, unlike haemoglobin, myoglobin molecules contain only one polypeptide chain rather than four, and therefore only one haem group. This haem group binds much more readily with oxygen than any of the haem groups in haemoglobin. So myoglobin will pick up and hold oxygen at much lower concentrations than haemoglobin does. This is shown by the dissociation curve – the myoglobin curve lies to the left of the haemoglobin curve (Fig 2.10). It has a very high affinity for oxygen.

What does this mean? It means that myoglobin makes an excellent oxygen store in a muscle. When the muscle is working hard, it may be using oxygen for respiration faster than the oxyhaemoglobin in the blood can supply it. The oxygen concentration gets lower and lower. Eventually, when it gets right down to about 1 kPa, the myoglobin begins to release its oxygen. You can see this on the curve. At concentrations of oxygen above 2 kPa, the

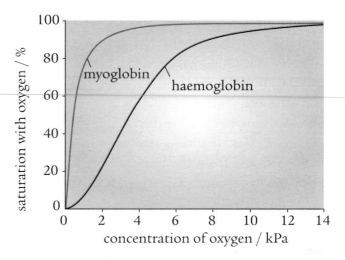

Fig 2.10 Myoglobin dissociation curve compared with that of haemoglobin.

myoglobin is still at least 80% saturated with oxygen. It only lets go of it when the oxygen concentration is really low. This way, it can provide extra oxygen to the muscle and allow it to keep respiring aerobically for a little longer before it has to switch to anaerobic respiration.

When oxygen debt has been repaid, myoglobin's higher affinity for oxygen means that it takes oxygen from haemoglobin to recharge the oxygen store.

Summary

1 A dissociation curve plots concentration of oxygen on the x-axis and the percentage saturation with oxygen on the y-axis. The dissociation curve for haemoglobin is S-shaped. This shows that haemoglobin readily combines with oxygen at high oxygen concentrations and readily releases it at low oxygen concentrations.

2 Haemoglobin combines with its first oxygen molecule with difficulty, but once one oxygen molecule is combined it makes it easier for three more to bind.

3 In the presence of higher concentrations of carbon dioxide, the haemoglobin dissociation curve shifts to the right (lower affinity for oxygen), which is known as the Bohr effect. This indicates that oxyhaemoglobin drops its oxygen more readily when carbon dioxide is present, which helps the supply of oxygen to respiring tissues.

4 Myoglobin is found inside muscle fibres, where it acts as an oxygen store, only giving up its oxygen at very low oxygen concentrations.

Enhancing performance

The Olympic Games in 1968 were held in Mexico City. This capital city is 2250 metres above sea level. At this height, the air is much thinner than at sea level. Each breath that you take brings much less oxygen into your lungs, and it is harder to supply your body tissues with all the oxygen that they need.

The 10 000 metres race took place on the first day of the games. An Australian runner, Ron Clarke, held the world record for this event. But on this occasion it almost killed him. He fell over the finishing line in sixth place, and collapsed unconscious.

Clarke was given oxygen, but even so he did not regain consciousness for an hour, and could not speak coherently for two days. His brain cells had clearly been affected by a lack of oxygen. However, he then recovered quickly, and was able to take part in a 5000 metre race later in the games. But none of the times in the long distance races were good, and no world records were broken.

The story in the explosive or sprint events was very different. Here, the athletes ran very fast times, jumped great heights or lengths, and threw long distances. It was at these games that Bob Beaman jumped a huge distance of 8.90 metres, a world record for long jump that was not exceeded until 1990. World records were also produced in the triple jump, and in all the men's races of 400 m or shorter.

Why such a difference in the performance in long distance races and sprints? In a distance race, the muscles are relying largely on aerobic respiration. The thin air and low concentration of oxygen meant that insufficient oxygen could be delivered to the muscles to keep them working. In sprint races, the muscles use anaerobic respiration, so they were not affected by the low oxygen concentration. In fact these athletes were all helped by the thinness of the air, which provided less air resistance to them or their projectiles moving fast through the air.

Altitude training

The times and distances achieved in the high-altitude 1968 Olympics raised awareness of the effect of altitude on athletic performance. Results for distance events were poor; results for explosive events were excellent. One group of athletes, however, appeared to perform especially well – the Kenyans, most of whom lived at moderately high altitudes.

The idea of training at altitude caught on rapidly. For athletes living at low altitude, trying to compete at high altitude made demands that their bodies could not meet. But over the long term, the low concentration of oxygen at altitude brings about physiological changes in the body that improve performances in distance events (Fig 2.11).

Increase in oxgyen-carrying capacity

The rate of production of red blood cells is controlled by a hormone secreted by the kidneys, called **erythropoetin**. As a person moves from low altitude to high altitude, the concentration of oxygen in their blood falls, because there is less oxygen in the air that they are breathing in. The kidneys respond to this by secreting more erythropoetin. This causes red blood cells to be produced more rapidly.

As well as the increase in the number of red blood cells, total blood volume also increases, as does the concentration of haemoglobin. Overall, this can result in the blood system containing well over 50% more haemoglobin than usual.

This extra haemoglobin means that more oxygen can be transported to the muscles. So VO$_2$ max increases. The effect is larger in some people than others, but on average it can enhance performance by 2 or 3% – a considerable advantage.

However, there are problems in training at high altitude. The lack of oxygen, until you have fully adapted, reduces your ability to work hard. The effects of this lack of hard training may outweigh the advantages. Many athletes now use a strategy called 'live high, train low'. They spend most of their time at altitude, but move to low altitude for training.

Increased ability to absorb oxygen

When a person moves from low altitude to high altitude, the low concentration of oxygen in their blood immediately stimulates breathing depth and rate to increase by up to 65%. However, if they then remain at high altitude for several days, their ventilation rate may increase by as much as five times (500%).

SAQ

2.11 The table below shows some of the winning times and distances in the 1964 Olympic Games held in Tokyo, and in the 1968 Olympic Games held in Mexico City. The letters WR mean that the performance took the world record.

Event	Winning performance in 1964	Winning performance in 1968
women's 100 metres	11.4 s	11.0 s WR
women's 400 metres	52.0 s	52.0 s
men's 100 metres	10.0 s WR	9.9 s WR
men's 200 metres	20.3 s	19.8 s WR
men's 400 metres	45.1 s	43.8 s WR
women's high jump	1.90 m	1.82 m
men's high jump	2.18 m	2.24 m
women's long jump	6.76 m	6.82 m WR
men's long jump	8.07 m	8.90 m WR
men's 5000 metres	13 min 48 s	14 min 05 s
men's 10 000 metres	28 min 24 s	29 min 27 s
men's marathon	2 h 12 min	2 h 20 min

a Sort these results and display them so that any patterns in the relative performances in 1968 and 1964 in different types of events can be seen.

b Describe these patterns.

c Tokyo is approximately 5.3 m above sea level. Mexico City is approximately 2250 m above sea level. Suggest explanations for the patterns that you have described in b.

Note: there are no entries for women's long distance running events because these were not held until 1984.

2.12 In an experiment carried out in 1987, 39 distance runners were allocated randomly to one of three training groups. All three groups first spent six weeks training at sea level. For the next four weeks, Group A lived and trained at an altitude of 2500 m (live high, train high). Group B lived at 2500 m and trained at sea level (live high, train low), and Group C lived and trained at sea level (live low, train low). For the last three weeks, all the athletes trained at sea level. Their performances in running 5000 m at sea level were measured at six times during their 13-week training period. Each performance was then rated against their performance at six weeks, the 'baseline' performance. The results are shown in the graph.

a i Describe the results obtained for Group C, the low-low group. In what way are these unexpected?

ii It was suggested that one reason for the unexpected performance of the low-low (and also the other two) groups towards the end of the training period could be that, whereas they trained in cool, dry conditions, the 5000 m was run in hot, humid conditions. How might this explain their performances?

b i Compare the performances of Group A, the high-high group, with Group B, the high-low group.

ii Suggest explanations for the differences you have described.

c What training programme would you recommend an endurance athlete to follow, and at what times, before they compete in an important event at sea level?

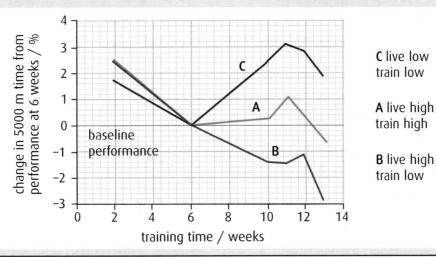

Fig 2.11 Training at altitude is now very common amongst athletes because of the extra haemoglobin that is produced in the blood over time, which improves performance at all altitudes in endurance sports.

Altitude sickness and adaptation to high living

A person moving from sea level to a high altitude, especially if they do this over a short period of time, may experience a number of very unpleasant and potentially fatal symptoms. This is known as mountain sickness or altitude sickness.

Mountain sickness happens because of the thin air at high altitude. Each breath brings in far less oxygen to the body than at low altitude. The person feels sleepy, cannot think properly, cannot make his or her muscles work properly and may have a fierce headache. They may vomit.

If they continue to stay at this altitude, or move even higher, they may undergo convulsions, and sudden death is quite common. The low concentration of oxygen in their blood may cause arterioles carrying blood to the brain to dilate, and this can cause fluid to leak into the brain tissue, leading to disorientation. Fluid also accumulates in the lungs, making it difficult for gas exchange to occur in the alveoli, and making the concentration of oxygen in the blood even lower than it is already.

Anyone showing symptoms of altitude sickness should be brought down to a lower altitude as quickly as possible.

However, if the ascent to high altitude is taken more steadily over a longer period of time, the body has time to adjust to the lowered oxygen concentration. A number of changes occur in the circulatory system, gas exchange system and in the muscle cells. After two or three weeks, more red blood cells are made, and normal breathing rates increase, both of which help to compensate for the low oxygen concentration by increasing the efficiency with which oxygen is obtained from the air and transported around the body.

Climbers going to very high altitudes – for example, on Everest – usually carry oxygen cylinders which they use for breathing in the later stages of the ascent.

Erythropoetin and blood doping

We have seen that the increase in erythropoetin secretion that occurs during altitude training helps sea level performance by increasing the number of red blood cells, and therefore the concentration of haemoglobin in the blood. Some professional sportsmen and women have tried to achieve a similar, or even better, effect on their body's ability to carry out sustained aerobic exercise by direct interference with their body chemistry.

In the 1990s, a procedure called **blood doping** began to be used by certain endurance athletes, including cyclists and skiers (*Human Biology for AS,* page 20). This involves removing 1 dm^3 of blood several months before the competition. The body responds to this by secreting extra erythropoetin, which stimulates red cell production and returns their number and concentration in the blood to normal over the next few days.

Meanwhile, the red cells in this sample are separated from the plasma, and stored at a low temperature. A few hours before the competition begins, the thawed cells are returned to the athlete's blood. This can greatly increase the red cell count, and therefore the haemoglobin concentration, in the blood, increasing the oxygen-carrying capacity of the blood and therefore the person's performance.

Blood doping is now officially banned, as it gives athletes who use it an unfair competitive advantage. It is very difficult to detect, because no foreign substances have been added to the body. The only possible method of detection (apart from actually catching an athlete doing it) is to measure the concentration of red cells in the blood. The percentage of the blood volume that is taken up by cells is known as the **haematocrit**. Haematocrit can be measured by centrifuging the blood (placing a sample in a tube and spinning it very fast). The red cells all accumulate at the bottom of the tube with the plasma above, so you can read off the haematocrit just by comparing the volume taken up by the cells and the plasma.

For men, the average haematocrit is about 42%, while for women it is 38%. A haematocrit above 50% is seen as being suspicious, although it is just possible that such a high value could occur naturally.

Another way – also officially banned – of achieving a similar effect is to inject the body with the hormone erythropoetin, which is known as Epo. The hormone is made by genetically engineered (recombinant) bacteria and is slightly different from the naturally produced human Epo. This has made it possible to detect its use and random tests are now carried out on cyclists and other athletes both in and out of competition.

Both blood doping and the use of Epo are dangerous. A high haematocrit increases the viscosity of the blood (Fig 2.12). This may reduce the supply of oxygen to some parts of the body, and also increases the risk of a blood clot developing, causing pulmonary embolism, heart attack or stroke (see *Human Biology for AS*, page 75). It is thought that more than 20 competitive cyclists may have died from these effects in the 1990s.

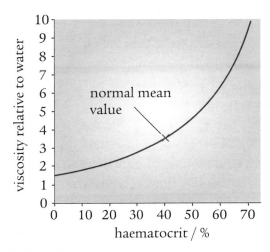

Fig 2.12 Haematocrit and blood viscosity.

Creatine phosphate

We have seen that muscles need ATP as an energy source for muscle contraction. They keep a very small store of ATP in the muscle fibres, which is used up very rapidly when exercise begins. They can produce more ATP by respiration. They also have a third source of ATP – a substance called **creatine phosphate**.

Muscles keep stores of creatine phosphate in their cytoplasm. This is their immediate source of energy once they have used up their small store of ATP. A phosphate group can quickly and easily be removed from each creatine phosphate molecule and combined with ADP to produce more ATP:

creatine phosphate + ADP $\longrightarrow$ creatine + ATP

Later, when the demand for energy has slowed down or stopped, ATP molecules produced by respiration can be used to 'recharge' the creatine:

creatine + ATP $\longrightarrow$ creatine phosphate + ADP

In the meantime, however, if energy is still being demanded by the muscles and there is no ATP to spare, the creatine is converted to creatinine and excreted in urine.

A muscle's store of ATP and creatine phosphate is enough to provide energy for up to 10 seconds, which is enough for a world-class sprinter to run a 100 m race. If the quantity of creatine phosphate in the muscle can be increased, this can improve the performance of sprinters and others who take part in events requiring short bursts of high-intensity performance. It has not been shown to have any beneficial effect in events lasting more than one minute.

It is possible to increase the creatine phosphate in muscles by taking supplements of creatine. It is usually sold as creatine monohydrate, which can be absorbed from the blood by muscle fibres and converted to creatine phosphate. One investigation showed that taking 20 g of creatine monohydrate for six days increases creatine phosphate stores in muscles by up to 20%. However, this amount taken over longer periods of time may damage the muscles' ability to take up and metabolise creatine, and studies have shown that, if the effect is to be maintained, then much lower doses of about 2 g are preferable.

Taking creatine supplements is perfectly legal in all sports. There is no evidence that it is dangerous, as the kidneys easily eliminate any excess in the form of creatinine. Fig 2.13 shows that the creatine phosphate naturally present in muscle gets used up quickly when the muscle is working hard; little is left after about 40 seconds.

Steroids

Steroids are substances that are synthesised from cholesterol, and their molecules are very similar to cholesterol molecules (Fig 2.14). Several hormones, including progesterone, testosterone and oestrogen, are steroids.

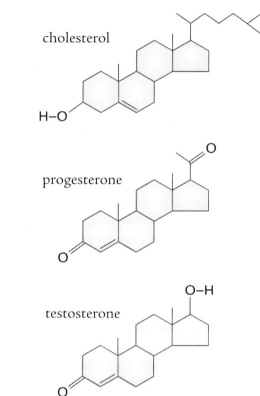

Fig 2.14 Steroids.

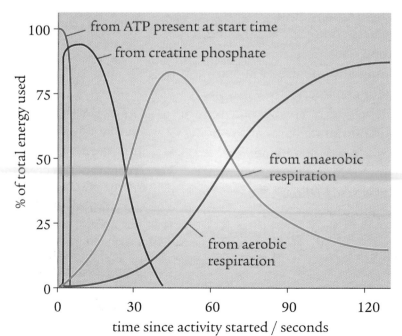

Fig 2.13 Energy sources used in muscle at high power output over a range of times.

Many steroid hormones stimulate **anabolic** reactions in body cells – that is, reactions in which large molecules are built from smaller ones. They are known as **anabolic steroids**.

Steroids are soluble in lipids, and they are therefore able to move relatively easily through cell membranes, despite the large size of their molecules. A steroid hormone enters its target cells, where it combines with a receptor molecule in the cytoplasm. This sets off a chain of events that results in transcription of a particular gene taking place, which in turn increases protein synthesis in the cell.

Testosterone, the hormone which is responsible for many male secondary sexual characteristics, and other similar substances such as stanazolol, have very great effects on protein synthesis in cells. They also increase aggression, which may be advantageous in making a person more competitive.

Athletes and others have illegally used anabolic steroids to try to increase their muscle size and strength. Athletes hope to increase their aggression when they take part in their event. Anabolic steroids reportedly have helped athletes to train harder and for longer. These uses are now banned, although, as we have seen (in the case study on page 1) some people have found the temptation of using them so great that they are willing to run the risk of being found out.

Moreover, the use of anabolic steroids is dangerous. In the long term, they decrease the body's own production of testosterone, and decrease the immune system's ability to respond to pathogens. They can damage the liver, whose cells take up the hormone and break it down to substances that are then excreted in the urine.

Athletes from a number of different sports are randomly tested, both in and out of competition, to check whether they have been taking anabolic steroids. The tests are thorough, but the interpretation can be unclear. For example, in 2003 a number of sprinters and tennis players were found to have a substance called **nandrolone** in their urine in quantities that were above the officially permitted level. Nandrolone is synthesised in the body from anabolic steroids, so its presence in abnormally large quantities suggests that these banned substances have been taken. However, it has proved difficult to be certain of just how much nandrolone is abnormal, or exactly where the nandrolone in a person's body might have come from, and therefore it is even more difficult to be certain what its presence in urine indicates about illegal use of anabolic steroids.

ACTIVITY 2.2

Blood doping in sport

Use the internet to find the current publication of the World Anti-doping Agency, called The Prohibitive List. Choose one drug from this list and investigate its use. You could consider any or all of the questions on the right.

- What does the drug do in the body?
- In which kinds of sports might it improve an athlete's performance?
- Can it cause harm?
- What methods can be used to detect its use by an athlete, and how do they work?
- Are there any cases of an athlete being banned for taking this drug?

Painkillers

Bruises and other injuries to muscles, tendons and ligaments can be very painful. Pain is a mechanism that is used by the body to indicate to the brain that damage has been done and that to continue the activity may cause even more damage. However, for some athletes, the danger of further damage may be less important than continuing with the activity. In these circumstances painkillers are used (Fig 2.15). Care must be taken, however, that serious injury through excessive use of an injured organ does not occur.

Fig 2.15 Pain killing spray can help a player continue in the game.

Summary

1. Training at high altitude can cause the number of red blood cells to increase, and also the total blood volume and VO_2 max. This can give an endurance athlete a competitive advantage over athletes who have trained at sea level. There is some evidence that living high and training low produces the greatest effect.

2. Blood doping is an illegal procedure in which $1\,dm^3$ of an athlete's blood is removed some weeks before competition, and stored at a low temperature. A few hours before the competition, the red cells from this blood sample are returned to the athlete's blood. This increases the supply of oxygen to muscles, and can therefore increase performance in endurance events. It is dangerous because it increases blood viscosity. It is almost impossible to detect with certainty.

3. Injecting erythropoetin (Epo) is another way of increasing the quantity of red blood cells in the body. It uses genetically engineered Epo, which is slightly different from normal Epo and so can be detected in the blood and urine. It is dangerous for the same reasons as blood doping.

4. Creatine phosphate is an energy store in muscle, which can be used to produce ATP when the small ATP store runs out. It does this more quickly than respiration, so it is useful in providing extra ATP before respiration is able to do so. Food supplements containing creatine monophosphate seem to increase the quantity of creatine phosphate in muscle, and may improve performance.

5. Anabolic steroids are drugs that speed up the synthesis of proteins in cells, including muscle fibres. Taken over a period of time, anabolic steroids can increase muscle bulk and strength, and may therefore improve athletic performance. They are illegal drugs in sport. They are usually detected by the presence of their breakdown products in urine. They are dangerous because they can produce a range of unwanted effects, including liver damage and a decrease in the effectiveness of the immune system.

CHAPTER 3

Monitoring visual function

Howard is 83. His wife died four years ago, and he lives on his own. Both of his children and their families live quite a distance away. They do come to see him every now and then, but it is a long drive and they are too busy to do it very often. He gets most of his food from the shop a little way down his road and likes to spend his spare time solving crossword puzzles, doing wood-carving, and reading – especially books about archaeology which is a great interest for him. He goes to an evening class about Bronze Age archaeology once a week, which he especially enjoys because there are people to talk to. He does get lonely in his house on his own.

But just recently something has happened that is going to completely change his lifestyle. He has started to notice that he can't see things clearly, even wearing his glasses. Words on the page have become blurred. He feels nervous going down stairs, as he can't see where the next step is. There is a dark area in the centre of his vision. He daren't make the journey to his archaeology class.

Howard is diagnosed with macular degeneration. The macula is a spot in the retina where light is focussed when you look directly at something. In Howard's eyes, the receptor cells in the macula are dying. It is happening in both his eyes, and he now can only read large-print books. He has had to stop most of his usual activities.

There isn't much hope of successful treatment for Howard. But, in years to come, there may well be. Macular degeneration is the leading cause of blindness in people over 55. Some success has been achieved in animals by transplanting cells from healthy parts of the retina into the damaged part. Researchers in several different countries have had success with extracting stem cells from the eye, and getting them to produce new receptor cells. The stem cells come from around the edge of the cornea and they are always there, no matter how old you are. They can be taken from eyes donated by people who have died, or possibly from a person's own eyes. One group of researchers have found that, by adding a gene called Crx to these stem cells, they can persuade them to make rhodopsin. As yet, they haven't managed to transplant these into damaged retinas, but there is great hope that this will be done eventually. But not in time, unfortunately, to save Howard's sight.

The eye is part of the **nervous system**. The nervous system is made up of:

- the brain and spinal cord, which form the **central nervous system**;
- the nerves and sense organs, which form the **peripheral nervous system** (Fig 3.1).

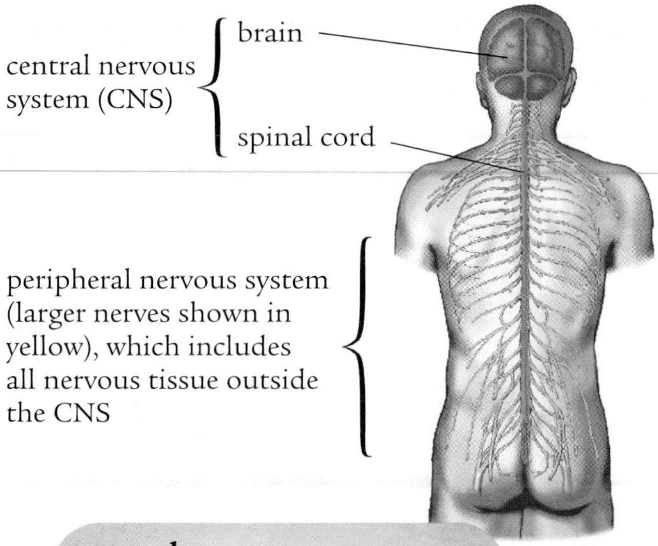

central nervous system (CNS) { brain

spinal cord

peripheral nervous system (larger nerves shown in yellow), which includes all nervous tissue outside the CNS

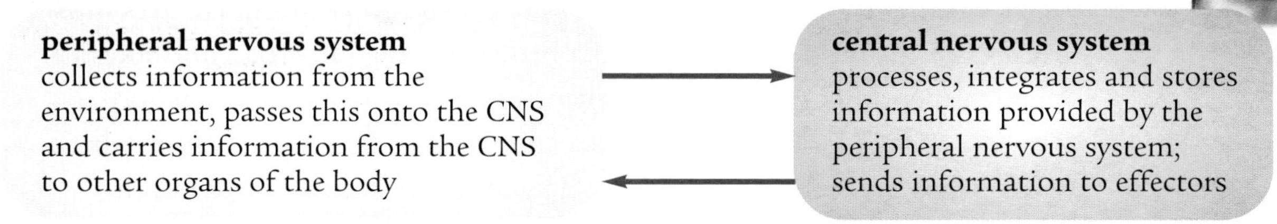

peripheral nervous system collects information from the environment, passes this onto the CNS and carries information from the CNS to other organs of the body

central nervous system processes, integrates and stores information provided by the peripheral nervous system; sends information to effectors

Fig 3.1 An outline of the organisation of the nervous system.

The eye is a sense organ. Like all sense organs, it contains cells known as **receptors**. These cells react to stimuli from their environment by generating nerve impulses – action potentials – that travel along nerve fibres to the central nervous system. The receptor cells change energy in the stimulus into energy in the nerve impulse. The energy in the stimulus that affects the receptors in the eye is light energy (Fig 3.2).

In this chapter, we will look at how the eye works, and at some of the tests which can be done to check its function and also, in some cases, problems in other areas of the body. Later, we will look at how the central and peripheral nervous systems work.

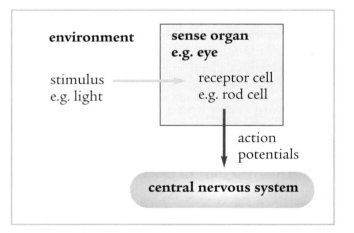

environment

sense organ e.g. eye

stimulus e.g. light

receptor cell e.g. rod cell

action potentials

central nervous system

Fig 3.2 Receptors in sense organs respond to a stimulus by producing action potentials, which carry information to the central nervous system.

COLEG LLANDRILLO COLLEGE
LIBRARY RESOURCE CENTRE
CANOLFAN ADNODDAU LLYFRGELL
087435

Structure and function of the eye

Fig 3.3 shows the structure of the human eye.

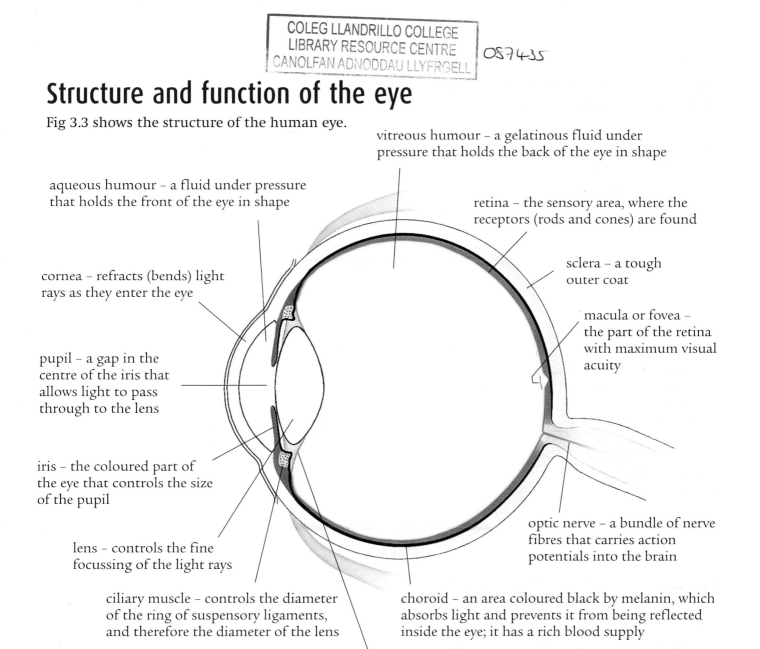

vitreous humour – a gelatinous fluid under pressure that holds the back of the eye in shape

aqueous humour – a fluid under pressure that holds the front of the eye in shape

retina – the sensory area, where the receptors (rods and cones) are found

cornea – refracts (bends) light rays as they enter the eye

sclera – a tough outer coat

pupil – a gap in the centre of the iris that allows light to pass through to the lens

macula or fovea – the part of the retina with maximum visual acuity

iris – the coloured part of the eye that controls the size of the pupil

optic nerve – a bundle of nerve fibres that carries action potentials into the brain

lens – controls the fine focussing of the light rays

ciliary muscle – controls the diameter of the ring of suspensory ligaments, and therefore the diameter of the lens

choroid – an area coloured black by melanin, which absorbs light and prevents it from being reflected inside the eye; it has a rich blood supply

suspensory ligament – holds the lens in position and enables any outward pull to change lens shape

Fig 3.3 Structure and function of the eye.

How the eye focusses light

Light enters the eye through the **cornea**. The receptor cells are in the retina at the back of the eye. For a clear image to be seen, the light must be perfectly focussed onto these receptor cells (Fig 3.4).

The light rays need to be bent inwards to be brought to a focus. The bending of light rays as they pass from one material into another is called **refraction**. Light rays are refracted as they pass from the air into the cornea. They then pass through the **pupil** and hit the **lens**.

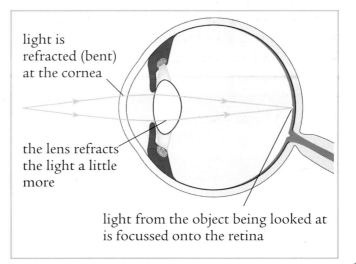

light is refracted (bent) at the cornea

the lens refracts the light a little more

light from the object being looked at is focussed onto the retina

Fig 3.4 How the eye focusses light.

51

The cornea does most of the necessary refraction of the light rays, but the lens is used to make fine adjustments. A thin lens does not refract the rays very much, whereas a fat one does.

A thick lens is needed when you are focussing on a nearby object. A thin one is needed when you are focussing on a distant object (Fig 3.5).

The shape of the lens is altered by the **ciliary muscle** (Fig 3.6). This ring of muscle is attached to the **suspensory ligaments** that hold the lens in position. When the muscles in the ring contract, they make the ring smaller. This releases tension on the suspensory ligaments and allows the lens to take up its natural shape, which is very curved and thick. When the muscles in the ring relax, they make the ring larger. This increases tension on the suspensory ligaments, which pull the lens outwards into a longer, thinner shape.

So, for close focussing the ciliary muscle is contracted, while for distant focussing it is relaxed. Many people find it restful to take their eyes away from their computer screen or book for a short while and let them relax by looking into the far distance.

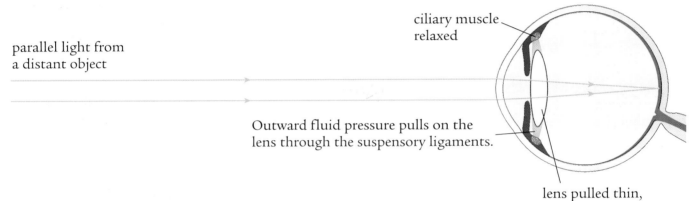

parallel light from a distant object

ciliary muscle relaxed

Outward fluid pressure pulls on the lens through the suspensory ligaments.

lens pulled thin, refracting the light less

Fig 3.5 Focussing on a distant object.

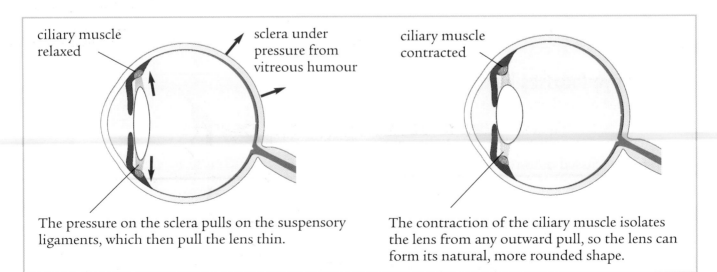

ciliary muscle relaxed

sclera under pressure from vitreous humour

ciliary muscle contracted

The pressure on the sclera pulls on the suspensory ligaments, which then pull the lens thin.

The contraction of the ciliary muscle isolates the lens from any outward pull, so the lens can form its natural, more rounded shape.

Fig 3.6 How the ciliary muscle affects lens shape.

The retina

The retina, as we have seen, is the part of the eye that contains the light-sensitive receptor cells. They are of two types – **rods** and **cones**. Their structures are shown in Fig 3.7.

Both rods and cones contain **pigments** whose molecules change shape when light hits them. In rod cells, there is only one type of pigment, called **rhodopsin**. However, there are three different kinds of cone cells, each with a different form of the pigment **iodopsin**. Here, we will concentrate on what happens when light hits a rod cell, but you can imagine very similar events taking place in cone cells.

The retina is quite puzzling. It looks as though it is all 'backwards' (Fig 3.8). Wouldn't it

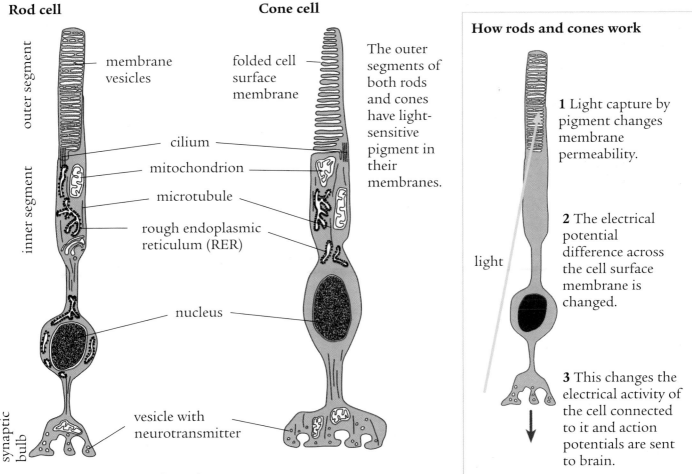

How rods and cones work

1 Light capture by pigment changes membrane permeability.

2 The electrical potential difference across the cell surface membrane is changed.

3 This changes the electrical activity of the cell connected to it and action potentials are sent to brain.

light

Rod cell

membrane vesicles

outer segment

inner segment

cilium

mitochondrion

microtubule

rough endoplasmic reticulum (RER)

nucleus

synaptic bulb

vesicle with neurotransmitter

Cone cell

folded cell surface membrane

The outer segments of both rods and cones have light-sensitive pigment in their membranes.

Fig 3.7 Rod and cone cells.

choroid

retina

rod

cone

bipolar cell

ganglion cell

action potentials to optic nerve and brain

Fig 3.8 The cells making up the retina.

light

53

be better if the rod and cone cells were on the outside so that the light hit them first, rather than the light having to go through the layers of bipolar cells and **ganglion cells** first? No-one has really thought of a completely convincing argument to explain this odd arrangement, and all we can say is that this is the way it has evolved, and it seems to work well.

How an action potential is generated

Information collected by rod and cone cells is transmitted to the brain in the form of **action potentials** along nerve cells in the optic nerve. (Action potentials are explained on pages 67 to 69.) Rod and cone cells act as transducers – that is, they transfer energy in light to energy in action potentials.

A rod cell, like neurones, maintains a **resting potential** across its cell surface membranes, i.e. there is a negative charge inside the cell compared with outside (see page 66). It does this by pumping out sodium ions and pumping in potassium ions. The difference in charge is produced because more sodium ions are moved out than potassium ions are moved in.

In the inner segment (Figs 3.7 and 3.9) the cell membrane is permeable to potassium ions, and they constantly flow out of the cell down their electrochemical gradient. However, in the outer segment, the cell surface membrane is permeable to sodium ions, so these constantly flow into the cell here. This constant flow of charge into and out of the cell in different regions generates a circulating electric current (Fig 3.9). So you can see that a lot is going on in a 'resting' rod cell.

While the rod cell is in this resting state, the synaptic bulb is secreting a steady stream of the neurotransmitter glutamate (see pages 72 to 74). This is an inhibitory transmitter. It diffuses across the synaptic cleft and prevents action potentials being generated in the bipolar cell.

When light hits a rhodopsin molecule in a rod cell, the rhodopsin changes shape. A rhodopsin molecule has two components – a protein part called **opsin** and another part called **11-*cis*-retinal**. Light causes the 11-cis-retinal to change to **all-*trans*-retinal**. This interacts with other proteins in the cell surface membrane, causing the sodium channels to close. This causes the circulating current to

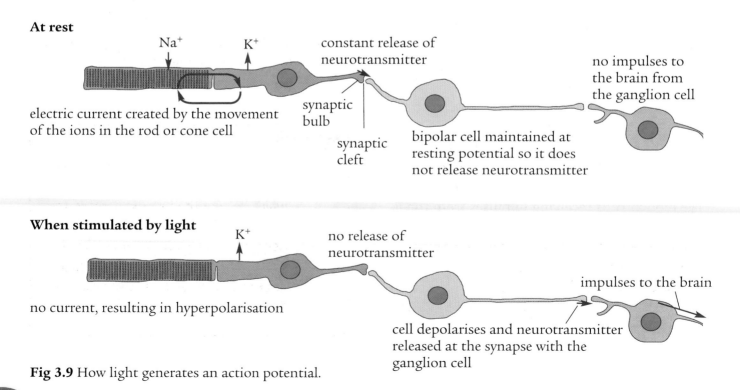

Fig 3.9 How light generates an action potential.

stop, and the cell becomes even more negative inside than usual. It is said to be hyperpolarised.

This causes the rod cell to stop secreting glutamate. Now there is no inhibition of the bipolar cell, and it becomes depolarised. This generates an action potential in it, which is transmitted across the synapse to a ganglion cell. From here, it is carried along the optic nerve to the brain.

Once a rhodopsin molecule has changed shape, it can no longer absorb light. In bright light, most rhodopsin will have changed shape. It then breaks down into opsin and retinal. If you move into a dark place, the opsin and retinal will be re-combined to form rhodopsin again. This takes a few minutes, which is why it takes a little while for your eyes to adjust so that you can see anything when you move from light to dark conditions.

Functions of rods and cones

Rod cells are very sensitive to even small amounts of light falling onto them. Even a single photon of light may be enough for them to produce an action potential in a ganglion cell. It is our rods that allow us to see in dim light.

Cone cells need more light to fall onto them before they respond. They are most useful to us in bright light. Moreover, we have three different kinds of cones, and this is why we have colour vision (Fig 3.10).

The three types of cones contain three types of the pigment iodopsin. Pigment B is most sensitive to blue light, pigment G to green light and pigment R to red light. For example, if the light falling onto the retina is blue, then it is the bipolar cells receiving impulses from the B cones that carry action potentials to the brain. The brain interprets action potentials from these cells as meaning 'blue'.

There is one part of the retina where there are no rods at all, and where the cone cells are most tightly packed. This is called the **fovea** or **macula**. This is the part of the retina where light is focussed when we look directly at an object, and from where the brain gets the most detailed information which it uses to form an image. It is degeneration of the cone cells in this area that causes the difficulty with vision known as macular degeneration.

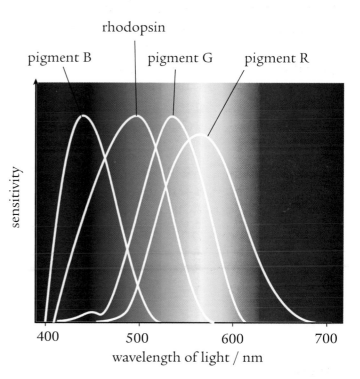

Fig 3.10 Sensitivity of the three cone pigments and rhodopsin to different wavelengths of light.

SAQ

3.1a Using the information in Fig 3.10, state the range of wavelengths of light to which each of the four pigments in the eye responds.

b Use your answer, and what you know about the sensitivity of rods and cones, to explain why we cannot see colours in dim light.

Visual acuity

Black-and-white or colour vision is not the only difference between the result of stimulation of rods or cones. There is also a difference in the degree of detail – the resolution – in the image that the brain 'sees'.

The diagram shows why this is so. Each cone cell is 'wired up' to a single ganglion cell, so the brain gets information from each cone individually. But this isn't the case for rods, where several rod cells all feed their information into the same ganglion cell.

So the brain gets 'pooled' information from a group of rod cells. The image that we see when using cone cells is therefore sharper than when using rod cells. We say that cone cells give us better visual acuity than rod cells.

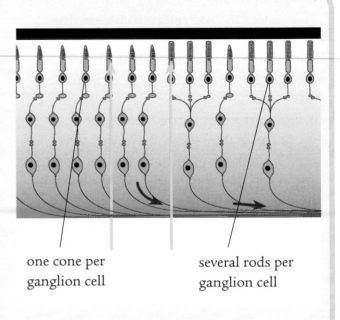

one cone per
ganglion cell

several rods per
ganglion cell

SAQ

3.2   We saw in the case study (see page 49) that it may be possible to transplant a healthy part of the retina into the region of the macula, in someone with macular degeneration. If this operation was entirely successful, would you expect the person to have his or her vision perfectly restored? Use the information about the structure of the retina to explain your answer. (You might also like to use the information in the Just for Interest section below entitled 'Visual acuity'.)

Getting the picture

The eyes and brain produce an image in a much more sophisticated way than a camera. The image that is focussed onto the retina undergoes much more 'digital processing' in the brain than you are aware of, in order to produce the image that we 'see'.

For example, if you are looking at a person standing one metre away from you, their image will cover a large amount of your retina. If the person is standing 100 metres away, their image will be much smaller. Yet your brain automatically interprets the small image as meaning that a person-sized object is standing a long way away from you, rather than that a very small person is standing close.

Optical illusions illustrate ways in which the brain puts its own interpretations onto images. They show that the brain is processing images in a sophisticated way.

Image processing has evolved to provide us with the most 'useful' information that can be gleaned from the simple image that appears on the retina. Illusions show that sometimes the final interpretation is 'sensible' and sometimes not. The information arriving from our eyes along the optic nerve is integrated with information arriving along pathways in the brain – from memory, for example – in order to produce the image we see.

How many black dots can you see? Where do you see them? Think about this illusion in terms of the use of cones in that part of the retina in the very centre of your field of view and the use of rods in more peripheral parts of your field of view. So far, however, this illusion cannot be fully explained.

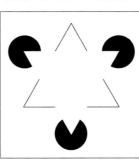

What do you see that is not really here? What visual information is the brain using to construct this 'imagined' object?

Which square is the lighter one, A or B? (See the bottom of the page for the answer.) What is the brain doing that makes us misinterpret the actual intensity of grey in A and B?

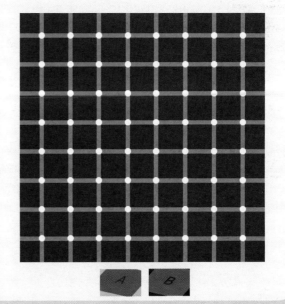

Summary

1 Receptors are part of the peripheral nervous system in which energy from a stimulus is changed to energy in nerve impulses. The nerve impulses are carried to the central nervous system – that is, the brain or spinal cord.

2 The part of the eye which contains light-sensitive receptors is the retina. Light is focussed on the retina by the cornea and lens.

3 The lens carries out fine adjustments to the focussing of the light. It is held in place by the suspensory ligaments, and the tension on these can be altered by the ciliary muscle. When this muscle contracts, the ligaments are loosened and the lens becomes relatively thick and rounded. When the muscle relaxes, the ligaments are pulled taut, which pulls the lens into a thinner shape.

4 The lens needs to be thin for focussing on distant objects, and thick for focussing on near objects.

5 The retina contains two types of receptor cells, rods and cones. Rods contain the pigment rhodopsin, while there are three kinds of cone cells with different types of iodopsin. All of these pigments are held in stacks of membranes inside the rod or cone cells. When light hits the pigments in a rod or cone cell, an action potential may be generated in the optic nerve, which carries it to the brain.

6 Rods are sensitive to dimmer light than cones, but do not distinguish between light of different colours. Cones only respond to relatively bright light, but as each of the three types respond to light of different wavelengths, the brain can interpret the action potentials from them to provide colour vision.

Eye tests

Testing eye function is used to assess a person's vision, so that they can be given glasses or contact lenses to help them to see more clearly. The people who carry out these tests are **optometrists**. Optometrists can also carry out tests that tell them about several aspects of a person's health, including level of consciousness, impairment of their brain and nerve function because of drugs that they have taken, and whether they have health problems such as diabetes or high blood pressure. And of course, they can detect conditions such as macular degeneration.

Routine eye tests

If you go to an optician to get glasses or contact lenses, several tests will be carried out on your eyes to find out what prescription you need. You will have tests for your visual acuity (how sharply in focus you can see things), your colour vision and how your pupil responds to light of different intensities.

Visual acuity test

For this test, you will be asked to read letters of different sizes on a chart known as a **Snellen chart** (Fig 3.11). You are asked to cover one eye (or it is covered for you) and then read out the letters you can see on the chart, starting from

Snellen chart

A
D F
H Z P
T X U D
Z A D N H
P N T U H X
U A Z N F D T
N P H T A F X U
X D F H P T Z A N
F A X T D N H U P Z

Fig 3.11 A Snellen chart scaled to be viewed at 3 m.

the top down. The optometrist will record the smallest row of letters that you can read. The test is then repeated with the other eye.

The letters on the chart are viewed from a distance of 6 metres (20 feet). If you can read them all, you have 20/20 vision. The first number is the distance, in feet, that you stand from the chart. The second number is the distance at which a person with 'normal' eyesight would have to stand to just be able to read the same smallest line that you could. So, if you are told your vision is 20/30, it means that your vision is not as good as that of a 'normal' person – they could stand ten feet further away from the chart than you did, and just be able to read the same line that you could.

For people who cannot read letters (for example, small children who have not yet learned to read, or people who use a language with a different alphabet) the Snellen chart may have pictures. For example, it might show cars where the patient is asked to identify which ones have a broken wheel.

The Snellen chart is used to test your ability to see things at a distance from you, but you might also be tested to see how good your near vision is. This uses a similar kind of card, but this time you will be asked to read it when it is about 30 cm from your eyes.

The results of these tests tell the optometrist what kind of glasses or contact lenses you need to help you to see more clearly.

Colour vision test

About 7% of men and 1% of women are red–green **colourblind**. They only have two types of cone cells, one sensitive to blue light and the other sensitive to red or green light. Their vision is usually completely normal in other ways – they just have a little trouble with such things as seeing holly berries in a holly tree and choosing the right tie to go with their shirt.

To test for colourblindness, a person is asked to look at a collection of cards made up of different coloured spots (Fig 3.12). The spots are

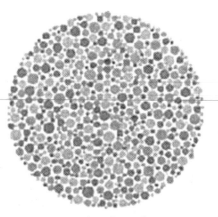

Fig 3.12 An example of a colour vision chart. Why are the size, arrangement and colour of each spot so varied in this chart?

arranged so the ones of a particular colour form images of numbers. If you can see the numbers, that means your eyes can see the different colours. If not, then you are colourblind with respect to a particular colour.

Colourblindness cannot be corrected with glasses, or indeed with any treatment at all. But it is useful for a person to know if they are colourblind, and in exactly which way, so that they understand what problems they may have.

Pupil response test

The pupil is the gap in the middle of the iris. The iris is made up of pigmented cells that won't let light pass through them. It also contains muscles – circular muscles arranged in rings, and radial muscles arranged like the spokes of a bicycle wheel.

If very bright light falls onto the retina, it may cause damage. The iris controls the amount of light that can reach the lens and retina, by adjusting the diameter of the pupil. Fig 3.13 shows how it does this. This is an example of a **reflex action** – that is, a rapid and automatic response to a stimulus that does not require conscious thought (see page 65). This test should perhaps be called the iris reflex test, because it is the response of the iris that is involved – the pupil is just a hole in the centre of the iris.

In the pupil response test, the person to be tested is seated in a dark room and a bright light is shone onto one eye. This is usually done by swinging a torch so that the light shines first

into one eye and then the other. There should be a very rapid response in which the circular muscles of the iris contract and widen the iris, so that it leaves only a tiny amount – perhaps just 1.5 mm – of the pupil exposed. The test is repeated with the other eye.

Light shone into one eye should make both pupils constrict equally. If there is a difference in the effect when the light is shone on one eye than when it is shone on the other, the person is said to have an **RAPD** – a **relative afferent pupillary defect**.

An RAPD can indicate damage to the optic nerve or the brain. It can also indicate that the person's nervous system is affected by alcohol or other drugs. In some states in the USA, it is measured by a computer and used to help to determine whether someone is sober or not, although it has proved not to be a very reliable indicator.

One of the advantages of this test is that it does not require the person to say what they see, so you can use it even on a baby or on someone who is unconscious.

Assessing level of consciousness

Eye examinations can help to determine the condition of a person who appears to be unconscious. Reflex actions have the advantage that they don't require the patient to communicate, and so both of the eye tests that can be used in this context involve reflexes. They are the pupil response reflex and the **blink reflex**.

We have already seen how the pupil response reflex is carried out. If the pupil size of an unconscious person does not change when a light is shone onto it, this can help a doctor to diagnose the underlying cause of the patient's condition. For example, someone who has taken amphetamines is likely to have dilated pupils which are fixed in that state, whilst a person whose condition is due to opiates, or who has suffered respiratory arrest as a result of barbiturate poisoning, will have small, fixed pupils.

The blink reflex is the rapid closing of the eyelid when something threatening approaches the eye. It is tested by suddenly moving a reflex hammer (the little tool that is tapped onto your knee if your doctor wants to test the knee-jerk reflex) towards the eyes. The blink reflex is still seen even in a patient who appears to be completely unconscious – it is one of the last to be lost as unconsciousness deepens. If it is not present, then this indicates that the person is in a coma and has lost all perception of their environment. It is probable that the brain has been very badly damaged.

Neither the pupil reflex nor the blink reflex are used on their own to assess consciousness, but will be part of a number of tests, including the ability of the patient to respond to speech.

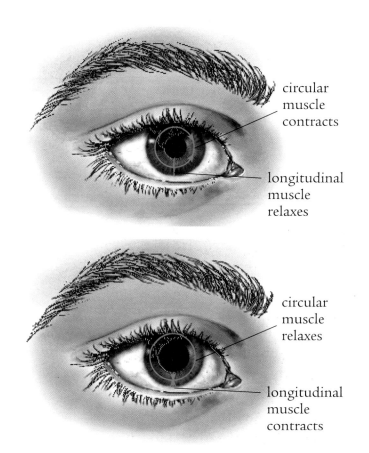

circular muscle contracts

longitudinal muscle relaxes

circular muscle relaxes

longitudinal muscle contracts

Fig 3.13 The pupil response.

SAQ

3.3   Most optometrists don't have a room as big as 6 m wide. Suggest how they could display the Snellen chart so that it looks as though it is 6 m away from you.

Summary

1. An optometrist tests a person's vision to determine whether they need to have their vision corrected.

2. Visual acuity is tested using a Snellen chart. The smallest row of letters that you can see, when at an effective distance of 6 m from the chart, is recorded.

3. Colour vision is tested using images made up of spots of different colours. If a person has colourblindness, they will not be able to see patterns that are visible to people with normal vision.

4. The pupil response test measures the response of the iris to a bright light shone into the eye. Both pupils should rapidly constrict when light is shone into either eye.

5. The pupil response test, sometimes known as the iris reflex test, and the blink reflex test, can be used to ascertain a person's level of consciousness. A poor iris reflex can indicate brain damage or the effect of drugs. The blink reflex is seen even in patients who are unconscious, and its absence indicates the very deep level of unconsciousness known as coma.

CHAPTER 4

Neurones

Josef is four years old. He lives in Nigeria, with his parents and four brothers and sisters. He loves swimming, and often plays in the small river that flows a few metres away from his home.

A few months ago, Josef woke feeling very ill, and his mother could feel that he had a fever as she held her hand against his forehead. As the day progressed he became even more unwell. He vomited several times. By the evening he could not move his legs.

By now his mother guessed what his illness might be. She had seen other children affected by it. She took Josef to hospital, where her diagnosis was confirmed. Josef had poliomyelitis.

There is no cure for polio; all that could be done for Josef was to keep him warm and rested and wait for his own body to fight the virus that was making him ill. He quite quickly recovered from feeling sick and running a temperature, but the loss of movement in his legs remained. Now Josef can still walk, but only very stiffly and he has trouble keeping up with his friends.

Polio has been eradicated in many parts of the world, following a vaccination campaign by the World Health Organization. Unfortunately, some countries in Africa have not taken up the offer of vaccination against polio for every child, because many people believe that the polio vaccine is the cause of their AIDS epidemic. As a result, countries that have been completely free from polio for years have seen a resurgence.

Polio used to be called 'infantile paralysis'. The virus enters the body in water that has been contaminated with human faeces, and then may invade the nervous system. It tends to infect the cell bodies of the motor neurones – that is, the cells that carry nerve impulses from the brain and spinal cord to the muscles. One in twenty infections leads to permanent paralysis, because these motor neurones are damaged beyond repair. Muscles that no longer receive nerve impulses along their motor neurones waste away and become useless. Sometimes the virus also destroys the neurones that carry impulses to the diaphragm and intercostal muscles, so that breathing stops. This happens to about 10% of children who are infected, and it can kill.

Neurones, otherwise known as nerve cells, carry information very rapidly from one part of the body to another. This information travels as a series of action potentials – fleeting changes in the electrical charge on either side of their cell surface membranes. Action potentials are also known as **nerve impulses**.

Neurones and the reflex arc

Neurones begin their lives as 'normal' cells, but as they differentiate they become very different in shape from any other cells in our body. They have many adaptations that give them the ability to transmit action potentials swiftly. All neurones have very similar adaptations, but there are recognisable differences between neurones that carry impulses to and from different parts of the body.

The structure of neurones

Fig 4.1 shows the structure of a **motor neurone**. (This is the type of neurone that is destroyed by the polio virus.) Motor neurones carry action potentials from the brain or spinal cord to muscles or to glands (see Fig 4.2a).

The cell body of a motor neurone lies within the spinal cord or brain. The nucleus of a neurone is always in its cell body. Often, dark specks can be seen in the cytoplasm. These are groups of ribosomes involved in protein synthesis.

Many thin cytoplasmic processes extend from the cell body. In a motor neurone, all but one of these processes are relatively short. They conduct impulses towards the cell body, and they are called **dendrites**. One process is much longer, and this conducts impulses away from the cell body. This is called the **axon**. A motor neurone with its cell body in your spinal cord might have its axon running all the way to one of your toes, so axons may be very long.

Within the cytoplasm of the axon, all of the usual organelles, such as endoplasmic reticulum, Golgi apparatus and mitochondria, are present. Particularly large numbers of mitochondria are found at the tips of the terminal branches of the axon, together with many vesicles containing chemicals called **transmitter substances**. These are involved in passing the nerve impulse from the neurone to a muscle, and their function is described on page 72.

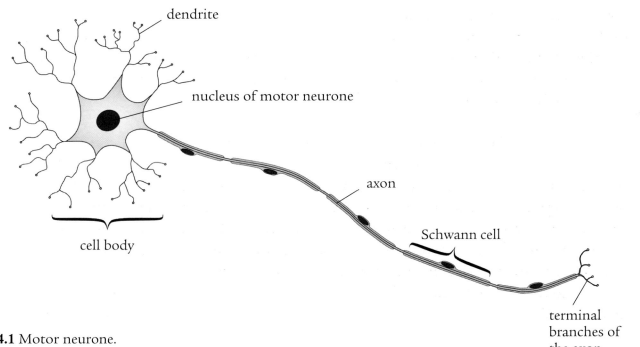

Fig 4.1 Motor neurone.

Sensory neurones (Fig 4.2b) carry information from sense organs to the brain or spinal cord. Their cell bodies are inside structures called dorsal root ganglia, just outside the spinal cord.

Sensory neurones are sometimes known as **bipolar neurones**, because they have two long cytoplasmic processes. You have met an example of bipolar neurones – the ones that carry impulses from the rod and cone cells to the ganglion cells in the retina of the eye (Fig 3.8).

Intermediate neurones (Fig 4.2c) have their cell bodies and their cytoplasmic processes inside the brain or spinal cord. They are adapted to carry impulses from and to numerous other neurones.

Myelin

In some neurones, cells called **Schwann cells** wrap themselves around the axon all along its length. Fig 4.3 shows one such cell, viewed as the axon is cut transversely. The Schwann cell spirals around, enclosing the axon in many layers of its cell surface membrane. This enclosing sheath, called the **myelin sheath**, is made largely of lipid, together with some proteins.

There are small uncovered areas all along the axons where there are gaps between the Schwann cells. These are known as **nodes of Ranvier**. They occur about every 1–3 mm.

About one third of our motor and sensory neurones are myelinated. The sheath increases the speed of conduction of the nerve impulses, and this is described on page 68.

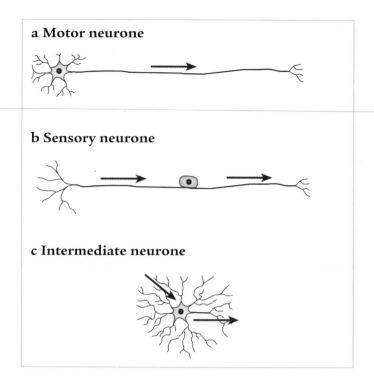

a Motor neurone

b Sensory neurone

c Intermediate neurone

Fig 4.2 Types of neurones.

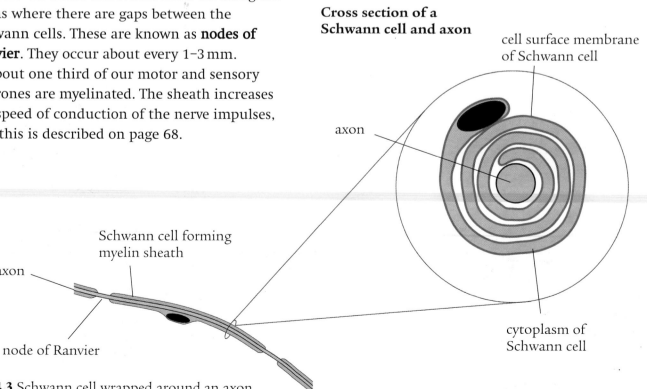

Cross section of a Schwann cell and axon

cell surface membrane of Schwann cell

axon

axon

Schwann cell forming myelin sheath

node of Ranvier

cytoplasm of Schwann cell

Fig 4.3 Schwann cell wrapped around an axon.

The reflex arc

Fig 4.4 shows how sensory, intermediate and motor neurones are arranged in the body to form a **reflex arc**. In the example in Fig 4.4, a **spinal reflex arc** is shown, in which the nerve impulses are carried into and out of the spinal cord. Other reflex arcs may involve the brain.

A reflex arc is the pathway along which impulses are carried from a receptor to an **effector**, without involving any conscious thought. An effector is a part of the body that responds to a stimulus. Muscles and glands are effectors.

The impulse arrives along the sensory neurone and passes through the dorsal root ganglion into the spinal cord. Here it may be passed directly to the motor neurone, or to an intermediate neurone and then the motor neurone. The impulse sweeps along the axon of the motor neurone, arriving at the effector within less than one second of the receptor having picked up the stimulus.

The response by the effector can be extremely rapid. It is called a reflex action. A reflex action can be defined as a stereotyped, fast response to a particular stimulus. Reflex actions help us to avoid danger, by allowing us to respond immediately to a dangerous situation without having to spend time thinking about it. For example, a sharp pinprick on the bottom of your foot will probably result in contraction of muscles in your leg, pulling the leg away from the stimulus.

SAQ

4.1   Some reflex actions seem to be innate (inborn). They appear to be 'hard-wired' into our brains from birth. Other reflex actions are learned during our lifetimes.

a   Think of a reflex action that almost everyone shows and that is therefore likely to be innate. Name:
- the stimulus;
- the receptor that picks up the stimulus;
- the effector that receives the nerve impulse;
- the response.

b   Do the same for a reflex action that you have learned.

c   What, if any, are the survival values of the reflex actions you have described?

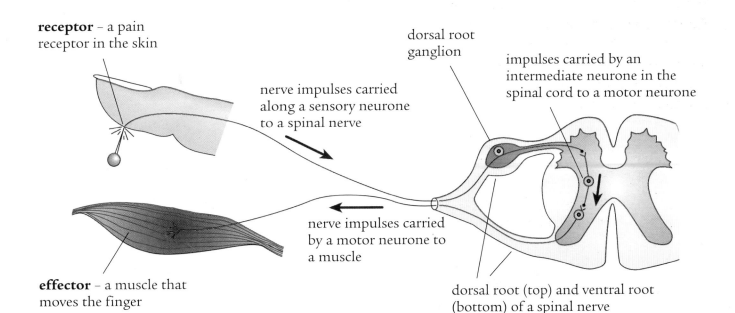

receptor – a pain receptor in the skin

dorsal root ganglion

impulses carried by an intermediate neurone in the spinal cord to a motor neurone

nerve impulses carried along a sensory neurone to a spinal nerve

nerve impulses carried by a motor neurone to a muscle

effector – a muscle that moves the finger

dorsal root (top) and ventral root (bottom) of a spinal nerve

Fig 4.4 A spinal reflex arc.

Summary

1 A neurone is a cell that is adapted for carrying impulses in the form of action potentials from one part of the body to another. A neurone has a cell body containing a nucleus and all the organelles normally found in a cell. It has two or more processes, one or more of which may be very long, which carry impulses either towards or away from the cell body.

2 Sensory neurones have their cell bodies in the dorsal root ganglia of the spinal cord. They carry impulses from a sense organ to the central nervous system. Intermediate neurones carry impulses between neurones within the central nervous system. Motor neurones carry impulses from the central nervous system to an effector, which may be a muscle or a gland.

3 The arrangement of neurones that can carry an impulse from a receptor to an effector is called a reflex arc. Reflex arcs may involve either the brain or the spinal cord. They may have only two neurones, the sensory and motor neurones, or they may involve an intermediate neurone as well.

Transmitting nerve impulses

We have seen that neurones transmit impulses as electrical signals. These signals travel rapidly from one end of the neurone to the other. They are not a flow of electrons like an electric current, which is even more rapid. Rather, the signals are very brief changes in the distribution of electrical charge across the cell surface membrane, caused by the very rapid movement of sodium and potassium ions into and out of the axon.

The resting potential

Even a resting neurone is very active (Fig 4.5). The sodium–potassium pumps in its cell surface membrane constantly move sodium ions out of the cell and potassium ions into the cell. These movements are against the concentration gradients, and so they are examples of active transport. Large amounts of ATP are used.

The sodium–potassium pump removes three sodium ions from the cell for every two potassium ions it brings into the cell. Both sodium and potassium ions carry a positive charge. This results in there being an excess of positive charge outside the membrane compared with inside.

The difference in charge is about −65 mV (millivolts), with the inside being more negative than the outside. This is called the resting potential of the neurone.

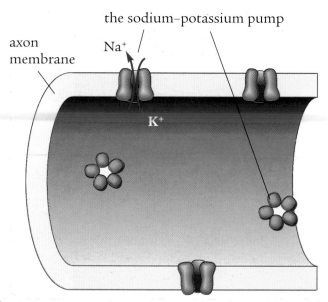

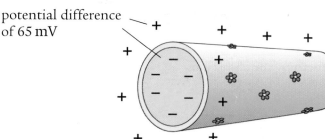

Fig 4.5 Activity in a resting neurone.

Action potentials

As well as the sodium–potassium pump, the cell surface membranes of neurones have other, quite separate, transporter proteins that allow sodium and potassium ions to pass through. Normally, these channels are closed.

Imagine a touch receptor in your hand. The receptor is actually the end of a sensory neurone. When the receptor receives a stimulus (touch), these sodium ion channels open. The sodium ions that had been pumped out rapidly flood back into the cell down their electrochemical gradient. Suddenly, the resting potential has gone – there is no longer a negative charge inside the axon compared with outside. The axon membrane is said to be **depolarised**.

So many sodium ions flood in so quickly that they 'overshoot'. For a brief moment, the axon actually becomes *positively* charged inside, rather than negatively. Then the sodium channels close, so sodium ions stop moving into the axon.

At this point, the potassium ion channels open. Potassium ions therefore diffuse out of the axon, down their electrochemical gradient. This removes positive charge from inside the axon to the outside, thus beginning to return the potential difference to normal. This is called **repolarisation**.

So many potassium ions leave the axon that the potential difference across the membrane briefly becomes even more negative than the normal resting potential. The potassium channels then close, and the sodium-potassium pump begins to be effective, restoring the normal distribution of sodium and potassium ions across the membrane, and therefore restoring the resting potential.

All these changes in electrical charge can be measured and displayed – for example, on an oscilloscope. Fig 4.6 shows what an action potential looks like.

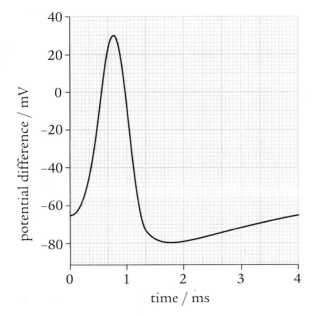

Fig 4.6 An action potential.

SAQ

4.2   Make a copy of Fig 4.6.

a   On your graph, draw a horizontal line right across it representing the resting potential.

b   The resting potential is said to be −65 mV 'inside'. What does this mean?

c   How does the cell maintain this resting potential?

d   As an action potential begins, the line on the graph shoots upwards from −65 mV to +30 mV.

  i   Why is this called 'depolarisation'?

  ii   Annotate your graph to explain what is happening in the axon membrane to cause this rapid depolarisation.

e   Annotate your graph to describe and explain what happens between about 1 ms and 2 ms.

f   Assuming the action potential begins at time 0, how long does it take between the start of depolarisation and the restoration of the resting potential?

Transmission of an action potential

The graph in Fig 4.6 shows the events that take place at one point in the axon membrane. However, the function of a neurone is to transmit information, in the form of action potentials, along itself. How do action potentials move along a neurone?

An action potential at any point in an axon's cell surface membrane triggers the production of an action potential in the part of the membrane just next to it. Fig 4.7 shows how it does this. The temporary depolarisation of the membrane where the action potential is causes a 'local circuit' to be set up between the depolarised region and the resting regions on either side of it. This depolarises these adjoining regions and so generates an action potential in them. In this way, the action potential sweeps all along the membrane of the neurone.

In normal circumstances, nerve cell axons only transmit an action potential in one direction. A 'new' action potential is only generated ahead of the action potential, not behind it. This is because the region behind it will still be recovering from the action potential it has just had. The distribution of sodium and potassium ions in this region is still not back to normal. It is therefore temporarily incapable of generating an action potential. The time it takes to recover is called the **refractory period**.

The all-or-nothing law

Action potentials are always the same size. A light touch on your hand will cause exactly the same size of action potentials to be generated in the sensory neurone as a strong touch. Either an action potential is generated, or it is not. This is called the all-or-nothing law.

So how does your brain distinguish between a light and a strong touch? This is done by having a different frequency of action potentials in the neurone. A heavy touch generates more frequent action potentials than a light touch. The brain interprets a stream of closely spaced action potentials as meaning 'strong stimulus'.

movement of positive ions (Na^+ or K^+) to negative areas will depolarise the membrane just outside the action potential

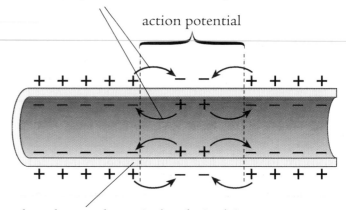

when the membrane is depolarised, ion channels open and the action potential 'appears' in this part of the membrane

Fig 4.7 How local electric circuits cause an action potential to move.

Saltatory conduction

The speed at which an action potential sweeps along the axon is not the same for every neurone. It depends partly on the diameter of the axon. The wider the axon, the faster the speed of transmission. For example, in a relatively small human axon it may be no more than $15\,\mathrm{m\,s^{-1}}$ but can be as high as $95\,\mathrm{m\,s^{-1}}$. Some invertebrates, such as earthworms, have some especially broad 'giant axons' and these can transmit action potentials at around $25\,\mathrm{m\,s^{-1}}$.

Giant axons work well for an earthworm, but humans use a different system for speeding up transmission of nerve impulses. As we have seen, many of our axons are myelinated. Myelin speeds up the rate at which action potentials travel by insulating the axon membrane. Sodium and potassium ions cannot flow through the myelin sheath, so it is not possible for depolarisation or action potentials to occur in parts of the axon which are surrounded by it. They can only occur at the gaps between the myelin sheath, the nodes of Ranvier.

Fig 4.8 shows how an action potential is transmitted along a myelinated axon. The local circuits that are set up stretch from one node to the next. Thus action potentials 'jump' from one node to the next, a distance of 1–3 mm. (Saltatory means 'jumping'.) This can increase the speed of transmission by up to 50 times.

The axons of many different neurones lie next to each other, in bundles called **nerves**.

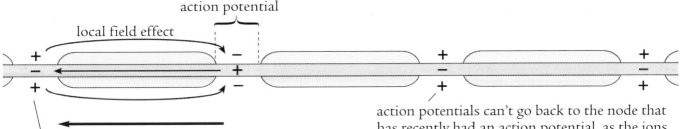

action potential

local field effect

action potential 'jumps' to the next node of Ranvier

action potentials can't go back to the node that has recently had an action potential, as the ions are not in the right place here

Fig 4.8 Saltatory movement of an action potential in a myelinated neurone.

Summary

1 A neurone maintains a voltage (potential difference) across its cell surface membrane, where the inside of the cell is approximately −65 mV with respect to the outside. This is called the resting potential.

2 The resting potential is produced by the sodium–potassium pump in the cell surface membrane, which constantly moves sodium ions (Na^+) out of the cell, and potassium ions (K^+) into it, by active transport. Three sodium ions are pumped out for every two potassium ions that are pumped in.

3 When a neurone is stimulated, an action potential is generated. Sodium channels open in the cell surface membrane. This allows sodium ions to flood in down their electrochemical gradient. This temporarily reverses the charge across the membrane, so that it becomes positive inside, and it is said to be depolarised.

4 Next the potassium channels open, so that potassium ions flood out. This brings the potential across the membrane back to being negative inside, and it is said to be repolarised.

The channels then close, and the sodium–potassium pump brings the potential back to normal (the resting potential) once more.

5 An action potential taking place at one point in a neurone sets up local circuits which depolarise the area of the membrane next to it. This sets up an action potential in that region. This continues all along the membrane.

6 The time it takes for a part of the membrane to revert to its normal resting potential after an action potential has passed is called the refractory period. During this time, it cannot produce a new action potential. This ensures that the action potential can only travel forwards, not backwards.

7 The axons of many neurones are surrounded by a fatty material called myelin, which is produced by Schwann cells. There are gaps in this sheath, called nodes of Ranvier. Action potentials jump from node to node, and so travel more swiftly than in a non-myelinated neurone. This is called saltatory conduction.

Nervous plants

Action potentials are found in plants as well as animals. In plants, they travel more slowly than in animal nerve cells. They move from cell to cell through plasmodesmata, which are tiny areas where one cell connects directly to another through gaps in the cell walls.

Most plants appear to have action potentials. The diagram shows an action potential that was produced in a plant after a stimulus was applied lower down the stem.

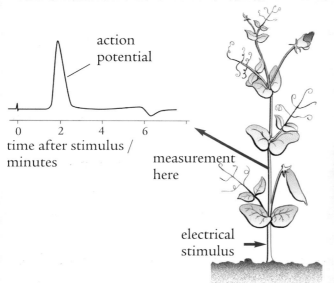

You may have come across the sensitive plant, a species of *Mimosa* which closes its leaves if you touch it. This stimulus is brought about by action potentials that travel from the point at which you stimulated it to the rest of the leaflets in that area. The action potentials move at about $2\,cm\,s^{-1}$, which is much faster than in most plants.

Another well-known example is the response of the leaves of the Venus flytrap. They have little sensitive hairs in the centre of their specialised leaves. If a fly touches one of these hairs, action potentials travel from the hairs to other parts of the leaf, making it fold over and trap the fly. The response time is about 0.5 s. The leaf then secretes juices containing digestive enzymes onto the trapped fly, and eventually absorbs the soluble molecules that are produced.

The fine hairs between the leaves (not the spines around the edge) are sensitive to touch.

When a fly, like this cranefly, touches the spines the leaves close quite quickly, trapping the fly. It is then digested.

Synapses

More than 30 species of sea snakes live in the waters off northern Australia. They spend most of their lives in the sea. Sea snakes have a very long right lung, which extends all the way to the base of the tail and is used to store air. They are excellent swimmers, and may stay submerged for hours.

Sea snakes are often caught in fishing nets, and people handling the catch must be careful not to touch one by mistake. Although they have only small fangs, and the bite itself is not painful at first, the venom is so toxic that it can kill an adult within hours. It works by interfering with the way that impulses are transmitted from a neurone to a muscle. Within hours of the bite, the neurotoxins in the venom will cause stiffness, muscle pain and spasm of the jaw, as well as pain in the area of the bite. Drowsiness and blurred vision will ensue, and may be followed by paralysis of the muscles that cause breathing movements. This can kill.

The venom of some sea snakes contains a protein called erabutoxin. It is a small protein, made up of only 63 amino acids. This protein binds to acetylcholine receptors at motor end plates – the tiny gaps between the end of a motor neurone and a muscle, across which the nerve impulse must pass to reach the muscle and cause it to contract. The blockage of these receptors by erabutoxin stops the impulses reaching the muscle and so causes muscle paralysis.

The toxicity of a venom is calculated by finding the quantity that is needed to cause death in 50% of organisms. This is called the LD50 (which stands for lethal dose in 50%). For most terrestrial snakes, LD50s range between 0.04 g and 0.01 g of venom for every kg of animal. Sea snake venom has an LD50 of between 0.04 and 0.01 mg kg^{-1}.

Sea snake bites need rapid treatment with anti-venoms. These are produced by injecting small amounts of venom into a horse, then increasing the dose until it becomes 'hyper-immunised'. Serum is then taken from the horse. The serum contains immunoglobulins (antibodies) that are broken down using the enzyme pepsin. The short peptide chains that are produced can bind with the venom molecules and stop them from functioning. In countries where bites from venomous animals are relatively common, stocks of various anti-venoms are kept in most towns.

The venoms of many poisonous animals contain neurotoxins. Many of these act at the junctions between one neurone and the next, or between a neurone and a muscle.

Where two neurones meet, they do not quite touch each other. There is a very small gap, usually about 20 nm wide, between them. This gap is called a **synaptic cleft**. The parts of the neurones near to the cleft, plus the cleft itself, make up a **synapse** (Fig 4.9).

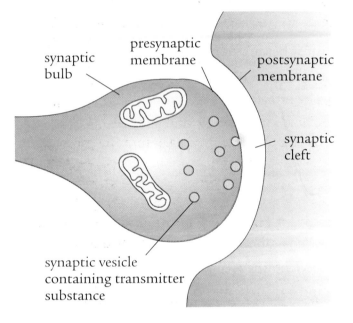

Fig 4.9 A synapse.

How impulses cross a synapse

Action potentials cannot jump across synapses. Instead, the signal is passed across by a chemical, known as a **transmitter substance**. In outline, an action potential arriving along the cell surface membrane of the first neurone, or **presynaptic neurone**, causes it to release transmitter substance into the cleft. The transmitter substance molecules diffuse across the cleft, which takes less than a millisecond as the distance is so small. This may set up an action potential in the cell surface membrane of the second, or **postsynaptic neurone**.

Now let us look at these processes in more detail. They are summarised in Fig 4.10.

The cytoplasm of the presynaptic neurone contains vesicles of transmitter substance. More than 40 different transmitter substances are known; **noradrenaline** and **acetylcholine (ACh)** are found throughout the nervous system, while others such as **dopamine** and **glutamate** occur only in the brain. We will concentrate on synapses which use ACh as the transmitter substance. These are known as **cholinergic synapses**.

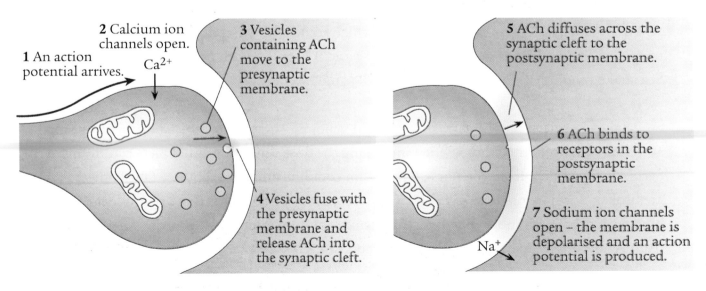

Fig 4.10 How impulses cross a synapse.

You will remember that, as an action potential sweeps along the cell surface membrane of a neurone, local circuits depolarise the next piece of membrane, opening sodium channels and so propagating the action potential. In the part of the membrane of the presynaptic neurone which is next to the synaptic cleft, the arrival of the action potential also causes **calcium ion channels** to open. Thus, the action potential causes not only sodium ions but also calcium ions to rush into the cytoplasm of the presynaptic neurone.

This influx of calcium ions causes vesicles of ACh to move to the presynaptic membrane and fuse with it, emptying their contents into the synaptic cleft. Each action potential causes just a few vesicles to do this, and each vesicle contains up to 10 000 molecules of ACh. The ACh diffuses across the synaptic cleft, usually in less than 0.5 ms.

The cell surface membrane of the postsynaptic neurone contains receptor proteins. Part of the receptor protein molecule has a complementary shape to part of the ACh molecule, so that the ACh molecules can bind with the receptors. This changes the shape of the protein, opening channels through which sodium ions can pass (Fig 4.11). Sodium ions rush into the cytoplasm of the postsynaptic neurone, depolarising the membrane and starting off an action potential.

A **neuromuscular junction** functions in just the same way. This is the synapse between the end of a motor neurone and a muscle. Here the sarcolemma of the muscle fibre is the postsynaptic membrane, and ACh sets up an action potential in it in just the same way as in a postsynaptic neurone.

Recharging the synapse

If the ACh remained bound to the postsynaptic receptors, the sodium ion channels would remain open and action potentials might fire continuously. To prevent this from happening, and also to avoid wasting the ACh, it is recycled. The synaptic cleft contains an enzyme, **acetylcholinesterase**, which splits each ACh molecule into acetate and choline.

The choline is taken back into the presynaptic neurone, where it is combined with acetyl CoA to form ACh once more. This resynthesis requires energy from ATP, supplied by the mitochondria. The ACh is then transported into the presynaptic vesicles, ready for the next action potential. The entire sequence of events from initial arrival of the action potential to the re-formation of ACh, takes about 5–10 ms.

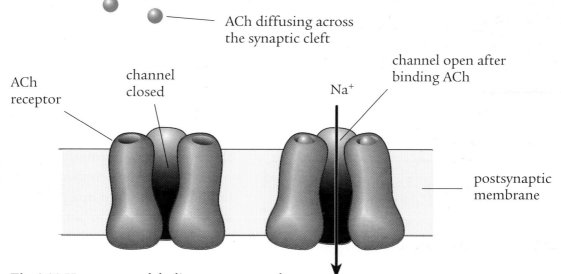

Fig 4.11 How an acetylcholine receptor works.

The actions of drugs and toxins at synapses

A bite from a sea snake (see the case study on page 71) introduces a toxin called erabutoxin into the blood. This toxin blocks the receptors on the postsynaptic membrane of cholinergic synapses, stopping nerve impulses from passing across.

Use the internet to find two more examples of drugs or toxins that act by interfering with the way that synapses work. Possibilities include nicotine, heroin, rattlesnake venom, funnel web spider venom, toxins from algal blooms, cone shells and poison arrow frogs, but there are many others.

Make a short presentation about your two examples. Describe the organism that produces the toxin, how the toxin may enter a person's body, what the toxin is, the symptoms that it causes, how it affects synapses and how this affects the bitten person, and how a bite is treated.

The functions of synapses

It isn't at first obvious why we have synapses. Action potentials could move much more swiftly through the nervous system if they did not have to cross synapses. In fact, synapses have numerous functions.

Ensuring one-way transmission

Signals can only pass in one direction at synapses. This ensures that signals can be directed along specific pathways, rather than spreading at random through the nervous system.

Interconnecting nerve pathways

Synapses allow a wider range of behaviour than could be generated in a nervous system in which neurones were directly 'wired up' to each other. At most synapses, many different neurones converge, so that many different potential pathways for the impulse are brought together.

It may be necessary for action potentials to arrive along several neurones simultaneously before an action potential can be set up in another.

Think for a moment of your possible behaviour when you see someone you know across the street. You can call out to them and walk to meet them, or you can pretend not to see them and hurry away. It is events at your synapses that determine which of these two responses, or any number of others, you decide to take.

Your nervous system is receiving information from various sources about the situation. Receptors in your eyes send action potentials to your brain which provide information about what the person looks like and whether or not they have seen you. Inside your brain, information is stored about previous events involving this person, and also about what you were about to do before you saw them. All of these pieces of information are stored in the myriad of synaptic connections between your brain cells. They are integrated with each other, and as a result action potentials will or will not be sent to your leg muscles to take you towards your acquaintance.

SAQ

4.3   Explain how the refractory period also helps to ensure one-way transmission of action potentials.

Summary

1 Neurones do not directly connect with each other, but are separated by a tiny gap called a synaptic cleft. The parts of the neurones on either side of this cleft, and the cleft itself, make up a synapse.

2 The arrival of an action potential at the presynaptic membrane causes calcium ion channels to open in the membrane and calcium ions flood in. This causes vesicles containing a transmitter substance such as acetylcholine to move to the presynaptic membrane and fuse with it. They empty their contents into the synaptic cleft. The molecules of neurotransmitter diffuse across the cleft and slot into receptor sites on the postsynaptic membrane. This may cause sodium ion channels to open, which depolarises the membrane and may set up a new action potential there.

3 When the impulse has passed, the acetylcholine is broken down by acetylcholinesterase. The choline part of the molecule is taken back into the presynaptic neurone and used to make more acetylcholine.

4 Synapses help to ensure that nerve impulses only pass one way along a neurone. They also help to link many different pathways within the nervous system, allowing for information from different sense organs or different parts of the brain to be integrated.

The autonomic nervous system

On page 50 we saw that the nervous system is made up of the central nervous system (brain and spinal cord) and the peripheral nervous system (nerves). The peripheral nervous system itself is also organised into different components. These are summarised in Fig 4.12.

The peripheral nervous system can be divided into the **somatic nervous system** and the **autonomic nervous system**. The somatic nervous system includes all the sensory neurones and also the motor neurones that carry impulses from the central nervous system to the striated muscles attached to the skeleton. So the neurones of the reflex arc in Fig 4.4 are all part of the somatic nervous system. All of the cell bodies of the autonomic nervous system are in ganglions outside the central nervous system.

The autonomic nervous system includes all the motor neurones that carry impulses from the central nervous system to the internal organs, often known as the **viscera**.

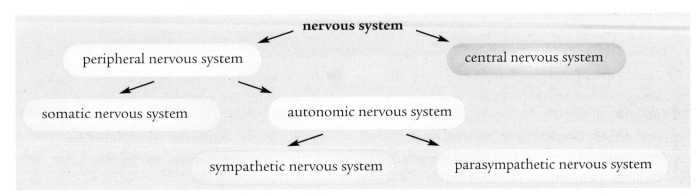

Fig 4.12 Organisation of the peripheral nervous system.

The sympathetic and parasympathetic nervous systems

The autonomic nervous system can itself be divided into two parts. Remember that both of these are made of up motor neurones only.

The **sympathetic nervous system** is made up of motor neurones that have their cell bodies in ganglia just outside the spinal cord. These motor neurones carry impulses from the spinal cord to each of the internal organs, Many of their synapses use a transmitter substance called noradrenaline, which is almost identical to the hormone adrenaline, while others use acetylcholine.

The **parasympathetic nervous system** is made up of motor neurones that have their cell bodies inside the spinal cord or the brain. They, like the neurones of the sympathetic system, innervate the viscera. Their synapses use acetylcholine.

Many of the axons of parasympathetic neurones are bundled together to form the **vagus nerve**, which runs from the brain to most of the body organs.

Nerve impulses from the sympathetic and from the parasympathetic nervous systems have opposite effects on body organs. For example, an impulse arriving along the sympathetic nerve that serves the sino-atrial node of the heart makes it beat faster and harder. An impulse arriving along the parasympathetic nerve (the vagus nerve) makes it beat more gently and more slowly.

Table 4.1 lists some of the effects of these two divisions of the autonomic nervous system. In general, you can think of the sympathetic system as preparing the body for 'fight or flight', while the parasympathetic system prepares it to 'rest and digest'.

Table 4.1 Effects of the autonomic nervous system.

Organ	Effect of sympathetic stimulation	Effect of parasympathetic stimulation
heart	increases rate and force of contraction	reduces rate and force of contraction
eye	pupil dilates ciliary muscle relaxes – lens thin for distant vision	pupil constricts (gets narrower) ciliary muscle contracts – lens thick for near vision
digestive system	little or no effect on glands sphincter muscles contract liver releases glucose	stimulates secretion from glands sphincter muscles relax liver increases glycogen production slightly
skin	sweat glands release more sweat hair erector muscles make hair stand up arterioles constrict	sweat glands in general not affected hair erector muscles not affected arterioles not affected

Summary

1. The peripheral nervous system is divided into two parts. The somatic nervous system includes all the sensory neurones and also the motor neurones that carry impulses to glands and muscles. The autonomic nervous system includes all the motor neurones taking impulses to the viscera.

2. The autonomic nervous system is once again divided into two parts. The sympathetic nervous system tends to bring about 'fight or flight' actions, while the parasympathetic nervous system prepares the body to 'rest and digest'.

CHAPTER 5

The central nervous system

The International Boxing Federation world featherweight champion Paul Ingle fought his last bout on Saturday December 16th 2000, at the Sheffield Arena, aged 28. Ingle was defending his title against South Africa's Mbulelo Botile. Ingle was knocked down in the 11th round, but got up as the bell went and made his way to his corner. He came out to fight in the 12th round, during which he collapsed unconscious at the feet of Botile.

Following a number of very serious injuries to boxers in the 1990s, rules were drawn up to ensure that an injured boxer would get rapid treatment. An ambulance and team of paramedics must be present at each bout, and neurosurgeons at nearby hospitals are informed that it is taking place. These precautions probably saved Paul Ingle's life. He was stretchered from the ring unconscious, and rushed to Sheffield Hallam Hospital where he had an emergency operation to remove a blood clot from his brain.

The blood clot was formed as a result of heavy blows to the head. Brain damage was inevitable, but the faster the clot could be removed the less extensive this was likely to be. Ingle was operated on by Robert Battersby, a consultant neurosurgeon. Drugs were used to put Ingle into a coma so that he could not move his head. Three weeks later, he was able to talk, but he still needed help with walking.

There was much speculation about whether the fight should have been stopped sooner. Some experts think that the damage was probably done in the first round. But Ingle's back-up team denied that they should have pulled him out earlier. "Nobody can make decisions just like that", a member of his team said. "He insisted on going out for the last round. He was talking perfect. It's such a short time to make that decision."

There are calls from the British Medical Association to ban boxing entirely. Although other sports can result in serious head injuries, boxing is one of the very few in which a legal and acceptable way of winning is through damaging another person.

Paul Ingle, featured in the case study on page 77, has made a full recovery. But many other boxers have not been so lucky. Steve Watt died in 1986 as did Bradley Stone in 1994, both as a result of injuries received during boxing matches. Several other boxers have received brain injuries that have caused permanent serious disability. No matter what protective headgear is worn, heavy blows to the head always run the risk of causing traumatic brain injury.

Structure and function of the brain

The human brain is perhaps our least well understood organ, and this is a direct result of its immense complexity. Psychologists study the science of human behaviour, while neurologists study the anatomy and physiology of the brain.

The great challenge is to bring these two sciences together, so that we can relate brain structure and function to our mental processes and behaviour. There has been much progress along this road, as new technologies such as MRI and PET scans have allowed us to see images of living brains, and have provided glimpses of what is happening in the brain as we perform tasks such as talking or remembering.

General structure of the brain

Fig 5.1 shows the structure of the human brain. The relationship between the main sections of the brain, however, is best illustrated in a simplified way, as shown in Fig 5.2. This shows the brain 'stretched out' into a line, rather than folded as it really is.

The brain is a cream-coloured organ, surrounded and protected by the bones of the cranium and also by three membranes known as meninges. These membranes help to secrete

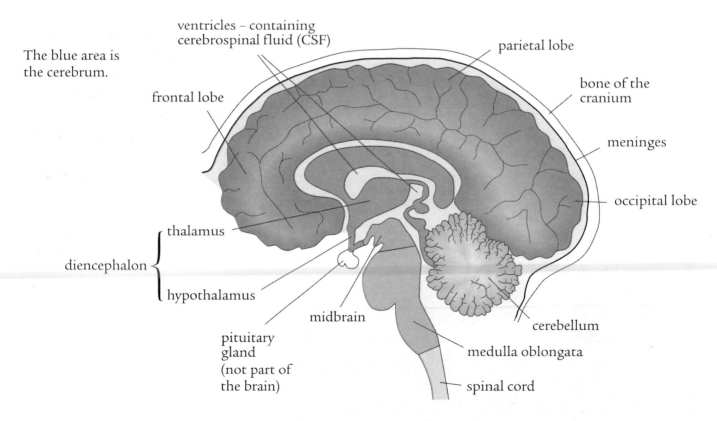

The blue area is the cerebrum.

Fig 5.1 The structure of the human brain.

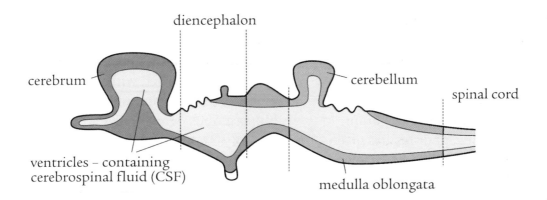

Fig 5.2 The arrangement of the main parts of the brain.

cerebrospinal fluid, which provides yet more protection and cushioning of the brain and also fills the spaces inside it, known as ventricles.

Most organs in the body are supplied with blood in capillaries with leaky walls – the leakiness helps the rapid transfer of substances between the blood and the tissues. In the brain, however, the capillaries are much less leaky, and many substances are not allowed through their walls. This barrier to easy exchange with the blood is known as the **blood–brain barrier**. It helps to isolate the brain from potentially damaging substances in the blood.

The tissue from which the brain is formed contains two different types of cells. **Neurones**, as we have seen, are specialised for the transmission of action potentials (Fig 5.3). However, these cells make up considerably less than 10% of the tissue in the brain. The rest consists of **glial cells**. Glial cells include the Schwann cells that form the myelin sheaths around some axons (see page 64) and also star-shaped cells called astrocytes. These may help to store potassium ions, preventing too many of them accumulating in the spaces between the cells, which might otherwise cause neurones to be depolarised.

The cerebrum

This is the highly folded area at the front of the brain, so large in humans that it covers most of the rest of the brain (Fig 5.6). It is made up of two **cerebral hemispheres**, connected to each other by a 'bridge' of tissue called the **corpus callosum**. The wrinkled surface (just a few millimetres thick) of the cerebral hemispheres is known as the **cerebral cortex**, and it is largely this part of the brain that is responsible for the characteristics that we consider to make us human – speech, emotions, logical thought and decision-making.

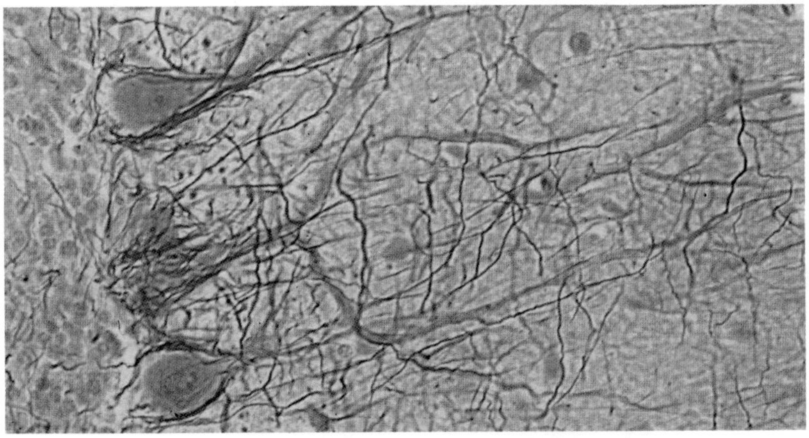

The pear-shaped structures are the cell bodies of neurones. Branching from the cell bodies to the right is a network of dendrites, which extend to the outer edge of the cerebellum (not shown). (×500)

Fig 5.3 Photomicrograph of neurones in the cerebellum.

In the past, the only way people could work out the functions of different parts of our brains was to study changes in the behaviour of people whose brains had been damaged, and link those changes to the particular area of damage. Now it is possible to watch live images of the brain using MRI or PET scanning, and this has given us much more information about how we use the various areas as we perform different activities by showing where there is most brain activity from one moment to the next.

The cerebral cortex receives information from sense organs, such as the eyes and ears. The left hemisphere receives nerve impulses from the right side of the body, and the right hemisphere from the left side.

The parts of the cortex that first receive this information are known as **primary sensory areas**. Nerve impulses from these areas and other parts of the brain are sent to **association areas**, where they are processed and integrated with other information coming from other parts of the brain (Fig 5.4). In the **motor areas**, nerve impulses are generated and sent to effectors.

A large association area in the parietal, temporal and occipital lobes is involved in determining what our sense organs tell us about the position of different parts of the body.

Another association area in the frontal lobe is involved in planning actions and movements. The third association area, known as the **limbic system**, is concerned with emotions and memory. The limbic system contains the **hippocampus**, which plays an important role in memory, and the **amygdala**, which coordinates the actions of the autonomic and endocrine (hormonal) systems and is involved in emotions.

There are some differences between the roles of the left and right hemispheres. The association areas of the left hemisphere, especially the parietal-temporal-occipital complex, are responsible for our understanding and use of language. One small area, called **Broca's area**, has long been known to be involved in the production of language in speaking or writing. **Wernicke's area** is responsible for the understanding of language. PET scans of active brains show that different parts of the brain are active depending on whether we are thinking of words, speaking them or listening to them (Fig 5.5). This is a good example of how different parts of the cerebral cortex must interact to carry out even the simplest of thoughts or actions.

The parietal lobe of the right hemisphere, however, is more concerned with non-verbal processes, such as being able to visualise objects in three dimensions, and in recognising faces.

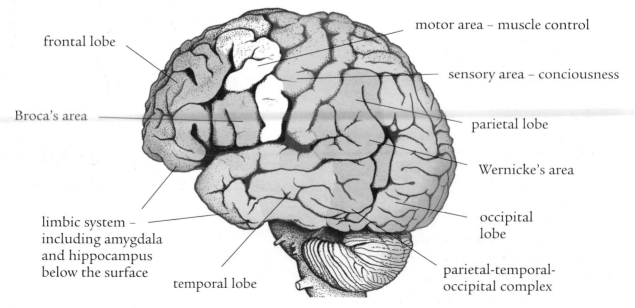

frontal lobe

motor area – muscle control

sensory area – conciousness

Broca's area

parietal lobe

Wernicke's area

limbic system – including amygdala and hippocampus below the surface

occipital lobe

temporal lobe

parietal-temporal-occipital complex

Fig 5.4 Primary sensory areas (green), association areas (blue) and motor areas (white) of the brain.

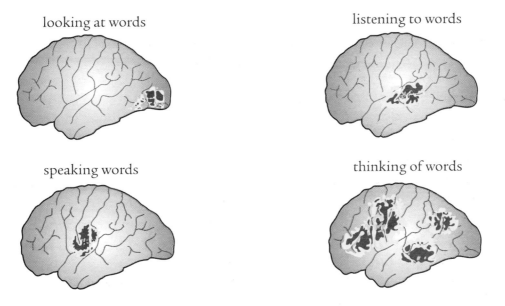

looking at words

listening to words

speaking words

thinking of words

Fig 5.5 PET scanning allows us to show how much work is being done in different areas of the brain while different tasks are done. Yellow – some activity; red – high activity; bright blue – most activity.

The cerebellum

The cerebellum, like the cerebrum, has a folded surface, but is much smaller. It is here that movement and posture are controlled. It receives impulses from the ears, eyes and stretch receptors in muscles and also from other parts of the brain. The information is integrated and used to coordinate the timing and pattern of skeletal muscle contraction and relaxation. Thus this area is responsible for balance, coordination, eye movement and fine manipulation.

The medulla oblongata

The medulla forms the link between the brain and the spinal cord. It coordinates and controls involuntary movements such as breathing, heart beat and movements of the wall of the alimentary canal.

The hypothalamus

This small region regulates the autonomic nervous system (see page 75), and also controls the secretion of hormones from the pituitary gland. In this way, it effectively controls many of our homeostatic processes, such as temperature regulation and the water content of body fluids. (It is not involved in the control of blood glucose levels.)

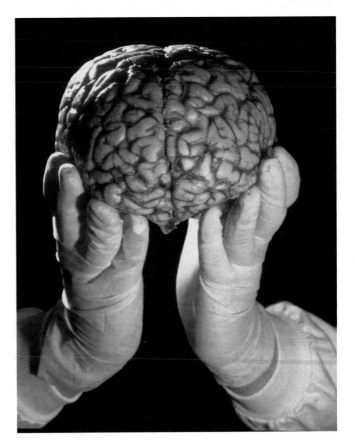

Fig 5.6 Front view of a normal human brain showing the cerebrum.

Memory

Most of us take memory for granted until we know someone whose memory is impaired and begin to understand how essential it is to us. A person with Alzheimer's disease loses the ability to form new memories and may not be able to remember what day it is or even what they ate for breakfast fifteen minutes ago. Without our memories, we cease to be the person we have previously been.

One area of the brain that is essential in forming new memories is a part of the limbic system called the hippocampus. This is used when we make new memories. We are not sure how it does this, but it is certain that synapses are involved. Synapses may be 'strengthened' in some way, or perhaps completely new synapses are made.

These memories are short-term memories, and most of us don't keep all of them for very long. But some are converted into long-term memories, and this involves other parts of the brain. Memories of events and facts are stored in the temporal and frontal lobes of the cerebral cortex. Facts or events are most likely to be converted into long-term memories if we 'play them back' in our heads. We may make an effort to replay them consciously, or it may happen while we are asleep. The involvement of the hippocampus in making new memories but not storing old memories of facts or events helps to explain why people with damage to this area may not be able to remember what happened five minutes ago but often still have vivid memories of the past.

We also store emotional memories – the kind of memory where a smell or a sound or an event can trigger emotions of love, fear or anger. These memories involve another part of the limbic system, called the amygdala. And spatial memories, our mental maps that help us to find our way from one room to another or from home to work, seem to be stored in the hippocampus itself. Yet another kind of memory, procedural memories, such as how to ride a bike, do not involve the hippocampus at all, and are formed and stored in the cerebellum.

Summary

① The brain is made up of neurones and glial cells. It is surrounded and protected by the meninges and the bones of the cranium. It is filled and surrounded by cerebrospinal fluid.

② The cerebrum is responsible for conscious thought, speech, emotions, language and decision-making. Association areas in the cerebrum integrate information from sense organs and from other areas of the brain. The limbic system is one of these association areas, and is closely involved with emotions and with the formation and storage of memories.

③ The cerebellum controls and coordinates the contraction and relaxation of skeletal muscles, so is responsible for movement and balance.

④ The hypothalamus regulates the autonomic nervous system, and controls the secretion of hormones from the pituitary gland.

Damage to the CNS

On May 27th 1995, an amateur show-jumping competition took place in Virginia, USA. One of the competitors was 'Superman' Christopher Reeve. As his horse stopped suddenly at a jump, he was flung forward and landed on his head. His two upper cervical (neck) vertebrae were shattered and the spinal cord in his neck was very badly damaged.

First impressions of the medical staff at the show-jumping arena and later at the hospital were that Reeve would die, or at least would be totally paralysed from the neck down and never able to breathe for himself. And for five years this prognosis was borne out, as he lay in bed, completely dependent on a ventilator to move air into and out of his lungs and on other people to feed him, wash him and care for him in every way. Feeling and ability to move were lost in all of his body below the neck.

At first, Reeve went into a deep depression, and wished that he had been killed outright. But as time went on he became more and more determined to live, and to do whatever was possible to help his body to mend as best it could. He knew that his relative wealth meant that he could pay for treatment that would not normally be available to patients, and he hoped that, as well as improving his own quality of life, he could perhaps make some contribution to developing new treatments for others.

Three days a week he was helped to exercise his legs using a technique called Functional Exercise Stimulation, or FES. His leg muscles were stimulated using computer-controlled electrodes in a rhythm matching the revolutions of 'bicycle' pedals on which his feet rested. This allowed his leg muscles to rotate the pedals, even though he had no voluntary control over them. This has proved to be much more beneficial than having the legs moved entirely passively.

Over time Christopher Reeve came to have feeling over 70% of his body. He developed some movement in the fingers of his left hand, in his right hand and in his feet. Perhaps most unexpected of all, he was able to breathe unaided for part of each day. This was the result of FES applied to the muscles of the diaphragm.

Reeve's experiences and improvements have shown that there can be at least some small improvements in the functioning of a damaged spinal cord. This gives hope for treatment in the future. Although no-one knows quite what is happening to bring about these improvements, at least it will provide researchers with some encouragement and direction for their studies into the recovery of function of a damaged central nervous system. Reeve died of a heart attack in 2004, aged 52.

Traumatic brain injury

Traumatic brain injury (TBI) can be defined as physical damage to the brain caused by a blow to the head. Men are 2.5 times more likely to suffer TBI than women, and those in the 14–21 age group are most susceptible.

Usually, TBI is the result of a single event – for example a car or motorbike accident, a fall from a horse or a criminal assault (Fig 5.7). A blow to the head can cause serious harm to the brain even if the skull is not fractured, but if parts of the skull penetrate the brain tissue then very severe damage is likely. The damage may be done directly to the neurones and glial cells making up the brain tissue, or it may break a major blood vessel within the head. This may starve cells of oxygen and glucose and so cause their death. Heavy bleeding into the cavities surrounding the brain can cause swelling and pressure on the brain. (This was the cause of the brain damage to Paul Ingle described in the case study on page 77. A similar example is shown in Fig 5.8.)

TBI can also be the result of the cumulative effect of damage over many years. There is considerable evidence that boxers are more likely to develop signs of brain malfunction than most people, such as memory loss and – in severe cases – illnesses such as Parkinson's disease. Footballers, too, are possibly at risk because of harm that can be caused by heavy contact of the ball with their heads.

Strokes

A stroke is an acute instance of damage to the brain caused by problems with blood vessels supplying it. About 80% of strokes are due to a blood clot forming in a vessel as the result of atherosclerosis. The remaining 20% are caused by bleeding into brain tissue.

The risk factors for strokes are, as might be expected, the same as those for coronary heart disease (see *Human Biology for AS*, pages 114–118). A person with hypertension (high blood pressure) has a considerably increased risk of having a stroke; the risk doubles with each 1 kPa rise in diastolic blood pressure.

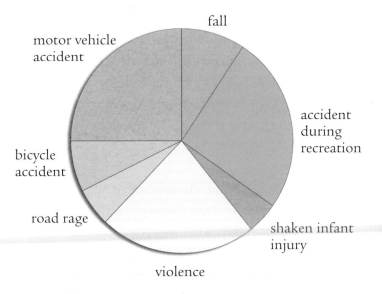

Fig 5.7 Causes of brain injury (data for USA).

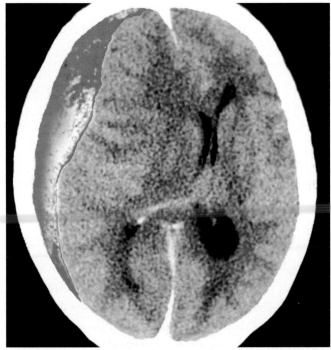

Fig 5.8 CT scan of a section through a head showing bleeding between the meninges, caused by impact to the head. This is a dangerous condition as it puts pressure on the brain.

5.1 The graph shows the incidence of stroke in males and females in Oxfordshire between 1981 and 1986.

a Describe the effect of age on the chance of having a stroke in women and in men.

b Suggest explanations for the patterns you have described.

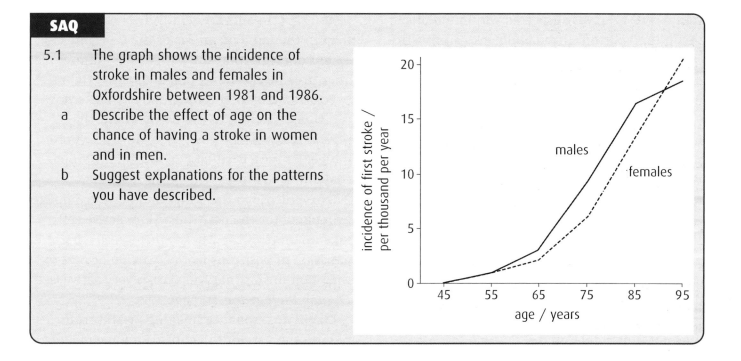

Brain cells have a high metabolic rate and must have good supplies of oxygen and glucose for respiration. They begin to die if deprived of these for more than a few minutes.

The effects of the stroke will depend on the parts of the brain in which neurones die. For example, a stroke in the right side of the cerebrum is likely to affect movement on the left side of the body. As this side of the brain is concerned with spatial awareness, the person may have problems in judging distance and so find difficulty with walking or picking up objects. A stroke in the left side of the cerebrum will affect language. Memory is often harmed no matter which side of the brain the stroke affects.

Spinal cord injuries

The spinal cord runs from the base of the medulla oblongata all the way down the back to the 'tail bone'. It lies in a channel formed by holes in the vertebrae and so is protected by bone. Like the brain, it is surrounded by meninges and cerebrospinal fluid. It has a central canal that runs along its length, also filled with cerebrospinal fluid (Fig 5.9).

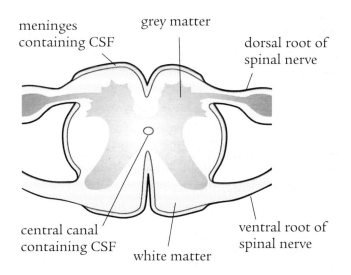

Fig 5.9 Cross-section of the spinal cord.

Spinal cord injuries are almost always the result of accidents. 80% of them occur in males. 40% are due to road traffic accidents, 35% to injuries received at work or at home and 20% to sporting injuries. Diving, horse-riding, rugby and gymnastics carry the greatest risk.

As for brain injuries, it is most important that treatment is given as soon as possible. Paramedics arriving at an accident scene where spinal cord injury is suspected will immobilise the injured person's head and neck using a stiff collar, because movement could cause further damage. Even so, many people with such injuries die before reaching hospital.

The spinal cord contains sensory, intermediate and motor neurones (see page 64), so injury to it can cause major loss of function. When axons are severed, they can no longer relay impulses to muscles or to other parts of the nervous system. Spinal nerves containing the axons of motor and sensory neurones emerge from it at intervals all down the body (see page 50), and so if the spinal cord is damaged all the parts of the body below the point of damage will not work normally and may not function at all.

Assessment of damage to the CNS

The extent and type of damage to the brain or spinal cord will be assessed as soon as possible after the patient's arrival at a hospital. There are many choices open to the medical staff, and they include scans and neurological tests.

Computer-assisted tomography or **CT scans** involve the use of X-rays which are sent through the body at different angles. A computer uses the images that these produce to build up a three-dimensional picture of that part of the body being scanned (see *Human Biology for AS*,

page 177). CT scans are relatively cheap, and can help in the rapid diagnosis of the type and extent of injury that the patient has suffered. They provide excellent images of the vertebrae.

Positron emission tomography or **PET scans** can show activities of the living brain. The person is injected with 2-deoxyglucose, whose molecules have been labelled with an isotope that emits positrons. The position of the 2-deoxyglucose in the body can be tracked down by looking for the positrons. More active cells take up more of the 2-deoxyglucose, so a high emission of positrons from a particular part of the brain means that this part is very active (see *Human Biology for AS*, page 177).

Magnetic resonance imaging or **MRI scans** require the patient to lie inside a huge magnet while computer-controlled equipment measures tiny differences between the strength of the magnetic field in different parts of their brain (Fig 5.10). Haemoglobin contains iron, and this has a small effect on the magnetic field. The effect is smaller when oxyhaemoglobin is present. The MRI scan therefore gives information about the distribution of oxyhaemoglobin in the brain, which represents the rate of respiration and therefore the activity of different areas. They are much better than CT scans at showing soft tissues (see *Human Biology for AS*, page 177).

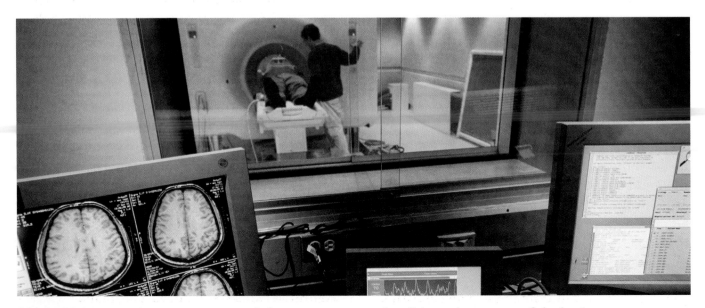

Fig 5.10 MRI scanning can capture real-time responses to stimuli in various parts of the brain.

Nerve conduction velocity test

This test is used to assess injury to a nerve. If a nerve is damaged, it conducts impulses more slowly than an undamaged nerve.

Electrodes are placed onto the skin a certain distance apart on the nerve pathway. A very mild electrical shock is then applied through one of them. This depolarises the neurones in the nerve, which produces action potentials that travel along the neurones. The time taken for the measurable depolarisation, due to the arrival of many action potentials, to be picked up by the other electrode is measured. The speed of this is calculated by dividing the distance between the electrodes by the time taken. This is normally done automatically by a computer.

electrode on the skin producing the shock

position of a major nerve that runs down the arm within the tissues

electrode on the skin detecting the arrival of the action potentials

Repairing damage to the spinal cord

In the peripheral nervous system, if an axon is cut, the part of the neurone without the cell body dies. The other part can slowly regrow, but may not be able to follow the original route. Until recently, it was thought that, if a neurone died, it could never be replaced, and that neurones could not be repaired or replaced in a severed spinal cord. This explains why severe damage to the spinal cord often results in permanent paralysis below the point of damage. However, there are now signs that it might be possible to encourage nerve cells to regrow, or new ones to form.

Scar tissue

Surviving nerve cell bodies in a damaged spinal cord appear to make attempts to regenerate by growing new axons, but these attempts normally fail. One reason for their failure is the production of scar tissue in the wounded region of the spinal cord. The scar tissue is formed by glial cells which multiply to form dense tissue, containing substances called proteoglycans.

This is probably useful because it protects the as-yet undamaged tissue near to the wound. But axons trying to regrow cannot cross this barrier.

Trials have been carried out to try to break down the scar tissue using an enzyme called **chondroitinase**, which is made by bacteria. The enzyme can cut a way through the scar tissue, so that axons can grow through it. This is very encouraging, and suggests that one day people with spinal injuries may be able to recover at least some of their capacity for movement. However, there are known to be many different inhibitors produced in the adult CNS that prevent regrowth, and as yet their importance and the way they have their effects are not understood.

Growth factors

Neurones need the presence of chemicals called **trophic factors** before they can regenerate. One such factor is **nerve growth factor (NGF)**. It seems that neurones from the central nervous system need a particular combination of trophic factors to be present if they are to regrow. In the future, it may be possible to use these factors to help damaged spinal cords to repair themselves at least partly.

Stem cells

The CNS contains stem cells that can divide and differentiate to form new neurones and glial cells. In the future, it may be possible to encourage these cells to form new tissue that could help to repair a damaged spinal cord.

Some success has been achieved in the USA in injecting foetal stem cells into the brains of stroke victims, with encouraging results. Similar trials have been carried out with people with Parkinson's disease. However, there is a long road ahead before any such treatment will become generally available.

Dealing with stroke damage

The effects of a stroke can vary tremendously. The stroke may be so small and localised that the person is completely unaware that anything has happened. In other cases, it may be fatal. In between these two extremes, many people suffer a stroke which leaves them unable to function normally.

A stroke often affects one side of the body more than the other. A stroke affecting the left side of the brain will affect movement of the right side of the body and vice versa. Damage to a particular part of the brain will result in the loss of abilities that are normally controlled in that area. For example, as the left cerebral hemisphere is important for the use and understanding of language, damage here may result in aphasia (for example, knowing what you want to say but not being able to get the word out) as well as difficulties in understanding written words or speech.

Immediate treatment for a stroke may include clot-busting drugs such as streptokinase or heparin, if the stroke is the result of a blood clot in the brain. This must be given no later than six hours after the onset of the stroke if it is to be effective. However, there is always a risk that this treatment may cause further bleeding in the brain, making things worse rather than better. Taking aspirin regularly in the days following the stroke is safer and can reduce the risk of recurrence. In severe cases, an artificial coma may be induced, to help to reduce further damage in the hours and days following the stroke.

As soon as possible, the patient undergoes rehabilitation therapy. This aims to help patients to relearn skills that they lost when their brain was damaged. The first priority is often to relearn motor skills – that is, being able to move parts of the body. This helps the patient to become independent, able to walk, wash, dress and eat again with no need for help. The degree of success of this therapy depends very much on the severity of the stroke, but many stroke victims can show enormous improvements in the weeks, months and years after their stroke. The therapy will also try to bring about improvements in speaking, writing and understanding speech or written words.

ACTIVITY 5.1

Nerve cell regeneration

New developments in our understanding of how nerve cells can regenerate, and so might help to repair damage to the spinal cord, are being made very rapidly.

Use the internet to find information about one line of recent research into nerve cell regeneration. You should try to use at least two different sources. Make a summary, incorporating diagrams and graphs if possible, of how and why the research was done and how the findings might contribute to therapies for people with spinal cord injuries. Explain what further work will be required before large-scale trials can take place on human volunteers.

Problems with memory and thought processes are often a significant result of a stroke. Cognitive therapy aims to help patients to recover some of these abilities. Patients frequently have problems with short-term memory, although their memories of long-ago events are less likely to be affected. The people caring for a stroke patient can do many simple things to help them to regain at least some degree of functioning short-term memory. For example, the patient may enjoy playing a game in which they are shown a tray of objects, then the objects are covered and they try to remember as many as possible. Carers can show the patient photographs, or look through a newspaper or magazine with them and help them to identify some of the well-known people shown there. Reminders can be posted around the house to help the stroke patient to remember how to do things – for example, simple directions about how to switch on the television or make toast. A large calendar in a very visible place with appointments and other events clearly marked on it may help them to keep track of what day it is.

Language and the brain

Although many animal species communicate with each other through sound, and some are able to learn to recognise words or even short sentences, none has such a complex and rich system of language as humans. Language is a vital part of our day to day existence, whether we read it, think about it, speak it, listen to it, sign it or watch it as we lip-read. We appear to be born hard-wired with the ability to understand language, including a basic grammatical system that is found in virtually every language in the world.

For most of us, language skills are controlled by the left hemisphere. Two small areas are especially important – Broca's area and Wernicke's area. If a person's Broca's area is damaged, perhaps by a stroke, they are still able to understand language but cannot produce it easily. This area controls grammar, speech and appropriate movement of the lips, tongue and larynx. Damage to Wernicke's area destroys a person's ability to understand either spoken or written language, although they are still able to speak fluently, albeit with difficulty in finding the right word or being able to convey the ideas that are in their head.

Language is a very complex skill involving many different parts of the brain (Fig 5.5 on page 81). The diagram below shows just how many different stages are involved in reading a word aloud.

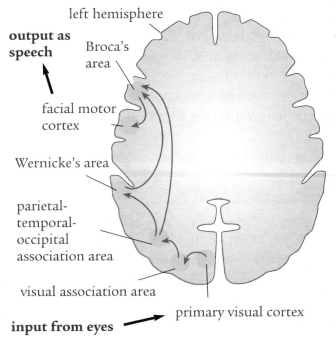

output as speech

left hemisphere

Broca's area

facial motor cortex

Wernicke's area

parietal-temporal-occipital association area

visual association area

primary visual cortex

input from eyes

Stroke rehabilitation

Following a stroke, a patient is likely to come into contact with a number of therapists. Research one of the following, and prepare a short presentation describing what they do and how they may help recovery from stroke damage:

- a rehabilitation nurse;
- a neurologist;
- a psychiatrist;
- a physiotherapist;
- an occupational therapist;
- a speech therapist.

Speech therapy for a man with aphasia following a stroke. He is practising producing sentences during a session with a speech therapist. He is describing what is happening in the photograph in front of him aided by a visual prompt of the necessary parts of the sentence.

Summary

1 Traumatic brain injury can be defined as physical damage to the brain caused by a blow to the head.

2 Brain injury may also result from a stroke. Most strokes are caused by a blood clot in the brain, while the remainder are caused by bleeding into or around brain tissue.

3 The spinal cord is protected inside the vertebral column, but if the vertebrae are damaged or displaced then the cord may be damaged. Severe damage may result in loss of sensation or ability to move from the point of the damage downwards.

4 CT scans, PET scans and MRI scans can help to diagnose the type and extent of injury. All three use computers to build up three-dimensional images of the parts of the body being scanned. CT scans are often used for the first diagnosis of an injury, and are good at showing bones. MRI scans are much better at showing soft tissue damage. MRI scans and PET scans can also show the activity taking place in different parts of the brain.

5 Nerve conduction velocity tests can assess injury to a nerve.

6 Damaged neurones do not easily regenerate, but it may be possible to help them to do so by using enzymes to break down scar tissue, reducing the activity of inhibitory molecules or providing the neurones with growth factors. It is also possible that stem cells could be used to produce new neurones.

7 The brain may at least partially recover after a stroke. Strokes often affect short-term memory, and cognitive therapy may help a patient to improve their memory.

Drugs and the brain

In the summer of 1984, neurologist James Langston found himself attempting to solve a very strange problem. Several young people were admitted to the hospital in which he worked, in California, showing most unusual and distressing symptoms. They had lost almost all control over their body movements; they had rigid limbs and motionless faces. Newspapers were later to christen them 'the living dead'.

Langston's experience of an illness called Parkinson's disease led him immediately to make a connection between what he was seeing in these young people and in the much more elderly people he often saw with similar symptoms. But Parkinson's is almost never seen in young people – some of these were only in their early twenties – and it was completely unheard of for a number of people to suddenly show full symptoms of a disease that normally develops gradually over many years.

Detective work quickly discovered that all of these young people were users of heroin and other opiate drugs. And there was an even tighter link between them. They had all bought an opiate called pethidine from the same source. Further investigations showed that the pethidine had been produced by an amateur chemist and that it was contaminated with a substance called MPTP.

Parkinson's disease is caused by the death of neurones in the brain that secrete a substance called dopamine. In this case, MPTP had killed the dopamine-producing cells almost instantly, bringing about a condition in the young people within hours, that would normally take many years to develop. And it was irreversible. The dopamine-producing neurones would never regrow.

Although the incident involving the young heroin users was catastrophic for the people affected, it did provide new leads to scientists trying to find out what causes Parkinson's disease and how it might be prevented or treated. Knowing the effect that MPTP had, and finding that it reduced the amount of dopamine in the brain, helped to guide people along research paths into the effects of dopamine in normal brains and also into finding out about chemicals which could reduce or enhance its secretions. This in turn has led to the development of drugs that can help to relieve some of the symptoms of Parkinson's disease.

A **drug** can be defined as a substance that alters the body's physiology. Drugs may be used to treat specific health problems, and this is known as **therapeutic** drug use. There are also drugs that some people may use to change their mood, such as caffeine, alcohol, cannabis and heroin. Although all of these drugs can have beneficial effects in some circumstances, the more powerful ones can create enormous problems for their users and others if they are abused. Table 5.1 lists some commonly used drugs.

Table 5.1 Some widely used drugs.

Drug	Why it is used	How it works	Some side effects
antibiotics	to cure infectious diseases caused by bacteria	kills bacteria or stops their cell division in various ways	may also kill 'useful' bacteria in the alimentary canal
antihistamine	to reduce the symptoms of hay fever and other allergies	blocks the effects of histamine, a chemical released by white blood cells which causes contraction of smooth muscle and contributes to inflammation	can cause drowsiness by blocking histamine receptors in parts of the brain responsible for wakefulness
aspirin	to reduce pain; can also be used to reduce risk of blood clotting and causing DVT or heart attacks	stops production of prostaglandins, by inhibiting the enzyme COX in body tissues; this reduces inflammation	may damage the stomach wall and cause it to bleed; may cause brain and liver problems in newborn and unborn babies
paracetamol	to reduce pain	inhibits COX in the brain	none
ibuprofen	to reduce pain	reduces inflammation	may cause bleeding in the stomach, especially in the elderly
caffeine (in coffee, tea and cola drinks)	to increase wakefulness and ability to concentrate	blocks receptors for adenosine, which is produced by most tissues, and tends to oppose their activity	may cause increase in heart rate and blood pressure
nicotine (in cigarettes)	can increase alertness and concentration, but most people who smoke do so because they are addicted to nicotine	binds to receptors at synapses that normally bind acetylcholine	nicotine causes addiction to tobacco smoking; other substances in cigarette smoke greatly increase risk of all types of cancer
alcohol	may have a calming effect and reduces inhibitions	enhances the effect of GABA in the brain, suppressing the activity of some neurones	many – for example, causes some people to become aggressive; increases reaction time so dangerous if driving; in large amounts can cause liver damage

Drug tolerance and dependency

Many drugs affect what happens at synapses, either in the brain or elsewhere in the body. Post-synaptic neurones contain receptors in their cell surface membranes into which the transmitter substance used at that synapse precisely fits (Table 5.2). Drugs that act at synapses may do so by mimicking the action of the transmitter substance; that is, they have the same shape and affect the post-synaptic neurone in the same way that the transmitter would. They may prevent the break-down of the transmitter – for example, by inhibiting the enzyme that normally does this. Or they may inhibit the action of the transmitter itself.

If the drug is taken over a period of time, then the body may adjust to its use. For example, if the drug blocks particular receptors at synapses, then new receptors may be produced to make up for the ones that are no longer in use. This means that more drug has to be taken to have the same effect. This is known as **tolerance** to the drug. An increasing tolerance is an indication of increasing dependence on the drug (see page 94).

The ways in which people use mood-changing drugs such as nicotine, heroin and alcohol can be classified according to how much control a person has over their drug-taking behaviour.

Recreational use involves a person taking a drug occasionally, in such a way that they do not suffer any health problems as a result, nor does their use of the drug affect their behaviour in ways that cause problems for anyone else. For example, having a glass of wine or beer with a meal would be classed as recreational use of alcohol.

Abuse occurs when the drug starts to damage the health of the person taking it, or of people around them or in their families. An example of drug abuse would be a person drinking enough alcohol to make them aggressive and act violently.

Table 5.2 Some neurotransmitters.

Neurotransmitter	Where it is found	Some of its effects
acetylcholine (ACh)	at synapses in the parasympathetic nervous system; also in the brain and some neurones in the sympathetic system	more secretion from salivary glands, more movement of alimentary canal, slower heart rate
noradrenaline	at synapses in the sympathetic nervous system; also in the brain	less movement of alimentary canal (constipation), dry mouth, faster heart rate
GABA (gamma amino butyric acid)	throughout the brain	an inhibitory transmitter that reduces the activity of neurones in the brain; counteracts the effects of dopamine and other transmitters
dopamine	throughout the brain, including the substantia nigra	involved in the control of voluntary movements and the integration of different kinds of information in the brain
5-HT (5-hydroxy tryptamine, serotonin)	brain	reduces the effects of ACh; slows the activity of some neurones; helps relaxation
glutamate	brain and spinal cord	involved in excitatory activity; important in memory formation
endorphins	brain and spinal cord	reduction of pain

Dependency occurs when, as a result of changes in the brain and other parts of the body, the person can no longer manage without the drug. Their life begins to revolve around getting the drug and using it.

Dependency can be classified as **physical** or **psychological**. This distinction is useful because it can help in working out the best way to help a person to escape from the hold that the drug has over them. However, there is no sharp dividing line between these two types of dependency, and in the end they both probably depend on changes that occur in the body as a result of taking the drug.

Physical dependency occurs because there have been changes in the structure and physiology of neurones in the brain. If the person stops taking the drug, they suffer from **withdrawal symptoms**. Withdrawal from heroin (see page 96) produces some of the very worst withdrawal symptoms. The person will feel anxious, restless and irritable. They will not be able to sleep. Their eyes water and nose runs, and they salivate excessively, and may vomit, have abdominal pain and diarrhoea. The pupils of their eyes dilate and they may feel pain all over the body. These extremely unpleasant symptoms start about 8 to 16 hours after withdrawal begins, and then can last for a week. The person will feel cravings for the drug for many weeks afterwards, as well as a general feeling of being unwell and being unable to relax or sleep (Fig 5.11).

Psychological dependency is also due to what is happening in the brain as a result of taking the drug, but the person does not experience unpleasant withdrawal symptoms when they stop taking it. They do, however, constantly crave the drug. It seems as essential to them as food or water does to you when you feel very hungry or very thirsty. They may have begun taking it to help them to get through a particular problem in their lives, and if that situation re-emerges they may start taking it again. Their drug-taking may also have led them to experience an environment that they enjoyed – for example, injecting drugs along with others; they may miss all the paraphernalia associated with this environment and feel a tremendous need to go back to it. Indeed, psychological dependency may be harder to get over than physical dependency.

Alcohol, (see pages 98–99) is an example of a drug to which both physical and psychological dependency may develop.

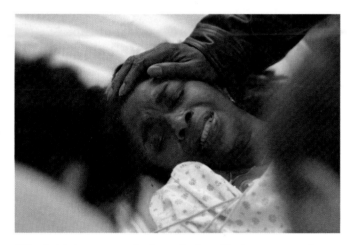

Fig 5.11 A woman in hospital suffering severe drug withdrawal symptoms.

Treating Parkinson's disease

Parkinson's disease was first described in 1817, in an essay by James Parkinson on the subject of the 'Shaking Palsy'. Parkinson's is common in Britain. It has a prevalence of between 1 and 2% overall, but occurs most frequently in people over 50.

The disease creeps up slowly. At first, a person may notice tremor in their arms or legs, which becomes progressively greater. As time passes, they will find movement increasingly difficult to control, and will walk slowly perhaps with an abnormal posture. Eventually their limbs may become rigid and refuse to move when they try to walk.

Parkinson's disease is caused by the death of a group of cells in a part of the brain called the **substantia nigra**. Normally, these cells produce a neurotransmitter called dopamine, and this enables them to transmit nerve

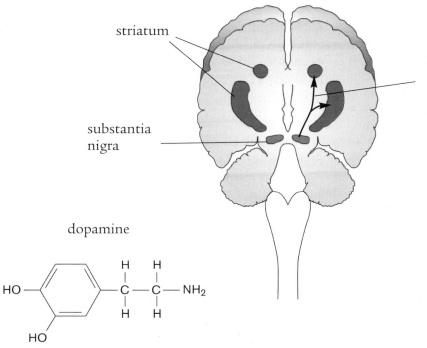

striatum

substantia nigra

dopamine

nerve impulses travel between the substantia nigra and the striatum for normal brain functioning

Fig 5.12 The substantia nigra of the brain and the neurotransmitter, dopamine, that is used at synapses there.

impulses to another part of the brain, the **striatum** (Fig 5.12). When the substantia nigra cells die, dopamine is not produced and so this communication cannot take place. The result is the loss of control of movement.

You cannot treat Parkinson's disease by giving someone dopamine, because dopamine cannot cross the blood–brain barrier (see page 79). Instead, a drug called **levodopa** is given. This drug does get into the brain, where cells are able to convert it to dopamine using the enzyme dopa decarboxylase. Levodopa has very beneficial effects in the early stages of Parkinson's disease.

One problem with giving levodopa is that the brain is not the only organ where dopamine acts as a neurotransmitter. Levodopa arriving at organs such as the kidneys, alimentary canal and liver can also be metabolised to produce dopamine, and this can produce unpleasant side effects, such as nausea and vomiting. However,

the enzymes that do this are different from the dopa decarboxylases in the brain. Levodopa is therefore usually taken in conjuction with carbidopa or benserazide, which inhibit the dopa carboxylases in organs other than the brain. This allows levodopa to be given in much higher doses without causing such unpleasant side effects.

As Parkinson's disease progresses, it is usually necessary to increase the dose of levodopa. This is because the cells that convert it to dopamine gradually die. However, if too high a dose is given then the rigidity and tremor can change to uncontrolled, jerking movements.

As we learn more about the disease it may become more possible to treat it successfully over a long period of time. For example, it is now known that there are at least five different types of receptors for dopamine, and if drugs can be targeted precisely to just one or two of these they might prove more effective in lower doses.

Heroin

Heroin is a powerful drug that can be used for the treatment of severe pain. It is also a drug that is abused. Heroin belongs to a class of drugs known as **opiates**.

The opiates

Opium is an extract from the seed capsules of oriental poppies, *Papaver somniferum*. It has been used for thousands of years to lessen pain. It also produces a feeling known as euphoria, in which all worries disappear and are replaced by intense happiness. Opium was a standard ingredient for a high proportion of the drugs and potions that were made and sold by apothecaries and herbalists in Britain for centuries. For example, a powder called 'diascordium', which supposedly could prevent you getting plague, was made up of:

cinnamon, cassia wood, scordium, dittany, galbanum, storax, gum arabic, opium, sorrel, gentian, Armenian bole, Lemnian earth, pepper, ginger, and honey

By the early nineteenth century, European chemists knew how to produce a much purer and more potent drug from opium, which was called **morphine**, after the name of Morpheus, the Roman god of sleep. In 1875, a slightly altered form of morphine called **heroin** was produced (Fig 5.13). Heroin enters the brain more quickly than morphine, so its effects are faster. It is used in medicine for pain relief, where it is known as **diamorphine**.

How opiates affect the brain

The brain uses many different transmitter substances that allow nerve impulses to cross synapses (Table 5.2 on page 93). Some of these neurotransmitters, in particular the **enkephalins** and **endorphins**, are involved in the reduction of sensations of pain. Their molecules are very like those of opiates. The receptors for endorphins and enkephalins, on the post-synaptic membranes of the synapses, have a shape that also fits opiates.

Opiates can therefore slot into these receptors and mimic the effects of our own naturally occurring endorphins. They not only reduce pain, but also affect our moods and reduce sensations of hunger or thirst. They have a depressive effect on heart rate and breathing rate.

The opiates are very useful drugs in medicine, because of their ability to reduce serious pain. However, they are also highly dangerous ones if used inappropriately, and can cause dependency. People who use them as recreational drugs (see page 93) may choose to inject them, because this gets them to the brain faster than if taken by mouth, and therefore provides a rapid and intense feeling of euphoria. While a few people seem to be able to use morphine or heroin like this and not become dependent on them, many others become unable to live without them.

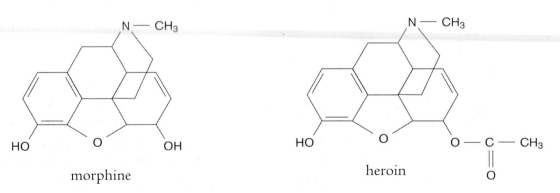

Fig 5.13 The chemical structure of morphine and heroin.

Craving the drug

Addictive drugs such as the opiates produce such a strong craving that it can completely take over a person's life. A person who is dependent on a drug may be driven to crime to get the money needed to buy the drug.

We are not absolutely sure how the craving is caused, but it does seem to involve the neurotransmitter dopamine. For example, heroin binds to receptors on neurones which inhibit GABA-secreting neurones (see Table 5.2 on page 93), therefore preventing them from carrying out their normal role in the inhibition of dopamine secretion. So more dopamine is secreted.

Nicotine, cannabis, amphetamines and benzodiazapines all seem to increase dopamine secretion, though each in different ways. Somehow, the extra dopamine produces the feeling of euphoria that these drugs can produce.

In a person who is addicted to heroin, the brain increases its production of an important messenger molecule, cAMP. This change in cAMP production tends to reduce the impact of the heroin on the neurones. However, on withdrawal from heroin, the cAMP production takes time to return to its normal level. The production of too much cAMP is thought to result in brain hyperactivity and the craving for heroin.

Cannabis

Cannabis is a preparation from the plants *Cannabis sativa* or *C. indica* (hemp and Indian hemp). It is thought to have been used for at least 3000 years. In England it was a commonly used drug in the nineteenth century, when it was prescribed as a painkiller, However, in 1928 its general use was made illegal. Despite this, it is a widely used recreational drug.

Cannabis is smoked, so the chemicals from it enter the body through the lungs. It is a mixture of thousands of chemicals, and research is going on into what all of these substances are and how they affect the body. They produce a feeling of happiness and self-confidence, relieve anxiety and heighten sensation. They also have a downside, because they reduce motivation, slow down logical thought, reduce coordination of movement and damage short-term memory. They may also cause mild hallucinations. Long-term use can, like smoking tobacco, cause lung cancer. Cannabis also suppresses the activity of the immune system.

One chemical isolated from cannabis appears to be particularly important in producing at least some of these effects. This is THC (delta-9-tetrahydrocannabinol). Several pharmaceutical companies are investigating possible useful effects of this and other substances extracted from cannabis. For example, THC helps to prevent too much fluid building up in the eye, and so could help to treat glaucoma, in which too great a pressure of fluid can cause blindness. Some of these substances can help to relieve severe pain, as they affect the same pain-regulating receptors as morphine. They may also be used to reduce nausea and vomiting caused by some cancer therapies. They may help people with multiple sclerosis, for whom they can reduce muscle cramps.

Although people may become tolerant to cannabis, they do not become physically dependent on it and only rarely become psychologically dependent. Withdrawal symptoms are mild. There is argument over whether there is long-term damage to the body.

Methadone

Getting a heroin-dependent person through the suffering of withdrawal is very difficult. It can last for days or even weeks, and is extremely unpleasant. In some cases, a different drug called methadone can be used to prevent these symptoms and help the person to beat their addiction.

Methadone, like heroin, is an opiate. As a person attempts to withdraw from heroin, methadone can be given to prevent the withdrawal symptoms. When they occur, the person is given a test dose of about 10 mg. When the symptoms recur, another 10 mg is given, and so on throughout one 24-hour period. Once it is known how much is needed in one day, in future it can be given in one dose a day, because the effects of methadone last for 24 hours. Now the patient no longer has to pay for heroin, and can instead be prescribed methadone. This can help the patient to get back to normal life.

The downside of this is that the patient is now addicted to methadone. If they want to beat this addiction, the methadone dose can be gradually reduced over a period of several days or weeks.

To help to stop them going back to taking opiates, they can be prescribed naltrexone. This binds to the opiate receptors in the brain, stopping the opiate drug from doing so. So naltrexone completely prevents the feelings of euphoria that result from opiate use and reduces the craving for the drugs.

Alcohol

Alcohol – more correctly **ethanol** – has been used by humans for thousands of years. It was drunk in beer, wine and other drinks produced by the fermentation of substances such as grapes by yeasts. It was also widely used as a solvent in the preparation of herbal remedies.

Alcohol molecules dissolve very easily in the fatty acid tails of phospholipids that make up cell surface membranes. This distorts the proteins that form channels in the membranes. In particular, it affects the shape of receptors in the membranes of neurones in the brain that respond to a neurotransmitter called **GABA**, which inhibits the formation of action potentials. Alcohol increases and prolongs the effects of GABA.

Alcohol also affects another, stimulatory, neurotransmitter called **glutamate**. This is the commonest neurotransmitter in the brain, and is responsible for much of the interaction between neurones. Alcohol blocks the receptors on cell membranes that glutamate would normally bind to.

So, alcohol increases the effect of the inhibitory neurotransmitter GABA and reduces the effect of the stimulatory neurotransmitter glutamate. Both of these actions reduce or depress the activity of the brain, so alcohol is a **depressant**. The effects are especially great in the cortex of the cerebrum and in the cerebellum. As the activity of the cortex is depressed, the person becomes less able to think clearly and logically and to make decisions. Inhibitions are reduced, and this helps some people to relax and interact socially. Depression of the activity of the cerebellum inhibits coordination of movements.

If drunk in large amounts, alcohol can kill. Inhibition of various areas of the brain causes drowsiness and eventually unconsciousness. It can cause coma. When the nervous stimulation of the muscles used in breathing is inhibited by alcohol, breathing movements stop and the person may die.

Alcohol is broken down in the liver by the enzyme **alcohol dehydrogenase**. Regular high consumption of alcohol over many years may damage the liver, causing **cirrhosis**. The liver cells have an enormous number of different functions in metabolism, and this condition can kill.

Long-term alcohol consumption also causes high blood pressure which in turn increases the risk of heart attacks and strokes. (However, there is evidence that regular consumption of small amounts of alcohol helps to reduce the risk of heart attacks, probably by increasing the amount of HDLs in the blood – see *Human Biology for AS*, page 112.) Alcohol can damage the lining of the stomach. It increases the loss of water in urine, so can cause dehydration.

Some people are able to drink large amounts of alcohol without becoming dependent on it, but others run the risk of developing dependency. It is not understood why some people become alcoholics (dependent on alcohol) while others do not. Alcoholics experience unpleasant withdrawal symptoms if they have to go for any length of time without drinking it. If they wish to give up drinking alcohol, they can be helped through these withdrawal symptoms with the use of drugs such as diazepam. However, a person who has once been dependent on alcohol can easily fall back into the same dependency again, unless they completely give up drinking alcohol or control their drinking very rigorously.

SAQ

5.2 The graphs show the number of people who were admitted to hospital in one part of the USA in the year 2000 for drug-related illnesses. In all cases, the drug was being abused and was a direct cause of the need for admission.

a Describe the pattern of alcohol abuse that resulted in hospital admission, amongst men of different ages.

b Compare the pattern you have described in a with that shown by cannabis.

c Compare the pattern you have described in a with the pattern of admissions for alcohol abuse seen in women.

d Explain why these data do not give useful information about the percentage of people who use these different categories of drugs.

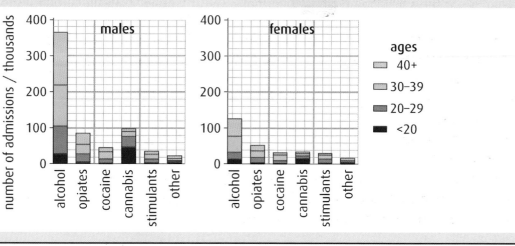

Summary

1. A drug is a chemical that changes the body's physiology. Drugs that affect the brain do so by interfering with neurotransmitters at synapses.

2. Over time, a person may need to take increasingly large amounts of a drug to have the same effect. This is known as drug tolerance.

3. When a person takes a drug to cause a desired mood change, this is known as recreational use. Recreational use may become abuse if the person begins to lose control over their use of the drug, and it causes harm to themselves or others around them. They may become unable to manage without the drug, when they are said to be dependent on it.

4. Dependency is classified as physical or psychological. Physical dependency means that withdrawal symptoms occur when the drug is stopped. Psychological dependency means that the person feels cravings for the drug, even though withdrawal symptoms are minor. Both physical and psychological dependency occur because of changes in the brain as a result of taking the drug.

5. Parkinson's disease is caused by the death of neurones in the substantia nigra that normally secrete the neurotransmitter dopamine. This causes loss of ability to move. It is treated by taking levadopa, which is taken into the brain and metabolised to form dopamine.

6. Heroin (diamorphine) is an opiate that is used to treat severe pain. It acts by binding with receptors in the brain that normally bind with endorphins. Heroin is also used as a recreational drug, and is dangerous because it can cause physical dependence. Withdrawal symptoms are severe.

7. Cannabis contains a large number of different chemicals, including THC. It may be used therapeutically to treat glaucoma, to reduce pain or to relieve the symptoms of muscle cramps. However, at present there are very tight restrictions on its use. Cannabis is also used recreationally because it can increase happiness and self-confidence. The use of cannabis represses activity of the immune system, and increases the risk of lung cancer.

8. Alcohol is a widely used recreational drug. It increases and prolongs the effect of the inhibitory neurotransmitter GABA and decreases the effect of the stimulatory neurotransmitter glutamate. This slows reactions and reduces the ability to think clearly and make rational decisions. While many people are able to use alcohol occasionally and have complete control over its use, others are prone to becoming psychologically or physically dependent on it.

CHAPTER 6

Controlling reproduction

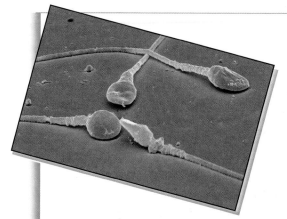

A large study made by the Aberdeen Fertility Centre in 2002 showed a 29% drop in sperm count since 1989.

Researchers at the Centre collected 16 000 samples of semen from 7500 men. They counted the number of sperm in 1 cm³ of semen. The average value was 62 million sperm per cm³. In 1924, this figure was 87 million sperm per cm³. Studies in the USA and elsewhere confirm the fact that sperm counts are dropping.

We don't really know why this happening. One research project in the USA has found a link between a man's body mass index (BMI) and sperm count. They measured the sperm count and body weight of 500 men, and found that obese men have much lower sperm counts than men of lower weight. Another investigation, also done in the USA, has looked into the effects of smoking cannabis. It tested sperm counts and sperm motility in 22 men who had smoked cannabis about 14 times per week for 5 years, and found that they produced relatively low volumes of seminal fluid, and the sperm moved 'too fast too early'. The sperm would have used up so much energy when they began their journey to an egg in the oviduct that, when they got there, they would not have had enough energy to complete their task and fertilise it. A study in Brazil found that caffeine also made sperm swim faster.

However, many people think there is no need to worry – yet. No-one has yet been able to check whether any of these changes have actually reduced a man's chances of fathering a child – in other words, his fertility. In general, a sperm count is only considered to be 'low' if it is below 20 million sperm per cm³, so the average sperm count is still well above this level. But the fall in sperm count does deserve some careful thought. There have been many suggestions put forward to try to explain it, including the use of artificial sweeteners, the addition of iodine to salt, eating food contaminated with pesticides, drinking too much alcohol, smoking cigarettes and being exposed to hormones used in the female contraceptive pill. More research is needed to discover whether these environmental factors are to blame, and whether they are actually affecting a man's fertility.

Most couples conceive a child within a year of trying, but approximately 10 to 15% are so unsuccessful that they are considered to be infertile. Whilst some couples will accept this and remain childless, others will be devastated by their infertility, and will do everything they can to conceive a child.

In this chapter, we will look at how the reproductive system works, and then consider some of the ways in which couples can prevent unwanted pregnancies and also how they can be given help if conception is proving to be very difficult for them.

Gametogenesis, fertilisation and pregnancy

Reproduction in humans involves:
- gametogenesis, which is the production of male gametes and female gametes;
- fertilisation, which is the fusion of the nuclei of two gametes;
- pregnancy and birth.

The urinogenital system

Figs 6.1 and 6.2 show the arrangement of the various organs that make up the reproductive system in males and females. As the organs of the urinary system (kidneys and bladder) are closely associated with the reproductive organs, this is sometimes known as the urinogenital system.

bladder – stores urine

ureter – carries urine from a kidney to the bladder

testis – makes and stores sperm and secretes sex hormones

seminal vesicle – secretes some components of semen

epididymis – sperm stored until they mature

prostate gland – secretes some components of semen

vas deferens – carries sperm to the urethra

erectile tissue – fills with blood to produce an erection

urethra – carries semen during sexual intercourse and urine during urination

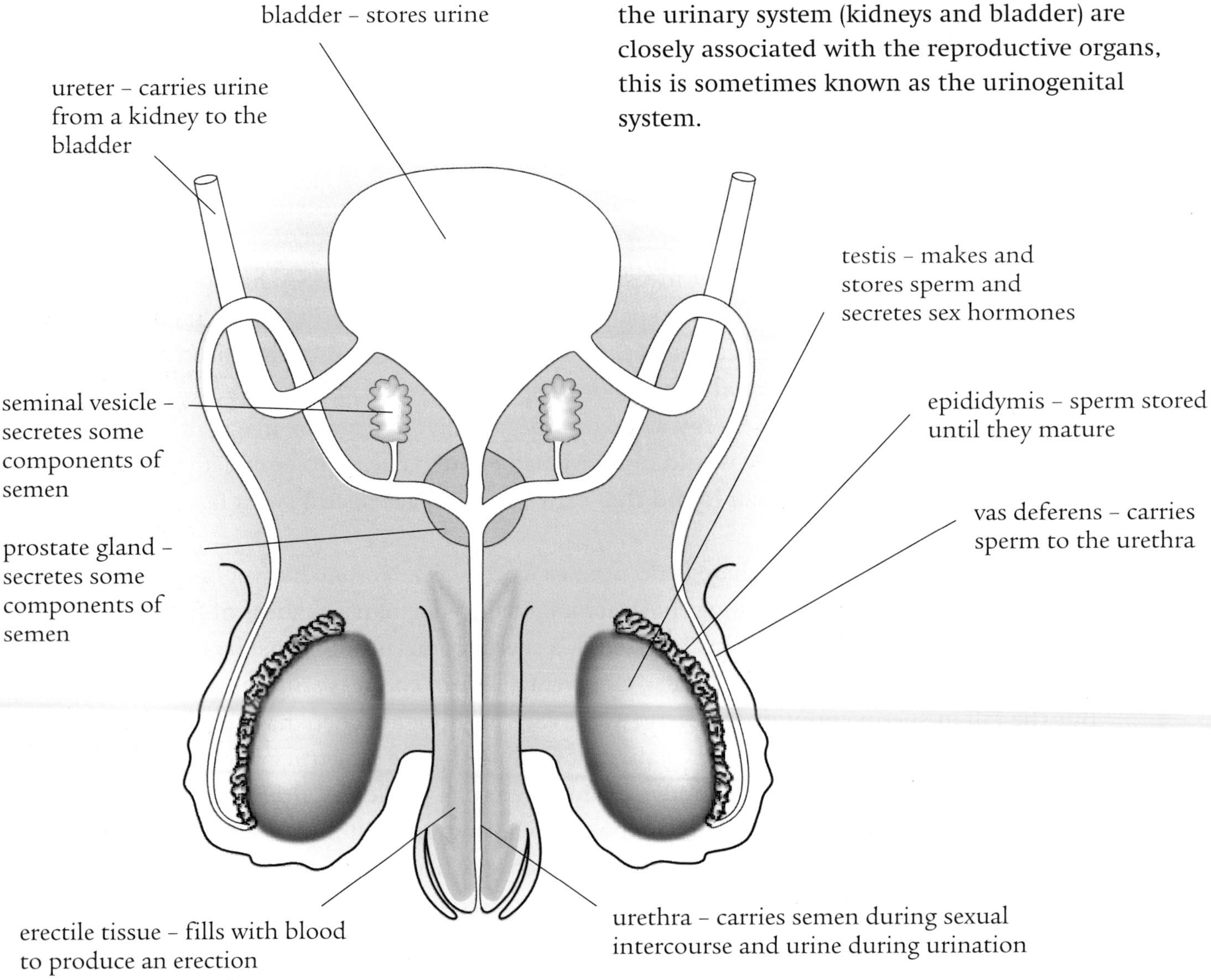

Fig 6.1 Structure and function in the male urinogenital system.

**side view of urinogenital organs
and surrounding organs**

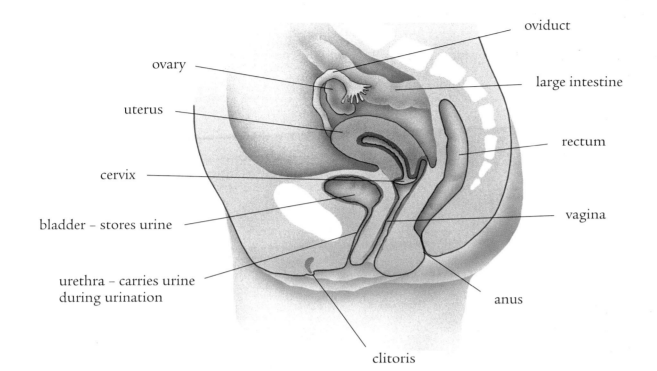

ovary

oviduct

large intestine

uterus

rectum

cervix

bladder – stores urine

vagina

urethra – carries urine
during urination

anus

clitoris

front view of reproductive organs

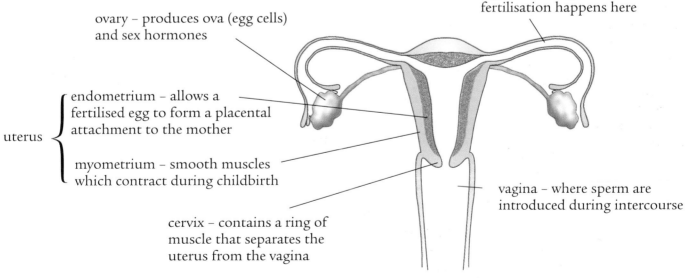

oviduct – allows sperm to enter
from the uterus and carries
eggs from ovary to the uterus;
fertilisation happens here

ovary – produces ova (egg cells)
and sex hormones

endometrium – allows a
fertilised egg to form a placental
attachment to the mother

uterus

myometrium – smooth muscles
which contract during childbirth

vagina – where sperm are
introduced during intercourse

cervix – contains a ring of
muscle that separates the
uterus from the vagina

Fig 6.2 Structure and function in the female urinogenital system.

Meiosis

The process of forming gametes is called **gametogenesis**. A gamete is a sex cell – an ovum (plural – ova) or a spermatozoon (sperm for short). At fertilisation, the chromosomes of both gametes join together to form the first cell of the new organism, the **zygote**.

Human cells contain two sets of chromosomes, so they are **diploid** cells. Each set is made up of 23 chromosomes (Fig 6.3). When gametes are formed, a diploid cell divides to form **haploid** cells, each with just one set of chromosomes. A gamete therefore contains 23 chromosomes, while body cells each contain 46.

The type of cell division that produces gametes must therefore share out the two sets of chromosomes in the parent cell so that the daughter cells get one complete set each. This type of division is called **meiosis**, and it is described in Fig 6.4. Meiosis is often known as 'reduction division', because it reduces the number of chromosomes from 46 to 23. There are actually two divisions in meiosis – meiosis I and meiosis II.

This is a micrograph of the chromosomes of a human cell from metaphase of mitosis, when chromosomes are most condensed (fattest).

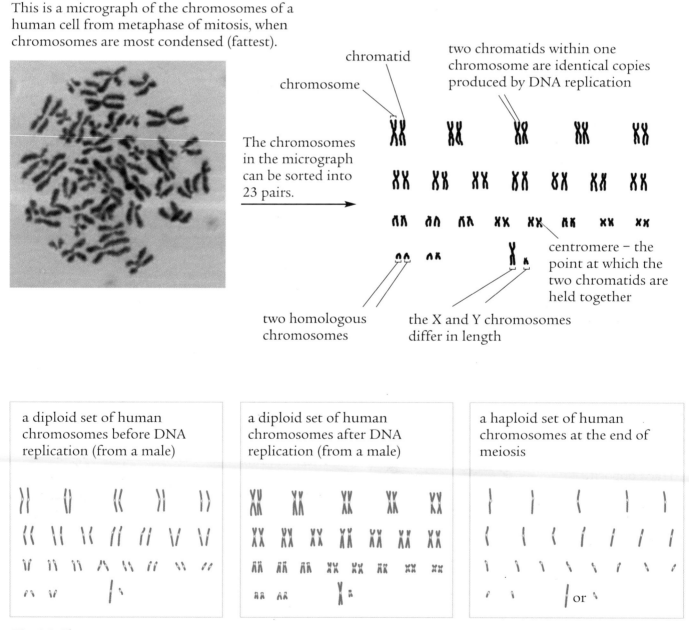

The chromosomes in the micrograph can be sorted into 23 pairs.

chromatid

chromosome

two chromatids within one chromosome are identical copies produced by DNA replication

centromere – the point at which the two chromatids are held together

two homologous chromosomes

the X and Y chromosomes differ in length

a diploid set of human chromosomes before DNA replication (from a male)	a diploid set of human chromosomes after DNA replication (from a male)	a haploid set of human chromosomes at the end of meiosis

Fig 6.3 Chromosome structure.

First half of meiosis (meiosis I)

1 Prophase I
(early)

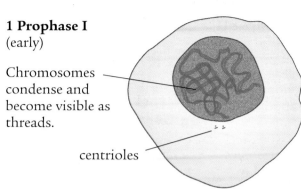

Chromosomes condense and become visible as threads.

centrioles

During condensation, but not visible at this stage, homologous chromosomes join into pairs called bivalents. A chromatid of one chromosome in a bivalent can cross a chromatid of the other forming a chiasma (cross-over point).

2 Prophase I
(late)

chromatid

Chromosomes have condensed enough to make them very visible.

A pair of homologous chromosomes is called a **bivalent**.

chromosome

chiasma (plural – chiasmata)

3 Metaphase I

Nuclear envelope disappears.

Centrioles have reached the poles.

The spindle has formed.

Bivalents are pulled to the equator by microtubules of the spindle attached to their centromeres.

4 Anaphase I

The homologous chromosomes of each bivalent separate. They are pulled to opposite poles by microtubules.

This is the step that halves the number of chromosomes.

5 Telophase I

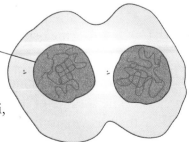

Chromosomes reach opposite poles and may decondense and form two nuclei, now with half the number of chromosomes in each.

6 Cytokinesis I

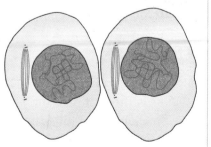

This stage runs immediately into prophase II (Fig 6.4b).

Fig 6.4a Meiosis I.

Second half of meiosis (meiosis II)

1 Prophase II

Chromosomes condense.

Spindle begins to form.

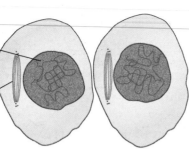

2 Metaphase II

Nuclear envelope disappears.

Chromosomes are pulled to the equator.

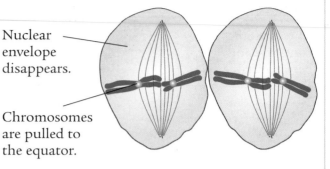

3 Anaphase II

Centromeres split so each chromatid is now a chromosome.

These chromosomes move to opposite poles.

4 Telophase II

Chromosomes reach the poles, decondense and nuclei form.

5 Cytokinesis II

The original cell has now produced four cells. Each of the four has half the number of chromosomes of the parent cell. Each cell has one chromatid (now chromosome) from each homologous pair in the original cell.

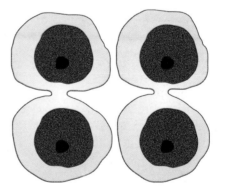

Fig 6.4b Meiosis II.

6.1 Do you agree with the statement that it is the first division, not the second division, of meiosis that can be referred to as a 'reduction division'? Explain your answer.

6.2 The bottom three diagrams in Fig 6.3 (on page 104) show images of human chromosomes arranged into their sets. Name a stage of the mitotic cell cycle or meiosis where the chromosomes would look like those in:

a the bottom left-hand diagram;
b the bottom central diagram;
c the bottom right-hand diagram.

SAQ

6.3   Make a copy of this table.

Feature	Mitosis	Meiosis
number of divisions that take place	one	two
appearance of chromosomes in prophase	chromosomes are made up of two chromatids joined by a centromere; homologous chromosomes do not pair up	
formation of chiasmata		

Extend the table to form as many more rows as you need, and complete it to summarise all the features of these two types of cell division that differ from each other.

6.4   Normally, mitosis occurs in diploid cells to form more diploid cells, while

meiosis occurs in diploid cells to form haploid cells. In principle, would it be possible for:

a   mitosis to occur in haploid cells;

b   meiosis to occur in haploid cells? Explain your answers.

Meiosis and variation

You may remember that when cells divide by mitosis the two new cells that are formed are genetically identical to their parent cell and to each other. This is not true for meiosis. When a cell divides by meiosis, *four* new cells are formed that are *genetically different* from their parent cell and from each other.

We have already seen one way in which the new cells that are formed by meiosis are different from their parent cell. The new cells are haploid whilst the parent cell was diploid.

But meiosis also produces variation amongst the genes that these cells contain.

There are two sets of chromosomes in the nucleus of a human cell. There are two chromosome 1s, two chromosome 2s, and so on. Both of the chromosomes of a pair carry genes for the same feature at the same place, or **locus**. For example, both chromosome 4s carry a gene that determines the production of red hair.

Most genes exist in different versions, or **alleles** (Fig 6.5). A human cell may therefore contain two different alleles for any gene. Figs 6.6 and 6.7 show how **independent assortment**

and **crossing over**, both of which happen during the first division of meiosis, produce this variation.

Fig 6.6 shows how independent assortment can shuffle alleles so that the new, haploid, cells differ from one another. Independent assortment happens because the two pairs of chromosomes can each lie either way up at the equator of the cell during metaphase I.

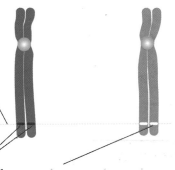

This line indicates the locus (place) where the gene determining red hair is found on chromosome 4.

The red line indicates the gene for red hair. Each chromatid will have the same gene, as it was copied during DNA replication.

The sister homologue could have a contrasting gene for 'not red hair', at this locus. The genes for red hair and not red hair are alleles.

Fig 6.5 Homologous chromosomes have genes for the same features at the same loci.

Imagine body cells containing one pair of alleles for red hair / not red hair and another for blue colour blindness / normal blue vision.

Chromosomes from the father are shown in blue shades and from the mother in violet shades.

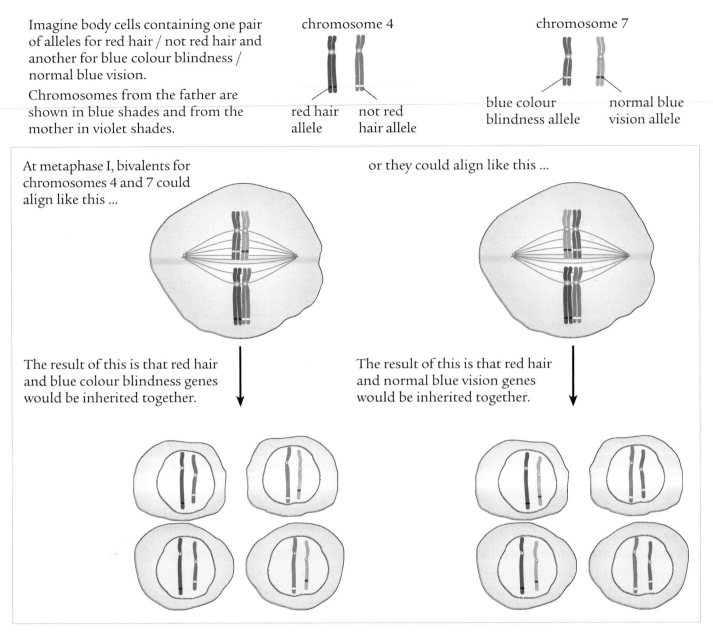

At metaphase I, bivalents for chromosomes 4 and 7 could align like this ...

or they could align like this ...

The result of this is that red hair and blue colour blindness genes would be inherited together.

The result of this is that red hair and normal blue vision genes would be inherited together.

Fig 6.6 How independent assortment produces variation. As a result of the randomness of the alignment at metaphase I, any allele of a pair of alleles can be inherited with any one of another pair that is on a different homologous pair of chromosomes.

We can calculate the number of different combinations of chromosomes that can be present in the gametes using the formula 2^2, where n is the haploid number of chromosomes. In the example shown in Fig 6.6, the haploid number is 2. The number of combinations is therefore $2 \times 2 = 4$. In this instance, these combinations of chromosomes mean that we also have four combinations of the alleles for hair colour and colour vision. They are:

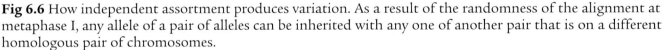

red hair / blue colourblindness
red hair / normal vision
not red hair / blue colourblindness
not red hair / normal vision

In a human cell, the haploid number of chromosomes is 23. The number of combinations of chromosomes is therefore 2^{23}. Try working this out (you have to multiply 2 by itself 22 times).

Crossing over is a result of the chromatids of one chromosome tangling up with the chromatids of the other one, during prophase I, forming **chiasmata** (singular – **chiasma**). The chromatids break and join at the chiasmata, producing a different arrangement of alleles on each one.

You can find out more about how this affects the genotype and phenotype of the offspring in Chapter 8.

As well as the red hair locus, chromosome 4 also has a locus for a gene coding for dopamine receptors. Imagine that there are two different alleles of this gene.

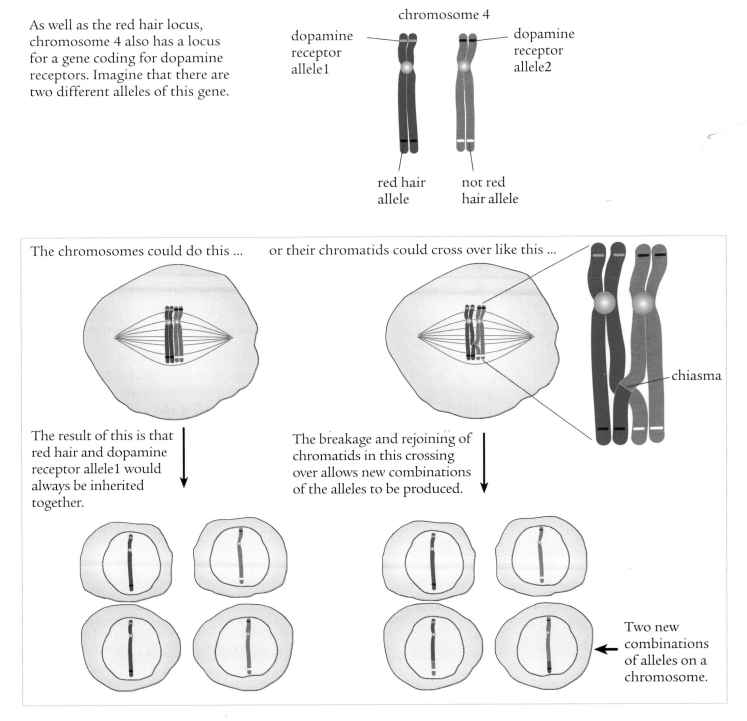

chromosome 4

dopamine receptor allele1

dopamine receptor allele2

red hair allele

not red hair allele

The chromosomes could do this ...   or their chromatids could cross over like this ...

chiasma

The result of this is that red hair and dopamine receptor allele1 would always be inherited together.

The breakage and rejoining of chromatids in this crossing over allows new combinations of the alleles to be produced.

Two new combinations of alleles on a chromosome.

Fig 6.7 How crossing over produces variation.

Spermatogenesis

Fig 6.8 shows how sperm are produced inside the testis. This process is called **spermatogenesis**. Sperm production begins in a boy around the age of 11, and then continues through the rest of his life. In most men, around 100 to 200 million sperm are made each day.

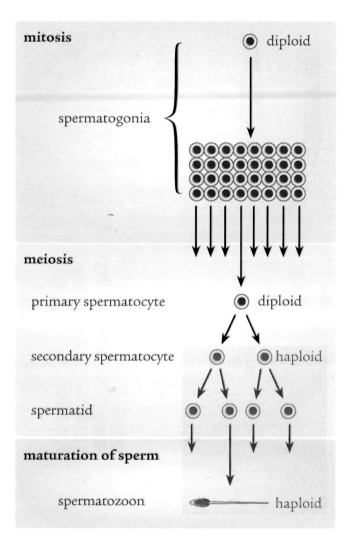

Fig 6.8 Spermatogenesis.

The testes are made up of many **seminiferous tubules**, and it is in the walls of these that spermatogenesis takes place. The process begins at the outer edge in the **germinal epithelium** and the new cells that are produced form towards the inner edge. So by looking at a cross-section of a tubule you can see all the stages in sequence.

The cells that begin it all are called **spermatogonia** (singular – spermatogonium). These are diploid cells, and they divide by mitosis to form more diploid cells. Some of these grow into new spermatogonia, whilst others grow much larger and are called **primary spermatocytes**.

Now meiosis begins. The two new cells that are formed by the first division are called **secondary spermatocytes**. They are, of course, haploid. After a few days, the secondary spermatocytes go through the second division, each forming two **spermatids**. These are also haploid.

That is the end of the cell divisions, and all that is now required is for the spermatids to differentiate into **spermatozoa**, usually known as sperm cells. They are all lined up with their heads attached to the wall of the tubule and their tails hanging free in the lumen. Fig 6.9 shows the structure of a fully developed sperm.

Throughout the process, the cells are protected by large cells known as **Sertoli** or **nurse cells**. These cells nourish and protect the cells that are developing into sperm, and are also responsible for helping to control and regulate spermatogenesis, as described on page 114.

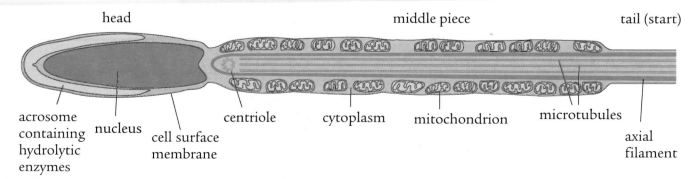

Fig 6.9 The structure of a spermatozoon (×14 500).

The histology of testes

1 Use high power (×10 eyepiece and ×40 objective lens) to look at a transverse section of a seminiferous tubule. Use the diagram and the micrograph to help you to identify the different structures. Make a labelled diagram of part of one tubule and a few of the cells between the tubules.

2 If available, use oil immersion to view and draw a few spermatozoa.

seminiferous tubule

Leydig cells (produce testosterone)

Sertoli cell (secretes fluid into the lumen and helps spermatids to become sperm)

germinal epithelium

spermatogonium

spermatocyte

maturing spermatozoon

Leydig cell

spermatocyte

germinal epithelium

spermatogonium

Sertoli cell

maturing spermatozoon

×800

Oogenesis

Fig 6.10 shows how ova are produced. The first stages of this process take place in the ovary, but the ova is not actually formed until fertilisation happens.

While a girl is still an embryo in her mother's uterus, germinal epithelial cells in her developing ovaries divide to form diploid **oogonia**. Within a few weeks, these oogonia begin to divide by meiosis. However, they don't get very far, only reaching prophase I. They are called **primary oocytes**. A lot of them disappear, but at birth the ovaries of a baby girl usually contain about 400 000 primary oocytes.

At puberty, some of these primary oocytes get a little further with their division by meiosis. They move from prophase 1 to the end of the first meiotic division, forming two haploid cells. However, one of these, the **secondary oocyte**, is much bigger than the other, the **polar body**. The polar body has no further role to play in reproduction. The secondary oocyte continues into the second division of meiosis, but gets no further than metaphase II.

Each month, one of the girl's secondary oocytes is released into the oviduct. If fertilised, it continues its division by meiosis. Strictly speaking, it is not really an ovum until this has happened. So the 'egg' that is released by an ovary during ovulation is actually a secondary oocyte, not an ovum. Fig 6.11 shows the structure of a secondary oocyte and the cells that surround it when it leaves the ovary.

Whilst all of these processes are taking place, up until ovulation, the developing oocytes are inside **follicles** in the ovary, also produced by the germinal epithelium. The wall of a follicle contains several types of cells including **granulosa cells** which surround and protect the oocyte, and secrete hormones.

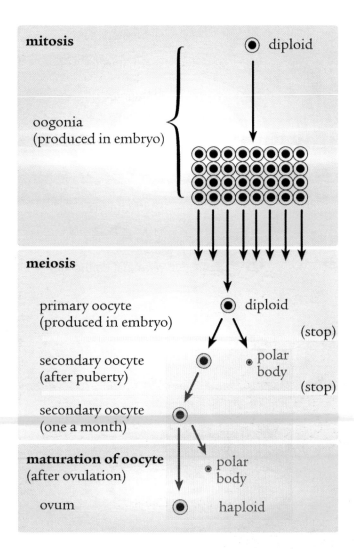

Fig 6.10 Oogenesis.

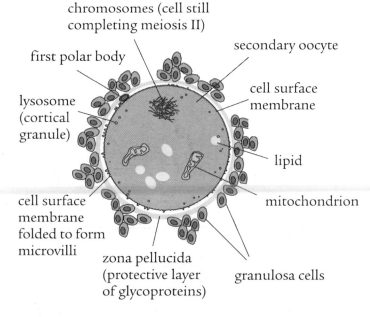

Fig 6.11 A secondary oocyte after ovulation.

The histology of ovaries

1 Use the naked eye to look at a slide of a section through an ovary. Identify the different structures using the diagram. Then place the slide on the microscope stage and view it using low power. Make a labelled, plan diagram of part of the ovary, showing at least three follicles in different stages of development.

2 Now use a suitable power to view one fully developed follicle. Make a labelled diagram of it, using these diagrams for reference.

3 Use an eyepiece graticule to measure the width of a fully developed ovarian follicle. Use a stage micrometer (or a calibration curve or formula if you have already made one) to convert the eyepiece units to mm.

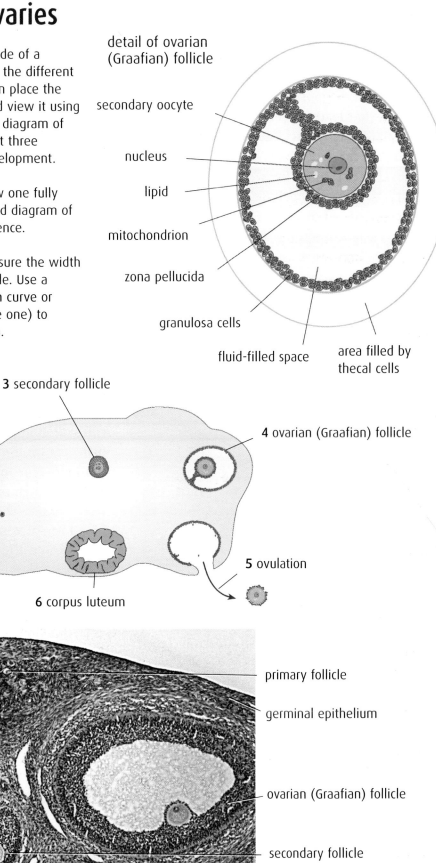

detail of ovarian (Graafian) follicle

secondary oocyte

nucleus

lipid

mitochondrion

zona pellucida

granulosa cells

fluid-filled space

area filled by thecal cells

3 secondary follicle

2 primary follicle

4 ovarian (Graafian) follicle

1 secondary oocyte

5 ovulation

6 corpus luteum

primary follicle

germinal epithelium

ovarian (Graafian) follicle

secondary follicle

×150

Hormonal control of spermatogenesis

Many of the same hormones are involved in the control of gametogenesis in both men and women.

Gonadotrophin releasing hormone, GnRH, is secreted from the hypothalamus. It passes into a blood vessel that leads directly to the anterior pituitary gland. Here it stimulates the gland to secrete the peptide hormones **luteinising hormone, LH** (sometimes known as interstitial cell stimulating hormone, ICSH, in men) and **follicle stimulating hormone, FSH**. These hormones are glycoproteins. They affect their target cells by binding to receptors in their cell surface membranes.

Testosterone, oestrogen and **progesterone** are secreted from the testes and ovaries. They are steroids (Fig 6.12) and so are soluble in lipids. This means that they can easily pass through cell surface membranes and into cytoplasm. They bind to receptors inside cells, which triggers a response from their target cells.

In men, testosterone is secreted by the **Leydig cells** (sometimes called interstitial cells) which are found between the seminiferous tubules (see Activity 6.1 on page 111). Testosterone secretion begins when a boy is still a foetus in the uterus, and it causes the embryo to develop male sexual organs. Its secretion is greatly reduced during childhood, but then increases at puberty, when sperm production begins.

This secretion of testosterone happens because LH is secreted. LH travels in the blood from the anterior pituitary gland, and binds to receptors on the Leydig cells. This causes them to secrete testosterone. The testosterone passes into the seminiferous tubules, where it binds with receptors in the Sertoli cells. This stimulates spermatogenesis.

At the same time, FSH is also secreted from the anterior pituitary gland, and this binds to the cell surface membranes of the Sertoli cells. This makes them more receptive to testosterone.

The level of all these hormones in the blood is controlled by negative feedback. If the concentration of testosterone in the blood rises too high, this inhibits the production of LH, which in turn reduces the secretion of testosterone. The level of testosterone in the blood remains fairly constant throughout a man's life, so sperm production is a continuous process. As the activity of Sertoli cells increases they release **inhibin**, a hormone which inhibits FSH secretion.

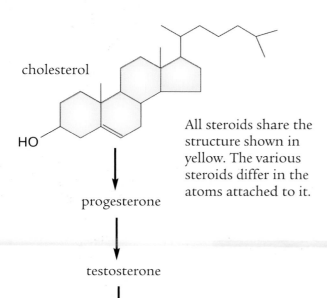

cholesterol

HO

All steroids share the structure shown in yellow. The various steroids differ in the atoms attached to it.

progesterone

testosterone

oestrogen

Fig 6.12 Steroid hormones are made from cholesterol.

SAQ

6.5   Explain how the structure of a sperm cell is adapted to suit its function.

Hormonal control of oogenesis

In women there is an approximately 28-day cycle, the **menstrual cycle**, of activity in the ovaries and uterus, in contrast to the steady production of sperm that occurs in men. The menstrual cycle (Fig 6.13) usually begins between the ages of 10 and 14, and continues until the woman reaches the menopause at around 50 years old.

The hormones that control spermatogenesis in men also control the production of eggs in women. Fig 6.14 shows the changes in these hormones during the menstrual cycle.

The cycle is considered to begin with the onset of menstruation. Menstruation usually lasts for about 4 to 8 days. During this time, the anterior pituitary gland secretes LH and FSH, and their levels increase over the next few days.

In the ovary, one follicle becomes the 'dominant' one. The presence of LH and FSH stimulates it to secrete oestrogen from the theca surrounding the follicle. The presence of oestrogen in the blood has a negative feedback effect on the production of LH and FSH, so the levels of these two hormones fall. The oestrogen stimulates the endometrium (lining of the uterus) to proliferate – that is, to thicken and develop numerous blood capillaries.

When the oestrogen concentration of the blood has reached a level of around twice to four times its level at the beginning of the cycle, it stimulates a surge in the secretion of LH and, to a lesser extent, of FSH. The surge of LH causes the dominant follicle to burst and to shed its secondary oocyte into the oviduct. This usually happens about 14 to 36 hours after the LH surge. The follicle then collapses to form the **corpus luteum** ('yellow body'), formed from granulosa cells, which secretes progesterone. This maintains the lining of the uterus, making it ready to receive the embryo if fertilisation occurs.

1 Uterus – most of the endometrium lining is lost during menstruation if fertilisation did not take place in the last cycle.

   Ovary – a follicle develops.

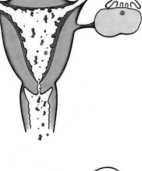

2 Uterus – the endometrium develops.

   Ovary – ovarian follicle produced.

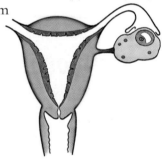

3 Uterus – endometrium is most developed and contains many blood vessels.

   Ovary – ovulation takes place.

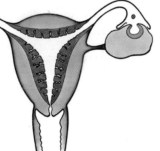

4 Uterus – endometrium maintained until corpus luteum degenerates.

   Ovary – a corpus luteum develops and then degenerates.

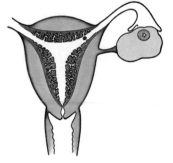

Fig 6.13 The menstrual cycle.

SAQ	
6.6 Explain how the structure of a secondary oocyte adapts it for its function.	6.7 Compare oogenesis and spermatogenesis.

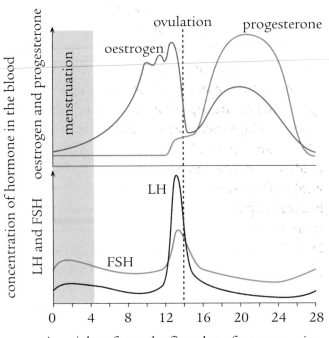

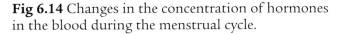

time / days from the first day of menstruation

Fig 6.14 Changes in the concentration of hormones in the blood during the menstrual cycle.

If fertilisation does not occur, the corpus luteum degenerates and so the secretion of progesterone and oestrogen falls. As the levels of these hormones plummet, the endometrium breaks down and menstruation occurs. The drop in the level of these hormones also removes the inhibitory effect on the secretion of LH and FSH, so the levels of these hormones begin to rise again and the cycle begins once more.

So, as in men, there is a negative feedback cycle involving interaction between the hormones secreted by the anterior pituitary gland and those secreted by the reproductive organs. But this cycle also has a *positive* feedback stage involved in it. This happens because, whereas lower levels of oestrogen inhibit the secretion of LH and FSH, very high levels stimulate it. This is why the surge of LH and FSH happens around day 12 of the cycle.

JUST FOR INTEREST

Hormonal infertility

The anterior pituitary gland secretes a number of hormones, often controlled by releasing hormones from the hypothalamus. These releasing hormones are produced in specialised neurones whose cell bodies are in the hypothalamus, and they secrete the hormones from the ends of their axons, as if they were neurotransmitters. But the releasing hormones are secreted into a blood vessel that takes them directly to the anterior pituitary gland just nearby.

Anterior pituitary gland hormones are not secreted steadily, but in pulses. The secretion of LH and FSH from the anterior pituitary is controlled by gonadotrophin releasing hormone, GnRH, of the hypothalamus and this, too, shows pulsatile secretion.

The frequency of these pulses determines which hormone or hormones will be synthesised and released from the pituitary. If there is one pulse of GnRH per hour, then both LH and FSH are secreted. If it is only one pulse every three hours, then FSH secretion is stimulated more than LH. If the frequency is increased above one pulse of GnRH per hour, then LH secretion is stimulated more than FSH secretion.

Infertility in some couples (see page 132) may be due to problems with GnRH synthesis or release that prevent the woman from ovulating. If so, then one way of helping her to conceive is for her to wear a portable pump with a catheter inserted into a blood vessel, delivering pulses of GnRH into her blood – like an 'artificial hypothalamus'.

Fertilisation

Fertilisation occurs when the nucleus of a sperm fuses with the nucleus of a female gamete in the oviduct.

We have seen that sperm production is a continuous process that takes place in the seminiferous tubules of the testis. The fully formed sperm move from these tubules into the **epididymis**, carried in fluid secreted by the Sertoli cells.

During sexual activity, stimulation of various parts of the body, and especially of the head of the penis, causes impulses to be sent from the brain through the parasympathetic nerve cells to an artery and its arteriole branches in the penis. They dilate, allowing blood to fill the spaces within the erectile tissue, so that the penis becomes hard and erect. Further stimulation causes impulses via sympathetic nerve cells to the vasa deferentia. Muscles in their walls contract and push the sperm within them into the urethra. At the same time, muscles around the prostate gland and in the seminal vesicles also contract, and this forces out fluid which mixes with the sperm to form **semen**. Semen contains citrate and calcium ions, and also fructose, which can provide the sperm with energy for their marathon swim towards a female gamete in an oviduct.

These muscles then contract in strong, rhythmic waves that force the semen along the vas deferens and out through the urethra. During sexual intercourse, the semen is ejaculated at the top of the vagina, near the cervix. A single ejaculation contains as many as 400 million sperm. These sperm are not yet ready to fertilise an egg. They can swim only weakly. Over the next few hours they gradually become **capacitated**, enabling them to swim more strongly and rapidly. During this process, a layer of glycoprotein around the sperm, and also plasma proteins in the seminal fluid, are hydrolysed by enzymes in the uterus. This appears to enable the tail to lash more strongly.

Changes also happen in the membrane around the **acrosome**, so that it can release its enzymes once an oocyte is reached.

The sperm gradually swim up through the fluid coating the inner walls of the uterus, towards the oviducts. Only a very small proportion of them, perhaps 0.025%, will complete the journey. And of these only one will be lucky to find and fertilise an oocyte, if there is one in the oviduct.

Fig. 6.15 shows how fertilisation takes place.

1 A sperm attaches to the secondary oocyte

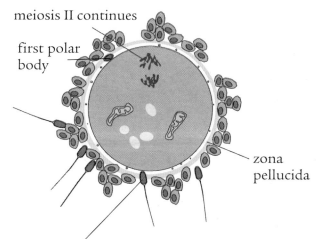

meiosis II continues

first polar body

zona pellucida

A capacitated spermatozoon digests a path through the zona pellucida, using enzymes from its acrosome, and fuses with the membrane of the secondary oocyte. The zona pellucida prevents another spermatozoon from binding.

2 A sperm enters

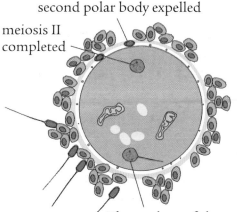

second polar body expelled

meiosis II completed

The nucleus of the spermatozoon combines with the ovum nucleus when this has completed meiosis.

Fig 6.15 Fertilisation.

Receptors on the sperm's cell surface membrane bind to proteins in the zona pellucida surrounding the secondary oocyte, and this stimulates release of the enzymes in the acrosome. They digest the zona pellucida, forging a pathway towards the membrane of the oocyte. As the membrane of the sperm makes contact with the membrane of the oocyte, the oocyte releases lysosomes (cortical granules) which rapidly pass into the zona pellucida and change the proteins there so that no more sperm can bind with them. This is known as the **cortical reaction**. The zona pellucida becomes an impenetrable barrier called the **fertilisation membrane**.

Contact of the sperm with its cell surface membrane stimulates the secondary oocyte to complete meiosis. A second polar body is formed, effectively acting as a 'dustbin' for the disposal of one set of chromatids. The nucleus of the successful sperm can now enter the egg, and the two nuclei fuse together to form a diploid nucleus.

The cell is now a diploid zygote. It has the full complement of chromosomes – two complete sets, one from the father and one from the mother. This mixture of chromosomes from two parents will make the child that grows from this single cell unlike either of them. Taken together with the variation in the genotypes of gametes formed as a result of meiosis, you can see that there is tremendous scope for variation in the children of any two parents. You will find out much more about this in Chapter 8.

Hormones during and after pregnancy

We have seen how hormones control the menstrual cycle, if an egg is not fertilised. But if conception does occur, then all of these hormones, plus several more, come into play to maintain the pregnancy and to control birth and lactation.

The first sign that fertilisation has occurred is the secretion of a glycoprotein hormone called **human chorionic gonadotrophin, hCG**. This is produced by the little ball of cells that has been formed by the repeated division of the zygote, known as a **blastocyst** (Fig 6.16). hCG is very similar to LH and has similar effects. It stimulates the corpus luteum to keep on secreting oestrogen and progesterone, which between them stimulate the endometrium so that its rich supply of blood vessels is maintained. This stops menstruation from taking place.

The blastocyst eventually arrives in the uterus and implants into the endometrium. A placenta is formed from the mother's and the foetus's tissues (Fig 6.17). (You studied this during your AS course, and you may like to look this up again to remind you of the parts and functions of the structures that are labelled on the diagram – see *Human Biology for AS*, page 183.) The placenta secretes oestrogen and progesterone, eventually taking over this role entirely from the corpus luteum.

Fig 6.16 A blastocyst.

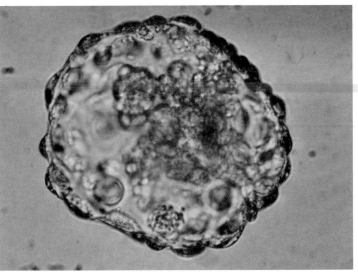

×500

hCG is secreted up until about the eighth week of pregnancy. As its levels decline, another protein hormone called **human placental lactogen** is secreted from the placenta. The function of this hormone is not yet fully understood, although it may possibly have a role in the control of blood sugar levels in the mother. It also enables oestrogen and progesterone to be effective on breast tissue.

The level of progesterone in the blood and also, to a lesser extent, that of oestrogen rises throughout pregnancy. These two steroid hormones cause enlargement of the breasts and maintain the endometrium. Progesterone also inhibits contraction of the muscles in the myometrium (outer, muscular layer of the uterus wall). As the pregnancy advances, the placenta increases its secretion of oestrogen.

Near the end of pregnancy, the peptide hormone **oxytocin** is produced by the hypothalamus and released from the mother's posterior pituitary gland. This hormone causes contraction of the uterine muscles, the myometrium, so that birth takes place.

Another steroid hormone, **prolactin**, is also secreted during pregnancy, from the mother's anterior pituitary gland. However, its actions are inhibited by the high levels of oestrogen and progesterone.

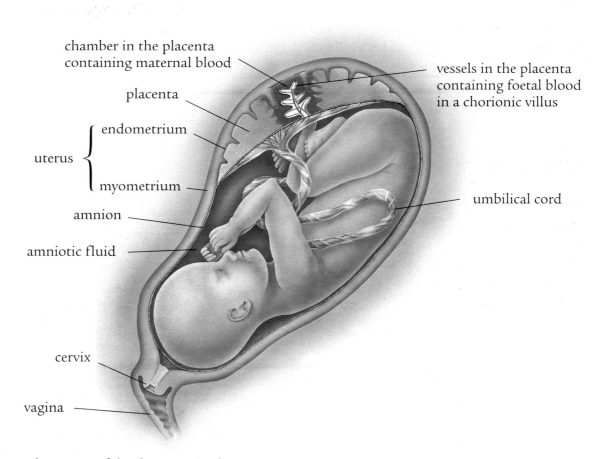

chamber in the placenta containing maternal blood

placenta

endometrium

uterus

myometrium

amnion

amniotic fluid

cervix

vagina

vessels in the placenta containing foetal blood in a chorionic villus

umbilical cord

Fig 6.17 Foetus at a late stage of development in the uterus.

After birth, when the placenta has been removed, the oestrogen and progesterone levels in the mother's blood plummet, and this allows prolactin to stimulate the breasts to secrete milk. The production and secretion of milk from the breasts (Fig 6.18) is called **lactation**.

The sucking of a baby on the breast causes prolactin to be released into the blood, and this increases milk secretion. Sucking also increases the release of oxytocin, and this causes the milk to be 'let down' – that is, allowed to flow out of the breast into the nipple. In some women, oxytocin production can be increased by hearing her baby cry. In this way, the amount of milk produced and released is neatly matched to the demands of the baby.

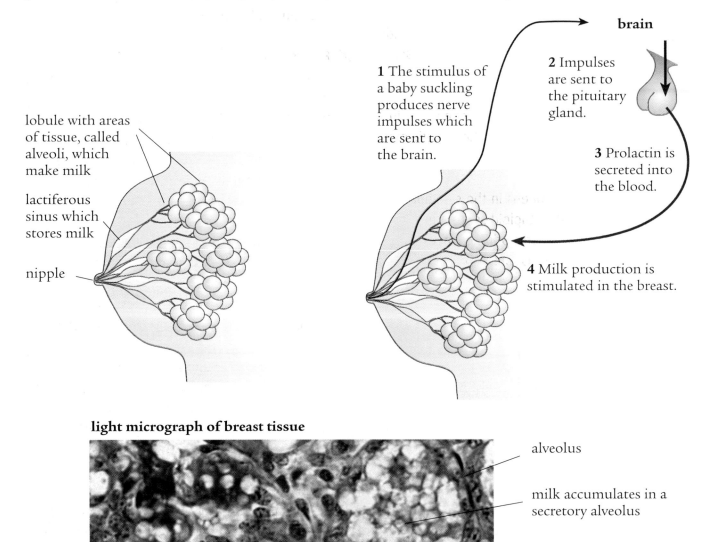

lobule with areas of tissue, called alveoli, which make milk

lactiferous sinus which stores milk

nipple

brain

1 The stimulus of a baby suckling produces nerve impulses which are sent to the brain.

2 Impulses are sent to the pituitary gland.

3 Prolactin is secreted into the blood.

4 Milk production is stimulated in the breast.

light micrograph of breast tissue

alveolus

milk accumulates in a secretory alveolus

globule of fat in a secretory cell

duct carrying milk away

Fig 6.18 The breast and lactation.

Summary

1. Gametogenesis happens within the testes and the ovaries. Cells divide by meiosis to form haploid gametes.

2. Meiosis involves two divisions. In the first, homologous chromosomes pair up and then separate. In the second division, the chromatids of each chromosome are separated. Meiosis forms haploid cells from diploid cells.

3. Independent assortment and crossing over in meiosis I produce variation in the genetic make-up of daughter cells.

4. Spermatogenesis happens in the seminiferous tubules of the testes. Diploid spermatogonia divide by mitosis to form primary spermatocytes. These divide by meiosis, first forming secondary spermatocytes at the end of the first division, and then spermatids at the end of the second division. These cells then develop into spermatozoa.

5. Oogenesis happens inside follicles in the ovaries. Diploid oogonia divide by meiosis, first forming primary oocytes at the end of the first division, and then secondary oocytes during the second division.

6. The hormonal control of spermatogenesis involves the glycopeptide hormones LH (ICSH) and FSH secreted from the anterior pituitary gland, and also the steroid hormone testosterone secreted by the Leydig cells. The levels of these hormones are kept approximately constant by a negative feedback mechanism.

7. The hormonal control of oogenesis involves LH and FSH, and also the steroid hormones oestrogen and progesterone secreted by the follicle cells in the ovary. When oestrogen levels are fairly low, their concentration causes a negative feedback effect on the secretion of LH and FSH. However, very high concentrations of oestrogen, as achieved on about day 12 to 13 of the menstrual cycle, cause a surge in the secretion of LH and this stimulates ovulation.

8. Fertilisation happens in the oviduct. During sexual intercourse, semen containing sperm is deposited near the cervix. After capacitation, the sperm swim through the uterus into the oviducts, where one of them may fuse with a female gamete. This stimulates the secondary oocyte to complete meiosis. The new cell that is formed is a diploid zygote.

9. The zygote divides repeatedly to form a blastocyst, whilst the now-empty ovarian follicle forms a corpus luteum. The blastocyst secretes hCG, which stimulates the corpus luteum to secrete oestrogen and progesterone.

10. As the placenta develops, it takes over the secretion of oestrogen and progesterone, which maintains the uterine lining. It also secretes human placental lactogen, which helps in the development of breast tissue. Progesterone inhibits the contraction of the myometrium, but near the end of pregnancy the mother's posterior pituitary gland secretes oxytocin, which stimulates this contraction and so birth takes place.

11. Prolactin is secreted from the mother's anterior pituitary gland throughout pregnancy, but is inhibited by oestrogen and progesterone until the placenta is lost from the body at birth. It is then able to stimulate lactation. Sucking of the baby on a nipple causes the release of prolactin and also oxytocin, which allows milk to flow to the nipples.

Birth control

CASE STUDY

India's population is second only to that of China. One sixth of the world's population lives in India, at a density ten times that of the United States of America. And the population is still growing rapidly, especially in the cities, where almost 25% of people live in slums. More than one third of India's population is made up of people less than 15 years old. The average number of children born to each woman between 2000 and 2004 – the fertility rate – was 2.85. The number required to keep the population constant is 2.

The United Nations Family Planning Agency (UNFPA) and the Indian government are continuing a programme begun in the mid-twentieth century to try to reduce the rate of growth of India's population. Health workers have trained local people to provide advice and help to couples wanting to prevent the size of their families from growing too large. Whilst this has had considerable success, there are still many shortfalls and more needs to be done to decrease overall population growth.

Do women and men in India actually want to have fewer children? For many couples, children are their health insurance for old age. They will need their children to help to provide for them when they can no longer work themselves. Before they desire to limit the size of their families, they will need to have some assurance that there will be ample support for members of small families. Men and women do not think of the population size of India when they decide how many children to have. They naturally think of themselves.

Nevertheless, about 42% of married Indian women are now using some form of contraception. Of these, about 75% have been sterilised, while the remainder rely on either oral contraceptives, condoms or an IUD. The government-led family planning programme is having a significant impact on birth rate, although this still has a long way to go before population size can be expected to level out.

The use of birth control gives couples control over the number of children that they have. **Contraception** means 'against conception', and specifically refers to methods that can be used to prevent fertilisation when sexual intercourse takes place. There are also several methods of birth control that do not prevent conception but rather prevent the tiny embryo from implanting into the lining of the uterus. These can be termed anti-implantation methods and they include the use of IUDs and the so-called 'morning-after pill'.

The term **family planning** refers to the ways in which a couple can control when to have their children, and how many they have, and it may involve contraception or anti-implantation methods.

Family planning in India and China

Use whatever resources you can access to research the history of the family planning programmes in India. You might like to look particularly for information about the compulsory sterilisation programme that took place in the 1970s.

Also research the ways in which China has succeeded in lowering its rate of population growth. You might like to find out something about the present day gender imbalance in the population, and people's predictions about the effects that this might have on people's behaviour and quality of life.

1 Compare the family planning programmes in India and in China from 1970 to the present day. Which has been more successful and why? What are the implications of the degree of success that the programmes have achieved?

2 One result of the success of China's programme has been an imbalance in the sexes, so that there are now more men in the population than women. What effects might this have on society?

Methods of contraception

The birth control pill

At the moment, the only birth control pill is prescribed for women, although considerable research is going into producing a pill that men could use as a contraceptive measure.

The 'pill' was developed in the 1960s, and its introduction had a huge impact on the freedom of women to have sexual intercourse without running the risk of becoming pregnant. While most would consider that this has been a great advance, it has also contributed to the rise in the incidence of sexually transmitted diseases, including HIV/AIDS, as more women have had unprotected sex with more than one partner.

The pill contains steroid hormones that suppress ovulation. Usually, synthetic hormones rather than natural ones are used, because they are not broken down so rapidly in the body and therefore act for longer. Some forms of the pill contain progesterone only, but most contain both progesterone and oestrogen and are known as **combined oral contraceptives**. There are many different types, with slightly different ratios of these two hormones, as women are not all alike in the way their bodies respond to the pill.

With most types of oral contraceptive, the woman takes one pill daily for 21 days, and then stops for 7 days during which menstruation occurs. In some types, she continues to take a different coloured, inactive, pill for these seven days.

6.8   The graph shows part of a woman's 28-day oral contraceptive cycle. The top row shows the days on which she took a progesterone and oestrogen pill. The part of the graph below this illustrates the changes in levels of progesterone and oestrogen (steroids) in her blood. The bottom graph shows the activity of the follicles in her ovaries.

a   How many days of the cycle are shown in these graphs?

b   Describe the patterns shown by the level of steroids in the woman's blood, and relate these to her pill-taking schedule.

c   Describe the patterns shown by the level of follicular activity. Explain how the levels of steroids in the blood can cause the patterns you describe.

d   A medical textbook states: "Towards the end of the 7-day pill-free period, some women can come dangerously close to ovulating." Using the data on the graph, and also your knowledge of the roles of hormones in follicle development and ovulation, discuss this statement.

e   One way around the problem described in part d would be for the women to take the pill all the time, without a 7-day break. Suggest why this is not the normal way in which oral contraceptives are used.

pill taking

menstruation

concentration of pill steroids in the blood

follicular activity

14 16 18 20 22 24 26 28 2 4 6 8

time / day number of the oral contraceptive cycle

Condoms

Condoms are a very widely used method of contraception. The use of a condom is a mechanical or barrier method of contraception, in which a physical barrier is placed between sperm and ova. Many people like to be able to use a contraceptive method as and when they need it, rather than altering their body physiology long-term as is done with oral contraceptives or sterilisation and also, to a lesser extent, using an IUD (see page 126).

Condoms are cheap and readily available. They are made from a material that does not allow the passage of sperm, nor of bacteria or viruses. So, apart from their contraceptive

effect, they also prevent the transmission of HIV/AIDS and other sexually transmitted diseases. With careful use, they have a very high success rate in preventing conception.

Condoms are the only method of contraception, apart from sterilisation, that is used by men. However, many women prefer to be in control of preventing their own pregnancy, and choose to use a femidom. Like a condom, this is an impermeable barrier, but it is placed inside the vagina instead of over the penis.

The effectiveness of both condoms and femidoms is increased even further if they are used with **spermicidal cream** inside the vagina.

Diaphragm

The **diaphragm** or **cap** is a flexible device which a woman can insert into the vagina so that it sits over the cervix. Like a condom, it provides a physical barrier preventing sperm from reaching an egg. Also like a condom, it should be used with spermicidal cream to be certain that no sperm can get past (Fig 6.19).

The diaphragm should not be worn all the time, but can be inserted some time before it is expected to be needed. It must be left in place for at least six hours after intercourse. A woman will need to be 'fitted' with a diaphragm initially, as it needs to be a snug but comfortable fit, but from then on she can easily put it into position herself. Nevertheless, many women find it a clumsy method and prefer to use a different method of contraception.

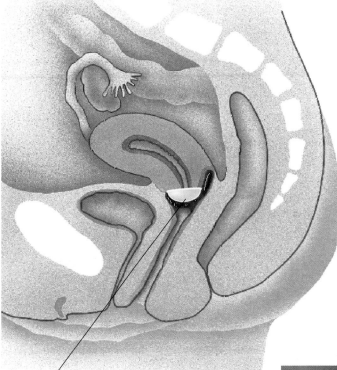

diaphragm over the cervix

Fig 6.19 The diaphragm method of contraception.

Implanon

Implanon is a contraceptive which is implanted into a woman's body and gives her protection against conception over a long period of time. It has replaced Norplant®, which has not been used since 2002 because it had unacceptable side effects including continual bleeding from the uterus. It consists of a small plastic rod containing progestogen, which has an action similar to progesterone – that is, it inhibits ovulation.

The hormone gradually diffuses out of the rod, providing a continuous low dose over a period of up to three years. It is therefore very convenient because the woman does not need to think about contraception at all. It also has some advantage over oral contraceptives in that it maintains a steady concentration in the blood that is lower than that seen soon after each pill is taken. On the down side, as in all the non-barrier methods, it does not have any protective effect against the transmission of bacteria or viruses. If the woman decides that she wants to become pregnant, the implant can be removed.

DMPA (Depo-Provera®)

Depo-Provera® is the registered trade mark of a contraceptive that is injected into a woman's body about once every 12 weeks. It provides continuous protection against conception throughout this time.

Depo-Provera® contains a synthetic hormone similar to progesterone called non-cyclic medroxyprogesterone acetate or DMPA. Like Implanon, it prevents ovulation. Its effects last

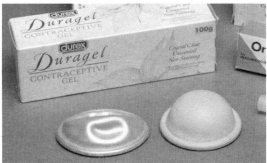

diaphragms and spermicidal cream

for about 12 weeks, at which time another injection will be needed if the woman still wants contraception.

Sterilisation

When a couple have had as many children as they want, they may opt for either the man or the woman being sterilised.

In men, sterilisation is achieved by **vasectomy**. In a relatively simple operation, usually done under local anaesthetic, the vasa deferentia leading from both testes are cut and tied, so preventing sperm from entering the urethra. In women, it involves tying the oviducts, a procedure called **tubal ligation**. It can also be done using a Filshie clip, which clips across the oviduct. Tubal ligation is normally done under general anaesthetic.

If properly carried out, both male and female sterilisation are 100% effective. Its big disadvantage is that it cannot normally be reversed, and this may cause problems for a person who, perhaps because they have a new partner, finds that they do still want to have more children. If a Filshie clip has been used, reversal is more likely to be successful.

Anti-implantation methods

Two widely used methods of birth control have their effect *after* fertilisation, although they do

this so early that the woman will never know that conception has taken place.

IUD

IUD stands for **intra-uterine device**. It is a small, folded piece of copper that fits inside the uterus (Fig 6.20).

The uterus responds to the presence of the IUD in the same way that it would respond to a slight bacterial infection. Leucocytes congregate in the uterus lining, and cytokines are secreted that bring about a low-level immune response. This helps to prevent sperm from passing through (and therefore it can also be considered to be a contraceptive) and prevents a blastocyst from implanting into the uterus lining. Moreover, the copper in the IUD is toxic to both sperm and the young embryo.

An IUD has to be placed in the uterus by a doctor or specialist nurse, and once in place it is left there. For some women, it is not suitable because it causes discomfort and also because it carries a small risk of infection. IUDs are therefore not usually recommended for young people who wish to have children later.

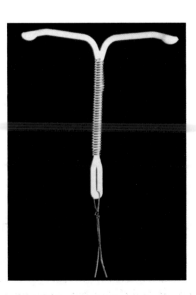

This IUD consists of a piece of moulded plastic that is inserted into the uterus. A coil of copper wire is wrapped around the stem. A piece of plastic string at the bottom passes through the cervix, allowing easy removal.

Fig 6.20 The IUD method of contraception.

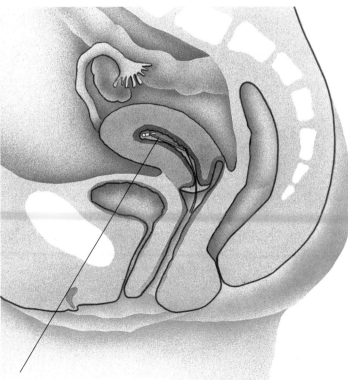

IUD in the uterus

The morning-after pill

This form of birth control is intended to be taken *after* a woman has had unprotected sexual intercourse and thinks that she might be pregnant. It might be taken by a woman who forgot to take her oral contraceptive pill, or if a condom broke, or by someone who was raped, as well as by a woman who simply did not take any precautions to prevent pregnancy. It works up to 72 hours afterwards, not just the 'morning after'.

The pill contains a synthetic progesterone-like hormone. If taken early enough, it reduces the chances of a sperm reaching and fertilising an egg. However, in most cases it probably prevents a pregnancy by stopping the embryo implanting into the uterus.

Ethical issues arising from birth control

People have used methods of birth control for thousands of years, but the last few decades have seen a huge increase in their efficacy and in the ease with which people can obtain and use them. This has led to disagreement between groups of people with strongly held views.

Some of the arguments against the widespread use of contraceptives include the following.

- The easy availability of a wide range of highly effective contraceptives appears to have led to an increase in promiscuity amongst people of all ages, but especially the young. Some people take the view that young people should wait until they are married before having sex, or at least should limit their sexual activities to a single partner.
- Parents are concerned that their children may be sexually active without their knowledge, because young people can get contraceptives easily and in privacy.
- Some people see the use of anti-implantation pills as being equivalent to 'unsupervised abortion on demand'.

Opinions on the other side of the debate are equally strongly voiced. Some of the advantages put forward include the following.

- It is likely that easy access to contraception prevents many unwanted pregnancies and many terminations that could cause great distress to young people and their families.
- Contraceptives have given increased control over their bodies and their lives to women in circumstances where their partners have no interest in preventing them from becoming pregnant.
- There is an urgent need to try to reduce world population growth.

ACTIVITY 6.4

Birth control issues

Chris is 16, and will be taking her GCSEs in a few months time. Her boyfriend, Nick, is doing his AS levels. They have been sexually active for some time. Nick uses a condom, but Chris isn't absolutely sure that they are always careful enough, and she worries about getting pregnant. She decides to try to get put onto the pill, but is nervous about visiting a family planning clinic, in case her parents find out.

Put yourself into the position of one of these people:
- Chris;
- Nick;
- Chris's mother;
- Chris's father;
- Nick's mother;
- Nick's father;
- a counsellor at the family planning clinic.

Get together with four other people taking different roles from you, and discuss what you think could and should happen in this situation.

6.9 The table shows data on the effectiveness of several different methods of birth control in a western country in the late 1990s.

Method	Percentage of women using this method who became pregnant in first year of use	Percentage of women who used the method for more than one year
none	85	
diaphragm	40	42
condom	14	61
femidom	21	56
combined pill	0	86
IUD	0.8	78
Depo-Provera®	0.3	70
Implanon	0.05	88
female sterilisation	0.5	100
male sterilisation	0.1	100

a Display these data graphically so that it is easy to compare the effectiveness of each method.

b Suggest explanations for the differences in success between the use of:
 i a condom and a diaphragm;
 ii a condom and Implanon.

c Suggest reasons for the difference in the percentage of women who continued to use:
 i a diaphragm and the combined pill;
 ii Depo-Provera® and Implanon.

Summary

1. Contraceptives prevent conception taking place, while anti-implantation methods prevent the young embryo from implanting in the endometrium.

2. The combined oral contraceptive pill contains oestrogen and progesterone, which suppress ovulation.

3. Condoms, femidoms and the diaphragm or cap are physical barriers that prevent sperm from entering the uterus, especially if they are used in conjunction with spermicidal creams. They also prevent the transmission of HIV/AIDS and other sexually transmitted diseases.

4. Implanon and Depo-Provera® provide long-term contraception by delivering a progesterone-like hormone into the blood.

5. Sterilisation is a permanent method of contraception that involves tying or cutting the oviducts or the vasa deferentia, or using a Filshie clip to close off the oviducts.

6. An IUD is a device that is placed in the uterus and prevents implantation. IUDs made of copper are also toxic to sperm and so may act as a contraceptive as well as an anti-implantation device.

7. The 'morning-after pill' contains a progesterone-like hormone that prevents implantation.

8. The widespread use of birth control has raised a number of questions relating to ethical issues, including an increase in promiscuity, the confidentiality between a doctor and young person that can prevent a parent knowing that their child is sexually active, and the possibility that the use of anti-implantation devices can be considered to equate to killing an unborn child.

Helping childless couples

"I gave them my all"

At the funeral of her eight babies Sheila Bowden told our reporter "I gave them my all and now I can rest with my conscience, even though I know I will have to deal with the 'told you so' brigade."

In August 1996, a 31-year-old mother – we will call her Sheila Bowden – made headlines in the *News of the World* and rapidly became a household name in Britain. Following fertility treatment, she had become pregnant with eight babies. Despite strong advice from her gynaecologist that she should have six of the embryos aborted so that there was a good chance that the remaining two would survive, she was adamant that she would not allow any of this to be done.

Sheila Bowden already had a five-year-old son who had been conceived naturally during her first marriage. Now she had a new partner, a married man who had two children by another woman. She underwent fertility treatment in London, resulting in the eight-fold pregnancy. She had had numerous miscarriages in the previous few years, and this probably influenced her decision to try to carry all eight babies to full term.

To her distress, she found herself a celebrity. While anti-abortion groups applauded her decision, there was a great deal of negative comment about her, especially for having sold her story to the *News of the World*. It did not help that her fertility treatment had been given free, on the National Health. She was seen as being a publicity seeker, positively wanting the notoriety that she received, but she insisted that she had no idea that her story would excite the media so much, and that she had never been motivated by the money. Her partner was also brought into the limelight; he had been unaware of Sheila's treatment.

As had always been predicted by her gynaecologist, she miscarried all eight babies. The media continued to follow her grief in the ensuing weeks. It took a long time for her story to fade away. Now she is still living with the man who was the father of the eight miscarried foetuses. They have three daughters, conceived without any need for fertility treatment – the treatment that she had stimulated her previously poorly functioning ovaries to produce oocytes and ovulate normally.

A couple is described as being infertile if they have failed to conceive a child after 12 months of trying. While the incidence of infertility has remained roughly the same over the last 20 years, the number of couples seeking help with conceiving a child has tripled.

Why such an increase? It is probably at least partly due to an increasing reluctance by couples to accept their infertility; there is perhaps a greater assumption now that they have a 'right' to have children and expect to be given help if it is required. Many infertile couples see their problem as a major life crisis, and feel devastated and powerless. Another factor is that many couples are delaying having their first child until much later than was the norm in the past. As a woman ages beyond 25, her fecundity – the probability of conceiving during one monthly cycle – falls considerably.

A couple seeking fertility treatment will first be assessed to try to find the root cause of their inability to conceive. Once this is known, it can guide the choice of the best way of helping pregnancy to be achieved (Fig 6.21).

Fig 6.21 A young couple are having a couselling session with a doctor in a fertility clinic. They are discussing the woman's impending artificial insemination. The doctor will explain the risks and chances of conception to the couple and allow them to decide whether or not to continue with the treatment.

SAQ

6.10   The graph shows the number of oocytes in a woman's ovaries between her conception and 50 years of age.

a   Describe the changes in the number of oocytes in a woman's body from conception up to the age of 50.

b   Suggest a reason for the rapid decrease in oocytes in a foetus between the ages of 6 and 9 months after conception.

c   Use the graph to explain one reason for the decline of a woman's fecundity with age.

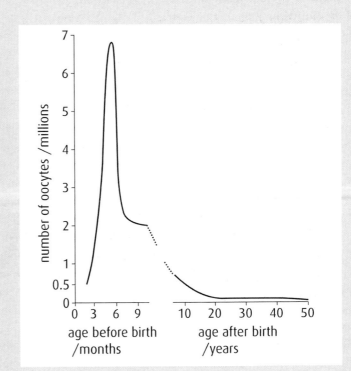

Causes of infertility

Of all cases of infertility in Britain, 50% are the result of problems in the woman's reproductive system, 35% are related to the man and the remaining 15% cannot be explained. Where the root cause is accurately diagnosed, 50% will eventually achieve pregnancy following treatment whilst almost 60% of those with no obvious cause will achieve pregnancy, even without fertility treatment, within five years.

Fig 6.22 shows the main causes of infertility in women and in men, and summarises the type of treatment that is most likely to be successful in each case.

Ovulatory disorders
Ovulation does not happen at all, or only very rarely. This is usually the result of an abnormal menstrual cycle in which some of the hormones are not secreted in sufficient amounts.
Treatment: use artificial hormones to induce ovulation.

Oviduct blockage
The oviducts may become blocked as the result of a bacterial infection (e.g. *Chlamydia*) which causes their walls to stick to each other.
Treatment: surgery to unblock the oviducts, or in vitro fertilisation (IVF).

Endometriosis
This is a condition in which the same tissue that is present in the lining of the womb – the endometrium – is also found in other parts of the body. It behaves in the same way as the endometrial tissue during the menstrual cycle. If present in the oviducts, this can cause them to become blocked.
Treatment: surgery to unblock the oviducts and use of hormones to prevent recurrence.

Antisperm antibodies
Some women develop an immune response against their partner's sperm. Antibodies are secreted by B lymphocytes, and destroy the sperm before they can reach an egg.
Treatment: IVF, or possibly intra-uterine insemination (insertion of semen into the uterus).

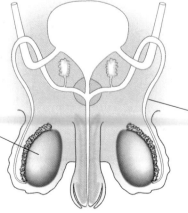

Abnormal sperm
Semen contains a significant proportion of sperm that appear abnormal when viewed using a microscope, or that cannot swim properly.
Treatment: in vitro fertilisation using selected sperm; if necessary, a sperm or spermatid can be injected into an egg during IVF treatment.

Absence of sperm
Semen contains a very low number of sperm. This could be caused by any one of several factors, including incomplete development of the testes, infection such as mumps or chlamydia or blockage of the vasa deferentia.
Treatment: surgery if blockage is suspected, otherwise IVF.

Fig 6.22 Causes of infertility.

Fertility treatments

Ovulation induction

Failure of ovulation is the cause of around 20% of all cases of infertility. It can be diagnosed in a number of ways – for example, by measuring hormone levels in the blood, or by using ultrasound or MRI to obtain images of the ovaries at different stages in the menstrual cycle. These images can show a fully developed follicle in the ovaries, ovulation actually happening, or the presence of a corpus luteum. The most common cause of failure of ovulation is a condition called **polycystic ovarian syndrome**, in which follicles are present in the ovary but don't develop as they should.

The first line of treatment will be to use hormones to induce ovulation. In many cases, a substance that interferes with the action of oestrogens, called an **anti-oestrogen**, will be given. The most commonly used one is **clomiphene**. This encourages the hypothalamus to produce **GnRH** (**gonadotrophin releasing hormone**), which in turn stimulates the secretion of LH and FSH from the anterior pituitary gland.

The anti-oestrogen is taken for five days, starting on day 5 of the menstrual cycle. Its success can be monitored by using an ultrasound scan to look for a developed follicle in the ovaries, and also by testing for progesterone in the blood. If it has not been successful, then increasing dosages of the drug may be given in subsequent cycles.

In some women, this treatment is not successful, and then other hormones can be tried. Usually, a mixture of LH and FSH is given. These are extracted from the urine of post-menopausal women and are sometimes known as 'hMG' – human menopausal gonadotrophin. This induces ovulation. A few days later, chorionic gonadotrophin (see page 118) is injected to stimulate the formation of the corpus luteum which will then secrete progesterone and help to maintain the endometrium.

The aim of **ovulation induction** is to allow the woman to conceive in an absolutely normal way, to achieve pregnancy with a single embryo and to give birth to a single, healthy child. However, it is difficult to judge the dosage of the hormones that will achieve ovulation of one oocyte and not several, and so it is quite likely that a multiple pregnancy will result.

Artificial insemination

If the woman is ovulating normally and the problem seems to lie with the sperm's inability to get past the cervix and swim to an egg, artificial insemination may be tried. Some of the male partner's semen is collected and then inserted into the woman's uterus via the vagina and cervix, just after she has ovulated. This is called **intra-uterine insemination**.

In some cases, the problem will lie with the inability of the man's semen to pass into the urethra, perhaps because the vasa deferentia are blocked. It may then be possible to collect sperm from the testes using surgery, which can then be used for artificial insemination.

In some instances, if the man is not producing active sperm, then semen may be taken from a donor. This can give rise to concerns by some people, who think it wrong that a woman should have a child by someone other than her partner. It might also cause discord in the family, even if the male partner is initially supportive of the process. Perhaps the biggest problem is whether the child should be told who their biological father is. Until April 2005, sperm donors in the United Kingdom had the right to remain anonymous, so that even the mother often did not know who was the father of her child. Now children born as a result of sperm or eggs donated after April 2005 have the right to find out about their biological parents once they reach 18 years old.

In vitro fertilisation (IVF)

'In vitro' means 'in glass'. In **IVF**, a woman's oocytes and her partner's sperm are mixed in a dish where fertilisation takes place.

Usually, ovulation will be stimulated using hormones as described on page 133. The dosages will aim to cause several follicles to develop simultaneously. The oocytes are collected from the woman using a tube that is inserted through the vagina and cervix and into the oviducts, using ultrasound for guidance.

On the same day, semen is collected from the man. The sperm are washed, and then placed into a liquid containing nutrients and substances that help them to become capacitated (see page 117). About four hours later, each oocyte is placed in a separate dish, and approximately 100 000 motile sperm are added to each. Alternatively, the DNA of a sperm is injected into an oocyte (Fig 6.23).

Three days after the oocytes were collected, they will be examined to see which ones have been fertilised. Two will be chosen and inserted into the uterus using a tube passed through the vagina and cervix. Two are used to give a greater likelihood that at least one will implant, but avoiding the risk of having triplets or even more babies.

The fate of the 'unused' embryos raises ethical issues. Some people believe them to be human beings, who should be treated as such. Others see things differently; it is certain that many early embryos conceived naturally are lost from the mother's body well before they implant in the uterus, so it can be argued that the loss of embryos after IVF is only mirroring natural processes. Another question to be addressed is whether these embryos can be used as a source of pluripotent stem cells, potentially a source of treatment for many different illness. While some countries allow this, others have passed specific legislation to prevent it.

Frozen embryo replacement

One possible use of any 'spare' embryos following IVF is to freeze them using liquid

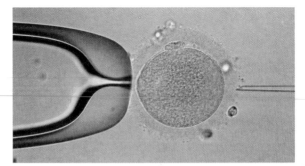

Fig 6.23 Photomicrograph of a microneedle (right) about to penetrate the oocyte to inject the DNA of a sperm cell. On the left, a flat-nosed pipette is used to hold the egg steady.

nitrogen, in which they can be stored for many years. About 70% of the frozen embryos survive.

The embryos remain in suspended animation, and can be thawed and transferred to the mother's uterus when needed. This process may be used when a woman has to undergo treatment that may damage her ovaries, usually when she is being given radiotherapy or chemotherapy as part of her treatment for cancer. It is also helpful when she has to undergo many cycles of fertility treatment before conceiving, as it avoids having to stimulate her ovaries repeatedly and having to undergo the collection of oocytes from her oviducts.

The ethical issues associated with this process are the same as those described for IVF. However, here another issue can arise. Normally, the permission of both members of the partnership will be required before implantation of the stored embryos can be carried out. This can cause difficulties if the male partner no longer wants the woman to have his child.

Yet another problem is the risk that the frozen embryos will get mixed up. There has been more than one known case where a woman was given embryos that were not hers, and there have probably been several more that never came to light. This causes great distress to the mother and her partner, who know that their biological child is growing up with another family, while the child that they are bringing up is not biologically theirs.

Diane Blood's story

Stephen and Diane Blood had been trying for a baby for only two months when Stephen caught meningitis, in February 1995. He quickly lapsed into a coma, and died without regaining consciousness.

Diane asked doctors to remove some semen from her husband while he lay in the coma, and this was frozen so that she could use it to father a child if Stephen did not survive. After his death, she was amazed to find that she could not do this. The Human Fertilisation and Embryology Authority ruled that Stephen needed to have given his written consent for his sperm to be used, and that Diane had had no right to ask for the semen to be collected without his permission.

But Diane Blood is not a person who gives in easily. She was absolutely certain that her husband would have wanted her to have his children, and she appealed against the decision. Having no success with that, she asked if she could take the frozen semen to another country, such as Belgium or the United States, where there were no laws preventing its use. But even this was denied to her. She still would not give up, and took her case to the Court of Appeal. In February 1997 she got the ruling she had always believed was right – she could take Stephen's sperm to another country in the European Community where she could have fertility treatment and conceive his children. Even so, it took another nine months before the Free University's Centre for Reproductive Medicine in Brussels agreed to give her treatment.

Mrs Blood gave birth to her first child in December 1998, and then her second – conceived in the same way – in July 2002. Still battling, in 2003 she eventually persuaded the courts that Stephen should be named as the legal father of her children.

GIFT

GIFT stands for **gamete intrafallopian transfer**. (The oviducts are also known as Fallopian tubes.) It is an alternative to IVF, used when infertility is caused by an inability of sperm and oocytes to arrive in an oviduct. It might be caused by a shortage of normal sperm, or by lack of ovulation in the woman.

Sperm and oocytes are passed into an oviduct through a tube inserted through the vagina and uterus. If oocytes cannot be obtained from the woman, then oocytes donated by another woman can be used.

A variant on this process is called ZIFT , where the Z stands for zygote. Here IVF is carried out as described on page 134, and a zygote placed into an oviduct.

Intracytoplasmic sperm injection

This process is known as ICSI. It is a modification of the normal IVF procedure in which a sperm is actually injected into an egg, rather than just allowing the sperm to fertilise the eggs by themselves. It may be used when the man's sperm are not able to do this, perhaps because they do not swim normally or because they do not become capacitated.

One problem with this procedure is that there is a slightly increased risk of abnormalities in a child that is born as a result. Normally, only 'fit' sperm will manage to fertilise an oocyte, and it is possible that a less than perfect sperm could carry genes that can cause a congenital abnormality.

Sperm banks

We have seen that very young embryos are able to survive freezing and thawing. The same is true of sperm. This has led to the setting up of **sperm banks**, consisting of samples of sperm that can be used in many of the infertility treatments described on pages 133 to 136. The technique of storing frozen cells is called cryopreservation.

The first successful use of frozen sperm took place in 1953, when previously frozen semen was used in a procedure involving intra-uterine insemination. Now it is the norm to use frozen sperm for IVF, even if the woman's own partner has donated them. This gives the opportunity to remove the sperm from semen, which could otherwise carry a risk of transferring HIV to the woman along with the sperm.

Most artificial insemination or IVF procedures use the sperm of the woman's partner. Sperm cryopreservation allows long-term sperm storage for a man who is perhaps facing medical treatment or a progressive illness which is likely to make him infertile.

However, we have seen that sperm from a donor may be used if the partner's sperm is incapable of fertilising an egg. Potential donors may be asked to give information about their family history, their interests, and their educational background. They undergo a thorough health check, looking for infectious diseases such as hepatitis and HIV/AIDS. They undergo genetic testing to check for hereditary diseases such as sickle cell anaemia. All of this information is used to build up a **donor profile**. If the profile suggests that the semen may be safe to use, then a sample will be taken and frozen. It will be kept for at least six months before use, during which time the donor will be repeatedly tested for infectious diseases, to reduce the likelihood that something was in an early and undetectable stage of development when the sample was collected.

Each sperm sample is labelled carefully and kept frozen in liquid nitrogen. The samples are kept in a secure area so that tampering is not possible, and the levels of liquid nitrogen are regularly checked.

A woman who is going to be given donated sperm is provided with the profiles of the donors, but not their names (see page 133), and she can use this to help her to choose the donor she would like to use.

Fertility treatment and natural selection

Within most populations of organisms, there are genetic differences between individuals. These differences may be small, but they are the raw material on which the process of **natural selection** takes place.

Natural selection happens when there are so many individuals in a population that there are not enough resources for all of them to stay healthy or to survive. This results in **competition**. There may be some organisms that have features which help them to survive in these conditions, giving them a competitive advantage over others without these features. These are the ones that are most likely to survive and to reproduce, passing their beneficial genes on to their offspring. Organisms without these genes are likely to die before they can reproduce.

It can be argued that fertility treatment is undermining natural selection processes that might act on human populations. People who cannot conceive naturally may not have the 'best' varieties of genes that influence their reproductive physiology. In most populations, organisms that have such genes would not hand

---

SAQ

6.11 The graph shows the charges for different procedures involved in fertility treatment at a hospital in Cambridgeshire (these exclude cost of drugs). These charges are directly related to the costs of the treatments.

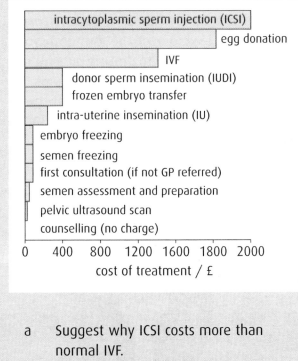

intracytoplasmic sperm injection (ICSI)
egg donation
IVF
donor sperm insemination (IUDI)
frozen embryo transfer
intra-uterine insemination (IU)
embryo freezing
semen freezing
first consultation (if not GP referred)
semen assessment and preparation
pelvic ultrasound scan
counselling (no charge)

0   400   800 1200 1600 1800 2000
cost of treatment / £

a   Suggest why ICSI costs more than normal IVF.
b   What is meant by 'semen assessment and preparation'?

c   The table shows the chances of a live birth following IVF treatment in women of different ages.

Age of woman / years	Chance of a live birth following IVF
below 23	unknown
23–35	more than 20%
36–38	15%
39	10%
40 and over	6%

i   Suggest why the chance of successful IVF treatment for women below 23 years of age is unknown.
ii Fertility treatment may not always be readily offered to women over the age of 40. Use these data, and also the information in the graph, to suggest why this is so.
iii What are your views on the provision of fertility treatment on the National Health for women over the age of 35? Use biological, ethical and economic arguments to support your opinion.

them on to the next generation because they would not reproduce. So, does fertility treatment mean that we are perpetuating 'bad' genes in human populations? Is it preventing natural selection from taking place?

There are undoubtedly some grounds to support this argument, but there are equal issues relating to almost all kinds of medical treatment. This, too, is preventing natural selection from 'weeding out' individuals who may be carrying genes that make them more susceptible to certain illnesses, just as much as fertility treatment does. It is difficult to argue that medical treatment should be denied so that natural selection can take place. And the genetic implications of reduced natural selection are likely to take a few hundred years at least to have a significant impact. By then, there may be a different and acceptable way of preventing some genes from being perpetuated in the population.

Multiple pregnancies and births

A multiple pregnancy can be defined as the presence of two or more embryos (or foetuses) growing in the uterus simultaneously. Nearly 98% of multiple pregnancies are twins. Fig 6.24 shows how **monozygotic** and **dizygotic twins** may be produced.

Not all multiple pregnancies lead to multiple births, as one or more of the developing foetuses may be naturally aborted at an early stage. Sometimes one of a pair of twins in the uterus may 'disappear' during the early stages of pregnancy, as it is reabsorbed into the mother's body, a phenomenon known as 'vanishing twin syndrome'.

As fertility treatments become more common, the incidence of multiple pregnancies and multiple births, especially ones involving three or more babies, are increasing (see Fig 6.26). This is a matter for concern, because a multiple pregnancy poses a greater health risk to both mother and babies than a singleton pregnancy. A multiple pregnancy is more likely to lead to premature birth and low birth weight. Complications develop in 80% of multiple pregnancies, compared with 30% of singleton pregnancies. The strain on the mother is greater, and this can result in her own ill health, such as the development of anaemia, diabetes or pre-eclampsia (see *Human Biology for AS*, pages 187–188). Miscarriage is much more likely in a multiple pregnancy.

Many gynaecologists consider that a quadruplet pregnancy should always be treated by removing at least one of the four embryos at an early stage, as failure to do this puts all four of them at great risk. There was never any realistic chance of the survival of any of the octuplets that Sheila Bowden (see page 130) was determined to keep.

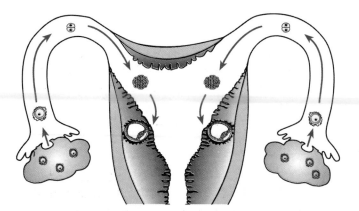

Dizygotic twins are produced when two oocytes are released at the same time and both fertilised.

Fig 6.24 Monozygotic and dizygotic twins.

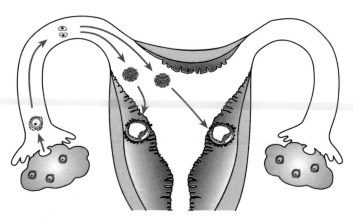

Monozygotic twins are produced when one oocyte is fertilised but the two cells produced by the first mitosis each develop into an embryo.

Pregnancy testing kits

Any couple trying for a baby will want to know as soon as possible if the woman has become pregnant. There are now many different pregnancy testing kits on the market which can be used at home. Most of them use **monoclonal antibodies** to test for the presence of human chorionic gonadotrophin in her urine (Fig 6.25).

Monoclonal antibodies are immunoglobulins that are all identical with one another. For pregnancy testing, antibodies are made that will bind with the hormone human chorionic gonadotrophin, hCG. This is done by injecting hCG into a mouse and then taking blood from it after its leucocytes have had time to respond to the hCG as an antigen, producing antibodies that are specific to hCG. One of these cells is isolated. It is then fused with a mouse myeloma cell (a type of cancer cell). The cell is grown and forms a clone in which all the cells secrete the one antibody – a monoclonal antibody.

For one type of kit, these hCG-specific antibodies are bound to atoms of gold. The antibody–gold complexes are then used to coat the end of a dipstick (Fig 6.25).

Another type of monoclonal antibody is also made, which will specifically bind with hCG-antibody–gold complexes. These are impregnated into a region further up the dipstick, called the Patient Test Result region, and immobilised.

To use the dipstick, it is dipped into a urine sample. Any hCG in the urine will bind to the antibodies at the end of the stick, and will be carried upwards as the urine seeps up the stick. As the hCG-antibody–gold complexes reach the test result region of the stick, they bind with the immobilised antibodies there and are held firmly in position. As more and more gold atoms arrive there, a pink colour (or another colour dependent on the brand) builds up.

There is also another strip, called the Procedural Control Region, that contains immobilised monoclonal antibodies. These are from goats, and they are anti-mouse antibodies. They bind with the antibody–gold complexes even if these have not encountered and bound with hCG in the urine sample. This strip therefore goes pink even if the test is negative.

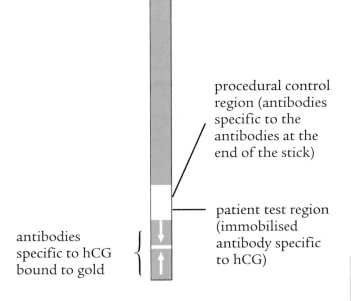

procedural control region (antibodies specific to the antibodies at the end of the stick)

patient test region (immobilised antibody specific to hCG)

antibodies specific to hCG bound to gold

How the pregnancy dipstick works

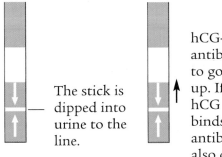

The stick is dipped into urine to the line.

hCG-specific antibodies bound to gold are carried up. If there is any hCG present, it binds to the antibodies and is also carried up.

Fig 6.25 How pregnancy test dipsticks work. Note that the appearance of the stick and colours produced will depend on the brand.

The results

If the stick is working, a pink line always appears in the control region – hCG-specific antibody bound to gold is carried upwards and captured by antibody specific to it, which was immobilised here.

If the urine contains hCG it binds to the hCG-specific antibody and gold at the end of the dipstick and is carried upwards. When this meets immobilised hCG-specific antibody, it is bound and a pink line appears. This shows the person is pregnant.

SAQ

6.12a Explain why the anti-hCG antibodies made by the mouse are bound to gold.

b Suggest how goat anti-mouse monoclonal antibodies could be made.

c Describe how the Procedural Control Region works, and explain why it is included on the dipstick.

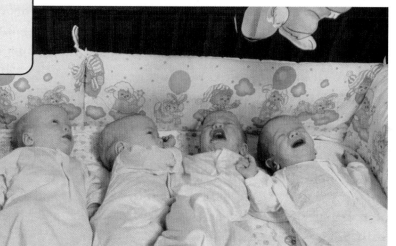

Fig 6.26
Multiple births.

SAQ

6.13a The table shows the relative number of singleton and multiple pregnancies arising from natural conception and five methods of infertility treatment. Display these data graphically.

b Explain how a multiple birth may occur when a woman conceives naturally.

ci How much more likely is it that a woman will have twins if she has IVF treatment than if she conceives naturally?

ii Suggest a reason for this.

d When IVF treatment is given, two embryos are put into the mother's uterus. Explain why two, rather than one or a number more than two, are used.

e Suggest why GIFT results in more multiple pregnancies than any of the methods that involve stimulation of ovulation alone.

Infertility treatment	Twins /%	Triplets /%	Quads and more /%
none (natural conception)	1–2	0.05 or less	0.001 or less
ovulation stimulated by clomiphene	5–10	0.5	0.05 or less
ovulation stimulated by hMG	15–30	5–8	0.5–4
ovulation stimulated by GnRH	5–10	2–5	0.1 or less
IVF	10–50	4–8	0.5–6
GIFT	20–25	2–8	0.1–2

Rhesus incompatibility

In your AS course, you may have read about the **Rhesus factor** and how it can cause problems in pregnancy. The Rhesus factor is an antigen that is held in the membranes of red blood cells. Some people have it, whilst others do not.

Problems can happen if a woman does not have the factor – that is, she is Rh negative – while her partner is Rh positive. The children that they have could be either Rh negative or Rh positive.

It is probable that at some stage, most likely at birth, there will be some contact between the mother's and baby's blood. If the foetus developing in the mother's uterus is Rh positive, the Rh antigens on the baby's red blood cells will be treated like any other antigens, and her B lymphocytes will make antibodies against them. These antibodies are a type of immunoglobulin called IgM and they cannot cross the placenta. So they do no harm to the developing foetus.

However, if the Rh negative mother becomes pregnant again with another Rh positive child, her body responds by producing a different kind of antibody called IgG. These antibodies are smaller, and they can cross the placenta. When they get into the embryo's blood, they cause its red blood cells to clump together and this may kill the child.

To prevent this from happening, the mother is immunised before she has a second child. She is given an injection of a preparation called RhoGAM. This contains IgG antibodies which act against the Rh antigen. If any Rhesus positive cells from her baby enter her blood, the RhoGAM will destroy them before they can stimulate the production of IgM antibodies.

Summary

1. Infertile couples may be given treatment to help them to conceive. Problems are a little more likely to be in the woman's reproductive system rather than the man's. They include ovulatory disorders, oviduct blockage, endometriosis, the production of antisperm antibodies, abnormal sperm and absence of sperm.

2. Fertility treatment often involves using hormones to stimulate ovulation. Oocytes may then be fertilised by artificial insemination, or in a container in a laboratory, which is known as in vitro fertilisation. In ICSI a sperm is injected into an egg.

3. Very young embryos or sperm can be kept for long periods of time in frozen nitrogen. This has allowed the production of sperm banks.

4. Some groups argue against fertility treatment because they believe it prevents the action of natural selection on human populations.

5. Fertility treatment is much more likely than 'normal' conception to result in a multiple pregnancy. Multiple pregnancies do not always lead to multiple births, as some of the embryos may fail to develop to term.

6. Pregnancy test kits often use dip sticks impregnated with monoclonal antibodies that bind specifically with human chorionic gonadotrophin.

7. If a Rhesus negative mother has a Rhesus positive baby, she may produce anti-Rhesus antibodies. If she has a second Rhesus positive baby, her antibodies may enter its blood and cause the red cells to clump together. This can be prevented by giving the mother an injection of antibodies which inactivate her own anti-Rhesus antibodies.

CHAPTER 7

Food and farming

CASE STUDY

It's Thursday afternoon. Carol is looking for beans in the supermarket. She is on a tight budget, and has to go carefully when she shops. As always, she goes for the cheapest beans that look good, which are from Kenya. Not the organic ones, as they cost way too much, and anyway, they don't look as perfect as the others. Not the ones that say they are grown in the UK, because they are also expensive in comparison with the imported ones.

Meanwhile, Mark Daniels is on his farm in Lincolnshire, where he grows a wide range of vegetables. He is looking at a field of runner beans that are in perfect condition for picking right now. But he is wondering if it is worth picking them at all. The supermarket chain which had a contract with him to buy the beans is paying such a low price that Mark calculates he will make no profit at all on the crop, and possibly won't break even. The supermarket says that they can't afford to pay him any more because their customers won't buy the beans if they are too expensive.

Farmers produce food that we eat. Like any other industry, they have inputs and outputs that they must manage carefully if they are to make a profit. Their inputs include costs of machinery, labour, fertilisers and pesticides. Their outputs are the money they get when they sell their crop.

In the UK, costs, especially labour costs, are higher than in many other countries. This makes it difficult for farmers to sell their produce at a profit, because the supermarkets can buy more cheaply overseas, even when transport costs are included.

Farming is a unique industry in that farmers share their 'factory floor' with all the rest of us. We enjoy looking at beautiful landscapes, walking in flower-rich meadows, hearing birdsong and seeing wild mammals such as deer. It is easy to forget that much of the landscape has been produced by hundreds of years of farming, and that it is managed by farmers. Keeping the countryside looking good, and in a condition that allows wildlife to flourish, costs money. If we want it that way, then someone has to pay.

In this chapter, we will look at the conflicts that can sometimes exist in the UK between farming and conservation, and how these conflicts can be avoided. And we will also consider what might happen in the future to the size of the human population, and some of the possible effects on the environment that we might see if this population continues to increase as rapidly as it is at the moment.

Farming and the environment

Farming practices have changed beyond all recognition in the last one hundred years. At the beginning of the twentieth century, most farms were mixed farms – some fields were used for growing crops such as wheat, barley or potatoes while others were used for raising cattle or sheep to give milk, meat or wool. However, the two World Wars brought about a major change. The difficulty of importing food from other countries influenced the government to encourage farmers to get the maximum possible yields from their land. Old meadows were dug up to grow cereal crops. More fertilisers were added to allow each hectare (ha) of land to give higher yields. Pesticides were used to reduce losses from insect damage. Horses were replaced with tractors; jobs done by several people were now done with one machine.

This pattern continued throughout most of the twentieth century, and not only in Britain. The European Union saw farming and the production of food as being so important that farmers were paid subsidies according to the area of the land that they farmed and how they used it – for example, how many sheep they kept, or how much wheat they grew.

Views of governments, farmers and consumers have now changed. There is increasing understanding that we value our countryside not only because it produces food for us but also because it is a habitat for plants and animals and a place that people like to visit for relaxation and enjoyment. More and more farmers are being encouraged to manage their farms for wildlife as well as for growing crops. It is now understood that farming and conservation can work together in providing not only food for humans but also habitats for wildlife.

Intensive and extensive farming

In Britain, some farms use **extensive** methods of rearing animals or growing crops (Fig 7.1). Extensive farming uses few inputs of bought-in feed and fertiliser and is usually carried out over a wide area with low stocking densities (Figs 7.3 and 7.4). For example, many farms in hilly or mountainous areas rear sheep or cattle extensively. The animals graze on relatively large areas of land. The farmers do not spend much on improving the grazing; they do not often apply fertilisers, herbicides or pesticides. Their inputs are therefore low. The farmer relies more on natural recycling of nutrients. The land can only support relatively small densities of livestock, even with some fertiliser and bought food, so the farmers do not get large returns.

In contrast, **intensive** farming methods involve high inputs in order to achieve high yields of crops and allow high stocking densities of animals (Fig 7.2). Considerable amounts of money are spent on improving the soil and using chemicals to reduce competition from weeds or losses of crop yields to insect pests. Cattle may be kept in a small area and fed on concentrates and silage rather than being allowed to graze outdoors. As a result, large yields can be obtained from each hectare of land. The extra income from these high yields more than offsets the extra spending.

extensive	**infertile upland grazing** – no inputs and 0.5 sheep per hectare
intensive	**upland grazing** – high inputs and 10 sheep per hectare (maximum)
	lowland intensive grazing – high inputs and 14 sheep per hectare (maximum)
extremely intensive	**housed sheep** – very high inputs and 1 sheep per 2 m^2 (maximum – the equivalent of 5000 sheep per hectare)

Fig 7.1 Extensive and intensive farming of sheep.

143

Fig 7.2 An example of intensively cropped lowland arable fields in Nothamptonshire. In the foreground there is a wheat crop ready to harvest. Barley and rape are crops grown in other fields in this area.

Fig 7.3 English hill farmland being extensively grazed by sheep. This is in the Cumbrian Lake District with the Langdale Pikes on the left.

Which type of system, extensive or intensive, is better for wildlife? Both types can work well if the farm is managed with sympathy towards conservation. Extensive farming of sheep in upland areas allows native wildlife to flourish alongside the sheep. Indeed, without the sheep grazing, many of the hillsides that people so much enjoy in places such as the Lake District would become covered with scrub and trees, instead of grass and other low-growing plants. But intensive farming, too, can be good for wildlife. Growing crops intensively on land that can sustain it means that less land is needed to produce a given yield, freeing up other areas that can be used for conservation.

Fig 7.4 English lowland farmland being extensively grazed by cattle. This is Otmoor in Oxfordshire.

Conservation on a farm

Mark Daniels (see case study on page 142) farms intensively – that is, he aims to produce high yields per hectare of land, and uses fertilisers, herbicides and pesticides to maximise the yield and quality of the crops. Most of his land is given over to growing vegetables. The Daniels family relies on the farm to provide them with their income. The crops grow best, and give the highest yields per hectare, if they are managed very carefully. The vegetables must be large, of even size and unblemished if the supermarkets and other outlets are to pay good prices for them. This costs money, because to get the vegetables in this condition Mark has to spray them with pesticides and add fertilisers to the soil.

However, Mark Daniels is also managing his farm for biodiversity. Together with a government organisation called the Farming and Wildlife Advisory Group, he has put together a Biodiversity Action Plan that is focussed on the conservation of several species, including reed warblers, barn owls and emerald dragonflies. He receives a grant for doing this, to compensate for the reduced income he will get. He can't grow as many crops if he spends time and money on conservation, or gives over some of the land to it.

The farmland is irrigated to increase productivity, and there is a network of drainage channels criss-crossing it. A wide variety of wildlife uses these channels as a habitat. They are periodically cleaned out to stop them from silting up, but only one side is cleared at a time so that the animals that live there still have somewhere to go.

The grass alongside them is left unmown, providing habitats, cover and food supplies for birds, small mammals and insects. One channel has been widened to produce a reed bed for the reed warblers to nest in. When fertilisers or pesticides are being applied to the land, they are kept well away from the ditches and hedges.

Within only a year or two of the beginning of the implementation of the action plan, the Daniels family are already enjoying seeing results. Several pairs of reed warblers are nesting in the reed bed. Barn owls, previously seen only rarely, are hunting for voles in the long grass and one pair is nesting in a nest box that has been put up for them. Several species of dragonflies and damselflies, including the emerald dragonflies, are breeding in the drainage channels.

Extensive farming

A farming system is said to be **sustainable** if it can be used over a long period of time and still be successful in producing whatever resource is being harvested. Both extensive and intensive farming practices can be sustainable if the land is managed appropriately.

If management is inappropriate, then the farming system may be unsustainable. For example, if there are too many sheep or cattle, then **overgrazing** may happen. This is a particular problem on poorer land. There may be extensive livestock farming on this land, but it can only be sustained if no more than a certain number of animals are grazing on it. If the stocking density is too high the grass will be eaten back so much that it does not regrow in some areas. Trampling by the animals and loss of vegetation cover exposes the soil to rain and allows it to be washed away (Fig 7.5). Over time, the soil cover and grass cover on a hillside can become so poor that it can hardly support grazing animals at all.

This kind of overgrazing was beginning to happen in many upland areas of Britain in the last half of the twentieth century. Farmers were paid subsidies by the European Union according to how many sheep or cattle they had. The more animals they put onto the land, the more money they got. Prices for wool, milk or meat were not high enough for a profit to be made from them, so many farmers depended entirely on their subsidies. Now changes in the way that subsidies are paid will allow hill farmers to graze fewer animals on the land. The idea is to keep the hill farmers in business so that we still have home-grown products from their enterprise, and also so that visitors to the upland areas will still see and be able to use beautiful countryside. Wildlife such as hares, butterflies and birds will have places to feed and breed. Farmers will effectively be paid to manage the countryside rather than to produce food.

However, there are suggestions that the grants available for hill farmers may encourage some farmers not to put stock on the hills at all, as the grant is modest and the returns are low. This land will slowly change to scrub, and then to woodland. For some people the open landscapes of our mountain areas are something they enjoy. A change to woodland may not suit them.

Intensive farming

Intensive farming can also be sustainable. Just as for extensive farming, the treatment of the land should ensure that it is not degraded, and that its ability to support grazing animals or to grow crops is not reduced in the future.

For example, because crops take mineral ions such as nitrates, potassium and phosphates out of the soil, fertilisers need to be added to replace them. These fertilisers may be inorganic,

Fig 7.5 Intensive cattle grazing has eroded the bank of this pond. At times the pond is filled with suspended mud as a result of the eroded soil being churned by the feet of cattle, which harms the pond life.

such as ammonium phosphate, or organic, such as farmyard manure. Both types work well if they are used carefully, but both can cause harm to habitats and wildlife if used inappropriately. It is now possible to analyse the soil on different parts of a farm very accurately to find out the concentrations of the mineral ions that it contains, and to compare this with the requirements of the crop that is going to be grown there. Then exactly the right quantity and type of fertiliser can be applied in each area, at exactly the right time of year to benefit the crop most. This helps the farmer because he does not spend money unnecessarily on wasted fertiliser, and also benefits wildlife because there is less likelihood that fertiliser will end up in water courses where it can cause eutrophication (see page 152).

Soil quality on the intensive farm can also be improved and sustained by adding humus to the soil. Humus is formed from rotted vegetable or animal matter, and it helps the soil to hold water and nutrients. A soil with a low humus content is more likely to become dry and powdery, which can increase the risk of erosion. The humus content of soil can be increased and maintained by adding materials such as farmyard manure. Most arable land in lowland England has a severely reduced humus content following the change from mixed farms to farms that are purely arable or purely for grazing animals.

SAQ

7.1 Since the 1950s there has been a fall in the number of mixed farms in the UK (having some arable fields and others grazed by stock). At the same time there has been an increase in the number of farms that are purely arable. Suggest how this may be connected with the falling level of humus in arable land.

7.2 An investigation was carried out to determine whether it would be better to use farmyard manure or an inorganic fertiliser when growing wheat and barley. The table shows the results.

a State two variables that would have been controlled in this investigation.

Fertiliser	Yield of wheat / t ha^{-1}	Yield of barley / t ha^{-1}
none (control)	2.1	1.0
farmyard manure	3.6	2.1
inorganic fertiliser containing N, P and K	3.1	2.3

b The percentage increase in wheat yield when using farmyard manure rather than no fertiliser can be calculated like this.

difference in yield
= 3.6 – 2.1 = 1.5
so percentage difference in yield
= $\frac{1.5}{2.1}$ × 100
= 71.4%

Calculate percentage increases in yield when:
- using inorganic fertiliser rather than no fertiliser when growing wheat;
- using farmyard manure rather than no fertiliser when growing barley;
- using inorganic fertiliser rather than no fertiliser when growing barley.

c Use your calculations to suggest which type of fertiliser should be used when growing these crops.

d Apart from percentage increase in yield, what other factors might a farmer consider when deciding which fertiliser to use? How might his choice affect wildlife in both the short term and long term?

The Broadbalk experiment

At Rothamsted in Surrey, the world's longest experiment into sustainability of intensive agriculture has been going on since 1853. Here, in a large field called Broadbalk, winter wheat has been grown continuously since 1843.

There have been several different experiments running in different parts of Broadbalk. On one part, winter wheat has been grown every year. This crop is sown in the autumn, allowing the grain to germinate and then spend the winter as small, green plants. In spring, the plants grow quickly and the wheat grain is ready for harvest in the summer.

Most farmers don't grow the same crop on the same land year after year, as it is thought that better yields are obtained if crops are rotated. Rotation involves growing different crops each year over a three or four year period. This should help to reduce problems from pests and diseases that otherwise might

build up, and also to help the soil to retain enough nutrients, because each kind of crop takes a different balance of nitrate, phosphate, potassium and magnesium ions from the soil.

On the Broadbalk plots, the soil has been regularly tested for nutrients, and various combinations of inorganic fertilisers and farmyard manure have been applied accordingly. At first, weeds were controlled by hand, but since the 1950s herbicides have been used.

Over the years, far from decreasing, the crop yields from Broadbalk have been increasing. The experiment shows that it is possible to obtain sustainable yields with intensive farming practices, even without using crop rotation.

Extensive and intensive farming

Research two examples of intensive farming, such as lowland wheat production or beef cattle grazing on an 'improved' grassland (sown with special grass varieties and fertilised with either manure or inorganic fertiliser). Briefly describe how they are managed, including a brief description of inputs and yield.

Describe how the two chosen examples would have to be managed in order to become examples of extensive systems of farming. Discuss the implications of the changes you suggest.

SAQ

7.3 The graph shows the yield of wheat grain from three areas of Broadbalk (see the Just for Interest panel on page 148) between 1855 and 1995.

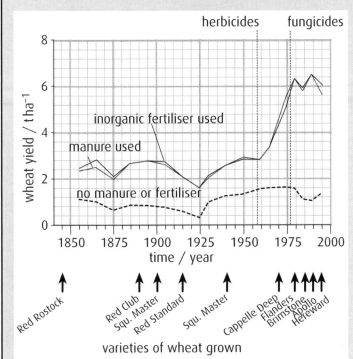

One part had no fertiliser added to it, another had farmyard manure, and the third was treated with inorganic fertiliser containing N, P and K.

a Describe the results obtained between 1855 and 1925 on the plot that had no manure or fertiliser added to it.

b With reference to the information on the graph, suggest reasons for the fact that the yield from this plot was higher from 1940 up to the present than in the early years of the experiment.

c Compare the results for the plot that had farmyard manure added and the plot that had inorganic fertiliser added.

d In another part of Broadbalk, the concentrations of nitrate ions leaching (being washed out) from the soil on areas treated with different amounts of inorganic fertilisers and with farmyard manure were measured. The results are shown in the graph below.

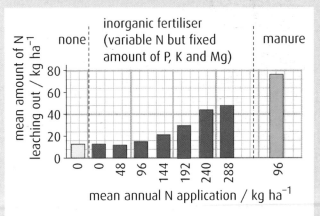

i Explain why it is undesirable for nitrate ions to leach out of the soil.

ii It is often thought that applying organic fertiliser to arable fields is better for the environment than applying inorganic fertilisers. Do these results support that view? Explain your answer.

Succession

We have seen how grazing by sheep helps to maintain the grassland that we enjoy seeing on many of the hills in the British landscape. If seeds of trees and shrubs germinate, the sheep will destroy them while they are still very small. If the sheep weren't there, first shrubs and then trees would grow. The hillsides would be covered with scrub and then, after some years, woodland.

A change like this that takes place in a community over time is called **succession** (Fig 7.6). If left alone, much of Britain would eventually be covered by woodland containing oak and ash trees. This is called the **climax community**.

The direction taken by succession is often very predictable. Imagine a field that has been ploughed for many years. Ploughing then stops

1 Marram grass can live in bare and mobile sand. Its roots stabilise the sand and help create dunes. It is a pioneer plant, able to colonise empty ground.

2 In the sand stablilised by marram grass some other plants can now begin to grow. Here they are small herbaceous plants, but often mosses, lichens or algae are some of the first colonisers.

3 Decay of plant remains adds humus and nutrients to the sand. This sandy soil can now support a range of other plants.

4 The soil eventually builds up so that even woody plants like this dwarf willow can grow.

Fig 7.6 An example of primary succession, that is, one that begins with bare ground. If bare sand is blown up onto a beach but not washed away, a succession may occur eventually leading to woodland as the climax community. At each stage of the succession the plants modify conditions, which allows different plants to colonise. Each stage of the succession is called a **sere**.

and the land is left to itself. The first plants to grow will probably be herbaceous (non-woody) ones such as grasses, thistles and docks which may have already been present as seeds in the soil, or whose seeds are blown there on the wind. These plants change the character of the land; they help to keep water in the soil and their dead leaves rot and form more humus. A few seeds of shrubs may also germinate at this time. These may grow to a significant size after a few years. Then tree seedlings appear amongst the shrubs. As the shrubs and trees grow taller, they shade the herbaceous plants so that they get only a little light and cannot photosynthesise effectively. Eventually, most of the grasses, thistles and docks disappear, having lost the competition for light, water and nutrients with the woodland trees.

Farming practices prevent succession from taking place. Grazing animals prevent shrubs from growing. Ploughing prevents even grass from growing. All through Britain, almost every landscape we see is the result of farming practices, some of which date back to well before a thousand years ago. Many of our upland areas, now covered with a thin layer of soil on which only grass and other small plants can grow, once supported mixed woodland. But this change is not *all* due to farming. Some of loss of woodland is also due to the climate being much wetter than it was when forest covered most of the UK. For example, in parts of Britain where there is a lot of rain, peat bogs and heather moorland are the climax community.

On land that has been affected by farming, we do not see the natural climax community that would have developed. Instead, we see a different one, sometimes called a **plagioclimax** (Fig 7.7). The flower-rich grasslands of the South Downs are a plagioclimax, that have only appeared and been maintained because people have grazed cattle and sheep on them for long periods of time. The process by which this plagioclimax has been formed is called **deflected succession**. Farming has altered the direction taken by succession.

Fig 7.7 Flower-rich downland plagioclimax.

Farming and conservation

In normal speech, we use the term 'conservation' to mean 'keeping the same'. In ecology, it doesn't quite mean that.

Imagine, for example, a pond that has been taken over by a Wildlife Trust. If the pond is in good condition, with clean water, lots of different plants growing and many different animals, the conservationists may, indeed, want to keep it just the same. But if it is polluted, choked with vegetation and mud and with only a few different species of animals, then they may want to change the pond. This is still called conservation.

Conservation often tries to maintain or improve the **biodiversity** of a habitat. Biodiversity is the number of different species that live there.

Farming practices usually decrease biodiversity. Obviously, a field growing a crop of wheat has very poor diversity. Almost all of it is covered by just one species of plant, which in turn will mean that only a few species of insects can find a suitable habitat there. This is unavoidable if we are to grow food efficiently. But we have seen, too, that even this kind of intensive farming can go hand-in-hand with conservation if the land is managed with sympathy towards wildlife.

Poor farming practices, however, can have wide and damaging effects on biodiversity. We will look at two examples of this – water pollution by farm waste and the removal of hedges.

Farm waste disposal

All kinds of farming produce waste, but by far the largest quantity is produced by livestock farming. Cattle, sheep and pigs all produce urine and faeces, which, even though they smell and look disgusting to us, are a rich source of nutrients for microorganisms such as bacteria and fungi, and also algae. These nutrients include organic substances such as urea and also ions such as ammonium and nitrate. If this waste is allowed to contaminate water courses, it can cause **eutrophication** (Fig 7.8).

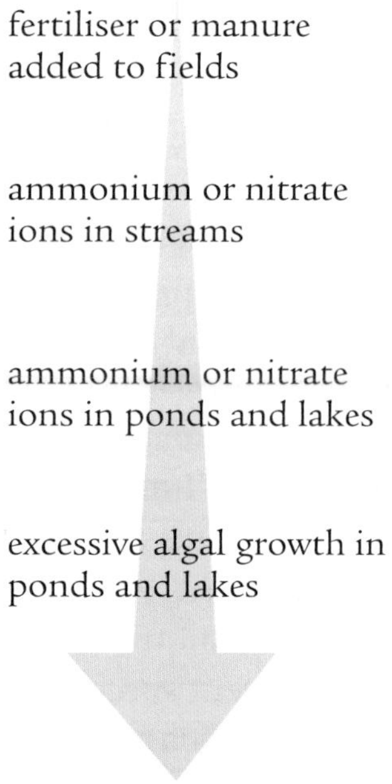

fertiliser or manure added to fields

ammonium or nitrate ions in streams

ammonium or nitrate ions in ponds and lakes

excessive algal growth in ponds and lakes

The decay of algae by aerobic bacteria, following the excessive growth of the algae, uses up oxygen in the water so fish and most animal life in the water dies.

Fig 7.8 Eutrophication.

The problem of safe disposal of animal waste is greatest when the animals are being kept in pens or buildings, rather than grazing over a wide area of land, because the waste is all concentrated in one place. The waste they produce is called **slurry**. If untreated slurry runs into a river, the organic substances that it contains provide a food source for bacteria. As they feed on the slurry, their populations increase. These bacteria respire aerobically, so they use up much of the oxygen that is dissolved in the water. As oxygen levels fall, fish and many different kinds of invertebrate animals can no longer live there.

The ammonium and nitrate ions may be used not only by bacteria but also by algae and water plants. These ions are used to make proteins and other nitrogen-containing molecules such as

DNA. Algal populations may therefore increase, forming a green soup in the water called an algal bloom. Some algae may form thick green mats on the water surface. Both of these algal growths stop light penetrating into the water, so plants living on the bottom cannot photosynthesise and therefore die. Their remains form yet more food for the aerobic bacteria, increasing the problem of oxygen depletion. Anaerobic decomposition may then set in, producing dark, smelly mud in which only a few specially adapted organisms, such as blood worms and rat-tailed maggots can live.

As well as causing problems in water courses, slurry can also cause air pollution because it emits **ammonia gas**, NH_3. This is a particular difficulty on pig and poultry farms and where cattle are raised indoors. 83% of air pollution by ammonia is caused by livestock farming. Programmes in the UK, in conjunction with the European Union, are working out the best way of keeping these and other animals to minimise the production of ammonia.

Ammonia is very soluble in water, and it is carried from the air to the ground when it rains. It forms **ammonium ions**, NH_4^+, and these are important nutrients for growing plants. You might imagine that this would be a good thing, but unfortunately the kinds of plants that we like to see in 'natural' landscapes – the short grasses and flowering plants such as harebells and orchids – are adapted to growing in soils with a low nutrient content. Adding ammonium ions to the soil encourages the grasses to grow tall and other, coarser plants to grow, such as nettles, thistles and docks. They soon crowd out the smaller plants, shading the light from them and inhibiting their growth.

Slurry may also contain **growth hormones** which have been used to increase the growth rate of cattle, and which may have harmful effects on other animals. Antibiotics may also be present, as they have also sometimes been used for a similar purpose. If slurry is stored and allowed to ferment in an enclosed tank, anaerobic bacteria can produce methane from it, which can be used as fuel.

SAQ

7.4 An investigation was carried out to see if housing pigs in different kinds of pens could affect ammonia emissions. The quantity of ammonia emitted was measured as the quantity of nitrogen lost (ammonia contains nitrogen). The table shows some of the results.

a State two factors that would be kept constant in this investigation.

b Describe the common features of the pattern of ammonia emissions throughout the year seen in all of these types of pen.

c Suggest reasons for the patterns you have described.

Type of pen	Ammonia emissions / g of nitrogen per day		
	Autumn	Winter and spring	Summer
fully slatted floor	41	42	60
fully slatted floor with rubber mats	37	40	75
traditional UK pen with partly slatted floor	22	21	73
new Dutch design of pen with partly slatted floor	19	23	29

Removal of hedgerows

Until the eighteenth century, there were few hedges in Britain. The Enclosure Acts from around 1720 to 1840 resulted in extensive planting of hedges throughout Britain, to mark ownership and to retain livestock. Now hedges have become an important habitat for many species of plants and animals, contributing greatly to biodiversity.

During the latter half of the twentieth century, when farmers were being encouraged to produce more and more food at the lowest possible cost, many hedgerows were removed. The large machinery that was used to prepare the soil and harvest crops could work more efficiently in these larger fields, and the land previously covered by hedges could now be used for growing crops. It is estimated that, between 1984 and 1990, about 21% of the hedgerows in England were lost.

By the late 1980s, people began to wake up to what was happening, and in 1995 parliament passed an Environment Act that required land owners to consult local authorities before they removed 'important' hedgerows. Since then, more legal protection for hedges has been approved, and the loss of hedgerows has been reversed. Some farmers are now planting new hedges, either to replace old ones that were ripped out, or even putting them in places where there was no hedge before. The Hedgerows Regulations, introduced in 1997, require a farmer to apply for permission before removing any hedgerow.

Why are hedges so important? Most obviously, they provide habitats for insects and birds that live and feed in them. The long grasses and other plants that grow around their bases provide nesting sites for birds such as yellowhammers and feeding areas for small mammals such as yellow-necked mice. The very oldest hedges, especially those planted even before the Enclosure Acts, are the most valuable in this respect, as they contain the greatest diversity of shrub species and therefore the greatest number of different habitats for different animal species.

Hedges act as wildlife corridors, a highway along which mammals and birds can travel from one area of woodland to another. They therefore help to maintain biodiversity in these woodlands.

Hedges need careful maintenance if they are to remain useful habitats. If nothing is done to them, the shrubs grow into trees, and the thick cover at their bases opens out. They need to be cut to let light into their bases so that the leaves on lower branches can photosynthesise and grow healthily. Cutting shrubs down low stimulates them to put out lots of new branches, making the hedge thicker (Fig 7.9).

Fig 7.9 This hedge is good for wildlife. It is cut once in every two years (to allow hedge plants more opportunity to flower and fruit). It is cut in late winter (to allow birds to eat the berries during the winter). It is cut with sloping sides so that the hedge has leaves right to the ground (to provide cover for wildlife).

Summary

1. Most of the food that we eat is produced by farming. Intensive farming involves high inputs such as fertilisers, pesticides, herbicides and concentrated animal feeds, in order to obtain a high return per hectare of land used. Extensive farming involves lower levels of inputs, so that more land is needed to obtain the same quantity of outputs as in intensive farming.

2. A farming method is said to be sustainable if it can be used over a long period of time and still provide the same quantity and quality of resources. Both intensive and extensive farming can be sustainable if the land is well cared for. For example, intensive arable farming requires care to be taken to maintain the structure and nutrient level of the soil. Extensive sheep farming on hillsides must avoid overstocking and overgrazing.

3. Succession is the directional change in a community over time, resulting in a climax community. The animals and plants in a community at each stage of the succession can alter the environment so that new species can live there. If undisturbed, succession leads to a final, stable climax community.

4. In Britain, the natural climax community in most areas would be mixed woodland. However, where land is managed or farmed, this does not normally appear. Farming causes deflected succession, in which a different, plagioclimax community appears. For example, sheep grazing on the South Downs has caused deflected succession resulting in species-rich grassland, instead of woodland.

5. Farm waste, such as slurry, can cause eutrophication if it is allowed to contaminate waterways. It contains nutrients which allow populations of algae or aerobic bacteria to increase, resulting in a lack of oxygen in the water and therefore loss of oxygen-requiring invertebrates and fish. Farm waste also emits ammonia gas, which is converted to ammonium ions and increases nutrient levels in the soil, encouraging the growth of a few species of plants and therefore decreasing biodiversity in grassland.

6. Hedgerows provide habitats for a wide variety of species of plants and animals, increasing the biodiversity in farmed areas of the countryside. They also act as corridors between woodlands, which can increase the diversity of woodland species. Many hedgerows were removed in the twentieth century, especially leading up to the 1990s, but legislation and a greater understanding of their importance has reversed this trend.

Photosynthesis

Arizona, USA, has an unusual tourist attraction in the hot, dry Sonoran desert. A huge structure of steel and glass covering 1.3 hectares rises out of the dusty soil. This is Biosphere 2, designed to be a miniature replica of the Earth's ecosystems in which experiments could be carried out that might one day help to work out ways of living in an inhospitable place such as the surface of Mars.

Many people volunteered to be the human guinea pigs in these experiments, and four men and four women were chosen. After two years of training, they entered Biosphere 2 on September 26th 1991. They were to stay there for two years, inside a completely sealed environment in which several different 'ecosystems' had been set up, including a tropical rainforest, a huge, eight-metre-deep 'ocean' and agricultural areas where they would grow crops and farm animals.

The idea was that their waste products would go into the soil and be recycled as plant nutrients. The carbon dioxide they breathed out would be taken in by plants and used in photosynthesis, producing food for them and their animals. Photosynthesis would produce oxygen for their respiration. All the water inside Biosphere 2 would be recycled over and over again. Nothing was supposed to be added or taken away.

But things did not work out quite so well as expected. The carbon dioxide levels soared to more than 0.3% (in normal air it is 0.04%). This huge rise happened because the low light levels of a cloudy winter slowed down photosynthesis, and this also caused oxygen levels to drop. By May 1992, the oxygen concentration of the air was dropping by around 0.3% per month. By January 1993, carbon dioxide 'scrubbers' had already been used several times to remove carbon dioxide from the air inside the Biosphere, and oxygen had also been added.

The Biospherians hung on until the end of their scheduled two-year stay. They had grown 80% of their own food and, although they had all initially lost around 16% of their body weight, this had stabilised and they were all fit and well.

The project had originally been intended to run for 100 years. But the scientific world viewed it with disdain, because it was not a controlled experiment, meaning that its findings were practically worthless. Biosphere 2's attempts to show that humans could live in such a sealed environment were brought to an end in 1994. Today, the site contains a conference centre and gift shops and restaurants for the tourists that visit. But still scientific research continues, monitoring changes in the various biomes inside the giant self-contained mini-world.

Photosynthesis happens in some kinds of bacteria, in tiny unicellular organisms called **phytoplankton** that float in the upper layers of the sea, and in green plants. We will concentrate on photosynthesis in green plants, because these are the ones that we live amongst and which we grow to produce our food.

How photosynthesis happens

Photosynthesis, like respiration, is a **metabolic pathway** – a series of reactions linked to each other in numerous steps that are each catalysed by enzymes. We can break it up into two main stages, the light-dependent stage and the light-independent stage.

The light-dependent stage

Photosynthesis is possible because of a substance called **chlorophyll** (Fig 7.10).

The chlorophyll molecule is large and complex.

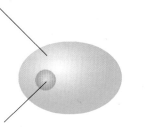

Inside a chlorophyll molecule there is a Mg²⁺ ion.

Fig 7.10 A chlorophyll molecule.

Chlorophyll molecules have a complex structure, and at the centre of each is a magnesium ion. Chlorophyll is a pigment, that is, a coloured substance. It is chlorophyll that makes plants look green. Chlorophyll is held in stacks of membranes inside organelles called **chloroplasts**. In most plants, the cells that contain chloroplasts are found in the mesophyll layers in their leaves, especially in the palisade cells (see page 14 in *Human Biology for AS*).

When light hits a chlorophyll molecule, some of the energy in the light is transferred to an electron in the chlorophyll. The electron is said to be 'excited', and it leaves the chlorophyll and passes to an electron acceptor that passes it down a chain of electron carriers held in the membranes inside the chloroplast (Fig 7.11). This should remind you of the electron transfer chain in respiration (see page 14) and it is actually very similar indeed. As the electron passes along the chain, energy is released from it and used to make ATP. So now some of the energy in the sunlight is trapped in an ATP molecule.

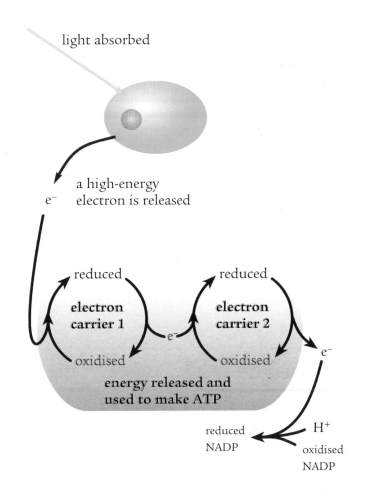

Fig 7.11 What happens when a chlorophyll molecule absorbs light.

The sunlight also has another effect inside the chloroplast. In the presence of sunlight, a water-splitting enzyme catalyses the break-up of water molecules (Fig 7.12). The oxygen from the water molecules is released as a waste product (that is where all the oxygen in the air around you comes from) and the hydrogen is picked up by a coenzyme called **NADP**. (This hydrogen acceptor is just like the NAD that you have already met in respiration, but it has an extra phosphate group.)

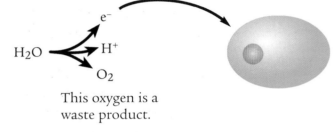

The electron from the splitting of water replaces the electron which was released after light absorption.

H_2O — e^-, H^+, O_2

This oxygen is a waste product.

Fig 7.12 The splitting of water in photosynthesis.

So, at the end of the light-dependent stage of photosynthesis we have ATP containing chemical energy that originally came from sunlight, and reduced NADP containing hydrogen from water (Fig 7.13).

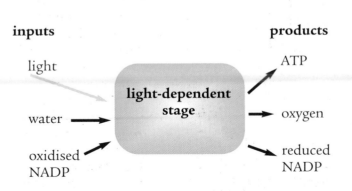

inputs

light

water

oxidised NADP

light-dependent stage

products

ATP

oxygen

reduced NADP

Fig 7.13 Summary of the light-dependent stage of photosynthesis.

The light-independent stage

The next parts of the metabolic pathway don't need light. They are therefore known as the light-independent stage, or the **Calvin cycle**.

Inside the chloroplasts of a green plant, there is an enzyme called **ribulose bisphosphate carboxylase**, or **Rubisco** for short. Rubisco is the commonest enzyme in the world. It catalyses the 'fixing' of carbon dioxide.

In this process, carbon dioxide from the air is made to combine with a substance called **ribulose bisphosphate** or **RuBP**. This substance has molecules that each contain 5 carbon atoms, so when a carbon dioxide molecule has combined with it the new molecule contains 6 carbon atoms. But these 6-carbon molecules immediately split apart to form two 3-carbon molecules, known as **glycerate 3-phosphate** or **GP**.

Now two products of the light-dependent stage come into play. The reduced NADP and some of the ATP are used to provide energy and phosphate groups to change the GP into a 3-carbon sugar, **triose phosphate** (Fig 7.14). This is the first carbohydrate that is made in photosynthesis.

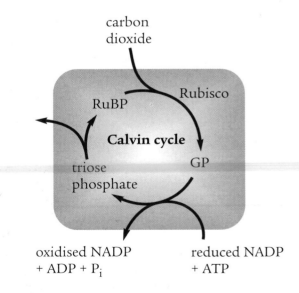

carbon dioxide

RuBP

Rubisco

Calvin cycle

triose phosphate

GP

oxidised NADP + ADP + P$_i$

reduced NADP + ATP

Fig 7.14 Light-independent stage of photosynthesis.

About five sixths of the triose phosphate is recycled to produce more RuBP, using up more of the ATP that was made in the light-dependent reactions. The remaining one sixth is used to make whatever the plant needs. Some will be converted to glucose and perhaps used in respiration, or to build up long molecules of cellulose to form new cell walls. Some will be made into lipids and used to make cell membranes or to provide food stores in seeds. Some will be made into amino acids and eventually proteins, using nitrogen atoms that have been absorbed from the soil in the form of nitrate or ammonium ions.

Food chains

Photosynthesis transfers energy from sunlight into organic substances such as carbohydrates, fats and proteins. This is where we get our energy from. The energy in the food that we eat was originally sunlight energy that was captured by plants and used in photosynthesis.

The way in which energy is transferred from one organism to another can be shown in a **food chain**. For example:

$$\text{maize} \longrightarrow \text{cattle} \longrightarrow \text{humans}$$

shows that energy in a maize plant is transferred to cattle when they eat maize, and that energy from cattle is then transferred to humans when they eat meat or drink milk (Fig 7.15).

The different stages in a food chain are known as **trophic levels**. The plants, at the first trophic level, are **producers**. They synthesise (produce) food which other organisms are able to use as an energy source. Animals which eat plants, such as cattle, are **primary consumers** (also known as herbivores) while in this food chain humans are **secondary consumers**. Some food chains also have **tertiary consumers**, but in Britain humans are not in much danger of being eaten by anything else, so this food chain stops there.

Efficiency of energy transfer

When cattle eat maize, the enzymes in their digestive system break down molecules from the maize. The resulting small molecules, such as glucose and amino acids, are absorbed into the blood stream and transported to all parts of the body. Cells absorb these molecules, and use them for various purposes. Some of the glucose molecules will be broken down in respiration to release useful energy that the cattle use for keeping themselves warm or for movement. Some of the amino acid molecules will be used to build protein molecules that may become part of muscle tissue.

Fig 7.15 The red tassles of the maize crop on the left are the stigmas of the flowers below which the maize cobs grow after the flower has been pollinated. The cobs are surrounded by green sheaths, which is why the cobs are not visible. Maize may be grown as feed for cattle. This is usually fed to cattle as maize silage (maize which has been partly fermented in bags).

However, cattle only actually take in a small proportion of the energy that the maize has trapped in its molecules (Fig 7.16).

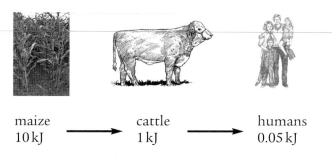

maize   cattle   humans
10 kJ   1 kJ   0.05 kJ

Fig 7.16 Most of the energy in maize does not get to humans in this food chain.

On average, about 10% of the energy in the maize is transferred to the cattle. Of the rest:

- some will be in parts of the maize plants that die and fall to the ground;
- some will be in parts of the maize plant that the cattle do not eat, such as the roots;
- some will be in parts of the maize that the cattle eat but do not digest, and this energy will be lost in the faeces.

More energy losses happen between the cattle and humans. For example:

- respiration in the cells of the cattle breaks down energy-rich molecules to produce ATP, and the energy in this is used for various processes in the cattle such as movement, eventually being lost to the environment as heat;
- excess amino acids that the cattle have eaten will be changed to urea in the liver and excreted in urine by the kidneys;
- we do not eat all parts of the cattle, such as their bones or hides;
- we are not able to digest all of the meat that we eat, and some energy-containing molecules are lost in our faeces.

At each step in a food chain, something like 90% of the energy at one level is lost as it is transferred to the next. Only about 10% is transferred between levels at each stage. We can say that the **efficiency** of energy transfer is 10%.

SAQ

7.5   In a 'natural' food chain, not involving humans, we would expect the efficiency of energy transfer between the primary consumers and the secondary consumers to be 10%.
a   Calculate the efficiency of energy transfer between cattle and humans shown in Fig 7.17.
b   Suggest why this efficiency is much lower than in a 'natural' food chain.

Fig 7.17 shows what this means in terms of the energy we can get from growing one square metre of maize plants which is harvested and fed to cattle.

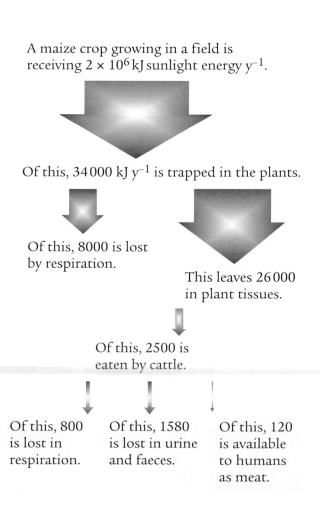

A maize crop growing in a field is receiving 2×10^6 kJ sunlight energy y^{-1}.

Of this, 34 000 kJ y^{-1} is trapped in the plants.

Of this, 8000 is lost by respiration.

This leaves 26 000 in plant tissues.

Of this, 2500 is eaten by cattle.

Of this, 800 is lost in respiration.

Of this, 1580 is lost in urine and faeces.

Of this, 120 is available to humans as meat.

Fig 7.17 Energy transfer into one square metre of maize, to cattle and then to humans.

160

The carbon cycle

Food chains show us how energy is transferred from one organism to another when they feed. But it is not only energy that we get from the food that we eat. We also get atoms which make up the molecules in our bodies.

These molecules include carbohydrates, fats and proteins. All of these contain carbon, hydrogen and oxygen. (Proteins also contain nitrogen.) All of the carbon, hydrogen and oxygen atoms in our bodies came from food we have eaten.

These atoms are passed around between different organisms and their environments. The atoms in your molecules will once have been atoms in something or someone else.

Fig 7.18 shows the carbon cycle, which is a representation of the pathways by which carbon atoms can be passed around between organisms. You can see the central role of plants in this cycle. They are the only way in which carbon atoms can be taken in from the air (in the form of carbon dioxide, during photosynthesis) and incorporated into molecules in living organisms.

Microorganisms in the carbon cycle

Microorganisms, including bacteria and fungi, are also of crucial importance in keeping the carbon cycle turning. Some species of these organisms act as **decomposers**, breaking down molecules in dead plants and animals, in faeces, in urine and in any other organic waste, and using them to make their own cells. Like all living organisms, decomposers respire, and so they return much of this carbon to the air in the form of carbon dioxide. Many of these microorganisms live in the soil. (Underestimation of this led to the initial problems in Biosphere 2, described in the case study on page 156.)

Most of these microorganisms respire aerobically, so they need oxygen. Sometimes the soil may not contain enough oxygen for them, and dead organisms do not fully decompose. Thick, peaty layers have built up in wetter parts of the country such as in the Peak District or on Dartmoor. The peat contains a great deal of carbon that, in a drier soil, would have been oxidised by microorganisms and released to the air as carbon dioxide.

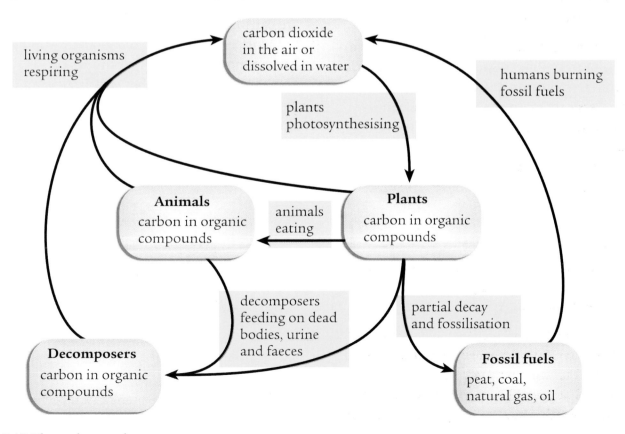

Fig 7.18 The carbon cycle.

Humans and the carbon cycle

The carbon cycle on Earth runs in an approximate balance – roughly the same quantity of carbon dioxide is taken out of the air by photosynthesis as is returned to it by respiration and other processes. However, there have been times in the Earth's history when this has not been so. Analysis of bubbles of air trapped deep in the ice in Antarctica has shown that the carbon dioxide content of the air has varied quite considerably in the past (Fig 7.19).

At the moment, the amount of carbon dioxide in the air is increasing. It makes up about 0.04% of the air now, compared with 0.03% in the mid-twentieth century. This increase might be quite natural – there are various processes that might account for it, such as more emissions from volcanic eruptions – but many scientists believe that we are at least partly to blame because we are burning more and more fossil fuels.

A fossil fuel is one that has formed from living organisms, buried deep in the ground in conditions where decomposers could not completely rot them. The carbon in the carbohydrates, fats and proteins in their bodies is still there, but is now in the form of other organic molecules that we can burn to release energy. Burning, like respiration, is an oxidation reaction. Combustion of fossil fuels is releasing carbon from them, in the form of carbon dioxide, which was stored away in the ground millions of years ago.

We have seen that photosynthesis is very important in taking carbon dioxide out of the air, and helping to stop carbon dioxide levels from increasing. Up to a point, plants on Earth may be able to make use of extra carbon dioxide and perhaps grow faster and larger. Unfortunately, we may not be helping this to happen. In many parts of the world, large areas of tropical forests are being cut down – for building materials, fuel or to clear land for growing crops or building homes and roads – and this **deforestation** can decrease the amount of photosynthesis that is happening in these places. We are just as much to blame in Britain as in tropical countries; we cut most of our forests down long ago.

So, by burning fossil fuels we are releasing extra carbon dioxide into the air, and by cutting down forests we are reducing the rate at which photosynthesis takes carbon dioxide out of the air. Between them, these two processes may be contributing to the rise in carbon dioxide concentrations that we are seeing now.

Why does this matter? It is very likely that these raised atmospheric carbon dioxide levels are causing the average temperatures on Earth to increase, a process called **global warming**. Carbon dioxide is one of a number of **greenhouse gases** (another very important one is methane) that help the temperature of the Earth's surface to remain higher than it would otherwise be (Fig 7.20).

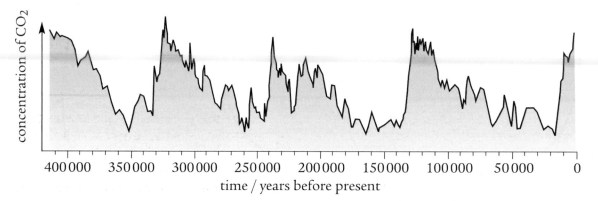

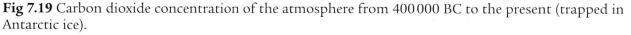

Fig 7.19 Carbon dioxide concentration of the atmosphere from 400 000 BC to the present (trapped in Antarctic ice).

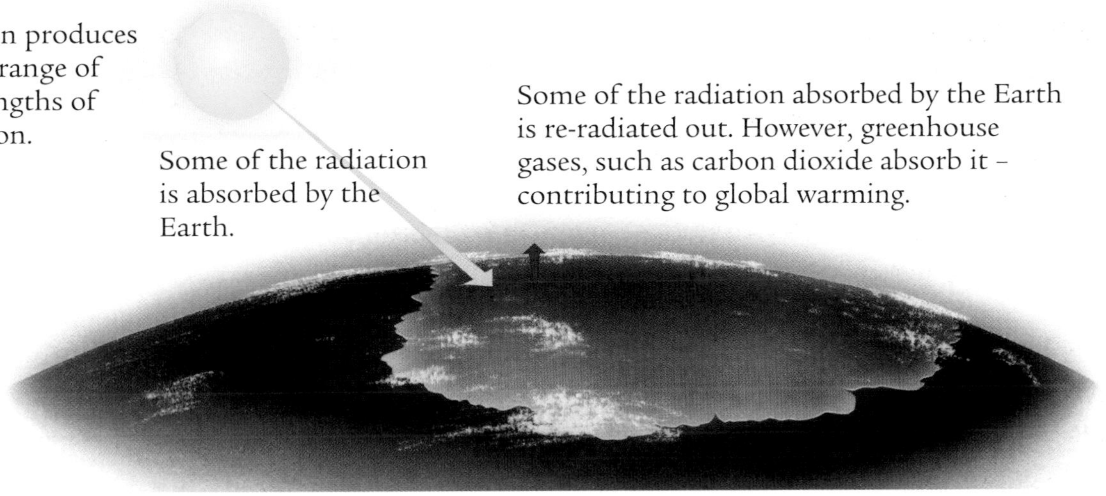

The Sun produces a wide range of wavelengths of radiation.

Some of the radiation is absorbed by the Earth.

Some of the radiation absorbed by the Earth is re-radiated out. However, greenhouse gases, such as carbon dioxide absorb it – contributing to global warming.

Fig 7.20 Global warming and greenhouse gases.

The radiation that we receive from the Sun has a wide range of wavelengths. Some of this radiation is absorbed in the atmosphere, but some reaches the ground and is absorbed there. Some of it is then re-radiated, back from the ground into the air, in the form of infra-red radiation – radiation with relatively long wavelengths that has a strong heating effect. Carbon dioxide in the atmosphere traps this long-wavelength radiation, stopping it from leaving the Earth and going off into space. It is estimated that without carbon dioxide in our atmosphere the Earth's surface would be so cold that no life could exist here.

The more carbon dioxide there is in the atmosphere, the more reflected infra-red radiation is trapped and the warmer the Earth becomes. This appears to be happening now, and it is alarming. We can't be sure just how much or how fast the temperature is rising, or what its effects might be. It is possible that so much ice on and around Antarctica and the North Pole might melt that sea levels could rise by many metres, completing submerging island groups such as the Maldives and perhaps even threatening low-lying coastal or estuarine cities such as London. Weather patterns might change, which in Britain might mean warmer and wetter winters, hotter summers and more extreme weather events, such as storms, floods and very high winds. Plants now living in southern Britain might no longer be able to survive there if they need cool temperatures, and may 'move' northwards, and some species of plants and animals might not be able to find a suitable habitat at all and would become extinct.

ACTIVITY 7.2

Global warming

1 Search the internet, magazines and newspapers for evidence that has been used to infer that global warming is happening. Choose one piece of evidence and use a range of sources of information to help you to assess its validity. How convincing is it? Discuss your findings with others and debate whether or not global warming is occurring.

2 Carry out a similar exercise to lead to a debate about whether or not our use of fossil fuels is contributing to changes in the carbon dioxide concentration of the atmosphere. Should governments make a reduction in fossil fuel use a priority?

Summary

1. In the light-dependent reaction of photosynthesis, chlorophyll absorbs energy from sunlight and helps it to be converted to chemical energy in ATP and reduced NADP.

2. In the light-independent reaction of photosynthesis, in the Calvin cycle, a 5-carbon molecule, RuBP, combines with (fixes) carbon dioxide to form two molecules of a 3C compound, GP. ATP and reduced NADP from the light-dependent reaction are used to convert GP into the carbohydrate triose phosphate. This is used to manufacture other substances in the plant, including other carbohydrates, lipids and amino acids.

3. Photosynthesis is almost the only way in which carbon atoms are taken from the atmosphere and made available to other living things. In the carbon cycle, carbon-containing organic substances made by plants provide a source of carbon atoms to other organisms from which they can build their cells. Respiration by all living organisms returns carbon to the atmosphere in the form of carbon dioxide. Microorganisms, some of which break down molecules in dead plants and animals and in their wastes, also respire and so return carbon atoms to the atmosphere that would otherwise remain in the soil.

4. Food chains are a representation of the flow of energy from producers to consumers. The different stages in a food chain are known as trophic levels.

5. Energy is lost between each trophic level in a food chain. For example, feeding maize containing 10 kJ to cattle provides only 0.05 kJ of energy to humans who eat beef or drink milk from these cattle. On average, energy transfer from plants to primary consumers, and from primary consumers to secondary consumers, has an efficiency of about 10%.

6. Millions of years ago, incomplete decay of dead plants and microorganisms led to the build-up of fossil fuels, which are now found deep beneath the ground. The combustion of these fossil fuels releases carbon dioxide to the atmosphere at a faster rate than the plants now living on Earth can remove it. This may be contributing to the current increase in the concentration of carbon dioxide in the atmosphere, which may be helping to cause global warming. Deforestation may be decreasing the quantity of carbon dioxide removed from the air by photosynthesis.

Human populations

The Black Death

In 1334, a new disease appeared in north-eastern China. Over the next few years, it steadily and inexorably made its way around the shores of the Black Sea and into Europe. In 1348, it arrived in Florence, Italy.

The Black Death, as it became known, usually began with the appearance of swellings called bubos which appeared on the neck, in the armpits and in the groin. Within a few days most victims would be dead. The disease was so feared that if one member of a family became ill they were often left abandoned in their home, as their relatives were too terrified to tend to them. Bodies were left unburied.

The disease spread from Florence at an average rate of 2 miles per day, all the way through Europe and into Britain, even reaching as far north as Iceland and Greenland. By 1352 it was almost burnt out, but new epidemics took hold in Britain and Europe at intervals up until the last major one in 1670.

It is thought that the 1348 epidemic killed about one third of the population of Europe. But, even now, there is argument about exactly what this disease was. It is usually thought to have been bubonic plague, an infectious disease caused by the bacterium *Yersinia pestis*, transmitted from person to person by bites from rat fleas. However, some researchers have questioned this, as it is difficult to see how this could have resulted in such a rapid spread.

Today, we would like to think that nothing like this could ever happen again. But we should not be too complacent. Bubonic plague is still around, and each year many people in Africa and some regions of eastern Asia die from it. And bubonic plague is not the only infectious disease that we should fear. In 1918 a new strain of influenza, Spanish flu, killed over 20 million people – more than died in the First World War. Today we have HIV/AIDS. In 2003, a new disease which we named SARS appeared, causing near-panic until it was realised that we could keep it under control, at least for the present.

The human population grew steadily from around 5000 years ago (3000 BC) until the Black Death killed so many in the fourteenth century (Fig 7.22). It was the increased size of the human population that allowed the Black Death to spread so rapidly – people were living more closely together in the towns and villages than ever before, presumably making it easier for rat fleas to carry the bacterium from one to the other. But since the temporary 'blip' caused by the Black Death, nothing else has happened to cause a significant decrease in the human population. Instead, it has grown at an increasing rate. In 1980, it was 4.5 billion (4 500 000 000), in 1990 5.3 billion and by 2000 6.1 billion. It is estimated that it will reach 6.8 billion by 2010 (Figs 7.21 and 7.22).

increases population

rising birth rate	falling birth rate
immigration	emigration
falling death rate	rising death rate

decreases population

Fig 7.21 Factors affecting a country's population size.

The effect of the human population on the environment

As human population increases, so does our effect on our environment. We cut down more forests so that more crops can be grown, more roads built and more houses constructed. We are burning more fossil fuels, which appears to be increasing the concentration of carbon dioxide in the atmosphere and contributing to global warming. We allow more pollutants such as pesticides, fertilisers and waste from industry such as heavy metals to contaminate soil and water. In some parts of the world, people kill large numbers of endangered animals for food or because parts of their bodies are thought to confer health benefits or sexual potency if they are consumed. Everywhere that humans live, we change the natural environment.

There is no doubt that our impact is decreasing biodiversity – the range of different species that live in a habitat. Cutting down a large area of rainforest, for example, removes the habitat for most of the plant and animal species that live there. They may be able to move to an undamaged piece of forest, or they may die. If this continues, the remaining areas of suitable habitat may become so scarce and so scattered that some species become extinct.

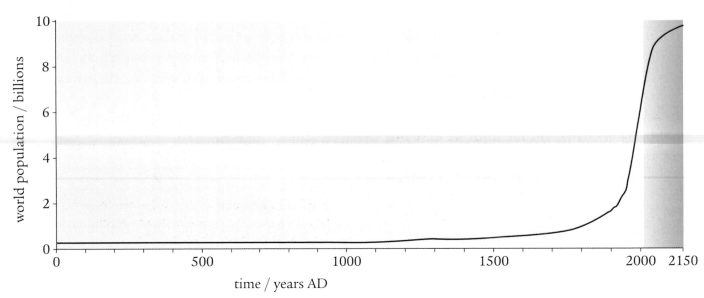

Fig 7.22 Global human population growth (estimated – yellow, predicted – blue). Data from the UN Population Division.

There have been mass extinctions of species in the past, thought to have been caused by such catastrophic events as a comet crashing into the Earth, or by huge volcanic eruptions. Many biologists think that we are now in the throes of another great mass extinction, but this time caused by ourselves.

The IUCN (International Union for the Conservation of Nature) exists to try to limit the harmful effects of humans on biodiversity. They publish a regularly updated Red List, listing the species that are currently under threat and that need protection if they are not to become extinct. The Red List for 2000 included more species than ever before. The number of critically endangered species of mammals on this list (the most threatened category) increased from 169 in 1996 to 180 in 2000. The IUCN estimates that 5435 animal species are threatened with extinction – about 25% of the known species. At least one in eight of all known plant species are also under threat. But we know that there are thousands of species out there which have never been named or described (including some large mammals as well as tiny insects and other invertebrates), so the actual number of threatened species must be huge. Some pressure groups have estimated that, if the current trend continues, around 50% of all living species will have become extinct by the year 2100.

National and international conservation groups, either funded by governments or by contributions from supporters, work constantly to reduce the harmful effects that we are having on biodiversity. But still the damage goes on, and probably will continue until we have our population explosion under control. Even in the UK, though we have controlled our population increase, we have not yet reversed the decline in biodiversity which was most severe after the 1930s due to changes in farming practices.

Causes of the human population increase

A population can be defined as a group of organisms of the same species that interbreed freely with one another. For humans, this includes all of us in every part of the Earth. The human population is a global population.

Populations of most species do not increase at the amazing rate at which our own is rising. Various factors help to keep them in check. Imagine, for example, a population of owls (Figs 7.23 and 7.24). The factors that might prevent the population from rising include:

- competition for food;
- an increase in infectious diseases, perhaps through weakened immune systems if they have not had enough to eat;
- an increase in aggression between the animals, increasing emigration;
- a decrease in reproductive success, perhaps through death of nestlings.

All of these factors have an increasing effect as the owl population gets bigger. They are said to be **density-dependent factors**, because their magnitude depends on the density of the owl

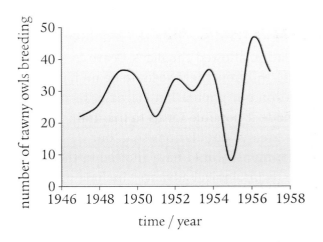

Fig 7.23 The fluctuation in the numbers of breeding tawny owls in Wytham Wood, Oxfordshire, from 1946 to 1958.

population. If the owl population rises, these factors become greater and cause the population to drop. When the owl population decreases, these factors decrease in effect and the population rises. Over time, the owl population remains roughly constant, oscillating around a fairly steady mean value.

Fig 7.24 Tawny owls.

When humans first evolved, our populations would have been controlled in this way. Various factors in our environment helped to keep the population stable. It also happened in the fourteenth century, when the relatively large population allowed the Black Death to spread so rapidly. But now there seem to be no natural checks on our population increase. Technology has made it possible for us to maintain much, much greater populations than our environments would have allowed in the past. These technological advances include methods of food production, advances in medical technology and disease control.

Food production

There are still some parts of the world where food production is not high enough to support a rise in population, and where so many people are short of food that high numbers die as a direct result of poor nutrition. Starvation and lack of protein, vitamins or minerals may prevent a woman from conceiving and giving birth, even if she does not die. It could be said that in these places lack of food is helping to keep the population stable.

Overall, though, the world produces more than enough food to feed everyone. The problem is that this food is not where it needs to be. In Britain, almost everyone gets enough to eat and our waste food is enough to feed thousands of others. Farmers in the European Union, using modern machinery, fertilisers and pesticides, produce far more food than the inhabitants of the EU require, so that a great deal of food can be exported.

Some of this excess food may find its way, with the help of international bodies such as the United Nations, or charities such as Oxfam, to parts of the world where populations are starving. It can help for a while, and perhaps reduce mortality rates until whatever caused the famine – perhaps lack of rainfall or war – allows the people to grow their own food once more.

Modern methods of food production are undoubtedly one of the factors that have allowed the human population to increase so rapidly in the past few hundred years. There still appears to be a very long way to go before global population increase will be halted by lack of food, even though this may be a stabilising factor in some small corners of the world where international aid cannot or does not intervene successfully in instances of famine.

Medical technology

Infectious disease, such as the Black Death, tends to have greater effects in a large population than a small one, and therefore can be a stabilising factor and help to prevent population growth. But as medicine has advanced, we have become much more successful in treating infectious diseases (with the use of antibiotics) and in limiting their spread (for example, with vaccination). In Britain, infectious disease causes the death of only a very small percentage of the population.

But every now and then something new emerges that we cannot control, and it is possible that some new infectious disease could emerge at any time and spread around the world out of control. HIV/AIDS in the 1970s and SARS in the 2000s are the most recent examples of infectious diseases that have emerged and spread rapidly around the world. We still have no cure for HIV/AIDS and it is still killing thousands of people each year. Luckily, SARS turned out not to be easily transmitted from one person to another, and quick, cooperative international action seems to have brought it under control.

Medical technology has also helped to reduce death rates from other diseases, such as cancers and inherited diseases such as cystic fibrosis. This may allow people to live longer than they would have done in the past, so the numbers on Earth at any one time increase. We have also seen that medicine has helped people to reproduce who would not have been able to do so naturally (see pages 130–136).

Birth rate and infant mortality

Birth rate can be defined as the number of live births per year per one thousand of the population. Fig 7.25 shows how birth rate in Britain has changed since 1911.

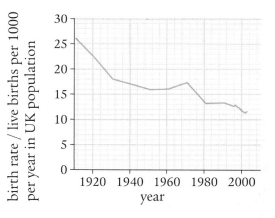

Fig 7.25 Birth rate in the UK from 1911.

In developing countries birth rate is high, mainly because parents want to have a large number of children to help the family to get food and to look after them as they age. Social and health changes have an immediate effect by reducing infant mortality but birth rate remains high for many years, resulting in high rates of population growth. The UK was in this position in the nineteenth and early twentieth centuries.

SAQ

7.6 The table shows the annual increase (increment) in the human world population in every tenth year from 1900. The figures are estimates to the present and predictions to 2040.

a Present the data graphically.

b Compare the data with the data for population size in the graph in Fig 7.22 on page 166. Why does population rise even when the annual increment is falling?

Year	Increment / millions	Year	Increment / millions
1900	10	1980	83
1910	11	1990	89
1920	21	2000	74
1930	23	2010	70
1940	23	2020	61
1950	50	2030	46
1960	67	2040	33
1970	74		

7.7   The graph in Fig 7.25 shows the birth rate in the United Kingdom between 1911 and 2003.

   a   Describe the changes during the period shown by the graph.

   b   Calculate the mean change in birth rate per year between:

    i   1911 and 1940;

   ii   1950 and 1970.

   c   Suggest reasons for these changes.

   d   Explain why the data shown in the graph do not tell us how the population in the UK was changing during this period.

Summary

1 As human populations increase, their impact on the environment increases. This endangers many species and reduces biodiversity.

2 Populations of organisms other than humans are normally kept in check by density-dependent environmental factors such as disease, competition for scarce resources or predation. As these factors increase, they tend to increase death rate and decrease birth rate.

3 Availability of food can limit the growth of human populations in parts of the world where supply of food does not meet demand, but overall there is more than enough food on Earth to feed everyone.

4 Advances in medical technology have increased life expectancy and reduced death rate from infectious and other diseases.

5 Birth rate tends to be high where mortality rates are high and availability of food, medicine and good health care facilities are limited, because parents want to have a large number of children to help the family to get food and to look after them as they age.

CHAPTER 8

Genetics and inheritance

In almost every country, and in almost every religion, there are laws and customs relating to marriages between closely related people.

In Britain and in Australia, marriage between brothers and sisters is banned, although marriage between first cousins is legal. However, in many states in the USA, and in China, marriage between first cousins is prohibited. First cousin marriages are also banned in some Islamic communities, but encouraged in others. In ancient Egypt, brother-sister marriages were commonplace amongst the ruling families, but probably extremely rare amongst the rest of the population. Amongst Hindus in southern India, one fifth of all marriages are between uncle and niece.

Why are there such laws, and why do they differ so much? Several theories have been put forward to explain why so many societies have rules and customs that prevent close relatives from marrying, of which the biological one has a strong case.

The more closely related two people are, the more of their genes are identical with one another. Brothers and sisters have identical genes at 50% of loci. For first cousins this value is 6.25% and for uncle and niece it is 12.5%. Close-kin marriages therefore increase the likelihood of rare, recessive alleles being brought together. This increases the risk of genetic diseases in the couple's children. It is possible that, over time, natural selection has favoured groups of people who did not allow such marriages, as they might have survived better in particular environments than those who did. One study found that marriages between close relations in Jordan resulted in 4% more children having an inherited illness than in marriages between unrelated people.

Perhaps the laws and customs differ because there are also gains to be had from marrying within the family. If you are part of a small group living amongst others with different beliefs and customs, marriage within the community (and therefore possibly with a relative if the community is small) may seem highly preferable to marrying a stranger with different customs.

We think that our chromosomes carry around 30 000 genes The postition on a chromosome at which a gene is found is called its **locus**. These genes help to make us who we are. They contain a code which determines the proteins that are synthesised in our cells.

Many of these genes exist in different versions, called **alleles**. If we have different alleles then our cells may make different proteins. This can have a considerable effect on our **phenotype** – the visible or measurable characteristics of how we look or how our physiology works.

In some cases, just one gene locus can have a significant effect on phenotype. In others, many genes are involved in producing the same characteristic. And many of our characteristics, although they are probably influenced by our genes, are also strongly affected by our environment.

Genetics is the study of inheritance. We will begin this chapter by looking at some of the characteristics that are affected by just one gene locus, and then consider the patterns of inheritance that are seen when alleles found at two different gene loci are inherited together.

Single gene inheritance

There are relatively few characteristics in humans that are known to be controlled by a single gene. Many of these involve alleles that can cause illness or disability.

Cystic fibrosis

Cystic fibrosis is a genetic disease in which abnormally thick mucus is produced in the lungs and other parts of the body. A person with cystic fibrosis is very prone to bacterial infections in the lungs because it is difficult for the mucus to be removed, allowing bacteria to breed in it. A person with cystic fibrosis needs daily therapy to help them to cough up this mucus (Fig 8.1). The thick mucus adversely affects many other parts of the body. The pancreatic duct may become blocked, and

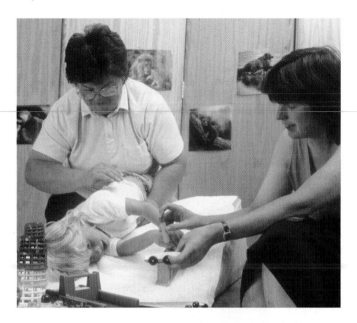

Fig 8.1 In cystic fibrosis the mucus produced in the airways is so thick that it cannot be cleared by ciliated cells or coughing. This obstructs the airway and increases the risk of infection. A physiotherapist is giving percussion treatment. This loosens the mucus, which is then coughed up.

people with this disease often take pancreatic enzymes by mouth to help with digestion. Around 90% of men with cystic fibrosis are sterile because thick secretions block ducts in the reproductive system.

Cystic fibrosis is caused by a recessive allele of the gene which codes for a transporter protein called **CFTR**. This protein sits in the cell surface membranes of cells in the alveoli (and also elsewhere in the body) and allows chloride ions to pass out of the cells. The recessive allele codes for a faulty version of this protein which does not act properly as a chloride ion transporter.

Normally, the cells lining the airways and in the lungs pump out chloride ions through the channel in the cell surface membrane formed by CFTR. This results in a relatively high concentration of chloride outside the cells. This reduces the water potential below that of the cytoplasm of the cells. So water moves out of the cells by osmosis, down the water potential gradient. It mixes with the mucus there, making it thin enough for easy removal by the sweeping movements of cilia.

However, in someone with cystic fibrosis this doesn't happen. Much less water moves out of the cells, so the mucus on their surfaces stays thick and sticky. The cilia, or even coughing, can't remove it all.

The CFTR gene

In each of our cells, we have two sets of chromosomes, one from our mother and one from our father. So we have two copies of this gene. The CFTR gene is found on chromosome 7. The CFTR gene consists of about 250 000 bases. Mutations in this gene have produced several different alleles. The commonest of these is the result of a deletion of three bases. The CFTR protein made using the code on this allele is therefore missing one amino acid. The machinery in the cell recognises that this is not the right protein, and does not place it in the cell surface membrane.

This allele is a **recessive** allele. The normal allele is **dominant**. A recessive allele has an effect on the phenotype only when the dominant allele is not present. A dominant allele has an effect no matter whether or not the recessive allele is also present.

We can use symbols to represent these two alleles. Because they are alleles of the same gene we should use the same letter to represent both of them. By convention, a capital letter is used to represent the dominant allele, and a lower case (small) letter for the recessive one. It is also a good idea to choose letters where the capital and small letters look quite different, so that neither you nor an examiner is in any doubt about what you have written down.

In this case, we will use the letter **F** for the allele coding for the normal CFTR protein and **f** for the allele coding for the faulty version. Because we have one gene from each of our parents, there are three possible gene combinations – **genotypes** – that may be present in any one person's cells.

They are:

Genotype	Phenotype
FF	unaffected
Ff	unaffected
ff	cystic fibrosis

A genotype in which both alleles of a gene are the same is said to be **homozygous**. A genotype in which the alleles of a gene are different is **heterozygous**. **FF** and **ff** are homozygous, and **Ff** is heterozygous.

Inheritance of the CFTR gene

When gametes are made by meiosis, homologous chromosomes first pair up and then are shared out between the daughter cells (see pages 105–106). Gametes contain only one set of chromosomes. A sperm or an egg can therefore contain only one allele for the CFTR gene.

Genotype of parent	Possible genotypes of their gametes
FF	all F
Ff	50% F and 50% f
ff	all f

At fertilisation, any gamete from the father can fertilise any gamete from the mother. We can show all of this using a **genetic diagram**. This is a conventional way of showing the relative chances of a child of a certain genotype or phenotype being born to parents having a particular genotype or phenotype. For example, the genetic diagram on page 174 shows the chance of a heterozygous man and a heterozygous woman having a child with cystic fibrosis.

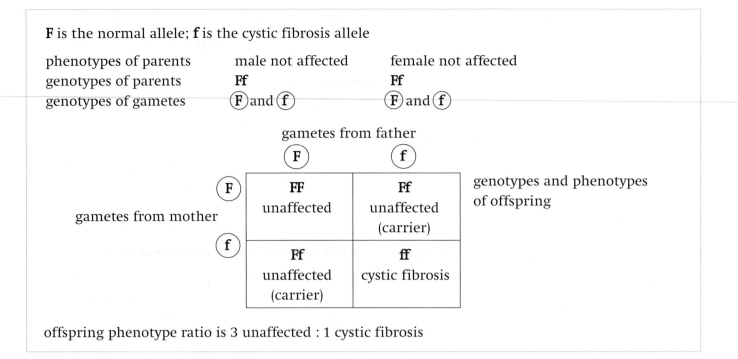

F is the normal allele; f is the cystic fibrosis allele

phenotypes of parents	male not affected	female not affected
genotypes of parents	Ff	Ff
genotypes of gametes	F and f	F and f

gametes from father

gametes from mother

	F	f
F	FF unaffected	Ff unaffected (carrier)
f	Ff unaffected (carrier)	ff cystic fibrosis

genotypes and phenotypes of offspring

offspring phenotype ratio is 3 unaffected : 1 cystic fibrosis

This shows us that each time the couple have a child, there is a 25% chance that the child will inherit the genotype FF and a 50% chance that they will inherit the genotype Ff. There is therefore a 75% chance that the child will not have cystic fibrosis. The chance of the child inheriting the genotype ff and having cystic fibrosis is 25%.

Another way of expressing this is to say that the probability of a child **not** having cystic fibrosis is 0.75, while the probability of having the disease is 0.25. This can also be stated as a probability of 1 in 4 that a child born to these parents will have this disease.

Yet another way of expressing this is to say that the expected ratio of children without cystic fibrosis to those with cystic fibrosis is 3:1.

SAQ

8.1 Copy and complete this genetic diagram to determine the chance of a heterozygous man and a woman with the genotype FF having a child with cystic fibrosis.

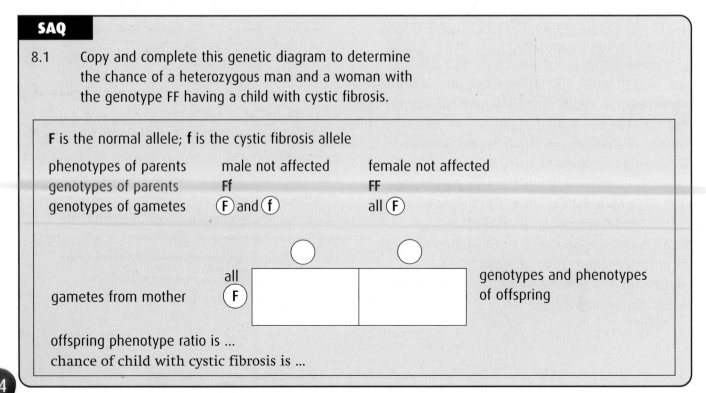

F is the normal allele; f is the cystic fibrosis allele

phenotypes of parents	male not affected	female not affected
genotypes of parents	Ff	FF
genotypes of gametes	F and f	all F

gametes from mother

	all F	

genotypes and phenotypes of offspring

offspring phenotype ratio is ...
chance of child with cystic fibrosis is ...

Huntington's disease

Huntington's disease is a genetic disease that affects the nervous system and muscles. An affected person's limbs and face may move uncontrollably, or they may become fixed and rigid. It is a progressive illness in which more and more neurones in the brain die, and it is eventually fatal. However, symptoms don't develop until the person is around 35 to 40 years old, and they may go on to live more than 20 years after these symptoms have first shown up.

The root cause of the disease has been tracked down to the gene that codes for a protein called **huntingtin**. We don't know what this protein does, but it is present in the brain and is thought to be directly related to the death of neurones there. The gene is on chromosome 4. The faulty allele of this gene has some extra CAG sequences, resulting in extra glutamines being included when the huntingtin protein is made. The number of CAG repeats is between 11 and 34, but a faulty gene may have up to 100. This is sometimes known as a 'gene stutter' – the same sequence is 'said' again and again. The more repeats in the gene, the earlier the onset of the disease.

Unlike the faulty CFTR allele, the faulty huntingtin allele is dominant. A zygote with two copies of the faulty allele does not develop, so homozygous dominant individuals never occur.

SAQ

8.2   With the help of a full and correctly laid out genetic diagram, determine the chance that a child born to a man with Huntington's disease and a woman without this disease will have Huntington's disease. (You should begin by choosing suitable symbols for the alleles and stating what your symbols represent.)

The Hardy-Weinberg equations

In Britain, approximately one baby in 3300 is born with cystic fibrosis. What does this tell us about the frequency of the cystic fibrosis allele in the population? The two Hardy-Weinberg equations allow this to be worked out.

In these equations, the letters p and q are used to represent the frequency of the dominant allele and the recessive allele in the population. So we can say:

p represents the frequency of allele **F**
q represents the frequency of allele **f**

The frequency of an allele can be anything between 0 and 1. If it is 0, then no-one has this allele. If it is 1, then it is the only allele of that gene in the population. If it is 0.5, then it makes up half of the alleles of that gene in the population.

The first Hardy-Weinberg equation is:

$$p + q = 1$$

The second equation is a bit more complicated. It is:

$$p^2 + 2pq + q^2 = 1$$

where:

p^2 is the frequency of genotype **FF**
$2pq$ is the frequency of genotype **Ff**
q^2 is the frequency of genotype **ff**

Using these two equations, and our knowledge of the frequency of cystic fibrosis in the population, we can work out p and q.

We know that 1 in 3300 babies are born with cystic fibrosis. So:

$$q^2 = 1 \div 3300$$
$$= 0.0003$$
$$q = \sqrt{0.0003}$$
$$= 0.017$$

We also know that p + q = 1. So:

$$p + 0.017 = 1$$
$$p = 1 - 0.017$$
$$= 0.983$$

Now we can use this to work out how many people in the population are carriers for the cystic fibrosis allele, with the genotype **Ff**. We know that the frequency of this genotype is $2pq$ (see above, where we introduced the second equation).

So:

frequency of genotype **Ff**
$$= 2pq$$
$$= 2 \times 0.983 \times 0.017$$
$$= 0.0334$$

This means that for every 100 people, 3.3 have the genotype **Ff**. In other words, about 1 in 30 people are carriers for the cystic fibrosis allele.

SAQ

8.3   Phenylketonuria, PKU, is a genetic disease caused by a recessive allele. About one in 15 000 people in a population are born with PKU.

Use the Hardy-Weinberg equations to calculate the frequency of the PKU allele in the population. State the meaning of the symbols that you use, and show all of your working.

8.4   Explain why we do not need to use the Hardy-Weinberg equations to calculate the frequency of the allele that causes Huntington's disease.

Gene mutations

The faulty alleles that are responsible for cystic fibrosis and Huntington's disease originally arise by gene mutation. But not all mutations in genes result in disease. It depends on where the mutation happens, and just how the mutation changes the base sequence in the DNA.

Site of the mutation

If a mutation of the CFTR gene took place in a skin cell, it would not matter at all.

- Firstly, because the genetic code is degenerate, the new base sequence might still code for the same amino acid sequence.
- Secondly, the mutation produces a recessive allele, and unless the person was heterozygous they would still have a copy of the normal, dominant allele in that cell.
- Thirdly, skin cells don't secrete mucus so it wouldn't make any difference to them even if they did have two copies of the mutant CFTR allele. The CFTR gene is not expressed (used to make proteins) in skin cells.
- Fourthly, even it did make a difference to that skin cell, there would still be thousands of other skin cells with the normal alleles. If the skin cell divided by mitosis it could pass its alleles on, but they still would only be a very small population of cells amongst a much higher number of smaller ones. Even where a dominant allele is involved, such as the mutant huntingtin allele, it is still unlikely that it will have any significant effect if it occurs in a body cell.

So, a mutation in a body cell isn't normally going to have much effect on the person in whom it happened. (The exception is when the mutation causes the cell to lose control over its rate of division, which can lead to cancer – see page 167 in *Human Biology for AS*.) It really has to take place in a cell that is going to form a gamete before we need to worry that it could cause a genetic disease. That gamete may fuse with another to form a zygote containing the mutated allele. And that single cell will divide repeatedly by mitosis to form all of the cells in the baby's body. Every one of them will contain the mutated allele.

For both cystic fibrosis and Huntington's disease, it seems that almost all mutated alleles are inherited from a parent or parents, rather than happening as a new mutation during gamete formation. If such a new mutation does occur, so that an affected child is born into a family in which there has been no previous history of the disease, it is known as a **sporadic case**.

Type of mutation

The most common faulty allele for the CFTR gene is the result of the deletion of three bases (Fig 8.2).

This results in the omission of phenylalanine from the CFTR protein.

However, more than 900 mutations have been discovered in the CFTR gene. Many of these don't have any effect at all on the protein that is made.

Codominance

So far, we have looked at examples where one allele of a gene is dominant and another is recessive. The alleles controlling the ABO blood group phenotypes, and those responsible for sickle cell anaemia, behave differently.

ABO blood group inheritance

Red blood cells contain a protein in their cell surface membranes that determines the ABO blood group. There are two forms of this protein, known as antigens A and B. The gene that encodes this protein is on chromosome 9. It has three alleles, coding for antigen A, antigen B or no antigen at all.

The symbols for these alleles are written differently from those for CFTR or huntingtin. Each symbol includes the letter I to represent the gene locus. It is then given a superscript to represent one particular allele.

part of the normal CFTR allele and the amino acids it codes for:

the most common mutation of this allele in which three bases are deleted:

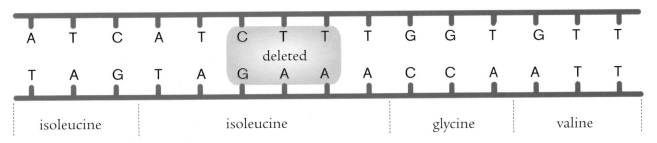

Fig 8.2 The mutation that is commonly associated with cystic fibrosis. Many other mutations have no effect. For example, if the third base pair from the left was changed from C–G to A–T, it would still code for isoleucine.

I^A	allele for antigen A	
I^B	allele for antigen B	
I^O	allele for no antigen	

They are written like this because alleles I^A and I^B are **codominant**. They each have an effect when they are together in a cell. However, both I^A and I^B are dominant with respect to I^O, which is recessive. So there are four possible phenotypes:

Genotype	Phenotype
$I^A I^A$	Group A
$I^A I^B$	Group AB
$I^A I^O$	Group A
$I^B I^B$	Group B
$I^B I^O$	Group B
$I^O I^O$	Group O

Inheritance of sickle cell anaemia

Sickle cell anaemia is a genetic disease resulting from a faulty gene encoding the B polypeptide chain in haemoglobin. The mutation and its effects are described on pages 198–199 in *Human Biology for AS*.

As the mutant and the normal allele are codominant, they should be written in the same style as the blood group alleles. The symbol **Hb** is used to represent the gene locus for this chain in the haemoglobin molecule, and a superscript for the allele. The normal allele is Hb^A and the sickle cell allele is Hb^S.

In a heterozygous person, *both* alleles are used as codes for making haemoglobin. There are therefore three phenotypes:

Genotype	Phenotype
$Hb^A Hb^A$	all normal haemoglobin
$Hb^A Hb^S$	half the haemoglobin is normal and half is sickle cell haemoglobin – sickle cell trait
$Hb^S Hb^S$	all sickle cell haemoglobin – sickle cell anaemia (disease)

SAQ

8.5 Using the correct symbols, draw a complete and fully labelled genetic diagram to find the chance of a child with blood group O being born to a heterozygous man with blood group B and a heterozygous woman with blood group A.

8.6 The diagram shows the known blood groups in three generations of a family. Squares represent males and circles females. What are the genotypes of 1 and 3 and the blood group of 2?

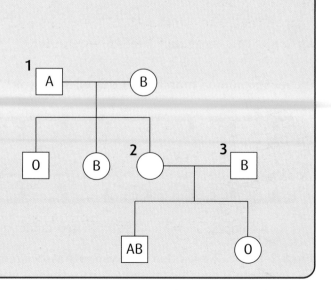

Sickle cell disease and malaria

The sickle cell allele is most common in parts of the world where malaria is present (Fig 8.3). This is not just chance – there is a causal link that explains the similarity in their distribution.

Sickle cell disease is a highly dangerous and potentially fatal disease, especially in countries where medical facilities are not easily available, such as some parts of sub-Saharan Africa. Children who are born with sickle cell disease, with genotype $Hb^S Hb^S$, are very likely to die before they reach reproductive age, and you would think that this would quickly remove the Hb^S allele from the population.

However, people who are homozygous for the Hb^A allele are also at a disadvantage in places where malaria is common. Malaria is caused by a single-celled organism called *Plasmodium*, which lives and breeds inside red blood cells. It causes recurrent fevers and can kill. Each year, more than 300 million people are infected with *Plasmodium* and 1.5 million of them die. Many of these fatalities are children. The allele Hb^S confers protection against malaria, because red blood cells containing sickle cell haemoglobin are much less likely to be infected with or damaged by *Plasmodium*. In evolutionary terms, we can say that the sickle cell allele has a selective advantage.

So having the genotype $Hb^S Hb^S$ or the genotype $Hb^A Hb^A$ decreases the chance that a person will live long enough to reproduce and pass on their alleles to their children. The best genotype to have is $Hb^A Hb^S$. You do not have sickle cell disease, nor are you very susceptible to malaria.

In each generation, children born with the genotype $Hb^A Hb^S$ are most likely to grow up and have children themselves. So both alleles are passed on to the next generation. If it were not for the protection that it gives against malaria, the Hb^S allele would slowly disappear. Perhaps we will see a slow change in the distribution of the allele in the future, if malaria can be brought under control.

There are some areas in which people have the allele but where there is no malaria. This may be due to migration of people with the allele into the area or the disappearance of malaria from that area, but not so long ago that selection against the allele has had a great effect on gene frequency.

Sex linkage

Genes whose loci are on the X or Y chromosome have different inheritance patterns from genes on all the other chromosomes, the **autosomes**. Women have two X chromosomes, while men have one X and one Y.

An X chromosome is much larger than a Y chromosome. It has many genes that are not found on the Y, that is, in the areas outside the homologous region (Fig 8.4). These genes are said to be **sex linked**, because their inheritance is affected by whether a person is male or female.

One such gene determines the production of a factor that is needed to enable blood to clot, a

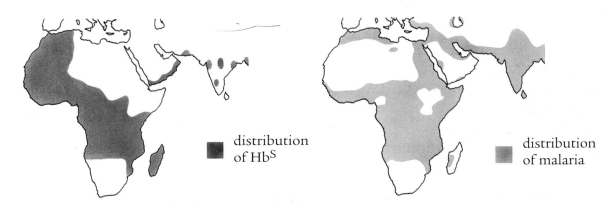

distribution of Hb^S

distribution of malaria

Fig 8.3 Distribution of the sickle cell anaemia allele and malaria in Africa and the near east.

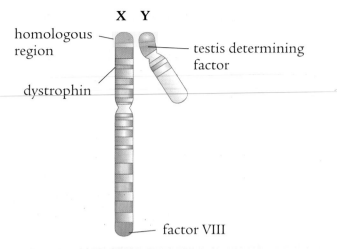

homologous region

testis determining factor

dystrophin

factor VIII

Fig 8.4 X and Y chromosomes.

protein called **factor VIII**. There is a recessive allele of this gene which codes for a faulty version of factor VIII. Without this factor, blood does not clot properly, a condition called haemophilia. Bleeding occurs into joints and other parts of the body, which can be extremely painful and eventually disabling. Haemophilia is treated by giving the person factor VIII throughout their lives.

When writing symbols of genes carried on the X chromosome, they are always written as superscripts. The symbol X^H can be used to represent the normal gene, and X^h for the haemophilia gene.

In women, there are two X chromosomes, so a woman always has two factor VIII genes. Her possible genotypes and phenotypes are:

Genotype	Phenotype
$X^H X^H$	normal blood clotting
$X^H X^h$	normal blood clotting (she has no symptoms, but is said to be a carrier)
$X^h X^h$	lethal

A foetus with the genotype $X^h X^h$ does not develop, so no babies with this genotype are ever born.

In a man, however, there is only one Factor VIII gene present, as he has only one X chromosome.

Genotype	Phenotype
$X^H Y$	normal blood clotting
$X^h Y$	haemophilia

The genetic diagram below shows how a woman who is a carrier for haemophilia, and a man who has normal blood clotting, can have a son with haemophilia.

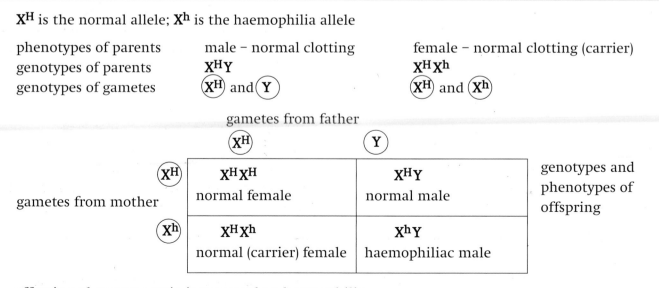

X^H is the normal allele; X^h is the haemophilia allele

phenotypes of parents — male – normal clotting — female – normal clotting (carrier)
genotypes of parents — $X^H Y$ — $X^H X^h$
genotypes of gametes — X^H and Y — X^H and X^h

gametes from father

gametes from mother	X^H	Y	
X^H	$X^H X^H$ normal female	$X^H Y$ normal male	genotypes and phenotypes of offspring
X^h	$X^H X^h$ normal (carrier) female	$X^h Y$ haemophiliac male	

offspring phenotype ratio is 3 normal : 1 haemophilia

The genetic counsellor

Where there is a possibility that a couple may have a child with a genetic disease, they may be referred to a genetic counsellor. The referral is normally done by their GP, but may also be made by a hospital doctor or any other health professional who is aware that there could be a problem. A couple may also refer themselves if they are worried.

A couple are likely to be referred if:

- either of them have genetic disease in their family;
- they belong to a group that is known to have a high risk of genetic disease (for example, a group in which marriage between close relatives is common);
- there is a history of recurrent miscarriages;
- the woman is over 38 (because the risk of the child having Down's syndrome is relatively high);
- as part of the management of a high-risk pregnancy.

The role of the counsellor is to provide the couple with information and help them to understand the risks involved in them having a child. The counsellor will then encourage them to make their own decision, based on this information, on what to do.

Parents may be very upset and shocked if they unexpectedly give birth to a child with a genetic disease. It is not uncommon for this to happen, because a recessive allele can be hidden in a family for many years. The cystic fibrosis allele, for example, is estimated to be present in 1 in 30 people, but only 1 in 3300 babies are born with cystic fibrosis. This is because most people who are carriers do not have partners who are also carriers. And even if they do, there is only a 1 in 4 chance that any one of their children will have the disease.

If parents find themselves in this situation, and if the disease is serious, they may question whether or not they should risk having another child. A genetic counsellor can give them the information they need to help them make this decision.

In other cases, a person may know that there have been instances of a genetic disease in their family, and is worried that they might have children with the disease. Here, too, the genetic counsellor can help to work out the possibility that this might happen.

Sometimes, as in the case of cystic fibrosis, it may be possible to take a tissue sample from the parents and test the DNA to find out which allele of a gene is present. This is called **genetic screening**, and it is explained in the next chapter.

The counsellor will apply knowledge of inheritance to the information she is given about relatives. It may involve a **pedigree analysis** in which this information going back for several generations is used. For example, a woman whose uncle had haemophilia wants to know if there is any chance that she could pass it on to her son. Women who are carriers for haemophilia will be unaware of this unless they have had a haemophiliac son. Blood testing in combination with pedigree analysis shows how haemophilia tends to pass from one generation to another (Fig 8.5).

If the woman's uncle was a haemophiliac, her grandmother was certainly a carrier. On average, half the daughters of a carrier are themselves carriers. So there is a 50% chance that her mother is a carrier. If her mother is a carrier then there is a 50% chance that she, as a daughter, is too. If she is a carrier, then there is a 25% chance she will give birth to a haemophiliac son. These make the chances of a haemophiliac son low, but certainly possible.

SAQ

8.7	Explain why a man with haemophilia cannot pass it on to his son.
8.8	Use genetic diagrams to explain the statements in the paragraph above.

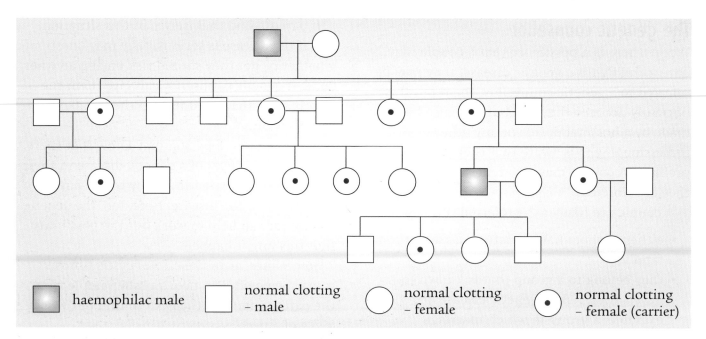

Fig 8.5 Pedigree for a sex-linked recessive disease, such as haemophilia.

SAQ

8.9   Use genetic diagrams to explain that the chance of a haemophiliac son being born to a mother who is a carrier, if her husband does not have haemophilia, is 25%.

i   Express this value as a **probability**.

ii   Give the expected **ratio** of normal to haemophiliac children born to this couple.

The role of the counsellor is not only to help the prospective parents to understand how a genetic disease is caused, and how it is inherited, but to help them think about whether it is truly undesirable for a child to be born with the disease. Many genetic conditions are relatively mild in their effects and many others can be effectively treated, and so the parents might decide to go ahead anyway (see Procedure 8.1 on page 183).

Another option for them is to use IVF rather than conceiving naturally. IVF (see page 134) could produce several embryos and it might be possible to test these for the allele in question. When embryos are chosen to be placed in the uterus, only those who do not have the allele might be used. However, many people find this unacceptable, and are concerned that it is a step onto the slippery slope leading to 'designer babies'.

SAQ

8.10   The family tree shows the occurrence of a genetic condition known as brachydactyly (short fingers). Use the tree to deduce:

a   whether the allele for this condition is dominant or recessive;

b   if it is sex-linked. Explain your answers.

Key to phenotypes
pink = brachydactyly
white = normal

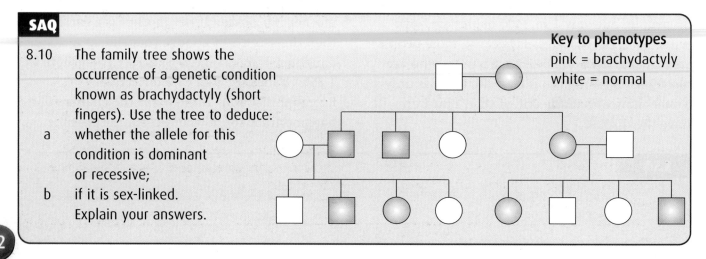

8.11   This family tree shows the incidence of the genetic disease phenylketonuria, PKU, in four generations of a family.

Key to phenotypes
pink = phenylketonuria
white = normal

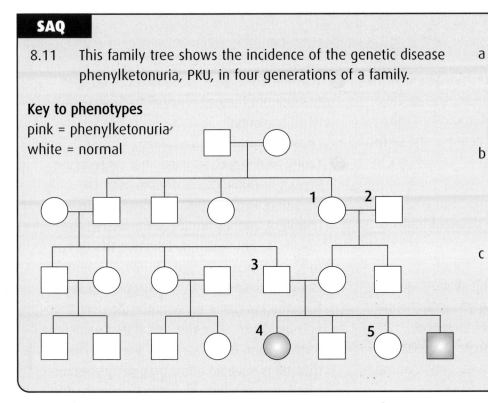

a   Describe **one** piece of evidence that shows:

i   that PKU is caused by a recessive allele;

ii   that PKU is not sex-linked.

b   Deduce the genotypes of 1, 2, 3 and 4. Use P to refer to the normal allele and p the recessive allele for PKU.

c   Person 5 talks to a genetic counsellor to find out the chance that she might have a child with PKU. What should the genetic counsellor tell her?

Genetic counselling

1   The counsellor talks to both parents or prospective parents and establishes rapport. Usually she talks to them together, but in some cases it may be better to do so individually.

2   She collects information that she can use to work out the inheritance pattern of the genetic disease. This involves asking about the families of both parents, and drawing up a pedigree. It is important to do this for both sides of the family. If the disease is not one whose inheritance pattern is already known (such as cystic fibrosis), analysis of the pedigree can then show whether the disease is caused by a recessive allele or a dominant allele, whether it is sex-linked, or whether it has arisen spontaneously.

3   The counsellor uses the pedigree analysis to determine the degree of risk that a child born to the parents will have the genetic disease, and explains this to the parents.

4   The severity of the disease is also discussed. The parents' perception of the disease may overestimate or underestimate the problem. The parents may be given the opportunity to meet doctors who deal with this disease, and with parents of children who have the same disease.

5   If available, and if the genetic disease is caused by a recessive allele, a test may be carried out on the DNA of both parents to find out if one or both of them is a carrier for the disease.

6   The counsellor will provide support to help the parents to decide whether or not to have a child. If they do decide to go ahead, they might choose to have IVF and genetic screening (see page 203) of the embryos before implantation, or to have amniocentesis or chorionic villus sampling with a view to having an early termination if the embryo is affected.

Summary

1. The position of a gene on a chromosome is known as a locus. Human cells are diploid, and so there are two of each type of chromosome in a cell. Chromosomes with the same genes at the same loci are said to be homologous.

2. Most genes have more than one form with slightly different base sequences. The different forms of a gene are known as alleles.

3. The genotype of a person is the alleles that they have in their cells. Their phenotype is the visible or measurable characteristics of their body structure or physiology. Phenotype is affected by genotype and environment.

4. A recessive allele of a gene only affects the phenotype if a dominant allele of that gene is not present. Dominant alleles always affect phenotype.

5. There are two copies of each gene in each diploid body cell. If these are the same, the genotype is homozygous. If they are different, the genotype is heterozygous.

6. Cystic fibrosis is caused by a recessive allele of the gene that encodes a transport protein called CFTR, which allows chloride ions to pass out of cells. Several such alleles have been discovered. In a homozygous person, a faulty form of CFTR is made and chloride ions do not easily pass out through the cell surface membrane. This results in the build-up of thick, sticky mucus in the lungs and other organs, which reduces efficiency of gas exchange and is often the site of repeated infections.

7. Huntington's disease is caused by a dominant allele of a gene that encodes the protein huntingtin. The faulty protein is associated with gradual death of neurones in the brain.

8. The Hardy-Weinberg equations can be used to work out the frequency of particular alleles in a population.

9. Faulty alleles such as those that cause cystic fibrosis or Huntington's disease arise by mutation. Most mutations, however, are harmless, as they are usually recessive and usually do not have any effect on the body if they occur in a body cell. Mutations are more likely to cause harm if they happen during the formation of gametes, because they will then be copied into all of the cells if that gamete is fertilised and forms a zygote. Even so, many mutations have no effect on proteins because more than one base triplet in DNA codes for the same amino acid.

10. Codominance, in which different alleles of a gene both have an effect in a heterozygote, is illustrated by the ABO blood groups and by sickle cell anaemia.

11. The sickle cell allele is relatively common in parts of the world where malaria is common because it confers resistance against infection with the malarial parasite, *Plasmodium*. Heterozygotes have a selective advantage over both types of homozygotes.

12. Genes found on the non-homologous part of the X chromosome, such as the gene coding for Factor VIII, are said to be sex-linked. As each male has only one copy, males are more likely than females to show the effects of a harmful recessive allele, in this case haemophilia.

13. A genetic counsellor helps parents to understand how a faulty allele can be inherited in their family, and to make informed decisions about having children.

Dihybrid inheritance

Yvonne can just remember her great grandfather on her mother's side of the family. He died when she was four, and she can remember how ill he was towards the end of his life – something to do with his kidneys, she thinks. She also remembers his hands, because he had odd fingernails on his middle fingers and none at all on his little fingers.

Her mother's parents are still alive. Her grandfather, John, also has odd fingernails and he has problems with his kneecaps as well. And so does her mother, two of her sisters and a cousin. Her eldest sister is having trouble with her kidneys, and is about to start having dialysis treatment.

It is fairly obvious to Yvonne that the odd fingernails and kneecaps must be an inherited condition. Yvonne herself has slightly odd fingernails that don't reach right to the ends of her fingers, although none are completely missing.

Yvonne is tracing her family tree, and she is interested in recording the occurrence of this feature and seeing if she can work out how it is inherited. The pattern of inheritance shows that the odd nails must be caused by a dominant allele.

She also includes other information on the family tree she is constructing. For those of her family who are alive, it is easy to record their hair colour, eye colour, and adult height, and with a little bit more work she also manages to find most of their blood groups. Between them, her family have three different blood groups – A, B and O. And a pattern immediately jumps out at her. All her relations with the odd nails have blood group B. But surely being blood group B can't make you have odd nails?

Yvonne is a bit worried by what she has found. She is beginning to wonder if perhaps the kidney disease is part of this pattern, too. She has the odd nails and is blood group B. Does this mean that she might get kidney disease, like her great grandfather and her sister?

It is indeed possible that Yvonne will develop kidney disease, though there is a very good chance that she won't. What Yvonne has discovered in her researches into her family tree is an example of linkage. Although she can't work it out from her family tree, the pattern of inheritance that she has found is caused by two different genes, one affecting blood group and one affecting the nails, kneecaps and kidneys.

A dihybrid cross

So far in this chapter, we have looked at examples of the inheritance of one gene. These are called **monohybrid crosses**. We can also look at the inheritance of two genes at a time. Crosses involving two genes are called **dihybrid crosses**.

For example, imagine that there is a gene on chromosome 4 that has two alleles, **A** and **a**. On chromosome 6, there is a different gene with two alleles **B** and **b**. Imagine that allele **A**, in the Rainbow family, codes for green ears and allele **a** for purple ears. Allele **B** codes for yellow hair and allele **b** codes for blue hair.

All the cells in the body have two complete sets of chromosomes. They will have two chromosome 4s and two chromosome 6s, so they will have two copies of each gene. There are nine different genotypes that any one person could have, and four different phenotypes:

Genotypes	Phenotypes
AABB	green ears, yellow hair
AABb	green ears, yellow hair
AAbb	green ears, blue hair
AaBB	green ears, yellow hair
AaBb	green ears, yellow hair
Aabb	green ears, blue hair
aaBB	purple ears, yellow hair
aaBb	purple ears, yellow hair
aabb	purple ears, blue hair

When meiosis happens and gametes are made, only one copy of each gene goes into the daughter cells. So, if a man has the genotype **AABB**, all of his sperm will get one of the **A** alleles and one of the **B** alleles. If he has the genotype **AaBB**, half of his sperm will get allele **A** and half will get allele **a**, and they will all get allele **B**.

We saw on page 107 that independent assortment in meiosis I means that each pair of chromosomes behaves entirely independently. If these genes **A/a** and **B/b** are on different chromosomes, then any allele of one may find itself in a gamete with any allele of the other (Fig 8.6).

parent genotype **AaBb**

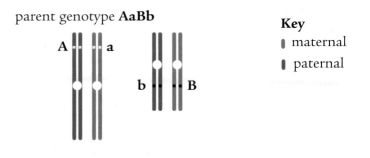

Key
- maternal
- paternal

A cell could go through meiosis and produce these gametes ...

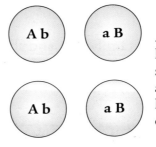

... if both paternal homologues go to the same pole in meiosis I, and both maternal homologues go to the opposite pole.

Or it could produce these gametes ...

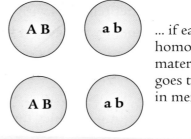

... if each paternal homologue and each maternal homologue goes to an opposite pole in meiosis I.

Fig 8.6 Independent assortment of chromosomes.

SAQ

8.12   Copy the two groups of four gametes in Fig 8.6 and draw the appropriate chromosomes inside each one.

We can work out the results of a dihybrid cross in just the same way as for a monohybrid cross, but showing the alleles of both genes. It is even more important now to put circles around the gametes, to help you to keep their alleles together. Notice, too, that we always write the two alleles for one gene next to other, and then the two alleles for the other gene.

In this example, both parents are heterozygous at both gene loci.

SAQ

8.13 If a woman has the genotype AAbb, what is the genotype of all the eggs that are made in her ovaries?

8.14 A man has the genotype AABb. What are the possible genotypes that his sperm may have?

A is the green ear allele; a the purple ear allele; B the yellow hair allele; b the blue hair allele

phenotypes of parents   green ears, yellow hair   green ears, yellow hair

genotypes of parents   **Aa Bb**   **Aa Bb**

genotypes of gametes   (AB) and (Ab) and (aB) and (ab)   (AB) and (Ab) and (aB) and (ab)

gametes from father

gametes from mother	(AB)	(Ab)	(aB)	(ab)
(AB)	**AABB** green ears yellow hair	**AABb** green ears yellow hair	**AaBB** green ears yellow hair	**AaBb** green ears yellow hair
(Ab)	**AABb** green ears yellow hair	**AAbb** green ears blue hair	**AaBb** green ears yellow hair	**Aabb** green ears blue hair
(aB)	**AaBB** green ears yellow hair	**AaBb** green ears yellow hair	**aaBB** purple ears yellow hair	**aaBb** purple ears yellow hair
(ab)	**AaBb** green ears yellow hair	**Aabb** green ears blue hair	**aaBb** purple ears yellow hair	**aabb** purple ears blue hair

genotypes and phenotypes of offspring

offspring phenotype ratio is –

    9 green ears, yellow hair :

    3 green ears, blue hair :

    3 purple ears, yellow hair :

    1 purple ears, blue hair

8.15   A woman with cystic fibrosis has blood
       group A (genotype $I^A I^O$). Her partner
       does not have cystic fibrosis and is not
       a carrier for it. He has blood group O.

a   Write down the genotypes of these
       two people.

b   With the help of a full and correctly laid
       out diagram, determine the possible
       genotypes and phenotypes of any
       children that they may have.

8.16   A man with sickle cell anaemia has a
       wife who shows no signs of sickle cell
       and has blood group AB. They have two
       children, neither of whom show any
       signs of sickle cell disease. One child has
       blood group A and the other has blood
       group AB.

a   With the help of genetic diagrams,
       determine the possible genotypes of the
       man.

b   The couple have a third child who has
       sickle cell anaemia and blood group B.
       Does this allow the genotype of the
       woman to be firmly decided? Explain
       your answer.

Autosomal linkage

In the case study on page 185, Yvonne thought that she could see a pattern in which her relatives with blood group B tended to have odd nails and kneecaps, and sometimes kidney disease as well. She had detected a pattern of inheritance called **autosomal linkage** (Fig 8.7). (Remember that autosomes are all the chromosomes except X and Y.)

The condition involving strange fingernails and kneecaps is called **nail patella syndrome** (NPS). (The patella is the kneecap.) The gene that causes this is found on chromosome 9. It codes for a protein that is involved in the development of limbs in the embryo. Most people with this syndrome do not need any medical treatment, but they are at a greater risk of developing kidney disease than other people. The allele that causes nail patella syndrome is dominant.

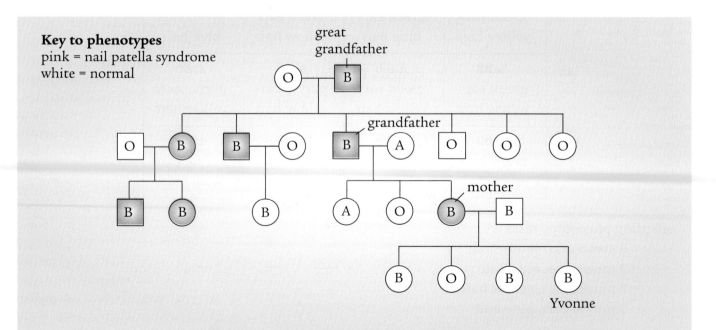

Fig 8.7 Autosomal linkage between nail patella syndrome and blood group B in Yvonne's family.

The gene locus that determines ABO blood group is also on chromosome 9, and it is very close to the nail patella syndrome gene. During meiosis, when the homologous chromosomes separate, the blood group and nail patella alleles stay together (Fig 8.8). Whatever the combination in which they were present in the parent cell, they stay in the same combination in the gametes that are formed.

So, when gametes are formed, the alleles do *not* assort independently. They stick together and stay in the same combinations as in the parent cell. This genetic diagram shows how blood group B and nail patella syndrome are inherited together.

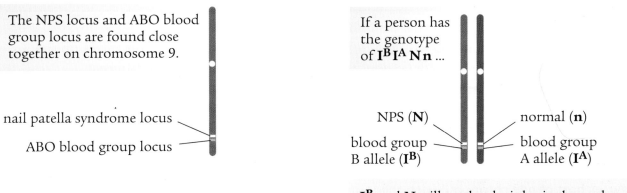

The NPS locus and ABO blood group locus are found close together on chromosome 9.

nail patella syndrome locus

ABO blood group locus

If a person has the genotype of $I^B I^A Nn$ ...

NPS (**N**)

blood group B allele (I^B)

normal (**n**)

blood group A allele (I^A)

I^B and **N** will tend to be inherited together and so will I^A and **n** – they are linked.

Fig 8.8 Linkage between the NPS and ABO group locus.

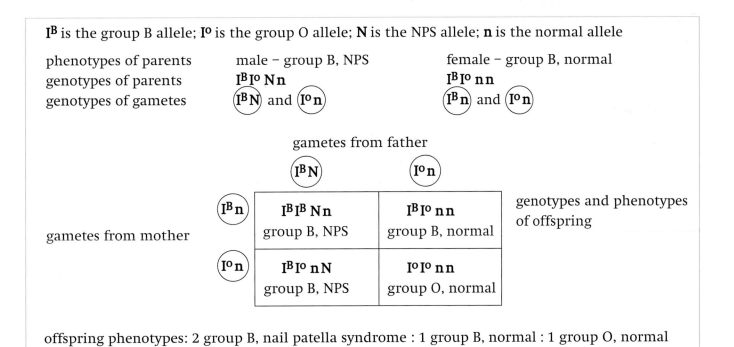

I^B is the group B allele; I^O is the group O allele; **N** is the NPS allele; **n** is the normal allele

phenotypes of parents	male – group B, NPS	female – group B, normal
genotypes of parents	$I^B I^O Nn$	$I^B I^O nn$
genotypes of gametes	$I^B N$ and $I^O n$	$I^B n$ and $I^O n$

gametes from father

		$I^B N$	$I^O n$	
gametes from mother	$I^B n$	$I^B I^B Nn$ group B, NPS	$I^B I^O nn$ group B, normal	genotypes and phenotypes of offspring
	$I^O n$	$I^B I^O nN$ group B, NPS	$I^O I^O nn$ group O, normal	

offspring phenotypes: 2 group B, nail patella syndrome : 1 group B, normal : 1 group O, normal

8.17 The Rainbow family only marry within the family. They have either yellow or blue hair, and either grey or orange toenails. The allele for yellow hair, **Y**, is dominant, as is the allele **G**, for grey toenails.

A man with the genotype **YyGg** has a partner who has the genotype **yygg**.

a Use a genetic diagram to find the possible genotypes and phenotypes of their offspring if these two genes are not on the same chromosome.

b Now construct another genetic diagram to find the possible genotypes and phenotypes of their offspring if the hair colour locus and the toenail colour locus are on the same chromosome.

Crossing over and recombination

The alleles of two different genes on the same chromosome are usually inherited together. But not quite always.

If you look back at page 109, you will see that the chromatids of homologous chromosomes can cross over, break and rejoin during meiosis I. This swaps part of one chromatid with the equivalent part of a chromatid on the other chromosome in the pair. This mixes up the alleles so that you can get different combinations in the gametes and therefore in the offspring.

For example, imagine a person who is blood group AB and who has nail patella syndrome. The possible gametes they could produce are shown in Fig 8.9 and in the genetic diagram on page 191.

Because the two loci are quite close together, crossing over between them doesn't happen very often. But sometimes it does, like this:

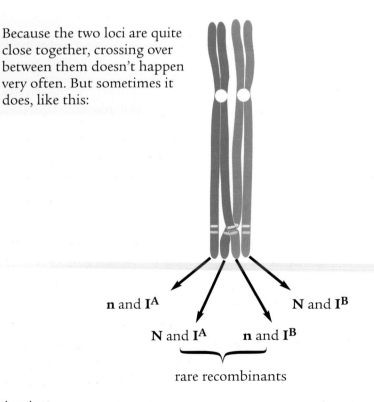

n and I^A **N** and I^B

N and I^A **n** and I^B

rare recombinants

Fig 8.9 Recombination.

We can show all of this in a partial genetic diagram.

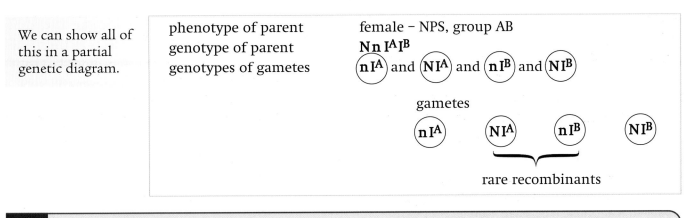

phenotype of parent
genotype of parent
genotypes of gametes

female – NPS, group AB

Nn I^{A}I^B

(nI^A) and (NI^A) and (nI^B) and (NI^B)

gametes

(nI^A)   (NI^A)   (nI^B)   (NI^B)

rare recombinants

SAQ

8.18   Look back at SAQ 8.17.
In part b, you worked out the possible phenotypes of this couple's offspring if the genes for hair colour and toenail colour were linked (i.e. on the same chromosome). Explain how crossing over could result in one of the children of this couple having a different combination of hair and toenail colour from either of their parents, even if the genes for these characteristics are linked.

Summary

❶ Dihybrid inheritance looks at the inheritance of genes at two different loci.

❷ Where the two genes are on different chromosomes, independent assortment means that either allele of one may be found with either allele of the other in a gamete. If two loci are being considered, and the genes at each locus have two alleles, nine different genotypes can occur in body cells, and four different genotypes in gametes.

❸ If the parents are heterozygous for both genes, the expected ratio of phenotypes in the offspring is 9:3:3:1. If one parent is homozygous recessive for both genes and the other is heterozygous, the expected ratio of phenotypes in the offspring is 1:1:1:1.

❹ If the two genes are on the same chromosome, they are said to be linked. This is known as autosomal linkage (to avoid confusion with sex

linkage). The combination of alleles that is present in the parent cells tends to be inherited by their children, so that particular characteristics tend to occur together within the family.

❺ If one parent is homozygous recessive for both genes and the other is heterozygous, and if the genes are linked, the ratio of phenotypes in the offspring is 1:1. The two phenotypes are the same as the parents' phenotypes.

❻ If crossing over occurs between two linked genes, new combinations of characteristics can be shown in the offspring.

❼ If one parent is homozygous recessive for both genes and the other is heterozygous, and if the genes are linked and there is some crossing over, then the ratio of phenotypes in the offspring will be not quite 1:1, because two new phenotypes may also be present.

Chromosome mutation during meiosis

Chromosome mutation can be defined as a random change in the number or structure of chromosomes. It is most likely to occur during meiosis, when it is easy for things to go wrong as the paired chromosomes line up on the crowded equator at metaphase and are pulled apart in anaphase (see page 105). Errors can result in the chromosomes not being shared equally between the daughter cells.

Klinefelter's and Turner's syndromes

You may remember that Klinefelter's syndrome and Turner's syndrome are caused by having an unusual combination of X and Y chromosomes. Fig 8.10 shows how these are caused. Both of them are the result of **non-disjunction** – a process in which faulty cell division means that one of the daughter cells gets two copies of a chromosome while the other gets none.

In the case of Klinefelter's syndrome, the mutation happens during oogenesis in the female parent. The two X chromosomes fail to separate as they should. One daughter cell gets both of them while the other gets none. This results in an oocyte with the genotype XX (it should really be X). It has 24 chromosomes instead of 23. When this oocyte is fertilised by a sperm carrying a Y chromosome, a zygote is produced with the genotype XXY. The number of chromosomes in the zygote is 47, that is, 2n + 1.

Turner's syndrome is caused if a faulty oocyte, with no X chromosomes, is fertilised by a sperm carrying an X chromosome. The resulting zygote has the genotype XO. It has 45 chromosomes instead of 46.

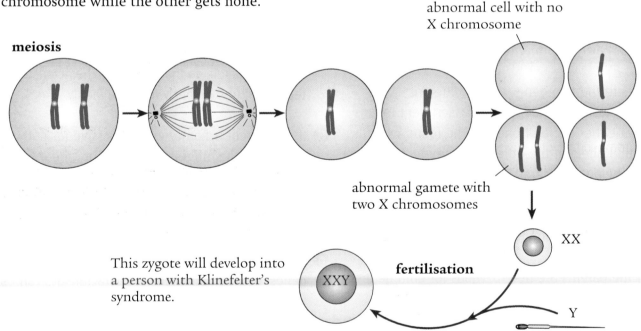

Fig 8.10 Non-disjunction of X chromosomes during oogenesis.

SAQ

8.19 Copy Fig 8.10 and complete it to show how Turner's syndrome can also arise from the non-disjunction shown in the diagram.

Down's syndrome

Non-disjunction may also affect chromosome 21, the shortest of all the autosomes. Sometimes both chromosome 21s go into one cell and neither into another. If this happens in an ovary, it results in an oocyte with either no chromosome 21 or with two copies instead of one. Oocytes with no chromosome 21 die, but those with two copies survive and may be fertilised. The resulting zygote has three chromosome 21s. This condition is known as **trisomy 21**. The zygote will grow into a child with Down's syndrome.

About 4% of cases of Down's syndrome are caused in a different way. During meiosis, part of the long arm of chromosome 21 breaks off and attaches to another chromosome. This is called **translocation**.

It is not known why having three copies of this chromosome produces Down's syndrome – there are clearly some ways in which genes interact that we do not yet understand.

Down's syndrome occurs in around 1 in 700 births. Its frequency greatly increases with the age of the mother, a result of the higher chance of mutation occurring during the formation of oocytes in older ovaries. Paternal age can also be a factor. Children with Down's syndrome have characteristically open, slightly flattened faces, and their eyelids have a fold in them. They are usually exceptionally happy and friendly people, though there are varying degrees of mental retardation. Indeed, some of the characteristics seen in Down's syndrome are very like the symptoms of Alzheimer's disease, but the reasons for this are not yet known. There are usually some health problems such as heart defects or muscle weakness, but these can often be kept well under control with appropriate medical treatment. Nevertheless, most people with Down's syndrome have a relatively short life expectancy.

Summary

1. During meiosis, it sometimes happens that both chromosomes of a homologous pair go into one daughter cell while the other daughter cell gets neither. This is known as non-disjunction.

2. Klinefelter's syndrome and Turner's syndrome are caused by non-disjunction of the sex chromosomes during meiosis in the ovary. The resulting genotypes are XXY and XO, respectively.

3. Most cases of Down's syndrome are caused by non-disjunction of chromosome 21. People with Down's usually have three chromosome 21s. It may also be caused by the long arm of chromosome 21 breaking off and re-attaching to another chromosome.

CHAPTER 9

Genetics and medicine

In July 2004, five-year-old Ben Hammond (not his real name) became the first person in the UK to receive a transplant from a brother who had been especially chosen to be a perfect donor for him. Ben has a rare blood disorder called Diamond-Blackfan anaemia. People with this illness have bone marrow that does not make red blood cells properly. They must have blood transfusions once every three weeks, and also painful injections into the abdomen three times each week. The only cure is a transplant of stem cells.

These stem cells needed to be an identical match for Ben's own cells, if his immune system was not to attack and destroy them. No donor could be found. So in 2001 Ben's parents asked the Human Fertilisation and Embryo Authority (HFEA) if they could use IVF to produce several embryos and then screen them to find one with a close tissue match for Ben. That embryo would then be implanted in his mother's uterus. When the baby was born, stem cells taken from the umbilical cord could be transplanted into Ben and hopefully cure his illness.

But the HFEA in Britain refused permission for this. Its stance was that it is fine to screen embryos to check that they do not have an inherited disease, because this would be for the benefit of the person who grew from that embryo. But it is not acceptable for the screening to be for the benefit of a different person.

In 2001, the HFEA changed its position, and made an exception to its ruling. If the embryos were being screened anyway for an inherited disease, then it would be acceptable to screen for a tissue match with an ill brother or sister at the same time. But this ruling was challenged in the High Court by the pro-life group CORE.

Refused permission in Britain, Ben's parents went to the USA where embryo selection is legal. Cord blood was collected from the resulting baby, Damon, at birth and was kept for a few months to check that Damon did not also have the disease before Ben was eventually given his transplant. And then in 2004 the HFEA changed its policy again. It is now allowable to screen and select embryos for a tissue match with a sibling – but only after all other possible treatments have been ruled out.

As the possibilities opened up by gene technology increase, so do the ethical dilemmas. In the UK, as the difficulties of matching technology, legality and ethical concerns became clear, the HFEA was set up specifically to tackle these issues. The case study opposite shows just how difficult it is proving for ethics and the law to hit the right balance between allowing new technologies to continue to push forward the boundaries and keeping them within limits that are acceptable to our society and in law.

The natural reaction of many people is that these new technologies are 'dangerous' because they 'work against nature'. Genetic engineering, including **genetic screening** of embryos, is often felt to be a threat to ourselves and to our environment. Some of these concerns are well-founded and deserve thorough debate, but there is also a great deal of ignorance of the science behind these new technologies, and therefore a danger that decisions might be made based on an incorrect assessment of the true facts. It is hoped that the HFEA, with members who between them have a good understanding of the science and an ability to see the ethical issues from the point of view of non-scientists, can bridge this gap between the point of view of the scientists and that of the general public.

In this chapter, we will look at some examples of the ways in which genetic engineering can be of direct benefit to human health, and some of the ethical issues associated with them. The medical and technical advances in this field are moving fast, and by the time you read this there will doubtless be other issues that require difficult ethical decisions to be made.

Using transgenic organisms

A transgenic organism can be defined as one to which DNA from an organism of another species has been added. For example, a human gene that encodes an enzyme called antitrypsin, an important treatment for cystic fibrosis, has been transferred to sheep which now produce milk

containing this enzyme. However, most of the transgenic organisms that have so far been produced are bacteria. For example, the bacterium *Escherichia coli* has been genetically engineered to produce **human growth hormone, hGH**.

Human growth hormone

Human growth hormone is a protein made up of 191 amino acids. It is secreted in short pulses from the anterior pituitary gland, especially during the first few hours of sleep and during exercise.

We produce hGH throughout life, not only when we are growing. The hormone does indeed stimulate growth in children, but it is also important in adults where it helps to maintain bone density and muscle strength.

Children who do not produce enough hGH, including those with Turner's syndrome (see page 192), are given regular injections of it to help them to grow to a normal height. It is also given to people with AIDS to help to slow down muscle wasting. Some drug companies advocate its use to prevent some of the gradual decrease in muscle and bone strength associated with ageing, but there is some controversy over its effectiveness and possible side effects. There is even more controversy over its use to enhance athletic performance, and it is hoped that regular testing of athletes in and out of competition will reduce or eliminate this use.

In the 1960s and 1970s, all of the growth hormone available came from the anterior pituitary gland of human corpses. Almost 80 corpses were required to provide just one year of treatment for a child. This source has a risk of transfer of infectious agents, especially the abnormal prion (a kind of protein) associated with Creutzfeldt-Jakob Disease (CJD).

In 1985, a new source of hGH appeared. Gene technology had inserted the gene for hGH into bacteria, and these transgenic organisms now synthesise it in such large quantities that there is more than enough for all people who require it. Now all of the hGH used is genetically engineered.

Isolating the gene

The way in which bacteria have been engineered to make hGH is typical of the techniques used for producing transgenic organisms.

First, the human gene for making hGH was found and isolated. This was done by first finding the messenger RNA that had been made by transcription of the gene. It is sometimes easier to do this than to find the right piece of DNA, because a cell only contains two copies of the DNA but may contain large numbers of molecules of mRNA that has been transcribed from it. This is especially true if cells can be used which are known to synthesise and secrete hGH.

Next, an enzyme obtained from viruses called **reverse transcriptase** is used to make a DNA copy of the mRNA. This is called **copy DNA** or **cDNA** (Fig 9.1). Many molecules of cDNA are made.

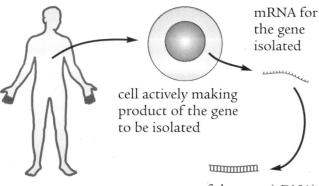

cell actively making product of the gene to be isolated

mRNA for the gene isolated

copy of the gene (cDNA)

Fig 9.1 Isolating and making a copy of a gene.

Making a recombinant plasmid

The next stage involves a **plasmid** – a small circle of DNA found in bacteria such as *E. coli*. The plasmid is used to transfer the hGH gene into a bacterium – it acts as a **vector**.

Many plasmids contain genes that confer resistance against antibiotics, and this fact is made use of at a later stage of the process, as we will see. One plasmid that is often used as a vector is called pBR322. This plasmid contains resistance genes for the antibiotics tetracycline and ampicillin (Fig 9.2).

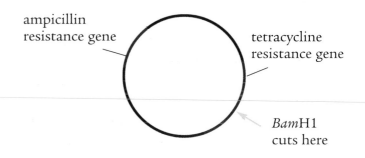

ampicillin resistance gene

tetracycline resistance gene

*Bam*H1 cuts here

Fig 9.2 Plasmid pBR322.

The plasmids are cut open using a **restriction enzyme**. This is a type of enzyme that helps bacteria to avoid infection by viruses, by cutting up viral DNA. There are many different restriction enzymes, each of which cuts DNA at a very specific target site. Fig. 9.3 shows the target site at which a restriction enzyme called *Bam*H1 cuts. This enzyme recognises the base sequence GGATTC, which occurs in the middle of the tetracycline resistance gene in the plasmid pBR322.

You can see that the enzyme cuts the two strands of the DNA at slightly offset positions. This means that short lengths of DNA are left with their bases exposed. These unpaired lengths are called 'sticky ends'. They are, of

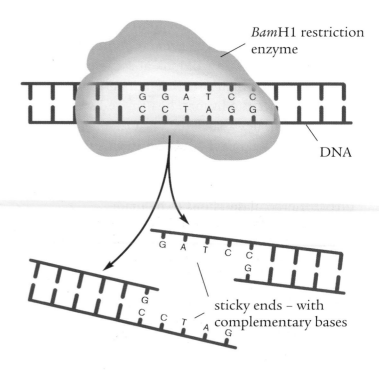

*Bam*H1 restriction enzyme

DNA

sticky ends – with complementary bases

Fig 9.3 Cutting DNA with a restriction enzyme.

course, complementary to each other. You can also see that the base sequence on one strand is the same as the base sequence on the other read backwards. The two base sequences are said to be **palindromic**.

The same restriction enzyme, *Bam*H1, is then used to cut the cDNA containing the human hGH gene. Because this enzyme always cuts at a GGATTC base sequence, the sticky ends that it leaves are exactly the same as those formed when it cut the plasmid. The cDNA and the plasmids are now mixed together, which provides the opportunity for the sticky ends of one to pair up with the sticky ends of the other, by complementary base pairing. An enzyme called **DNA ligase** is added, and this links up the sugar-phosphate backbones of the newly paired sections, forming a complete circular plasmid that contains the hGH gene (Fig 9.4).

However, this won't happen to *all* of the plasmids. Some of them will just stick themselves together again, rejoining their own sticky ends. So these plasmids won't contain the hGH gene.

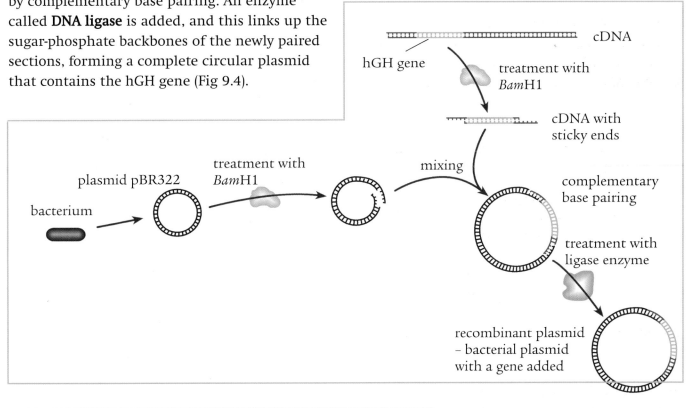

In the diagram above only one recombinant plasmid is shown, for simplicity. In reality lots of different ones are produced, depending on the number of points at which the restriction enzyme cuts the plasmid and cDNA.

Fig 9.4 Making a recombinant plasmid.

Inserting the gene into bacteria

The recombinant plasmids are now used as vectors to carry the hGH gene into the cells of bacteria. They are mixed with *E. coli* in a solution containing calcium ions. The calcium ions affect the wall and membrane of the bacteria, enabling them to take up the plasmids (Fig 9.5).

The hGH gene is inserted into the tetracycline resistance gene of plasmid pBR322, inactivating the tetracycline resistance gene.

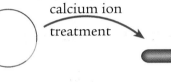

calcium ion treatment

One bacterium with the plasmid carrying the hGH gene is selected.

Fig 9.5 Inserting a gene into a bacterium.

Now the fact that pBR322 contains antibiotic resistance genes becomes very useful indeed. It is likely that only a few of the bacteria have actually taken up the recombinant plasmid. These few have to be identified and separated from the majority that have not.

The plasmid contains a gene that makes the bacteria resistant to the antibiotic ampicillin. So any bacteria that have taken up the plasmid will be resistant to this antibiotic.

However, there is still a possibility that the plasmid a bacterium has taken up is one that did not pick up the hGH gene, and had just re-stuck its own sticky ends together. But these, too, can be identified. The *Bam*H1 cutting site is right in the middle of a gene for resistance to the antibiotic tetracycline. If the hGH gene was successfully inserted, it will have split this tetracycline resistance gene in two, inactivating it. So any bacteria that have taken up the

recombinant plasmids, as opposed to ones that didn't pick up the hGH gene, will not be resistant to tetracycline.

The bacteria are therefore first grown on agar plates containing ampicillin. All the ones that have not taken up the plasmid are unable to grow. Small samples from some of the surviving colonies are then transferred onto plates containing tetracycline, in a way that keeps the colonies in exactly the same positions on the new plate. This is called **replica plating** (Fig 9.6). The ones that have taken up the recombinant plasmid won't be able to grow, whilst those that have taken up plasmids that don't contain the hGH gene will grow.

1 A sample of bacteria, which have been treated with transgenic plasmids, is spread on the master plate containing ampicillin. Ampicillin resistant bacteria grow.

sterile cloth which bacteria can stick to

2 touch master plate bacterial colonies

3 touch the tetracycline plate

4 incubate

5 Colonies that grow on the master plate but not on the tetracycline replica plate have definitely taken up the transgenic plasmid.

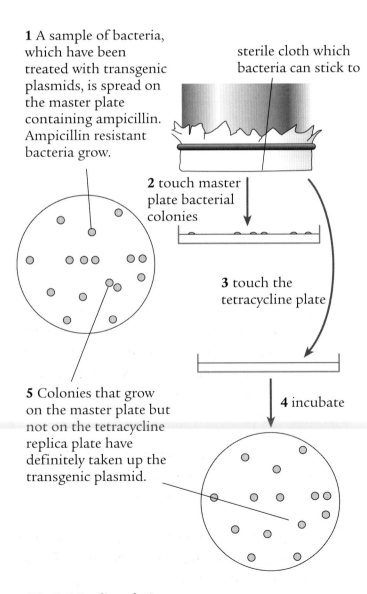

Fig 9.6 Replica plating.

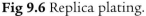

Any colonies of bacteria that grow on the ampicillin-containing plates, but that don't grow on the tetracycline-containing plates, are almost certain to have taken up the recombinant plasmids and therefore to contain the hGH gene.

Producing recombinant hGH

The chosen bacteria are cultured and allowed to multiply, therefore making many copies of themselves and the recombinant plasmid inside them. This **clones** the gene (Fig 9.7).

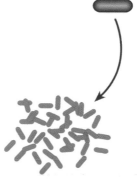

The selected bacterium containing hGH is grown. All the cells will contain the same recombinant plasmid carrying hGH.

Fig 9.7 Cloning.

Transgenic *E. coli* are now cultured in large fermenters on a commercial scale. The bacteria follow the code on the human DNA that they contain, synthesising hGH. The hGH is extracted from the bacterial culture and purified.

SAQ

9.1 Explain why each of the following is done when engineering bacteria to produce hGH.
   a Messenger RNA, rather than DNA, is isolated from human cells.
   b The same restriction enzyme is used to cut the human DNA and the bacterial plasmid.
   c Sticky ends are left on the plasmid and on the DNA.
   d Bacteria that have taken up the plasmid are cloned.

Summary

1 Human growth hormone is synthesised by bacteria (*E. coli*) into which the human gene for this protein has been added. These bacteria are said to be transgenic organisms, because a gene from another species (in this case, humans) has been inserted into them.

2 To do this, messenger RNA for hGH was isolated. Reverse transcriptase made a DNA copy of this mRNA. This DNA is called cDNA.

3 The restriction enzyme *Bam*H1 was then used to cut the cDNA and also the plasmid. This left the same sticky ends on both.

4 The plasmids and cDNA were then mixed, so that some of their sticky ends could pair up with each other. DNA ligase was used to link the sugar-phosphate backbones.

5 The plasmids were inserted into *E. coli*. The bacteria were cloned, and tested so that those into which the hGH gene had been successfully inserted could be isolated.

6 These genetically engineered bacteria are cultured on a large scale, and the hGH that they make is purified and sold.

Gene therapy

As you saw in Chapter 8, there are many diseases that are caused by faulty alleles of genes. When genetic engineering really began to get going in the 1990s, it was envisaged that it would not be long before gene technology could cure these diseases by inserting 'normal' genes into the cells. But this has proved to be far more difficult than was originally thought.

Gene technology, and the success of the Human Genome Project in mapping the human chromosomes, has given us the opportunity to identify precisely many more genes responsible for genetic diseases. The problems for gene therapy lie in getting normal versions of these genes into a person's cells and making them work properly when they get there.

SCID

SCID stands for severe combined immunodeficiency disease. There are several different causes of this rare inherited disease. In some cases, it is caused by a faulty allele of a gene coding for an enzyme called **adenosine deaminase** or **ADA**. This enzyme is essential for proper working of the immune system. Without it, the immune system is unable to fight off infections, and without treatment a child born with this disease will almost certainly die in infancy or early childhood.

In 1990, a four-year-old girl from Ohio, in the USA, became the first patient to be successfully treated using gene therapy. Some of her T lymphocytes were removed from her body, and copies of the normal ADA allele inserted into them, using a retrovirus (see *Human Biology for AS*, page 221) as vector. They were then replaced in her body. The treatment worked. She still needs to have regular transfusions of these genetically engineered cells every few months, but otherwise has been able to lead a reasonably normal life.

Another form of SCID is caused by a gene on the X chromosome that codes for the production of a protein called **interleukin 2**, also essential for the functioning of the immune system. This disease is sex-linked, occurring only in boys. Gene therapy trials are being carried out to try to insert a correct version of the gene into boys with the faulty gene.

In 2002, however, the hopes for this treatment suffered a major setback. During trials in France, a boy in whom the interleukin gene had successfully been inserted developed leukaemia (a cancer involving uncontrolled division of cells that produce leucocytes) and died. The trial was immediately halted, as were three trials in the USA that were using similar techniques. A second boy in the French trial also developed leukaemia in 2003, resulting in suspension of 30 more trials in the USA.

The trouble is that, when the vector inserts the gene into the DNA in the human cells, you cannot control exactly where it goes. It seems that in these cases the virus had inserted the interleukin gene right next to one that controls cell division. Even if this happened in only one of the treated leucocytes, it might be enough to cause leukaemia, because that one cell could proliferate.

However, many researchers think that these two cases should not halt research into the use of gene therapy as a treatment for SCID. They point out that, without gene therapy, boys with SCID will die anyway. Gene therapy, despite the risk of developing leukaemia, is their best hope of a relatively normal life.

SAQ

9.2a   Explain what is meant by:
i   a retrovirus;
ii   a vector.
b   Suggest why a retrovirus was chosen as a vector in gene therapy for SCID.

Cystic fibrosis

The success with the SCID treatment raised everyone's hopes. SCID is a rare disease, but there are many other genetic diseases that affect a much larger number of people. Cystic fibrosis was an obvious candidate for gene therapy.

We have seen that cystic fibrosis is caused by a faulty allele of the CFTR gene (see page 172). This allele is recessive, so if the normal dominant allele could be inserted into cells in the lungs, the correct CFTR should be made. In theory, there is no reason why this should not happen. In practice, there have been major problems in getting the gene into the cells.

In the UK, trials began in 1993. The normal allele was inserted into liposomes (tiny balls of lipid molecules) which were then sprayed as an aerosol into the noses of nine volunteers. This succeeded in introducing the gene into a few cells lining the nose, but the effect only lasted for a week.

Researchers in the USA tried a different vector. In a trial involving several people with cystic fibrosis, they introduced the gene into normally harmless viruses and then used these to carry the gene into the passages of the gas exchange system. The gene did indeed enter some cells there, but some of the volunteers experienced unpleasant side effects as a result of infection by the virus. As a result, the trials were stopped.

To be used as a treatment, the gene really needs to get into many cells throughout the respiratory system, including the ones that divide to form new surface cells. This has so far not been achieved.

Duchenne muscular dystrophy

Duchenne muscular dystrophy (Fig 9.8) is a genetic disease caused by a faulty allele of a gene encoding a protein called **dystrophin** (see the Just for Interest on page 8). The gene is on the X chromosome, so this is a sex-linked disease that occurs only in boys. In the UK, one in every 3500 boys born has this illness.

Like the faulty CFTR gene, the faulty dystrophin allele is recessive. If a copy of the correct allele could be inserted into muscle cells, then they should make proper dystrophin and prevent the disease from developing. But the same problem blocks the way – how can the gene be put into all the muscle cells in the body?

Trials with mice in 2004 showed a possible solution. Researchers used a virus that homes in on striated muscle cells rather than any other cells in the body, and does not cause an immune response. They injected this into the bodies of mice with muscular dystrophy, together with a growth factor called VEGF, which helps the virus to get into the muscle cells. They found that the gene had been successfully inserted into striated muscle cells all over the body – muscles in the limbs, the breathing muscles and the heart muscle.

Before a possible new treatment such as this is used in humans, many trials must be undertaken, first in other animals and then in humans.

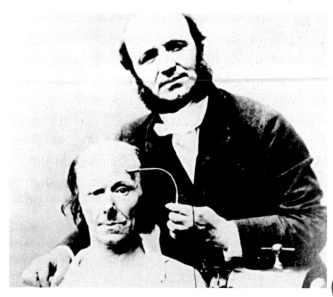

Fig 9.8 Guillaume Duchenne, the French doctor, who did important work on Duchenne muscular dystrophy, photographed in 1861. He is holding an electrode to a patient's head for the electric therapy he pioneered. He also developed a method of removing small pieces of muscle (a biopsy) for microscopic examination.

ACTIVITY 9.1

The future of gene therapy

The future of gene therapy through treatment of body cells is not easily predictable. In the first instance there are the scientific problems to overcome and in the second, there are the decisions to be made by society about what should be allowed and what should not be allowed.

The scientific literature now contains a wide range of examples of gene therapies for body cells which have either been suggested or are being researched.

Choose one example (excluding therapies involving modification of a developing human embryo). Research that example using the internet, science journals and any other appropriate sources of information and present a concise, illustrated description of the technique, assuming that it could be applied to humans.

Consider the ethical implications of this technique and put the case both for and against it.

Make a brief presentation to the class.

Discuss the future potential for gene therapy in the light of the information presented.

Summary

1. Gene therapy is the treatment of a person with a genetic disease by correcting the genetic problem. This currently involves attempting to insert a copy of the 'normal' allele of the gene into their cells.

2. In one method, some cells are taken from a tissue in which the gene is expressed. These are cultured outside the body, and a copy of the 'correct' allele of the gene inserted into them using a vector. These genetically engineered cells are then replaced in the person's body. This has been done successfully to treat SCID. However, a major setback has been the development of leukaemia in some patients.

3. An alternative approach is to use a vector containing the 'correct' allele to place the gene into cells within the body. This has been attempted with the CFTR gene, but viral vectors have sometimes caused illness themselves.

Genetic screening

In 1989, the first 'designer baby' was created. Officially known as pre-implantation genetic diagnosis (PGD), the technique involved mixing the father's sperm with the mother's oocytes in a dish – that is, a 'normal' IVF procedure. It was the next step that was new.

At the eight-cell stage, one of the cells from the tiny embryo was removed. The DNA in the cell was analysed, and used to predict whether or not the embryo would have a genetic disease for which both parents were carriers. An embryo that was not carrying the allele that would cause the disease was chosen for implantation, while embryos which did have this allele were discarded.

Since then, over 1000 babies have been born following this technique. It has been used to avoid pregnancies where the baby would have Duchenne muscular dystrophy, thalassaemia, haemophilia, Huntington's disease and others. In 2004, it was first used in the UK to produce a baby that was a tissue match with an elder sibling, with a view to using cells from the umbilical cord as a transplant into the sick child.

A study published in 2004 showed that this technique was safe for the mother and the child. Removing one cell at the eight-cell stage did not appear to harm the embryo at all. The study compared the percentage of problems amongst 754 children born as a result of this technique with others conceived and implanted 'naturally', and found no significant difference between them.

Genetic screening is the analysis of a person's DNA to check for the presence of a particular allele. This can be done in adults, in a foetus or embryo in the uterus (see *Human Biology for AS*, pages 203–204) or – as in the case study above – in a newly formed embryo produced by in vitro fertilisation. Perhaps more than any other medical technique, genetic screening has generated some major ethical issues about which there is much debate.

For some time, genetic testing of embryos has been leaving prospective parents with very difficult choices to make if the embryo is found to have a genetic disease such as Down's syndrome or cystic fibrosis (see *Human Biology for AS*, pages 202–205). The decision about whether or not to have a termination is very difficult to make. Now, though, advances in medical technology have provided us with even more ethical issues to consider.

Somatic and germ cell gene therapy

As we have seen (see page 200), gene therapy involves introducing a 'correct' allele into a person's cells as a treatment for a genetic disease. So far, all attempts to do this in humans have involved placing the allele in body cells, otherwise known as **somatic cells**. However, another possibility would be to insert the allele into **germ cells** – that is, cells that are involved in sexual reproduction – gametes or an early embryo. For example, in theory a woman with cystic fibrosis could opt to try to conceive a baby using IVF. Eggs (secondary oocytes) would be harvested from her in the normal way. Then the 'correct' allele of the CFTR gene could be injected into an egg, and then this egg could be fertilised by a sperm to produce a zygote.

At present, this is illegal in humans. However, it has been successfully done in other animals, although it looks as though there is a high chance of offspring produced in this way having other, unpredicted, diseases.

The problem that many people see with germ cell therapy is that *all* the cells of the child are produced from this genetically engineered zygote, and therefore will all carry the gene that has been inserted. When the child grows up and produces eggs or sperm, these gametes will also contain the allele and therefore it will be passed on to their children. We say that the allele is in the **germ line**, being passed on from generation to generation.

The ethics of genetic screening

In 2004, the law allowed an embryo to be chosen that did not have an allele for a genetic disease, and also one that *did* have a tissue type that would allow a successful transplant into a sick elder brother or sister. But it did not allow the addition of an allele to an egg, sperm or zygote. A line has to be drawn somewhere, but feelings can run high about this and many people believe that the law is allowing too much while others think that it should allow more.

There is still controversy over other, long-established outcomes of genetic screening. For example, a foetus can now be screened for a genetic disease while in the uterus, using amniocentesis or chorionic villus sampling. The parents may then decide to have the pregnancy terminated if the embryo is found to have a genetic disease. However, there have been cases where this decision has been made even though the 'defect' has been a relatively minor one, such that the child could be expected to lead a fairly normal life.

ACTIVITY 9.2

Debating the ethics of genetic screening and gene therapy

1 Write three statements about the ethics of genetic screening and gene therapy. For example:

'I think selecting an embryo that doesn't have a genetic disease is OK.'

One should be a statement with which you definitely agree, another should be one about which you are uncertain, and the third should be a statement with which you definitely disagree. Write each statement on a separate piece of card.

2 Join two or three others, and discuss all of your statements. Organise the cards into three heaps, depending on whether you all agree, all disagree, or have differing opinions.

3 Now collate all the decisions within the class. Are there any statements with which you all agree or all disagree?

4 Finally, debate the issues in the whole class. You could also consider the question of who should make these decisions. Should it be individual people, doctors, religious groups, judges, Parliament, the government or an organisation such as the Human Fertilisation and Embryo Authority?

Allele frequencies in the population

We have seen that the frequency of a recessive allele in the population can be calculated using the Hardy-Weinberg equations (see page 175). If everyone is free to marry anyone else, and if the likelihood of each person reproducing is the same, then we would expect these allele frequencies to remain the same in each generation.

However, in humans this is not always the case. Medical intervention can greatly affect selection pressures. For example, medical assistance may help people with genetic diseases to live longer with their illness than would have happened in the past, and so be able to reproduce. This could rapidly increase the frequency of that allele in the population.

On the other side of the coin, genetic screening and choice of embryos produced by IVF could decrease the frequency of faulty alleles, because fewer babies would be born with that condition and therefore there would be less chance of the allele being passed on to future generations.

Genetic engineering of somatic cells, of course, does not directly affect allele frequencies because the engineered cells are not passed on to the next generation.

ACTIVITY 9.3

The effect of selection on allele frequency

In this activity, you will use beads to represent two different alleles in a population. Each group will exert a selection pressure of a different value on their population, and then pool results for analysis.

1 You will need a large pot containing around 100 beads of one colour and 100 beads identical with the first ones except that they are a different colour. Each bead represents an allele of the same gene. You also need to draw a table with three columns – AA, Aa and aa. Decide which colour beads represent each allele.

2 First, use the Hardy-Weinberg equations to predict the frequencies of each genotype that you would expect in a population where alleles A and a are present in equal numbers.

3 Now you will try producing the 'next generation' without exerting any selection. Without looking, take two beads at random from the container. Score the genotype in the table. Keep doing this until all the beads are used up.

4 Do your results match your prediction? If not, suggest reasons for this.

5 Now you will produce another generation, but this time you will exert a selection pressure against the homozygous offspring. Organise groups so that each one tests a different selection pressure.

6 Take beads at random as before, scoring their frequencies in a results chart. However, this time discard a proportion of the homozygous recessive offspring. If you are exerting a 100% selection pressure, discard every one. If you are exerting a 50% selection pressure, discard every second one. If you are exerting a 25% pressure, discard every fourth one, and so on.

7 Continue this for several more generations, remembering not to return the discarded homozygotes to the pot.

8 Collect and collate class results. Draw graphs to display them clearly.

9 Discuss the results you have obtained.

9.3 In the fruitfly, *Drosophila*, flies may have normal brown bodies or darker ebony bodies. Ebony body is caused by a recessive allele.

An investigation was carried out to find the effect of 80% selection against the ebony-bodied flies over 20 generations. The results are shown in the graph.

a Describe the effect of selection on the frequency of:

i ebony-bodied flies;

ii the allele for ebony body.

b If this selection continued, would the allele ever disappear completely from the population? Explain your answer.

c This investigation was carried out with fruitflies. Write one or two paragraphs explaining how its results provide insights into the frquency of the sickle cell allele in human populations.

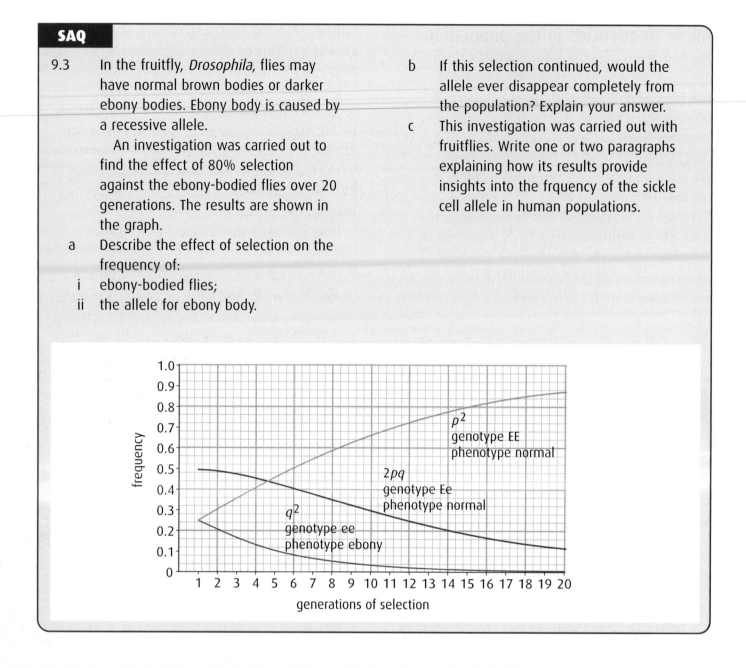

ebony body

ACTIVITY 9.4

The public perception of genetic engineering

Construct a short questionnaire that you can use to find out how much students in your college or school understand about genetic engineering.

Your questions should be short and easy to understand. Think about how you will analyse the answers as you write the questions.

What are the main conclusions? What were the problems experienced in the design and in the implementation of the questionnaire?

Summary

1. Genetic screening involves testing an embryo or adult for a particular allele of a gene.

2. If screening is done on a foetus in the uterus, the mother may ask for a termination if the baby will have a genetic disease.

3. If the test is done on an embryo produced by IVF, the results can be used to ensure that the embryo chosen for implantation does not carry the faulty allele.

4. It is also legal to check whether an embryo produced by IVF is a good tissue match for a sick sibling, as long as the embryo would have been checked anyway for the presence of a faulty allele that might have affected the future of the child.

5. In theory, it would be possible to choose embryos for characteristics other than genetic diseases – for example, with a particular hair colour. This is not allowed.

6. It is also theoretically possible to change the genotype of an embryo produced by IVF by inserting DNA into it. This is not allowed.

7. Genetic screening and genetic engineering could alter the frequency of a particular allele in a population. For example, parents who are both carriers for cystic fibrosis could have their children by IVF, each time rejecting any embryos which have two copies of the faulty allele. If this happened on a wide scale it would reduce the frequency of the allele in the population.

Transplant surgery

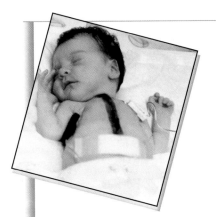

In 1984, a tiny baby was born in a hospital in California. She had a major defect in her heart, and everyone knew that she would not live unless she could have a heart transplant. Her parents, hoping for a miracle, named her Fay.

But how do you find a suitable heart for a very small baby? There is a shortage of hearts available for transplant anyway, and the chance of finding one that would fit in Fay's tiny body was practically zero.

Surgeons at the hospital decided to try out an audacious new technique. They took a heart from a baboon and transplanted it into Fay. The hope was that the heart would keep Fay alive until a human heart could be found for her. The medical team even talked about her living long enough to go to university. The hope was short-lived. Despite treatment to suppress the activity of Fay's immune system, her body rejected the baboon heart. She died within weeks of her birth.

CASE STUDY

Today, transplant surgery is almost taken for granted. Many people owe their lives to a kidney transplant or a heart transplant. But a shortage of donors still means that people in need of transplant surgery often have to wait many years before a suitable organ becomes available, and many die before the transplant can be done.

Tissue typing

For a transplant to be successful, it is important that the donor and the recipient have similar tissue types. If so, then the recipient's immune system is less likely to mount an all-out attack on the transplanted organ. Rejection is by far the commonest factor that limits the success of organ transplant.

You have already seen (see *Human Biology for AS*, page 18) that before blood transfusion is carried out care must be taken to use blood of a group that will be accepted by the recipient's body. This involves two antigens, A and B, which may be found in the red cell membranes. However, other body cells also have antigens in their surfaces. The most important ones are known as the human leucocyte antigen system, or **HLA**. These antigens are found in the cell surface membranes of all body cells except red blood cells.

The HLA antigens are encoded by a group of six gene loci, all found very close to one another on chromosome 6. Because they are so close, they all tend to be inherited together – that is, they are linked. These genes are known as the **major histocompatibility complex, MHC**. The block of six gene loci is known as a **haplotype**.

There are many different alleles of each of these six genes. The immune system responds to cells with a different set of HLA antigens to those of 'their own' body just as it would respond to the invasion of any antigen. T lymphocytes attack the invading cells, producing cytokines to encourage other leucocytes to attack and destroy them. This is what happens when a transplanted organ is rejected.

So, for a good chance of a transplant being successful, the donated organ must have an identical or at least very similar set of HLA antigens to the recipient. Checking this is called **tissue typing**.

The loci are given letters to identify them, from A to F. Each gene has several different alleles. A has 59 alleles, B 27, C 24, D 10, E 9 and F 6. This makes the possible different combinations absolutely huge ($59 \times 27 \times 24 \times 10 \times 9 \times 6 = 20\,645\,280$). However, because some of the alleles are quite rare, the chance of finding a perfect match with an unrelated person is not as small as one in $20\,645\,280$, but nearer to one in $200\,000$. This is still very, very small.

But within a family the chance of a perfect match is much, much greater, because the whole set of genes is inherited together. For example, imagine that a mother and father have these haplotypes for the MHC complex:

mother	father
A52 B20 C13 D7 E8 F2	A33 B4 C19 D9 E5 F1
A23 B17 C19 D4 E9 F5	A7 B21 C9 D10 E8 F3

gametes:

A52 B20 C13 D7 E8 F2	A33 B4 C19 D9 E5 F1
and	and
A23 B17 C19 D4 E9 F5	A7 B21 C9 D10 E8 F3

offspring:

A52 B20 C13 D7 E8 F2
A33 B4 C19 D9 E5 F1
and
A52 B20 C13 D7 E8 F2
A7 B21 C9 D10 E8 F3
and
A23 B17 C19 D4 E9 F5
A33 B4 C19 D9 E5 F1
and
A23 B17 C19 D4 E9 F5
A7 B21 C9 D10 E8 F3

You can see that it is not possible for a child to have the same haplotype as either of their parents, if both parents are heterozygous for their haplotypes. But it is possible for two of the children to have the same haplotype. There are four different haplotypes that the children may have, so the chance of any one child having a particular haplotype is one in four (that is, 0.25 or 25%). If a second child is born, the chance is one in four that he will have the same haplotype as the first child. Using a donor from within the family therefore gives a much better chance of finding a tissue match than with an unrelated donor. But this is not usually possible. Many people have to wait months if not years before a kidney with a similar tissue type to their own is found.

The species concept

The case study on page 207 describes the first example of a **xenotransplant** – that is, a transplant from one species into another. Xenotransplants have been discussed many times since then, and there is even a suggestion that pigs could be genetically engineered so that their organs could be used for transplantation into humans. Pigs are of particular interest because their organs are a similar size to those of humans. Already several people with severe burns have been given skin grafts using pig cells and some people with diabetes have had cells from a pig's islets of Langerhans transplanted into their livers. Nevertheless, the risks from such transplants – not only of rejection, but also of the transfer of viral or other diseases from pigs to humans – are as yet seen as far too high for it to be used other than in exceptional cases. There are also major ethical and religious issues associated with transplants from pigs (see also page 212).

Pigs and humans are clearly different **species**, as are cats, giraffes and gorillas. In everyday life, most people have no difficulty in understanding what a species is. In biology, however, there has to be a universal understanding of the meaning of the term. For example, are horses and zebras different species, or is a zebra just a stripey version of a horse? The answer is that they are different species, and the reason is that they do not normally breed together to produce fertile offspring. But carthorses and Shetland ponies do both belong to the horse species as (with a few technical difficulties) they are able to breed together to produce horses or ponies that are fertile and can have offspring of their own. We can define a species as a group of similar organisms that can successfully interbreed with each other, but that do not successfully interbreed with other organisms.

Though this definition works well with animals it does not work as well with other living organisms such as bacteria.

Linkage and the HLA system

We have seen that the genes coding for the HLA antigens are found on chromosome 6. There are other genes on this chromosome, too, and therefore their inheritance tends to show linkage with the HLA genes.

For example, a genetic disease of the connective tissues called ankylosing spondylitis is closely linked with an HLA allele known as HLA-B27. More than 90% of people with this illness also have this allele. Ankylosing spondylitis is a disease that gets progressively worse through life, as the joints in the spine and pelvis suffer from inflammation and eventually fuse together.

However, there are many more people who have HLA-B27 but don't have ankylosing spondylitis. About 5% of people in Britain have HLA-B27, while only 1% of these have the disease. We don't know why there are these differences.

Taxonomy

Placing an organism into a particular species is an example of classification, or **taxonomy**. Taxonomy can be defined as the naming and classification of organisms. Each species is given a two-word Latin name that is used by scientists all over the world.

For example, the Latin name for our species is *Homo sapiens*. The first name is the group of similar species – the **genus** – to which we belong. There are currently no other members of the genus *Homo* on Earth, but in the past there have been other species which we think should also be classified in this genus. They include *Homo habilis* and *Homo erectus*, whose fossil remains suggest they were sufficiently different from us that we would not be able to interbreed with them if we chanced to be on Earth at the same time.

Taxonomists classify organisms according to how closely related they are. The more closely related, the more genes we would expect them to have in common. Two organisms in the same species will have almost all of their genes in common, allowing them to interbreed successfully. Classifying two species into the same genus means that they are sufficiently genetically different to prevent them from interbreeding, but we still think that they are closely related, and have descended from a common ancestor (Fig 9.9).

Genera (the plural of genus) are grouped into families, then orders, then classes, then phyla (singular – phylum) and finally kingdoms. The full classification of ourselves is shown in Fig 9.10.

Classification of humans

subspecies	*Homo sapiens sapiens*
species	*Homo sapiens*
genus	Homo
family	Hominidae (humans)
order	Primates (apes, monkeys, lemurs)
class	Mammalia
phylum	Chordata
kingdom	Animalia

Another example

Aeshna grandis (The Brown Hawker dragonfly)
Aeshna
Aeshnidae
Odonata (dragonflies and damselflies)
Insecta
Arthropoda
Animalia

Fig 9.10 Groupings used in classification.

Many taxonomists classify us to one more level below that of species, the subspecies. They use the full name *Homo sapiens sapiens* for our subspecies, to distinguish this subspecies from *Homo sapiens neanderthalensis*, Neanderthal man. Neanderthal man lived around 100 000 years ago, and was very human in appearance, but generally more stocky and strongly built than ourselves (Fig 9.11). Neanderthals used a

These two dragonflies have a lot of features in common. However, they never interbreed – they are different species.

At some point in the past there was a common ancestor of both species. They both evolved from this ancestor, explaining why they have so many features in common.

Fig 9.9 Two species in the same genus.

wide range of tools, lived in caves or shelters made from tree branches and animal skins, and hunted wild animals such as woolly mammoths and wild deer for food. Burial sites have been found that suggest they followed religious or cultural practices, and lived together as communities. Some taxonomists classify them as a separate species from us, *Homo neanderthalensis.* No-one will ever know which is the correct classification according to the definition of a species given on page 209, as we will never know if they could interbreed with our species.

Models of a Neanderthal man (above) and woman holding a baby wrapped in animal skins (right). The model of the man is in the Field Museum, Chicago, and the model of the woman is in the Naturkundemuseum in Stuttgart, Germany.

The name *Homo erectus* means 'erect man'. This is an extinct species of hominid. We are not sure if it was an ancestor of *Homo sapiens* or just a relative. *Home erectus* lived from 1.8 million years to 200 000 years ago and was the first hominid to spread from Africa to Asia. We believe they used fire and were nomadic hunter-gatherers.

Fig 9.11 *Homo sapiens neanderthalensis* and *Homo erectus* reconstructions. We have good skeletal remains of Neanderthals, so our knowledge of their body form is sound, but we don't know details of hair growth or skin colour. We know far less about earlier human ancestors, such as *Homo erectus.* Therefore, reconstructions of extinct hominids have to be taken as being, in part, educated guesses.

Speciation

We can, of course, only guess whether or not we would have been able to breed with members of the genus *Homo* who lived long ago, and who we only meet as bones and fossils. It seems that each time new finds are made, the taxonomists change their ideas about our possible relationships. These questions also raise another one – how did our species first appear on Earth?

The appearance of a new species is called **speciation**. There are several different ways in which this can happen, some of which involve **geographical isolation**.

There are several different ideas about how our species evolved, but we don't yet know how it happened. One possibility is that *Homo sapiens* evolved when a splinter group of an ancestral species became separated from the rest and gradually became adapted to a different environment. Perhaps the ancestral species was adapted to living in dense tropical forest, while the splinter group became adapted to living in savannah (grassland).

Imagine, for example, a population of a human-like species living in Africa hundreds of thousands of years ago. They could all potentially interbreed with one another, although in practice it is likely that most of them only interbred with others of their close community. We can imagine that one adventurous group managed to cross a large river and develop a community some distance from the rest. Over time, the river became larger and almost impossible to cross, so that the splinter group was now completely isolated from the rest of their species.

After maybe thousands of years or perhaps less, different features gradually evolved in the two groups. On one side of the river, people lived in thick forest, and those who were best able to climb trees and get food in these conditions were the most likely to survive long enough to breed and pass their genes on to their children. On the other side, there were few trees and the splinter group lived in grassland, spending their time on the ground and hunting the large herds of grazing animals that they found there. In this habitat, people with different characteristics were most likely to survive. For example, those standing upright would be able to see better over tall grass and be more capable of long-distance walking.

Different selection pressures on the two geographically separated populations would have resulted in their genomes becoming different from each other. If, eventually, the river had become fordable and they met up again, they would no longer interbreed. The two groups, although no longer geographically isolated, would have become **genetically isolated**. A new species would have been formed.

Today, although we live in many different environments in every corner of the world, there is no chance that genetic isolation and speciation will happen again. We are all much too mobile for that. Even before travel by air, road and sea became possible, people had spread all over the world and no population was isolated from any other for long enough for their genes to diverge sufficiently to cause genetic isolation and therefore the emergence of a new species.

Genetically engineered organs

So where does all of this leave us regarding the use of other species as a source of transplant organs? Clearly if there are difficulties of organ rejection even if an organ from another member of our own species is transplanted, then the chance of rejection becomes even stronger if xenotransplantation is carried out. The only advantage of using such a source is that there are always plenty of organs available (Table 9.1).

There is, however, a possible way around this. There has been some success in using genetic engineering techniques to produce pigs whose cells are lacking the antigens which cause the strongest immune response in the recipient. If this could be done, then animals could be bred especially to serve as a source of organs for transplant into humans. However, this would be unacceptable to some people for ethical reasons, while others would not wish to be given organs from pigs for religious and cultural reasons.

Perhaps a more acceptable and potentially more successful method could involve the use of stem cells. It might be possible, for example, to take stem cells from the umbilical cord of every baby when it is born, and store these for future use. If the person needs a transplant later in life, these stem cells could be used to grow new tissues or organs that would be a perfect genetic match.

SAQ	
9.4	Explain the difference between each of these pairs of terms. Use examples to illustrate your answers.
a	restriction endonuclease and reverse transcriptase;
b	gene therapy and genetic screening;
c	somatic cells and germ cells;
d	blood grouping and tissue typing;
e	*Homo sapiens sapiens* and *Homo erectus*.

Table 9.1 Sources of organs for transplantation.

Source	Advantages	Disadvantages
Living relative	It may be possible to find a very closely matched tissue type.	Taking an organ from a living donor has a low but measurable risk to their health.
Unrelated person who has just died	The use of the organs to help to save another life may help the donor's family to cope with their grief.	There is a shortage of such organs, as not many people carry donor cards. It is difficult to find a closely matched tissue type.
Unrelated person who is willing to sell an organ	Could provide a good reward for the donor.	There is great risk of exploitation of poorer people by dealers.
An animal of another species	There is a limitless supply of such organs available. It may be possible to use this as a stop-gap measure until a suitable human organ becomes available for transplant.	Many religious groups, cultural groups and individuals find this unacceptable. The organ will have a very different tissue type from the recipient and will eventually be rejected even if immunosuppressant drugs are used. There is a significant possibility that viruses or other pathogens in the organ could be transferred from the other species to humans, possibly resulting in the emergence of a new infectious disease.

Summary

1 A species can be defined as a group of similar organisms that can interbreed successfully with each other but not with members of another species.

2 The naming and classification of living organisms is known as taxonomy. Our species is *Homo sapiens*.

3 Some taxonomists classify us as a subspecies, *H. sapiens sapiens*, to distinguish us from Neanderthal man, *H. sapiens neanderthalensis*.

4 Our species may have evolved as a result of geographical isolation from an ancestral species. In different environments different selection pressures acted, eventually making us so different from the ancestral species that interbreeding was no longer possible.

5 Transplanted organs must be a close tissue match if the recipient's immune system is not to reject the organ. In particular, an organ from a donor who has the same HLA system tissue type should be used.

6 The HLA antigens are encoded by a set of six closely linked genes at the MHC loci on chromosome 6. Each of these genes has many different alleles.

7 It may be possible to genetically engineer animals of other species so that their cells do not carry antigens that our immune system would attack. This is being researched in pigs. However, there are major ethical issues associated with this, and many people would not be prepared to accept this new technology.

CHAPTER 10

Homeostasis

CASE STUDY

On February 24th 2001, Edmonton was experiencing the extremely low winter temperature so typical in this part of Canada. At –20 °C, going outside involved covering most parts of the body with insulated clothes, and breathing the super-cold air made you gasp.

Suki, 13-months old and wearing only her nappy, was playing in the warm living room in her house. She could already walk quite well, but perhaps her mother had not realised just how mobile she was. Suki found her way to a door that had not been quite pulled shut, and wandered outside into the garden. It was snowing, and Suki's tiny footprints were quickly obliterated by the fresh snowfall.

It was quite a little while before Suki's mother suddenly realised that she had heard nothing from Suki for a while. She peeped round the door to the living room but could not see her. She wasn't alarmed – perhaps she had toddled off to another room. It wasn't for another ten minutes that she began to be worried. And two minutes after that she began to panic.

Outside, there was nothing to be seen except falling snow. Suki's mother called her friend next door, who rushed round to help. Now they found the partly opened door. Had someone come in and taken Suki? How could this have happened without her mother hearing something? Surely the child would not have wandered outside into the snow.

Several hours later, a search team found the toddler. She was lying face-down in the snow, apparently not breathing and with no detectable heart beat. Paramedics measured her core temperature as 15 °C.

Within minutes, she was admitted to the paediatric intensive care unit at the large teaching hospital. There, her body temperature was slowly, slowly raised back towards normal. And, equally slowly, her body came back to life. Within hours her heart beat was normal, she was conscious and apparently had suffered no brain damage. "She was essentially in a cold-induced coma," explained the doctor in charge of the unit. "If your body slows right down like that, then even brain cells don't need much oxygen. We caught her before any long-term harm had been done."

Remarkably, most of the incidences of recovery from the kind of incident described in the case study involve small children. This is no coincidence. The faster the body cools, the shorter the time during which body cells are demanding oxygen which cannot be supplied by the slowing breathing and heart rates. If it cools quickly, then everything shuts down so fast that neurological damage is far less likely to happen. The body of a small child cools much faster than that of an adult, because a child has a much greater surface-area-to-volume ratio. Heat is lost rapidly through the large surface area, while the smaller volume of cells inside the body cannot produce sufficient heat to replace it.

The principles of homeostasis

Humans are mammals, and we share one of the most distinctive mammalian characteristics – the ability to control core body temperature. Whatever the temperature of the environment outside the body, the cells deep within it are kept at a temperature close to 37 °C. This ensures that metabolic reactions taking place inside them do not speed up or slow down just because the external temperature changes.

Temperature is not the only feature of our internal environment that is kept fairly constant. We also have mechanisms that control the concentration of glucose in the blood and tissue fluid, and also their water potential.

The maintenance of a steady internal environment around body cells is called **homeostasis** – meaning 'staying the same'.

Negative feedback

The way in which each aspect of the internal environment of the body is maintained involves a mechanism called **negative feedback**. This is illustrated in Fig 10.1.

A negative feedback system requires a **receptor** and an **effector** and an efficient means of communication between them. The receptor monitors the factor that is being controlled – for example, the temperature of the blood. If the value of this factor is not what it should be, then the receptor communicates with the effector. The effector then brings about an action that brings the factor back towards normal.

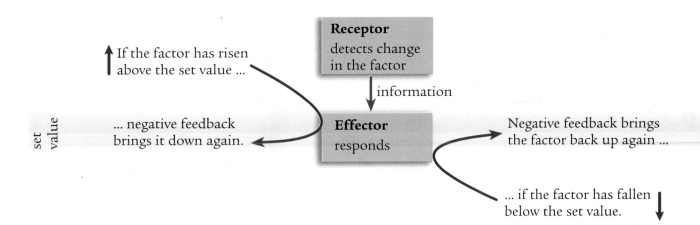

Fig 10.1 Negative feedback.

In the human body, the communication between the receptor and effector may be via the nervous system or via the endocrine (hormonal) system. In some instances – such as the control of temperature – both are involved. In this case, as we will see, the nervous system helps to bring about rapid, short-term changes while the endocrine system can control longer-term ones.

Because there is inevitably a short time delay between a change in the factor, its detection by the receptor, communication with the effector and the response of the effector, the control does not happen instantly. This results in an oscillation around a set value, rather than an absolutely unchanging one.

Role of the autonomic nervous system

The **autonomic nervous system** (see page 75) plays a very important role in the control of many of the factors of the internal environment. This part of the nervous system includes all of the motor neurones that carry impulses to the internal organs, such as the heart and the digestive system. A summary of some of its effects are shown in Table 4.1 on page 76. Its role in the control of body temperature is described on pages 219–220.

Many of the activities of the autonomic nervous system are regulated by the **hypothalamus** (see page 81). This small area of the brain contains numerous types of receptors that monitor factors such as blood temperature and water potential. It also receives information, in the form of nerve impulses, from receptors elsewhere in the body. Yet more information is received via hormones that are carried to it in the blood that flows through it. The hypothalamus can be thought of as a central information-collecting centre that measures many factors of the internal environment, and then uses this information to control the actions of effectors that can help to keep these factors close to their normal values.

In this chapter, we will look at one of these factors – internal temperature – and another, the water content of the blood, will be covered in Chapter 11. However, it is important to note that not every factor of the internal environment involves the hypothalamus or the autonomic nervous system in such a central role, and this is true of the other example of homeostasis that is described in this chapter, namely the control of blood glucose concentration.

Summary

1. Homeostasis is the maintenance of a relatively constant internal environment.

2. Homeostasis does not keep each factor exactly the same all of the time. It maintains a dynamic equilibrium, in which the factors may oscillate around a mean value and where this mean value itself may change in different circumstances.

3. Homeostasis is brought about by negative feedback mechanisms.

4. Negative feedback involves a receptor, an effector and a communication system between them.

5. The hypothalamus contains receptors which measure certain features of the blood, and also receives impulses from other receptors in different parts of the body. It coordinates this information and sends nerve impulses, via the autonomic nervous sytem, to effectors.

Temperature regulation

France in crisis as death toll hits 3000

The national holiday in early August sees many Parisians heading out of the city to holiday homes or camp sites. Families often take their pets with them but – perhaps because they don't always want to go – the most elderly members of the family may be left behind in their houses or apartments in Paris.

This mass exodus happened as usual in August 2003. But something much less usual also happened at the same time. Temperatures rose into the high 30s and then kept on rising, hitting values of up to 42 °C. The heat wave continued on and on, roasting Paris in a drying, enervating heat.

Parisian buildings are generally built to keep heat in, not to keep it out. Few had air conditioning. Old people left alone at home had no way to keep themselves cool. No-one had understood just what danger they were in. It was not until more than 3000 had died that full realisation of the crisis sank in. In mid-August, Prime Minister Jean-Paul Rafin returned from his alpine holiday and at last declared a state of emergency, recalling holidaying hospital staff and instigating a coordinated effort to try to stop any more deaths taking place and to deal with those that already had.

The deaths were due to hyperthermia (a body temperature raised well above normal) and dehydration. Undertakers and funeral parlours did their best to cope with a 37% increase in demand, but could not always do so; there were several stories of bodies being left in apartments for up to eight days before they were collected. Early reports that 3000 people had died turned out to be an underestimate. By the end of the month, figures showed that there were 11 435 more deaths in the first two weeks of August than would normally be expected – an increase of 55%.

In Britain, we are perhaps more familiar with deaths of old people from hypothermia (a lowered body temperature) than from hyperthermia, as described in the case study. The elderly are often less able to regulate body temperature than younger people, in part because they are less mobile but also because older bodies don't work quite so well as younger ones.

There are three ways in which heat can be transferred from one point to another – **conduction**, **convection** and **radiation**. Understanding them is important in explaining the maintenance of body temperature (Fig 10.2).

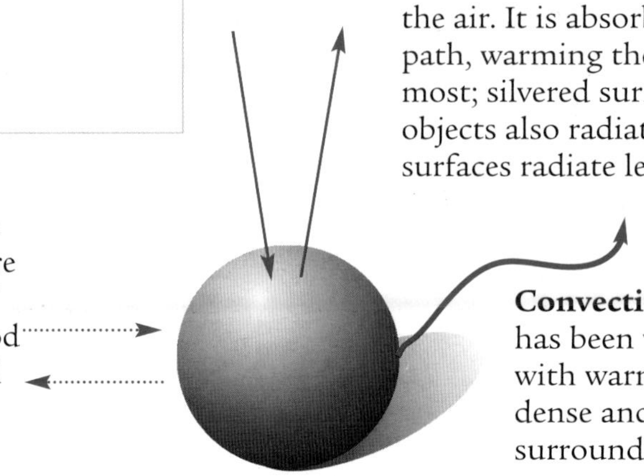

Radiation – This is infrared radiation (e.g. the main heat of an electric bar fire or the Sun). All objects emit infrared radiation. The hotter they are, the more they emit. This radiation travels in straight lines through the air. It is absorbed by solid objects in its path, warming them. Black objects absorb most; silvered surfaces reflect it. Black objects also radiate most and silvered surfaces radiate least.

Conduction – Heat passes from one particle to another if they are next to each other. The speed of transfer will depend on how good a conductor of heat the material is. Air is quite a poor conductor of heat. Water is a better heat conductor.

Convection – If a fluid like the air has been warmed (e.g. by contact with warm skin) it becomes less dense and so will rise through surrounding cooler air. If there are movements in the fluid, heat is transported away more rapidly.

Fig 10.2 Conduction, convection and radiation.

All mammals are able to generate heat inside their bodies, and so are said to be **endothermic**. ('Endo' means 'inside'.) Body temperature is controlled by ensuring a balance between the production of heat inside the body and the loss of heat to the environment (Fig 10.3). We are perhaps better at keeping the body warm in a cold environment than we are at keeping it cool in a hot one. We have several different ways of keeping warm, but if the external temperature rises above our internal one, the only physiological way of keeping cool is through sweating.

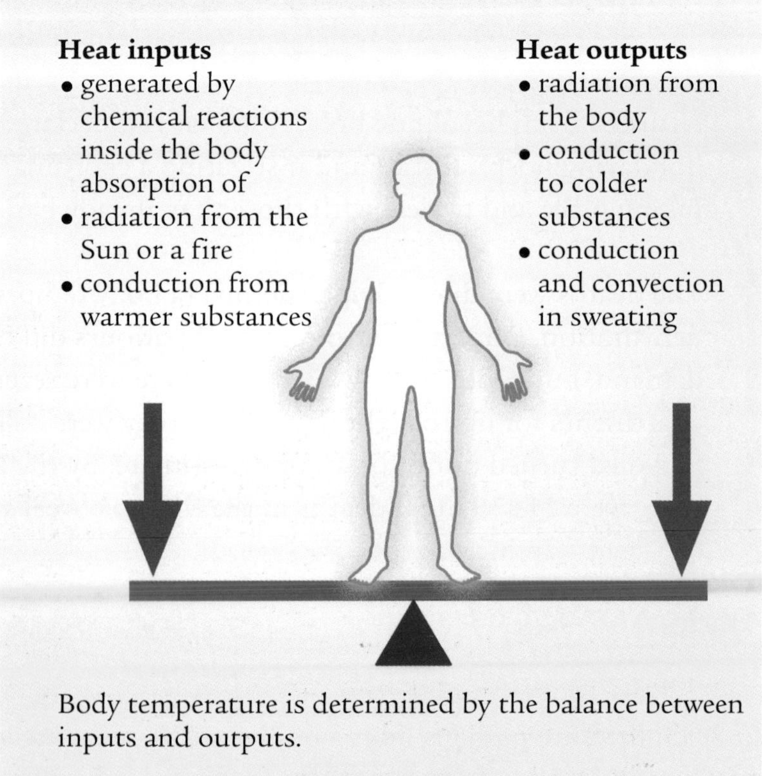

Heat inputs
- generated by chemical reactions inside the body absorption of
- radiation from the Sun or a fire
- conduction from warmer substances

Heat outputs
- radiation from the body
- conduction to colder substances
- conduction and convection in sweating

Body temperature is determined by the balance between inputs and outputs.

Fig 10.3 Heat inputs and heat outputs.

Temperature receptors

The hypothalamus never stops monitoring the temperature of the blood flowing through it. The temperature it monitors is our **core temperature** – the temperature within the body. This should remain at around 37 °C, although this value varies between different people and also depends on the level of activity that is taking place, the time of day and – for women – the stage of their menstrual cycle (Fig 10.4).

Effectors that help to control temperature

When temperature receptors sense a change in external or core temperature, the hypothalamus sends impulses via the autonomic nervous system to various effectors that help to resist or reverse the change.

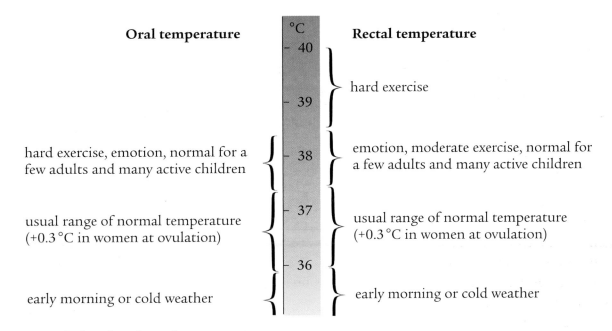

Oral temperature

hard exercise, emotion, normal for a few adults and many active children

usual range of normal temperature (+0.3 °C in women at ovulation)

early morning or cold weather

°C
- 40
- 39
- 38
- 37
- 36

Rectal temperature

hard exercise

emotion, moderate exercise, normal for a few adults and many active children

usual range of normal temperature (+0.3 °C in women at ovulation)

early morning or cold weather

Fig 10.4 Typical oral and rectal temperatures.

The hypothalamus also receives information, in the form of nerve impulses, from sensory neurones in the skin, known as **peripheral receptors**. These sense changes in the temperature of the environment around the body, and so can give 'early warning' that the body temperature might change. When you walk out of a warm room into a cold one and say that you 'feel cold', it is the nerve impulses from these surface receptors that you are responding to – your core temperature probably has not changed at all.

There are also peripheral receptors in other parts of the body, particularly in the spinal cord, the organs within the abdomen and the walls of the vena cava.

When the body is too cold

Impulses arriving in the hypothalamus from the skin surface as a result of exposure to a cold external environment bring about a rapid reflex action. A similar response occurs if the core temperature begins to fall. You shiver as muscles in several parts of the body contract and relax rapidly, generating heat within themselves. This heat is conducted into the blood, which carries it around the body.

Arterioles can control the proportion of blood that passes through different organs. The reflex response to feeling cold involves smooth muscle in the walls of arterioles delivering blood to the skin surface. This muscle contracts, narrowing the lumen of the arterioles and shutting off blood supply to the surface capillaries. This is known as **vasoconstriction**. It ensures that less heat is lost to the surroundings by radiation from the body surface.

Sweat glands reduce their output of sweat, or stop it entirely. **Erector muscles**, attached to the base of hair follicles, contract, pulling the hairs up on end. We are not very hairy, so this does nothing to help us to keep warm. In other mammals, it traps a layer of air next to the skin, which insulates the body from changing temperatures around it. For us, all that happens is that we get goose bumps.

Other organs have a part to play. Impulses carried along nerve axons cause some cells to alter the outcome of aerobic respiration inside their mitochondria. You may remember that electrons from the Krebs cycle are passed down an electron transfer chain, releasing enough energy to form ATP as hydrogen ions pass through the inner mitochondrial membrane (see page 15). Now this is 'uncoupled' – that is, the energy released when the hydrogen ions pass through the membrane is not used to make ATP. Instead, it is released as heat. (See Just for Interest, page 16). This is sometimes referred to as **chemical thermogenesis**. It is especially important in babies, where brown fat contains mitochondria in which the generation of heat is more important than the generation of ATP.

When the body is too hot

When a rise in environmental temperature is detected by skin receptors, or a rise in blood temperature is detected by receptors in the hypothalamus, all of the actions described above go into reverse.

The arterioles supplying blood to the skin now dilate, a process known as **vasodilation**. This allows more blood to flow close to the skin surface, so that heat can radiate from it or be conducted to the air. This is why a pale skin tends to go pink in hot conditions.

Sweat glands are stimulated, by neurones of the sympathetic nervous system, to secrete more sweat (Fig 10.5). Plasma from the blood passing through is extracted in the sweat gland and passes up through the sweat ducts to the skin surface. This liquid is mostly water, but also contains many of the solutes present in blood plasma, in particular sodium ions, chloride ions and urea. As it lies on the surface of the skin, the water in it evaporates. Water has a high latent heat of vaporisation and so, as it changes from liquid to gas, it absorbs heat from the skin. Shivering and chemical thermogenesis are strongly inhibited when temperature rises.

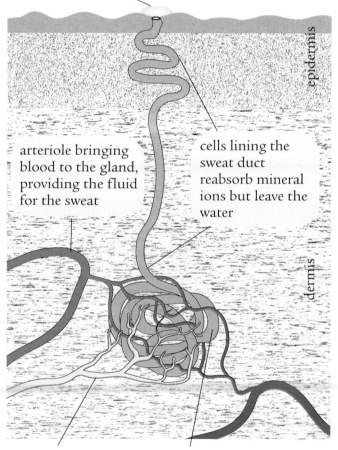

sweat secreted – mainly water but contains some mineral ions

epidermis

arteriole bringing blood to the gland, providing the fluid for the sweat

cells lining the sweat duct reabsorb mineral ions but leave the water

dermis

sympathetic nerve stimulates secretion

cells of the glandular tube secrete fluid without protein but with mineral ions

Fig 10.5 A sweat gland.

Longer-term temperature control

The responses described on pages 219–220 are all short-term ones. They can swing into action quickly and equally quickly be switched off as temperature is brought back towards the norm.

However, if we find ourselves subjected to a longer-term change in the temperature of the external environment, then another system of control becomes important. This involves a hormone called **thyroxine**, which is secreted by the **thyroid gland** (Fig 10.6). Thyroxine increases metabolic rate and **thermogenesis** (heat production).

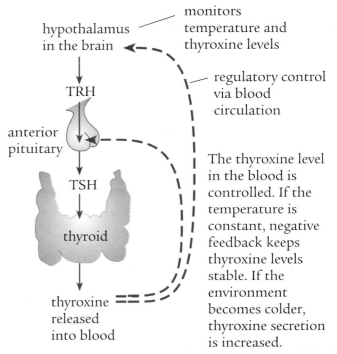

Fig 10.7 The regulation of thyroxine secretion.

monitors temperature and thyroxine levels

regulatory control via blood circulation

The thyroxine level in the blood is controlled. If the temperature is constant, negative feedback keeps thyroxine levels stable. If the environment becomes colder, thyroxine secretion is increased.

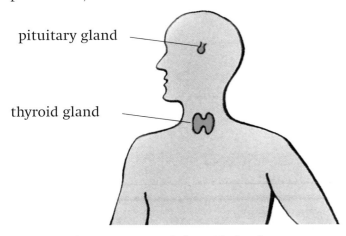

Fig 10.6 The pituitary and thyroid glands.

When the hypothalamus senses a drop in temperature, it secretes a hormone called **thyrotrophin releasing hormone, TRH**. This is secreted into the blood and carried to the nearby anterior pituitary, where it stimulates the secretion of **thyroid stimulating hormone, TSH**. This, in turn, stimulates the release of thyroxine by the thyroid gland (Fig 10.7).

This gland lies in the neck, on either side of the trachea. It is made up of many follicles, each surrounded by cuboidal epithelium. They secrete a precursor of thyroxine into the lumen of the follicle, where it is stored. When TSH reaches them, they take up droplets of liquid from the follicle by pinocytosis and change the precursor to thyroxine which is then secreted into the blood (Fig 10.8). Thyroxine contains iodine, and this is why we need some iodine in the diet.

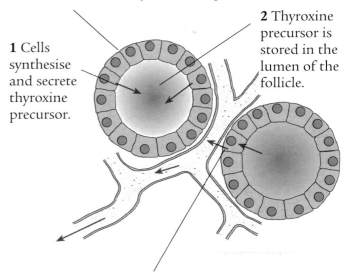

follicle, surrounded by cuboidal epithelium

1 Cells synthesise and secrete thyroxine precursor.

2 Thyroxine precursor is stored in the lumen of the follicle.

3 When more thyroxine is needed in the body, the precursor is absorbed by the cuboid cells of the follicles and made into thyroxine. It is then secreted into blood capillaries.

Fig 10.8 Thyroid tissue.

Thyroxine is able to pass through the cell surface membranes of its target cells. It enters the nucleus, where it stimulates the transcription of a number of genes. One of the many effects of this is the production of more mitochondria inside the cell. More respiratory enzymes are synthesised, especially those of the electron transfer chain. Glucose and fat metabolism is increased, so producing more respiratory substrate. Overall, this results in a greater rate of respiration and therefore of heat production. Thyroxine has a general effect of increasing metabolic rate throughout the body.

The effect of thyroxine is not immediate, because it takes time for a gene to be transcribed and for protein to be synthesised. Equally, the effect cannot be turned off immediately either. We tend to secrete extra thyroxine when exposed to the cold for a few days – for example, when on a skiing holiday or when living in an inadequately heated house in winter. As the heat-generating mechanisms of the body become more active, we become **acclimatised** to the new, low-temperature environment.

PROCEDURE 10.1

Measuring core temperature

Core temperature is the temperature deep inside the body. We cannot measure this directly and accurately in a routine way, as this would require surgery. Instead, we can measure peripheral temperature at various sites, chosen because they do give readings that are reasonably close to the true core temperature. The results from these sites vary in accuracy and precision. The skill of the nurse or doctor is an important factor in deciding which site to use and there is no universal agreement as to which is the best site to use.

A standard mercury-in-glass clinical thermometer is normally used. However, there is increasing use of electronic infrared sensors, which have the advantage of rapid response. The precision of temperature measurements using a clinical thermometer is much affected by the time the thermometer is left in position. The times quoted below are recommendations in the light of research. The thermometers must be disinfected between use with different patients.

Oral temperature
This is the simplest peripheral measurement but is the least accurate estimate of core temperature. The bulb of the thermometer is placed under a person's tongue on one side or other of the midline. It is left for 7–8 minutes. The person should not have smoked, taken vigorous exercise, or hot or cold drinks in the previous 15 minutes.

This technique is not suitable for an unconscious person, or an uncooperative child or baby.

Rectal temperature
This is often considered to be the site most likely to give an indication of core temperature, giving results which are about 0.5 °C above oral temperature. The thermometer should remain for 2 minutes.

However, some authorities suggest that this site responds slowly to any induced heat change in the body. The thermometers used rectally should be clearly identified as such and kept separately from other thermometers, for obvious health reasons.

Axillary temperature
This is the skin temperature measured in the armpit. Care needs to be taken to ensure the thermometer makes good contact with the skin for accuracy. The thermometer should be left for 9 minutes.

The use of this site is least likely to result in trauma.

Tympanic membrane of the ear
There are conflicting views on the accuracy and precision of measurements using this site. By some, it is considered to be a good site to use and suitable for electronic temperature measurement.

Care has to be taken to ensure no trauma is caused to the tympanic membrane (ear drum).

Hypothermia

Hypothermia is a condition in which the body temperature drops significantly below normal – usually considered to be below 35 °C – and where the normal temperature-regulating mechanisms are unable to bring it back up.

As body temperature drops, all metabolic reactions slow down, because the reduced kinetic energy of the reactant molecules slows down their movement and therefore reduces the likelihood of them colliding with each other. Thus, the very thing that could bring temperature back up again – an increase in metabolic activity – is slowed down.

Hypothermia can be the result of exposure to extreme cold. A very cold environment means that there is a steep temperature gradient between the skin and the air around it, so that heat is lost rapidly. A strong wind increases the loss of heat; this is known as **wind chill**. Heat is conducted from the skin to warm the still air next to the skin. Air is a poor conductor of heat but convection or wind takes this warm air away. As the wind speed increases, the depth of the layer of still, warm air is reduced and rate of heat loss increases. Walkers and climbers trapped by injury or other difficulties on a windy, exposed mountainside can quickly suffer a dangerous fall in body temperature. Crawling inside a plastic survival bag can make a huge difference to the likelihood of survival.

Getting thoroughly wet or being immersed in water can also lead to hypothermia. Wet clothes should be removed as soon as possible and replaced by dry ones.

Hypothermia is a particular risk for elderly people, even in their own homes. Many older people are very concerned about saving money, and may be reluctant to switch on heating. They may not be very mobile, so will spend much of the day sitting in one place. Their lack of movement means that their bodies do not produce much heat. They may not eat well enough to provide their cells with sufficient fuel for respiration and therefore heat generation. Every winter, many elderly people die from hypothermia.

A person who is suffering from hypothermia often does not recognise it. They will have been feeling very cold, but now may feel sleepy and relaxed. This is a danger sign to others, who should recognise that their companion is at risk and attempt to reverse the loss of body heat.

The first line of treatment is to prevent any further heat loss, by wrapping the victim in warm, dry blankets and providing a hot water bottle if possible. In most cases, a person who is taken into a warm environment will recover from hypothermia if they simply lie there for a period of some hours. Sugary drinks should not be given until temperature is close to normal, as when cells are too cold they are not able to metabolise glucose.

SAQ

10.1 With reference to the properties of air, water and other materials and the methods of heat transfer (conduction, convection and radiation) suggest reasons for each of the following.

a Hypothermia is a severe risk when a person is immersed in water.

b Hypothermia is possible if a person is wearing wet clothes.

c Silver-surfaced thin plastic 'survival bags' are useful in preventing hypothermia in a person immobilised on a high mountain.

d A blanket reduces heat loss from the body.

10.2 Explain why eating food helps to prevent hypothermia.

Hyperthermia

They didn't really look like the sort of people who ought to be thinking of walking along a canyon in the Sinai Desert: some were clearly well into their sixties and early seventies. They had, at least, all got hats on and all were carrying a water bottle. Their young guide hurried them along – he wanted to get the walk along the Painted Canyon done and be back in the luxury hotel in time for the next meal.

As they walked, the Sun rose higher, so that even in the depths of the canyon they were hit by its harsh heat. At first it was relatively easy going, but as it got rougher some of the older tourists began to struggle. A team spirit developed, with younger or more agile members helping others to clamber over rocks. There was a lot of laughter, though it was clear that some people were in genuine difficulty.

As they emerged from the canyon, an open stretch of sand greeted them, with a short but steep rise at the end of it. Just one small tree stood ahead of them, at least promising a little shade. As the party slowly made its way across the sand, it was very clear that one of the oldest ladies was in real difficulties. She was weaving from side to side and seemed to have no idea where she was. She muttered to herself. One of the younger men in the party got his shoulder under her arm and virtually lifted her up the path.

At the top was a Bedouin tent, manned by three local tribesmen who knew exactly what ill-prepared British tourists needed at this point in their adventure. Cool shade, and even cooler drinks from a fridge (powered by a small generator), at a price. But the elderly lady was too far gone to notice. Her skin was red and dry, she was talking nonsense, and could not be persuaded to drink. Someone poured ice-cold cola onto her head and neck and the party was hustled back to the hotel. Here she lay in an air-conditioned room as her companion bathed her skin with cold water. By night-time she was fine, although the next day she had no memory at all of what had almost been a fatal accident in the Painted Canyon.

So what had happened? It turned out that she had wanted to urinate and had been too embarrassed to go behind one of the few possible rocks they had passed on the walk. Instead, she had chosen not to drink any water. Dehydrated, she had been unable to sweat. It was difficult for any of the party to recognise what real danger she had been in. After all, you don't expect to run the risk of death on a short walk organised by a reputable holiday firm.

Hyperthermia is a condition in which the body temperature rises significantly above normal. Like hypothermia, it can easily be fatal if not brought under control.

Hyperthermia may be caused by an infection in which toxins produced by bacteria or viruses affect the hypothalamus. It is probable that this reaction of the body to infection has evolved as an effective way of fighting off the pathogens. In most cases, a fever of this kind is fairly short-lived, and the body returns to a normal temperature within a few days.

Very high external temperatures can also cause hyperthermia. The only method that we have of bringing body temperature below that of the environment is by sweating. In humid conditions, however, the air may already be saturated with water vapour, so that sweat simply lies on the skin and cannot evaporate. In those circumstances, the body has no natural way of bringing temperature down to normal. This is why we feel much more uncomfortable in humid conditions than when the air is dry.

Sweating involves the loss of a great deal of fluid from the body, and it is very important to keep drinking large quantities of water when in hot conditions. This is especially true if you are being active because muscular activity produces heat. Lack of sufficient water in the body will reduce the ability to sweat, and therefore will allow body temperature to rise uncontrollably.

As core temperature rises much above 38 °C, the person will feel ill. If core temperature rises above a certain value, usually around 41 °C, then the ability of the hypothalamus to coordinate temperature regulation becomes seriously reduced. Body temperature just keeps on rising and the person is said to be suffering from **heat stroke**. They will feel dizzy and sick and may lose consciousness.

Treatment should involve bringing the body temperature down quickly, with cold drinks if the person can swallow them and with cold water applied to the body, exposing the skin so that the water can readily evaporate from it. Heat stroke is very dangerous, and can be fatal if not treated rapidly.

SAQ

10.3   When a person falls into cold water, the body temperature drops much faster than in cold air. An investigation was carried out to see if it is better to stay still if you are in cold water, or to swim.

   An indoor swimming pool was filled with water. The air in the building and the water were kept at a steady temperature of 15 °C.

   Two volunteers stayed in the building for one hour. For the first 30 minutes they sat still next to the pool. They then both got into the pool. Person A swam for the next 30 minutes while person B lay still in the water.

   The core temperatures of both volunteers were measured at intervals. The results are shown in the graph.

   a   Compare the results for the two volunteers.
   b   Suggest reasons for the differences that you have described.

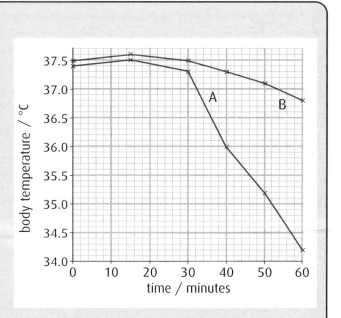

10.4   The graph shows the mean core temperatures of two groups of athletes running at a steady speed. One group was allowed to drink fluids during the trial, while the other group was not.

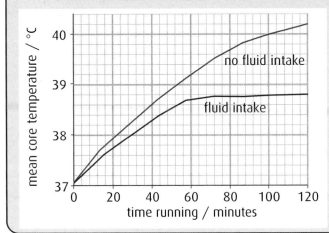

a   Describe the change in core temperature of the group who were allowed to drink fluid during the 120 minutes of exercise.

b   Suggest an explanation for the pattern you have described.

c   Describe the differences between the pattern shown by the group who drank fluids and the group who did not.

d   Suggest explanations for these differences.

e   How might you use these results to advise each of the following athletes on whether or not they should drink fluids during their race?

   i   a 5000 metre runner

   ii   a marathon runner

Summary

1 The temperature deep inside the human body, known as the core temperature, is maintained at approximately 37 °C.

2 The maintenance of a steady temperature involves keeping a balance between heat loss and heat gain.

3 The hypothalamus coordinates temperature regulation. It contains receptors that measure blood temperature, and also receives information from peripheral receptors such as those in the skin. It sends impulses to effectors along neurones of the autonomic nervous system.

4 When the body is too cold, shivering helps to increase heat production. Heat is also released in several different tissues as the movement of hydrogen ions through the inner mitochondrial membrane is uncoupled from ATP production and releases heat instead. Heat loss is reduced by vasoconstriction, which lowers the rate of heat loss by radiation from the skin.

5 When the body is too warm, sweat glands secrete sweat onto the surface of the skin. As the water in it evaporates, it cools the skin. Vasodilation allows more blood to flow close to the skin surface, so that more heat is lost from the blood by radiation.

6 In the longer term, exposure to cold stimulates the release of thyrotrophin releasing hormone (TRH) by the hypothalamus. This in turn stimulates the secretion of thyroid stimulating hormone (TSH) from the anterior pituitary gland, and this then stimulates the secretion of thyroxine from the thyroid gland. Thyroxine switches on genes that increase metabolic rate.

Summary continued ...

7 Core temperature can be estimated by measuring peripheral temperature. Choice of site and care taken with the temperature measurement reduces error. Rectal temperature is often taken to be the most reliable of core temperature estimates.

8 Hypothermia is a condition in which core temperature drops below 35 °C, from where the normal temperature-regulating mechanisms cannot raise it. It is treated by steadily warming the body.

9 Hyperthermia is a condition in which core temperature rises above 38 °C. If caused by an infection, it may return to normal without outside help. However, above around 41 °C the temperature-controlling mechanisms are no longer able to function, and heat stroke may result. It is treated by cooling the body by applying water to its surface, and getting the patient to drink if at all possible.

Controlling blood glucose level

CASE STUDY

At the Sydney Olympics in the year 2000, Steve Redgrave made history as the first person to win a gold medal in five consecutive Olympic Games. His achievement was the culmination of years of hard training and the maintenance of an outstanding level of fitness.

World-standard rowing takes a huge amount out of the body. Sir Steve Redgrave's event involved sitting in a boat with three other rowers, working at a rate that took them over the 2 km course at speeds of around 6 metres per second. The energy output is very large – around 2 kJ per stroke – and maintaining this rate over such a long course puts demands on the body that are far beyond the imagination of most of us.

Yet, in 1997, Steve had been diagnosed as having diabetes. His body had become unable to control his blood glucose level unaided, so now he has to help it along. For his last Olympic appearance, he had to plan his training schedule and his food intake meticulously. Each day, he gave himself seven insulin injections.

Steve Redgrave's example shows us that, although the development of diabetes later in life is most common in overweight and unfit people, it can occur in almost anyone. And, perhaps even more importantly, it illustrates the fact that having diabetes does not have to stop you doing whatever you want to do.

The pancreas

The pancreas is a soft, red organ that lies close to the stomach, just beneath the diaphragm (Fig 10.9). It is unusual because it has two quite different functions. Some of its cells produce and secrete pancreatic juice, which is carried to the small intestine along the pancreatic duct, and which helps to complete the digestion of proteins, carbohydrates and fats in the food we eat. This makes the pancreas an **exocrine gland** – that is, one whose secretions go into a duct that delivers them to a particular place in the body.

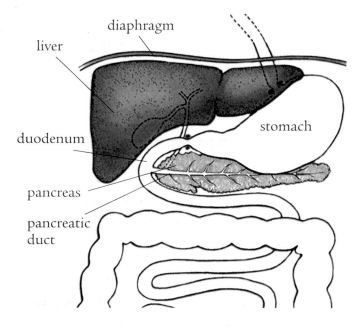

Fig 10.9 The pancreas and associated organs.

Other cells in the pancreas produce and secrete two hormones which are central to the control of blood glucose level – **insulin** and **glucagon**. The secretion of these two hormones is done by cells in little clumps within the pancreas called **islets of Langerhans** (Fig 10.10). There are two types of cells, **alpha** cells that secrete glucagon and **beta** cells that secrete insulin. The islets have many blood capillaries associated with them, and the secretions of the islet cells go into these capillaries. This makes the pancreas an **endocrine gland** – that is, one whose secretions go directly into the blood.

islet of Langerhans containing α and β cells

cells secreting pancreatic juice

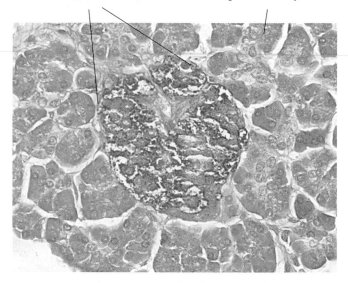

Fig 10.10 Light micrograph of an islet of Langerhans and surrounding pancreatic cells (×300).

The blood glucose control mechanism

As in all cases of homeostasis, the control of blood glucose concentration involves a negative feedback mechanism. This is outlined in Fig 10.11.

Normal values of blood glucose concentration lie somewhere between 70 mg and 110 mg per 100 cm^3 of blood (4.2 to 6.6 mmol dm^{-3}). The receptors that measure this are the islet cells themselves.

Imagine that a person has just eaten a meal containing a lot of sugar. In the digestive system, this is broken down to monosaccharides, including glucose, and these are absorbed into the blood. As this blood flows through the pancreas, the alpha and beta cells detect the raised blood glucose level. The alpha cells respond by stopping the secretion of glucagon, and the beta cells respond by secreting insulin.

Insulin is a small protein, made up of a single polypeptide chain. It dissolves into the blood plasma, and is carried all over the body. Some cells have receptors in their cell surface membranes into which the insulin molecules fit. These **target cells** include liver cells, muscle cells and cells in adipose (fat) tissue.

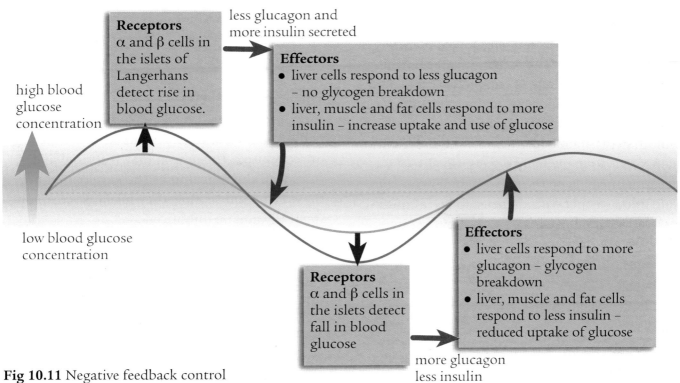

Fig 10.11 Negative feedback control of blood glucose concentration.

The arrival of insulin at the target cells causes more transporter proteins for glucose to be inserted into their cell surface membranes. This allows more glucose from the blood to pass into them by facilitated diffusion. The insulin also causes the cells to metabolise glucose faster, using some of it for respiration and converting the rest to the insoluble polysaccharide glycogen, for storage. All of this brings the blood glucose level down.

After a while, the blood glucose level may fall below the norm. Now it is the alpha cells in the islets of Langerhans that are stimulated, and they secrete glucagon into the blood. Glucagon causes liver cells to break down some of their stored glycogen into glucose and to secrete this glucose into the blood. The glucagon also causes the liver cells to make glucose from fats, which again can be released into the blood and help to raise the blood glucose level towards normal.

SAQ

10.5   Explain the difference between each of these pairs of terms:

a   an exocrine gland and an endocrine gland;

b   beta cells and B lymphocytes;

c   glycogen and glucagon;

d   facilitated diffusion and active transport.

ACTIVITY 10.1

Histology of the pancreas

Using the photograph in Fig 10.9 to help you identify cells, examine a slide of pancreas tissue under the microscope. Move to the highest power objective and find, examine and draw a small islet of Langerhans and one small area of surrounding tissue. Avoid drawing too many cells.

Using a stage micrometer and eyepiece graticule, measure the diameter of several islet cells and several cells of the surrounding tissue. Are they different in size?

Diabetes mellitus

Diabetes mellitus, usually just called diabetes, is an illness in which the blood glucose control mechanism has partly or completely broken down. It is very important to diagnose and control this disease as early as possible, because wildly swinging blood glucose levels are highly dangerous to many body organs. Good treatment can keep things well under control and allow people with diabetes to live almost entirely normal lives.

There are two types of diabetes. **Type 1 diabetes**, sometimes known as insulin-dependent diabetes, begins at a very early age. The pancreas appears to be incapable of secreting enough insulin, so that blood glucose levels may soar uncontrollably after a carbohydrate-containing meal. **Type 2 diabetes** normally begins later in life. The pancreas does secrete insulin, but the liver and other target cells are unable to respond fully to it.

Risk factors for diabetes

The risk factors for Type 1 diabetes are not known. It is thought that the development of this illness may be affected by a person's genes, but there also seem to be some environmental risk factors. In particular, it has been suggested that the person's own immune system may attack their beta cells, although why this should happen is not yet understood.

Type 2 diabetes is most likely to develop in people with an excessively high body weight, especially those with a BMI (body mass index) above 27. (To calculate your BMI divide your weight in kilograms by your height in metres squared.) People with 'apple-shaped' figures (most fat carried around the middle) are at greater risk than those with 'pear-shaped' figures (most fat carried around the hips and thighs). A sedentary lifestyle also increases the risk.

There is even more evidence for a genetic link for Type 2 diabetes than there is for Type 1. In the year 2000, the first gene that could be involved in this was found. It lies on chromosome 2 and is one of probably many – mostly as yet unknown – genes that affect the risk of developing Type 2 diabetes.

Symptoms of diabetes

Many people have Type 2 diabetes for years without knowing it. First symptoms can go unrecognised. The person may feel tired and thirsty all the time, but as the development of these symptoms is slow they may just creep up stealthily and be unnoticed.

An understanding of what is going wrong can explain these symptoms. Imagine that a diabetic person eats a meal containing a lot of sugar. As this is absorbed, blood glucose levels go well above normal, but the liver and muscle cells are not alerted about this and do not take corrective action.

The very high blood glucose levels mean that the kidneys (see page 239) are not able to stop it from being excreted in the urine. Instead of being stored in the liver as glycogen, much of the glucose is lost from the body. Later, when the glucose in the blood has been used in respiration, and if the person does not eat again, blood glucose levels may drop well below normal. The liver cells have not stored any as glycogen, so they cannot release glucose to bring up the level in the blood. The person feels very tired and may even become unconscious.

Having a high blood glucose level is known as **hyperglycaemia**. It is usually defined as a level above 262 mg per 100 cm^3 (15 mmol dm^{-3}). In the short term, hyperglycaemia makes the person feel unwell. They may have a dry mouth, blurred vision and feel very thirsty. They may be confused. Sometimes hyperglycaemia is associated with **ketoacidosis**, caused by the presence of substances called ketone bodies in the blood. The ketone bodies are produced from fatty acids in the liver, and can be used as respiratory substrates. However, in diabetes they may be produced faster than they are used and high concentrations of them can be dangerous. Up to 10% of diabetic people admitted to hospital with ketoacidosis die.

There is no first aid treatment that non-medical staff can carry out for hyperglycaemia. Symptoms of hyperglycaemia are warm, dry skin and rapid breathing and high heart rate. The breath is sickly sweet and the person will have a powerful thirst. If you think someone has hyperglycaemia, you should dial 999 for an ambulance. If the person is unconscious, lie them on their side, with head resting on one of their hands (the recovery position).

Having a low blood glucose level is known as **hypoglycaemia**. The person feels exceptionally tired and may become confused and show irrational behaviour. Hypoglycaemia is not restricted to people with diabetes. Many normal people can become mildly hypoglycaemic if they have not eaten for a while, and be quite unaware that their mood and behaviour has been changed as a result. However, a person with diabetes is more likely to suffer severe attacks of hypoglycaemia.

If severe hypoglycaemia is caught early, it can be easily treated by eating something sugary, containing glucose that can be quickly absorbed. If it is untreated, then coma may result. In that case, admission to hospital will be necessary, where glucose can be administered intravenously.

Glucose levels that regularly swing too high and too low can cause significant damage to many different organs in the body. High blood glucose levels cause damage to blood vessels, to the kidneys and to the eyes.

PROCEDURE 10.2

The fasting blood glucose test

This test is used to diagnose suspected diabetes.

A person is requested to fast overnight and for breakfast (water is allowed, but no other drinks or foods). In the morning a blood sample is taken at a doctor's surgery or at a hospital.

The sample is analysed by a pathology department where the glucose concentration is measured. Normal values should be between 80–100 mg 100 cm^{-3} (4.8–6.0 mmol dm^{-3}).

If the level is above 110 mg 100 cm^{-3} (6.6 mmol dm^{-3}), the person may have diabetes. However, newborns and some pregnant women may have higher blood glucose levels and not have diabetes.

If there is doubt about the diagnosis, a glucose tolerance test can be carried out (see Procedure 10.3, below).

PROCEDURE 10.3

The glucose tolerance test

This test is also used to diagnose suspected sufferers of diabetes.

A person is requested to fast overnight as in Procedure 10.2. At the visit to the surgery or hospital the person is asked to drink 75 g of glucose dissolved in water over a 10-minute period. A blood sample is taken at the start and then each 30 minutes for the next 2.5 hours.

Blood glucose levels are measured in the samples. If the blood glucose is 120 mg 100 cm^{-3} (7.2 mmol dm^{-3}) or more at 2 hours, the person has diabetes.

In a normal person, though blood glucose levels rise after drinking the glucose, they quickly fall back to normal.

10.6 A glucose tolerance test was carried out on a normal person and a person with Type 2 diabetes. Each person was given a drink containing the same mass of glucose, and their blood glucose levels and insulin levels were measured over the next four hours.

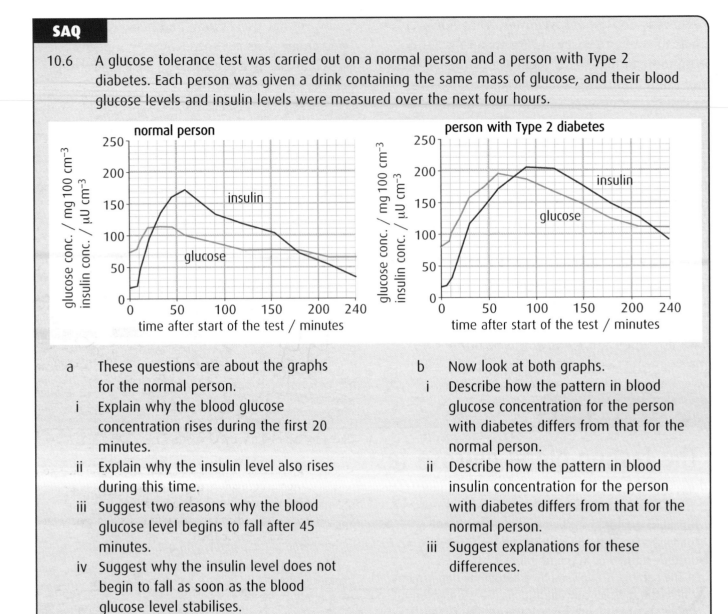

a   These questions are about the graphs for the normal person.

i   Explain why the blood glucose concentration rises during the first 20 minutes.

ii   Explain why the insulin level also rises during this time.

iii   Suggest two reasons why the blood glucose level begins to fall after 45 minutes.

iv   Suggest why the insulin level does not begin to fall as soon as the blood glucose level stabilises.

b   Now look at both graphs.

i   Describe how the pattern in blood glucose concentration for the person with diabetes differs from that for the normal person.

ii   Describe how the pattern in blood insulin concentration for the person with diabetes differs from that for the normal person.

iii   Suggest explanations for these differences.

Treating diabetes mellitus

As yet, there is no cure for diabetes. However, research into the use of gene therapy and also the use of stem cells gives hope for the future.

The management of diabetes mellitus revolves around keeping blood glucose concentrations reasonably constant. The patient may need to check blood glucose regularly, using a simple sensor such as that shown on page 38 in *Human Biology for AS*. Urine should also be tested regularly for the presence of glucose; if the illness is under control, then there should be only very small amounts of glucose present (Fig 10.12).

In Type 2 diabetes, a well controlled diet may be able to keep symptoms at bay. If the patient is obese, then weight loss through diet and exercise will be the first target. It is often possible to manage the condition, at least in the early stages, by diet alone. The person needs to eat small meals at reasonably regular intervals, never flooding their blood with excess glucose and never allowing it to drop too low.

Almost all people with Type 1 diabetes, and many with Type 2 diabetes, use insulin injections to help them to control their blood glucose level. Most insulin now available is produced by transgenic bacteria which contain and express the human gene for insulin, although some people use insulin derived from pigs. Different people may need one, two, three or more injections each day.

Meals should contain carbohydrates that are absorbed steadily over a period of time, rather than rushing a high dose of carbohydrate into the blood. This type of carbohydrate is provided by polysaccharides, so the diet should contain such foods as beans, wholemeal bread and cereals, potatoes and pasta. Sugar should generally be avoided.

The right balance of food intake, exercise and insulin injections will be worked out for each individual. If they know they are going to undertake exercise (going for a long walk, playing a game of football), they should eat carbohydrate-containing food beforehand.

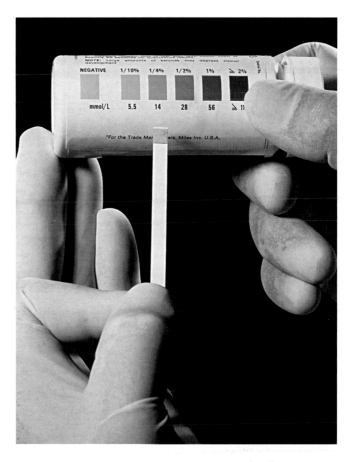

Fig 10.12 Glucose sensor for urine. However, urine tests are not an accurate guide of blood glucose concentration because the blood glucose concentration at which glucose begins to appear in urine can vary significantly.

SAQ

10.7 The graph shows the changes in blood glucose concentration in a person who ate 50 g of carbohydrate as wholemeal bread and others who ate 50 g of carbohydrate as lentils and as soya beans.

a Explain the shape of the curve when bread was eaten.

b Describe the differences between this curve and the ones showing the results after lentils and soya were eaten.

c Suggest reasons for these differences.

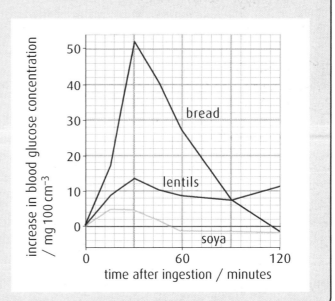

Summary

1. Normal blood glucose concentration is between 80 and 100 mg 100 cm^{-3} (3.89–5.83 mmol dm^{-3}). It is kept at this level by a negative feedback mechanism.

2. Blood glucose concentration is sensed by the alpha and beta cells in the islets of Langerhans in the pancreas.

3. If blood glucose is too high, the beta cells secrete insulin. Insulin causes cells in the liver and muscle and adipose tissue to take up more glucose from the blood, and to use it faster in respiration. Glucose is also used to form glycogen which is stored in these cells.

4. If blood glucose is too low, the alpha cells secrete glucagon. Glucagon causes cells in the liver to break down glycogen to glucose and to release glucose into the blood. They also synthesise glucose from fatty acids.

5. Diabetes mellitus is an illness in which blood glucose is not controlled. Type 1 diabetes develops early in life, and is caused by a lack of secretion of insulin by the pancreas. Type 2 diabetes develops later, and is caused by an inability of liver and muscle cells to respond to insulin.

6. Both types of diabetes appear to have some genetic risk component, but the evidence for this is greater for Type 2 than for Type 1. Being overweight is a strong risk factor for Type 2 diabetes.

7. A person with untreated diabetes will experience large swings in blood glucose levels. An abnormally high level is known as hyperglycaemia. An abnormally low level is known as hypoglycaemia.

8. The fasting blood glucose test can usually detect a person who is suffering diabetes, as the blood glucose concentration is higher than normal. The glucose tolerance test can confirm this diagnosis. A person with diabetes will have blood glucose levels higher than normal 2 hours after ingestion of a glucose solution and having fasted overnight.

9. Treatment for diabetes involves attempting to maintain a relatively constant blood glucose level by means of a controlled diet and, in many cases, insulin injections.

CHAPTER 11

The kidneys

James was Sally's second baby, so she noticed quite quickly that something wasn't right. The birth had been fine, and the baby boy seemed perfect. Sally had been allowed to go home from hospital just a couple of days afterwards.

But he wasn't feeding properly, and had become very listless. When she did manage to get anything inside him, he vomited. She took him to her GP, who sent her on to the hospital so tests could be done.

The paediatrician that she saw was very concerned and admitted James immediately. A blood sample was taken, and fast-tracked through the path lab. The first set of results came through within an hour. James's blood had a pH of 7.55, well above the top end of the normal range of 7.35 to 7.45. However, the urea content was abnormally low.

The paediatrician hadn't ever seen a case like this before, but she had read about it and thought that she recognised what the problem was. She got a second opinion from a colleague before she gave Sally her diagnosis. She told her that she thought James had a genetic illness, and that his body wasn't producing an essential enzyme. This enzyme, usually present in the liver, would normally change ammonia to urea. Because James didn't have this enzyme, ammonia, a very toxic substance, was building up in his blood. Fast action was needed to prevent even more damage than had been done already, and James was given haemodialysis straight away.

Over the next few days, his condition visibly improved. He was more alert and able to feed reasonably normally. But Sally was told the outlook was not good. James must always eat a special diet, low in proteins, if he was to avoid high ammonia levels in his blood. There was a substance that he could take, called arginine, to help him to get rid of the ammonia. All the same, this was going to be a condition that would be very, very difficult to control. The fact that it had been caught so early was in his favour, although it was possible that the high ammonia levels might already have caused some brain damage.

The production of urine by the kidneys is the way in which we get rid of unwanted substances, including urea, from the blood. However, in the case study, it wasn't the kidneys that were at fault but the liver. The liver metabolises toxins and other unwanted chemicals, while the kidneys remove them or their products from the blood.

Excretion

Urine is a liquid that is made from blood plasma. The kidneys make urine by extracting many of the components of plasma from the blood, and then allowing some of them to return to the plasma. The rest are lost from the body in the urine.

This process is part of **excretion**. Excretion can be defined as the removal of unwanted products of metabolism from the body. Some of these are toxic, while others are simply present in larger quantities than required.

One of our main excretory products does not involve the kidneys and is not excreted in urine. This is carbon dioxide, a waste product of respiration, and therefore produced in all our cells. Carbon dioxide is excreted by the lungs. If it is allowed to build up, it increases the acidity of the blood. At first, a raised carbon dioxide concentration in the blood causes an increase in breathing rate. If it continues to rise, breathing rate reaches its maximum and the person struggles hard for breath. They may then become lethargic and eventually unconscious. Death usually occurs if the concentration of carbon dioxide in the blood rises above 16 kPa (120 mm Hg).

It is important to realise that defaecation – the removal of faeces from the body – is not excretion. Faeces are largely made up of undigested food, especially cellulose from plant material. These substances have never been absorbed into the blood, and are not products of metabolism. The term for the removal of faeces is **egestion**.

Nitrogenous waste

'Nitrogenous' means 'containing nitrogen', so nitrogenous waste is material within the body that we don't need, and that contains nitrogen.

The human body is unable to store any excess protein that we eat. As most people eat significantly more protein than required, something needs to be done with the excess. This happens in the liver, and it is called **deamination** (Fig 11.1).

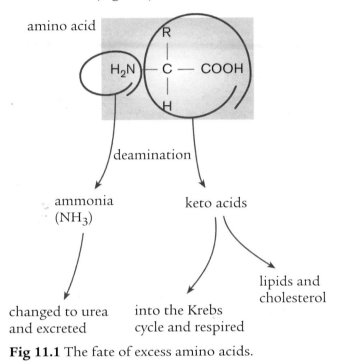

Fig 11.1 The fate of excess amino acids.

In deamination, excess amino acids (from excess protein) are broken down. The amino group is removed, and forms **ammonia**, NH_3. The rest of the amino acid molecule forms a keto acid, which can be respired to release energy, or converted to fat to be stored.

As we saw in the case study on page 235, ammonia is very toxic and cannot be allowed to remain in the body. Still in the liver, it is combined with carbon dioxide to form **urea**, $C(NH_2)_2O$. Urea, although still toxic, is nowhere near as dangerous as ammonia. The liver releases urea into the blood, where it dissolves in the plasma and is transported all over the body. Most of it is removed from the blood as it passes through the kidneys.

The structure of the kidneys

The two kidneys lie against the back of the abdominal cavity (that is, close to the backbone). A long, white tube runs from each of them to the **bladder**. These are the **ureters**, and they carry urine away from the kidneys and into the bladder where it is stored.

Each kidney is supplied with blood through a **renal artery**, which branches off from the aorta. A **renal vein** returns blood to the vena cava.

Fig 11.2 shows the gross structure of a human kidney. Kidney tissue is a deep, dark red. Seen with the naked eye, the surface of a kidney section shows it to be made up of an outer **cortex** and an inner, paler **medulla**. A whitish area, the pelvis, lies in the centre of one edge.

The nephrons

Each kidney is made up thousands of tiny tubes, called **nephrons** (Fig 11.3). These are much too small to be seen with the naked eye, and even with a microcscope it is not easy to see them clearly. This is because the nephrons take a very winding route from the outside of the kidney to the pelvis; when the kidney is cut through the cut will go through tiny bits of lots of different nephrons.

Ultrafiltration

Ultrafiltration, as its name suggests, involves filtration on a molecular scale. This process removes small molecules from the blood and into the lumens of the nephrons.

Ultrafiltration happens in the **renal capsules** of the kidneys. These are each made up of a **Bowman's capsule** (the starting point of the nephron) and a tangle of tiny blood capillaries called a **glomerulus**.

The blood in the glomerular capillaries is separated from the lumen of the Bowman's capsule by two cell layers and a basement membrane (Fig 11.4). The first cell layer is the lining, or endothelium, of the blood capillary. This, like that of most capillaries, has many small pores in it through which plasma can escape. Lying closely against this endothelium is a basement membrane and against that is the layer of cells making up the lining of the

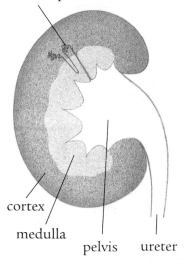

Fig 11.2 The structure of the kidney.

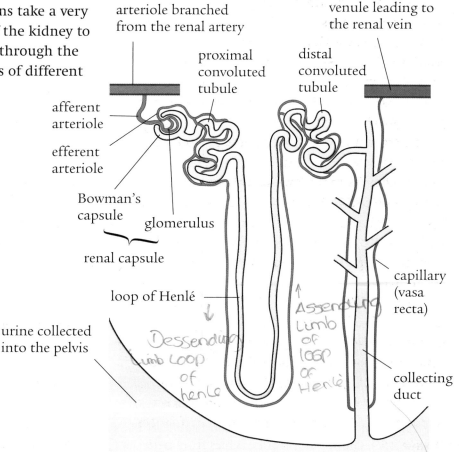

Fig 11.3 A kidney nephron.

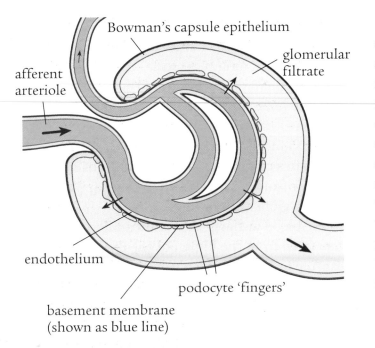

afferent arteriole

Bowman's capsule epithelium

glomerular filtrate

endothelium

podocyte 'fingers'

basement membrane (shown as blue line)

Fig 11.4 Renal capsule.

Bowman's capsule, called **podocytes**. 'Pod' means 'foot', and these cells have a very unusual structure: they have many projecting fingers that wrap themselves closely around the capillary loops of the glomerulus (Fig 11.5). Tiny slits are left between the interlocking podocyte fingers.

Blood arrives at the glomerulus in an **afferent arteriole**, and flows away from it in an **efferent arteriole**. The diameter of the efferent arteriole is less than that of the afferent arteriole, making it difficult for blood to flow away as easily as it flowed in. This results in a build-up of hydrostatic pressure inside the glomerular capillaries. Consequently, blood plasma is forced out through the pores in the capillaries, through the basement membrane and then through the slits between the podocytes. The fluid that passes through, into the cavity of the Bowman's capsule, is known as **glomerular filtrate**.

Not quite all the components of plasma can pass through this filter. No cells can pass through and proteins with a relative molecular mass greater than about 65 000 to 69 000 cannot get through, and they stay in the blood. Table 11.1 shows the composition of blood plasma and of glomerular filtrate.

Table 11.1 Concentrations of substances in blood plasma and glomerular filtrate.

Substance	Concentration in blood plasma / g dm^{-3}	Concentration in glomerular filtrate / g dm^{-3}
water	900	900
inorganic ions	7.2	7.2
urea	0.3	0.3
uric acid	0.04	0.04
glucose	1.0	1.0
amino acids	0.5	0.5
proteins	80.0	0.05

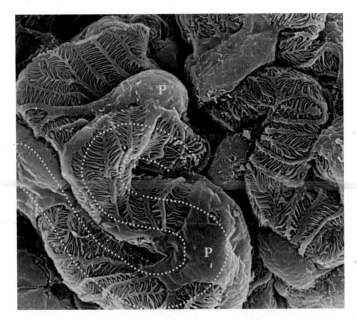

Fig 11.5 SEM of podocyte cells. A blood capillary runs inside the cylinder formed by the podocytes (yellow line). Glomerular filtrate issues from between the tiny fingers of the podocytes, as shown by arrows. The main cell bodies of two podocytes, in which the nucleus is found, are show by 'P'.

Selective reabsorption

As glomerular filtrate is simply blood plasma minus large proteins, it is inevitable that it will contain many substances that the body should keep, as well as others that it should get rid of. Selective reabsorption, which happens as the filtrate flows along the nephron, takes these wanted substances back into the blood.

Most of this reabsorption takes place in the **proximal convoluted tubule**. The walls of this part of the nephron are made up of a layer of cuboidal cells with microvilli on their inner surfaces (Fig 11.6).

Blood capillaries lie very closely against the outer surface of the capsule. The blood in these capillaries has come directly from the glomerulus, so it has much less plasma in it than usual and has lost many of the ions, small proteins and other substances that it was carrying as it entered the glomerulus.

The outer membranes of the cells of the proximal convoluted tubule actively transport sodium ions out of the cytoplasm. This lowers the concentration of sodium ions inside the cell, so that they passively diffuse into it from the filtrate, down their concentration gradient. In doing this, they pass through a transporter protein. There are several different sorts of these, and each one transports something else at the same time as sodium. They can even do this against a concentration gradient. For example, a sodium ion diffusing through one kind of transporter might carry a glucose molecule with it, up the concentration gradient for glucose. This is called **co-transport**.

In this way, all of the glucose in the proximal convoluted tubule is reabsorbed into the blood. Amino acids, vitamins, sodium ions and chloride ions are also reabsorbed here.

The removal of all these solutes from the glomerular filtrate greatly increases its water potential. But the water potential inside the cells in the nephron walls, and inside the blood capillaries, is *decreasing* as these ions and

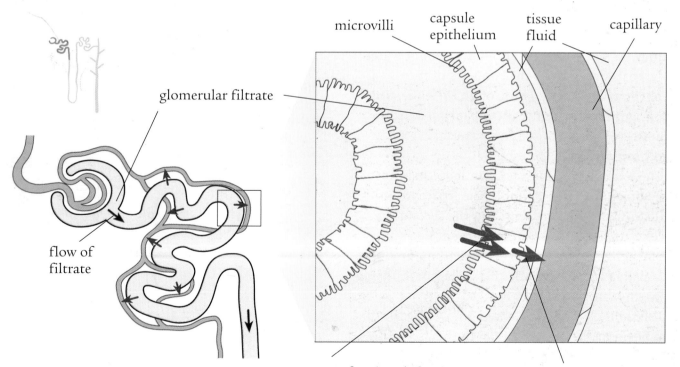

microvilli   capsule epithelium   tissue fluid   capillary

glomerular filtrate

flow of filtrate

co-transport of Na$^+$ and glucose across the inner membrane

active transport of Na$^+$ across outer membrane of tubule wall

Fig 11.6 Selective reabsorption from the proximal convoluted tubule.

molecules move into it. So a water potential gradient builds up. Water molecules move down this gradient, out of the nephron and into the blood. About 65% of the water in the filtrate is reabsorbed here. As the blood flows away, the water and other reabsorbed substances are taken with it.

Surprisingly, quite a lot of urea is reabsorbed too. Urea is a small molecule, which passes easily through cell membranes. Its concentration in the glomerular filtrate is considerably higher than in the capillaries so it diffuses passively through the wall of the proximal convoluted tubule and into the blood. About half of the urea in the filtrate is reabsorbed in this way.

All of this reabsorption greatly decreases the volume of the liquid remaining in the tubule. In an adult human, around $125\,cm^3$ of filtrate enters the proximal tubules each minute, and all but $45\,cm^3$ is reabsorbed.

The loop of Henlé

The function of the **loop of Henlé** is to create a very high concentration of sodium and chloride ions in the tissue fluid in the medulla of the kidney. As you will see, this allows a lot of water to be reabsorbed from the contents of the nephron when they pass through the collecting duct. This means that very concentrated urine can be produced, conserving water in the body and preventing dehydration.

The loop of Henlé is a hairpin loop that dips deep down into the medulla. The first part is called the **descending limb** and the second the **ascending limb**. These differ in their permeabilities to water. The descending limb is permeable to water, while the ascending limb is impermeable to it (Fig 11.7).

It is a bit easier to understand how it works if you begin at the 'wrong' end – in the ascending limb. The cells in the upper part of this limb actively transport sodium and chloride ions out of the nephron and into the surrounding tissues. This increases the water potential of the fluid inside the nephron and decreases the

water potential outside it. Water cannot pass out of the nephron at this point, because the walls are impermeable to it.

Now think about the descending limb. We have seen that its walls are permeable to water. As the fluid from the proximal convoluted tubule flows through the descending limb, it passes through the area into which sodium and chloride ions have been pumped. So there is a water potential gradient, and water flows down it from inside the descending limb into the tissues outside it.

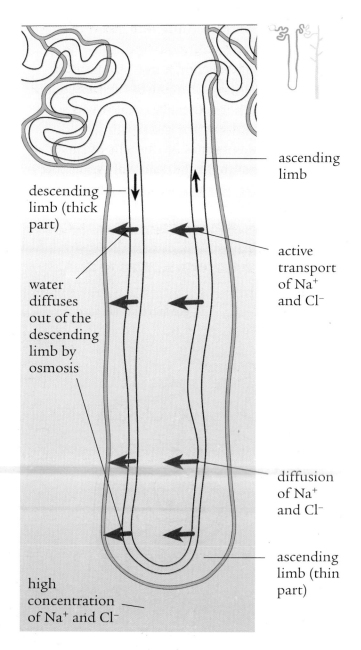

descending limb (thick part)

water diffuses out of the descending limb by osmosis

high concentration of Na$^+$ and Cl$^-$

ascending limb

active transport of Na$^+$ and Cl$^-$

diffusion of Na$^+$ and Cl$^-$

ascending limb (thin part)

Fig 11.7 The loop of Henlé.

As the fluid continues onwards, down the descending limb, it loses more and more water. By the time it gets to the bottom and goes around the hairpin, it is very concentrated indeed (that is, it has a very low water potential). And so is the tissue fluid outside it.

We have now arrived back at the ascending limb. The fluid that begins to go up this part of the loop is very concentrated – it has lost a lot of its water, so the concentration of the ions that remain is large. This makes it relatively easy to pump these ions out of the tubule as the fluid moves up.

Having the two limbs of the loop running next to each other like this, with the fluid flowing down one side and up the other, enables the maximum concentration to be built up both inside and outside the tube at the bottom of the loop. It is called a counter-current system.

The longer the loop of Henlé, the greater the concentration that can be built up. In humans, about one third of our nephrons have long loops of Henlé. In desert-living animals, such as gerbils, almost all of the loops are very long. This, as we shall see, is because the very low water potential that they build up in the medulla helps water to be conserved and not lost in the urine.

Reabsorption in the distal convoluted tubule and collecting duct

The fluid now flows through the distal convoluted tubule and into the **collecting duct** of the nephron. The cells in the walls of the distal convoluted tubule actively transport sodium ions out of the fluid, while potassium ions are actively transported into it.

As the fluid flows down the collecting duct, deeper into the medulla, it passes through the same regions as the deep parts of the loop of Henlé. The very low water potential in this region once more provides a water potential gradient, so that water flows out of the collecting duct and into the tissues around it. It moves into the blood capillaries (the vasa recta) and is transported away (Fig 11.8).

Now you can see how the loop of Henlé helps to conserve water. The lower the water potential it can build up, the greater will be the water potential gradient between the fluid inside the collecting ducts and the tissues outside the duct. This enables more water to be drawn out of the collecting duct, resulting in a smaller volume of more concentrated urine.

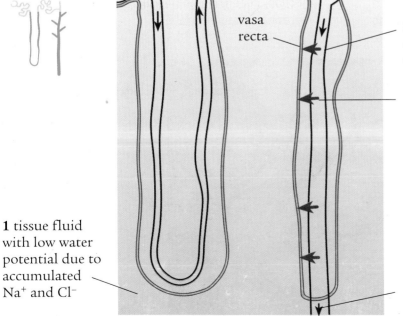

vasa recta

2 Water diffuses out of the collecting duct by osmosis when the collecting duct wall is permeable to water.

3 Water is collected and removed by the capillaries of the vasa recta.

1 tissue fluid with low water potential due to accumulated Na^+ and Cl^-

4 Urine with a very low water potential can be produced.

Fig 11.8 Reabsorption of water from the collecting duct.

Histology of the kidneys

Examine a stained slide of kidney tissue with the naked eye. See if you can identify the cortex and medulla by intensity of colour. This will help you make an early identification of these areas when the slide is being observed under the microscope.

1 Examine the slide under the lowest power objective. Identify the cortex and the medulla.

2 In the cortex, observe a glomerulus and proximal convoluted tubule. Move through the objectives to the highest power available. Look for signs of microvilli (a brush border) on the inside membrane of the proximal convoluted epithelium. Blood capillaries are always difficult to see in tissues, but you may be able to see the capillaries in a glomerulus. Draw and label.

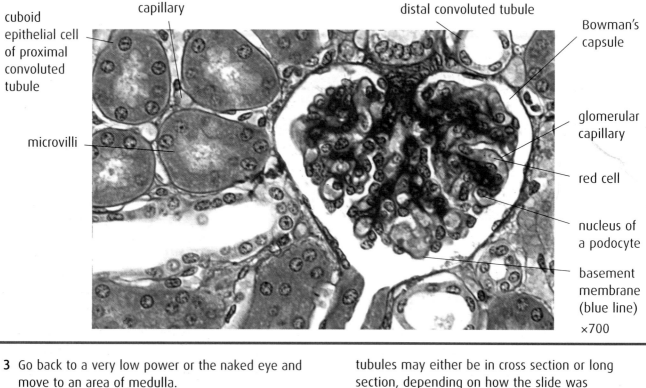

cuboid epithelial cell of proximal convoluted tubule

capillary

microvilli

distal convoluted tubule

Bowman's capsule

glomerular capillary

red cell

nucleus of a podocyte

basement membrane (blue line)

×700

3 Go back to a very low power or the naked eye and move to an area of medulla.
Examine at the highest power. Look for collecting duct, loop of Henlé and capillaries. Note that the tubules may either be in cross section or long section, depending on how the slide was sectioned. Draw and label.

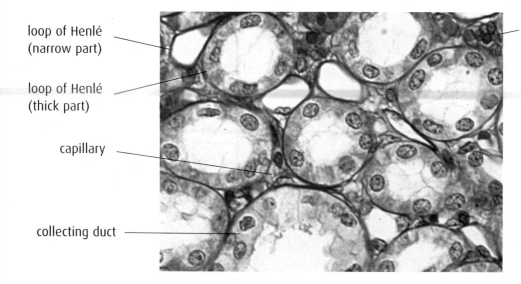

loop of Henlé (narrow part)

loop of Henlé (thick part)

capillary

collecting duct

venule containing red cells

×700

11.1 Although almost half of the urea in the glomerular filtrate is reabsorbed from the proximal convoluted tubule, the concentration of urea in the fluid that remains inside the nephron actually increases. Explain why.

11.2 The graph shows the relative concentrations of four substances as they pass along a nephron.
   a What is unusual about the y axis (vertical axis) of the graph? Why is it shown this way?
   b Take each curve in turn, and explain why it is this shape.

The control of water balance

As well as their role in excreting nitrogenous waste substances, the kidneys also play a central part in the control of the water content of the blood and tissue fluid. This is a vital part of homeostasis, and is known as **osmoregulation**.

Osmoregulation, like temperature regulation, is under the control of the hypothalamus. Like both temperature regulation and the regulation of blood glucose levels, it works by means of negative feedback.

The hypothalamus contains sensory neurones called **osmoreceptors**. They are sensitive to the water potential of the blood that passes through the hypothalamus. Their cell bodies produce a hormone called **anti-diuretic hormone**, or **ADH**. ADH is a small peptide, made up of just nine amino acids.

However, the osmoreceptor cells don't secrete this hormone directly into the blood. Instead the ADH passes along their axons which terminate in the posterior pituitary gland. (Oxytocin is secreted in the same way.)

If the water potential of the blood is too low (that is, it does not contain enough water) then some of this ADH will be released from the ends of these axons, just like a transmitter substance at a synapse. However, it is released into the blood, not into a synaptic cleft. The ADH is therefore secreted from the posterior pituitary gland, even though it was synthesised in the hypothalamus.

We have seen that water is reabsorbed from the fluid in the nephron and back into the blood as the fluid passes through the collecting ducts. Water is drawn out of the collecting ducts by osmosis, moving down its concentration gradient. The water balance of the body can be controlled by adjusting the permeability of the cell membranes of the collecting duct cells to water. Make them more permeable, and more water is reabsorbed and less is lost in the urine. Make them impermeable and no water is reabsorbed and more is lost in the urine.

These cells are the target cells for ADH. ADH molecules slot into receptors on their cell surface membranes. This causes little groups of protein molecules in their cytoplasm, called **aquaporins**, to move to the cell surface membrane and insert themselves into it (Fig 11.9). They form channels that allow water molecules to pass through.

So, with ADH in position, water can move freely out of the collecting ducts and back into the blood. A small volume of urine is therefore formed, and the body conserves water.

Everything goes into reverse if the blood contains too much water. The osmoreceptors in the hypothalamus are not stimulated, and so only a little ADH is released into the blood. Much less ADH binds to receptors in the cell surface membranes of the collecting duct cells, and the aquaporins move back into the cytoplasm. Now the walls of the collecting ducts are quite impermeable to water, so most of the water in the fluid inside the collecting ducts flows along and into the bladder. Large volumes of dilute urine are produced.

no ADH – no water reabsorption

ADH – water reabsorption

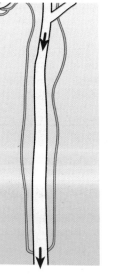

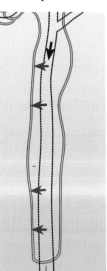

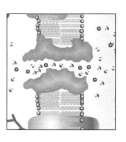

an aquaporin – this channel allows water molecules to move through cell surface membranes

large volume of urine with high water potential

small volume of urine with low water potential

Fig 11.9 ADH and water reabsorption.

JUST FOR INTEREST

Two similar hormones

Oxytocin, which is responsible for muscle contraction of the uterus during childbirth and expressing breast milk when a baby suckles, and ADH are very similar to each other. Both are peptides containing just nine amino acids. Their gene loci are close to one another on chromosome 20.

Their similarities are so great that oxytocin can actually bind to the ADH receptors in the cell surface membranes of the collecting duct cells in the kidneys. Infusion of oxytocin into the blood is used to induce labour in women where it is believed to be overdue. Sometimes this can lead to water retention, so that body fluids become much more dilute than they should. If unchecked, this can lead to convulsions.

Urine as a diagnostic tool

A sample of a patient's urine can be very helpful in the diagnosis of illness. Urine contains many of the waste products of metabolism, and if a doctor knows what these are then he or she is often given useful clues about the nature of the patient's illness.

Urine is easy to obtain and easy to test. There is no need for any invasive procedure or technical skill, such as is needed for taking a blood sample. A quick urine test, even though it may not give a definite diagnosis, can be very helpful in pointing a doctor towards a likely one, and therefore in deciding what further tests should be done.

Urine for testing should be collected 'mid-stream' – that is, not right at the beginning of urination nor right at the end. If collected at the beginning of urination, the sample could contain bacteria or other contaminants that are present in or close to the urethra, which could confuse the results.

Medieval use of urine

In medieval times, urine inspection – a procedure known as uroscopy – was one of the very few tools that a physician could use to help him to diagnose illness. Between the seventh and seventeenth centuries, large numbers of manuscripts explaining its use were published.

When a physician arrived at the house of a patient, the first thing he would be shown would be the chamber-pot. Many physicians advocated the collection of urine in a pot that had the same shape as the bladder, so that it would have the same shape as the urine in the body and thus give a more accurate diagnosis. The urine would be studied straight after urination when it was hot, again after one hour and then for a third time when completely cold.

Just looking at urine was not always enough. Many physicians also tasted it. Sweetness indicated diabetes mellitus.

To help physicians in their diagnosis, colour charts were produced with up to 20 different shades. Bright gold was good;

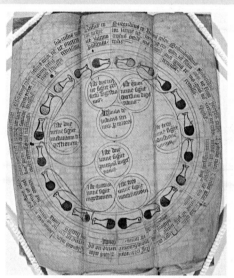

14th century physician's belt book. The dark colored samples at five o'clock are linked to a caption reading, "these urines signify death."

colourless was bad. There is a not dissimilar present-day chart that some athletes use.

Urine was also a component in the production of several important materials in medieval times. It was used in fulling, a process in which wool was made softer. Large vats were partly filled with urine, the wool added and then trodden by people standing up to their knees in it. In the leather industry, urine was used to tan leather; hides were soaked in a mixture of urine and cattle dung. Urine was also used for making dyes, as a fertiliser (said to be especially good for apple trees) and in a number of medicines.

We have seen that a person with diabetes mellitus is likely to excrete glucose in their urine after a carbohydrate-containing meal. Only a small sample of urine is needed to test for the presence of glucose. Dip-sticks for glucose testing can be bought at any pharmacy, and they are very easy to use. Colour charts supplied with the dip-sticks make interpretation of the results very straightforward.

Urine can also enable the diagnosis of another kind of diabetes – **diabetes insipidus**. This illness has nothing to do with diabetes mellitus. Diabetes insipidus is the result of a malfunction of the mechanism for control of water balance in the body. A person with diabetes insipidus excretes large amounts of dilute urine, even when their blood water content is low. There are several causes of this illness. In some cases it is a genetic disease, caused by a mutation in one of the genes coding for the production of aquaporins. In others it is a result of a malfunction in ADH secretion, perhaps because the hypothalamus has been damaged by injury or a tumour.

Other tests can be done on urine, such as looking for the presence of hGH in pregnancy testing. Breakdown products of most hormones are present in it, and – as well as helping to diagnose disease – these can indicate use of performance-enhancing drugs by athletes.

Summary

1. Excretion is the removal of waste products of metabolism from the body, some of which are toxic.

2. Carbon dioxide is a waste product of respiration, and is excreted by the lungs.

3. Excess amino acids cannot be stored, and they are deaminated by the liver to form first ammonia and then urea. Urea is our main nitrogenous excretory product.

4. The kidneys are supplied with blood through the renal artery, and the renal vein takes blood back to the vena cava. Ureters connect the kidneys with the bladder. In section, they can be seen to be made up of an outer, dark cortex and an inner, paler medulla.

5. A kidney contains thousands of tubules called nephrons. These begin in the cortex as Bowman's capsules, which are in very close contact with a knot of capillaries known as a glomerulus.

6. Ultrafiltration takes place because of a relatively high blood pressure that builds up in the glomerulus, which forces ions and molecules with a molecular mass less than about 65 000 out of the capillaries and into the lumen of the Bowman's capsule. Red and white cells and large proteins remain in the blood.

7. Selective reabsorption takes place throughout the nephron. In the proximal convoluted tubule, active transport of sodium and co-transport of glucose allows almost all glucose to be reabsorbed, along with much of the water and most amino acids and vitamins.

Summary continued...

8 In the loop of Henlé, a counter-current mechanism helps to build up a high concentration (low water potential) in the tissues in the medulla. As the fluid flows through the collecting ducts, this high concentration causes water to pass out of them down its water potential gradient.

9 Water content of the blood is sensed by osmoreceptors in the hypothalamus, and controlled through a negative feedback mechanism.

10 The degree to which water passes out of the collecting ducts is controlled by ADH. This is secreted by the posterior pituitary gland and increases the permeability to water of the cell surface membranes of the cells of the collecting duct. Much of the water is therefore reabsorbed into the body.

11 Analysis of urine can give clues that help with the diagnosis of disease. A person with diabetes mellitus may have glucose in their urine. A person with diabetes insipidus passes large amounts of very dilute urine.

Kidney failure

Kidney failure is an illness in which the kidneys stop working properly. It may be acute, suddenly happening in the space of a few days or even hours. Or it can be chronic, developing slowly over perhaps many years.

Causes of kidney failure

There are very many possible reasons why the kidneys stop functioning. Acute kidney failure often happens when the patient already has some other illness or following surgery. Sometimes it is caused by an inflammation within the glomerulus or happens as a result of sepsis (infection of the blood and body tissues by bacteria).

Chronic kidney failure is usually caused by inflammation in the glomeruli. There often is no clear reason to explain why this has happened. It is most common in older people, and people with diabetes stand a greater risk of chronic kidney failure than others.

Diagnosing kidney failure

A person with acute kidney failure will be feeling extremely ill. There will usually be very little output of urine, because ultrafiltration isn't happening. However, some types of failure may have exactly the opposite effect, resulting in the production of large volumes of urine. Chronic kidney failure is usually characterised by more urine than normal being produced. The patient will probably have coped with it for a long time, drinking more to compensate for the loss of liquid.

The failure of the kidneys to extract and excrete unwanted substances from the blood means that the contents of blood and urine will be different from those of a person whose kidneys are working correctly. Blood tests may show that there is too much water present, or too few potassium ions (because potassium ions are not being excreted and because all the water in the blood dilutes it so much). Urine samples, if any urine can be obtained, may show very unusual concentrations of various ions and molecules, and may contain blood. In chronic renal failure, urine usually contains large proteins that would not normally be there. Ultrasound tests may be used to see if there are any obstructions (such as kidney stones) that are preventing urine leaving the kidneys or flowing along the ureters.

Treating kidney failure

A person with acute renal failure is likely to recover completely from it, but this is not so for chronic renal failure. So, while treatment for acute renal failure will aim to keep the person alive until the kidneys start working normally again, treatment for chronic renal failure will try to slow the progression of the illness.

In both cases, fluid intake will be carefully controlled to try to do the usual job of the kidneys in keeping the water balance in the body correct. Ideally, the volume of urine produced in one day will be measured, and then this same volume of liquids will be drunk on the next day. Intake of sodium ions and proteins in the diet will also be controlled. If too much fluid is being lost in urine, then a saline drip may be used to restore the blood to its normal volume and water potential.

Renal dialysis

In severe cases of renal failure, the patient will be treated using **dialysis**. This treatment mimics the role of the kidneys in ultrafiltration.

In **haemodialysis**, blood from the patient's vein is passed through very small tubes made from a partially permeable membrane. On the other side of the membrane, dialysis fluid flows along in the opposite direction (Fig 11.10). This fluid has the water potential and concentration of ions and glucose that the patient's blood should have if their kidneys were working properly (see Table 11.2). As their blood flows through the tubes, water, ions and glucose are able to diffuse freely through the membrane so that concentrations of each of them become the same as in the dialysis fluid. Blood cells and protein molecules are too large to pass through the membrane, so they remain in the blood.

Peritoneal dialysis is now used more commonly than haemodialysis. The peritoneum is the layer of tissue that lines the abdominal cavity. This cavity contains fluid, which bathes the internal organs. In peritoneal dialysis, a catheter is inserted into the peritoneal cavity and dialysis fluid is passed through it, filling the cavity. It is left there for some time, allowing exchange between the blood and the fluid, and then drained off. It takes around half

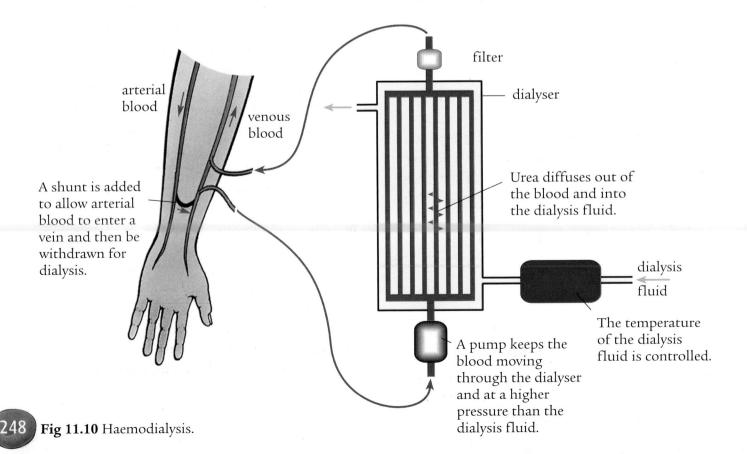

arterial blood

venous blood

A shunt is added to allow arterial blood to enter a vein and then be withdrawn for dialysis.

filter

dialyser

Urea diffuses out of the blood and into the dialysis fluid.

dialysis fluid

The temperature of the dialysis fluid is controlled.

A pump keeps the blood moving through the dialyser and at a higher pressure than the dialysis fluid.

Fig 11.10 Haemodialysis.

Table 11.2 The composition of dialysis fluid and plasma.

	Dialysis fluid /mmol dm^{-3}	Blood plasma /mmol dm^{-3}
sodium ions	130–135	136–145
potassium ions	1.5–3.0	3.5–5.0
calcium ions	1.6–1.8	1.0–1.4
magnesium ions	0.5–0.75	0.75–1.0
chloride ions	95–100	95–105
hydrogencarbonate ions	35–40	22–28
glucose	0–10	3.8–6.1
urea	0	6.5–8.2

Note: The composition of dialysis fluid is modified to suit individuals.

to three quarters of an hour for the fluid to be introduced to the abdomen, take up wastes from the blood and then be drained off again. In most cases, patients can walk around with the fluid inside them, though they do need to have fluid introduced and removed several times each day.

These two types of dialysis each have their advantages and disadvantages.

Haemodialysis is more efficient at removing unwanted substances from the blood, but it does take several hours and a patient has to be connected to the machine for that time. Kidney dialysis machines are very expensive, and in short supply. Moreover, if haemodialysis is done intermittently, then the patient may experience wide fluctuations of water content of the blood and also the concentrations of various dissolved substances within it, in between treatments. Another problem is that it becomes progressively harder to find a suitable blood vessel because scar tissue builds up.

Peritoneal dialysis, on the other hand, allows the patient to walk around freely while dialysis is happening. It is a continuous process, so there should be no large swings in blood volume or content. However, it does run a much greater risk of infection, because pathogens might enter the abdomen through the catheter.

Kidney transplants

By far the best treatment for a person with kidney failure is a successful kidney transplant. However, as we have seen (see page 207), finding an organ with the correct tissue type is very difficult. Many kidney patients have to wait years for a transplant. Table 9.1 on page 213 summarises the main sources of organs, including kidneys, for transplant and some of the problems associated with them.

As a person can survive perfectly well with one kidney, it is often possible to take a kidney from a living relative and transplant it into the person with kidney disease. This can work well, because there is a good chance of a close tissue match, and the relative may really want to help the patient.

However, the shortage of kidneys available for transplant and the fact that the donor can manage with only one kidney has fuelled the growth of a global trade in human kidneys. International rings have been uncovered where people living in poverty are persuaded to sell a kidney for cash. The kidneys are then sold on to a recipient, with the middle-man making a considerable profit on the transaction. This raises a number of ethical questions. It can be argued that these people are being exploited, that they run a greater risk of illness if their remaining kidney fails or if the operation to remove the donated kidney is done badly, and that they do not receive much money for it. On the other hand, many of the people who donate their organs are desperately poor, and the money they get for the sale may be as much as a year's normal salary for them. If they live a normal life afterwards, then they are happy with the arrangement. It is likely that this type of sale in body parts from living donors will continue, going underground in countries where laws are passed against it. The best way to stop it may be to increase the number of organs available from people who have died, but as yet little real progress has been made with this.

Summary

1. Kidney failure is an illness in which the kidneys stop working normally. There are many different causes, including inflammation of the glomeruli and side effects of surgery.

2. Kidney failure can be diagnosed by blood tests and urine tests. Different types of failure give different results to these tests. A patient with acute kidney failure may be producing very little urine, so that toxic waste products and water build up in their blood. However, in chronic kidney failure it is more normal for too much urine to be produced, and it may contain large protein molecules.

3. Initial treatment will try to maintain the concentration and content of the blood as normal as possible, by controlling fluid and nutrient intake, possibly using a saline drip.

Acute kidney failure may not need any further treatment, but chronic kidney failure may require dialysis.

4. Haemodialysis passes blood through tubes made of partially permeable membranes, with dialysis fluid flowing in the opposite direction on the other side of the membranes. In peritoneal dialysis, the abdominal cavity is filled with dialysis fluid, which is removed and replaced several times a day.

5. Kidney transplants are the best treatment, but there is a shortage of kidneys and tissue matches are difficult to make. The fact that a person can live a healthy life with one kidney has meant that living donors may be used. Most people are happy with the ethics of this if the donor is a family member, but the sale of organs for cash raises several ethical issues.

CHAPTER 12

Ageing

Who is the person who has lived to the greatest age? That's an impossible question to answer. In many countries there are still no reliable records of births and deaths, and even in developed countries these have only been available within the last 100 years or so.

One contender must be Elizabeth Israel. She was born in Dominica (in the West Indies) on January 27th 1875 and died on October 10th 2003. If her birth record is correct, she was 128 years old at the time of her death. She was the daughter of a slave, and worked in sugar plantations until she was 100.

In Europe, the oldest known person was Jeanne Calment, a French woman who died on August 4th 1997 at the age of 122. Her birth certificate recorded her date of birth as February 21st 1875. She outlived not only her husband, but also her only child and her only grandson. For the last 12 years of her life she lived in a retirement home in Arles. Despite being blind and nearly deaf, Jeanne retained her sharp mental faculties. She remembered Van Gogh, as being "dirty, badly dressed and disagreeable" when he visited her father's art supplies shop in Arles. She smoked until she was 120, but kept active; she began fencing lessons when she was 85.

Japan seems to be a place where you can expect to live to a very old age. On October 31st 2003, Kamato Hongo died aged 116, and on November 13th in the same year, Mitoyo Kawate died at the age of 114.

Did any of these people have special secrets? It seems not. The Japanese diet, which contains a lot of rice, oily fish and vegetables, may perhaps explain the relatively long life expectancy of Japanese people. But Jeanne Calment's smoking and Elizabeth Israel's fondness for dumplings don't quite fit in with what most people consider to be a healthy lifestyle. The only factor that they all seem to have in common is their sex – they are all women. If you want to live a long life, then being female is your best bet.

We all begin to age as soon as we are born. 'Ageing' simply means getting older. None of us can escape that. However, we may be able to affect **senescence** – the deterioration of our bodies as they succumb to age-related changes and to disease.

Factors affecting life expectancy

The case study shows that being female is very helpful if you want to live to a ripe old age. Your nationality also has a large effect on life expectancy. Fig 12.1 shows the average life expectancy of babies born in six different countries in 2004.

We don't thoroughly understand what causes the differences shown in Fig 12.1. Certainly lifestyle does have an effect. For example, the so-called 'Mediterranean diet', rich in olive oil and vegetables and low in red meat, seems to be associated with increased life expectancy. The low expectancies in many countries in sub-Saharan Africa are largely due to the high incidence of HIV/AIDS. But genes are also important, and there is evidence that if your parents lived a long life then this increases the chances that you will, too.

Ageing is a hot topic for research in the twenty-first century. Most of us think we would like to live longer, and drug companies see the development of drugs that might help us to do so as being potentially highly lucrative.

In this chapter, we will look at some especially important issues related to ageing in the United Kingdom. These include the changes that take place in women's bodies as they reach and pass the menopause, and also the changes that occur in several body systems in all of us as we age.

The menopause

The **menopause** can be defined as the time of the last menstrual cycle of a woman. It normally occurs between the ages of 50 and 54, but it can happen as early as 35 years of age and as late as 59. The timing of the menopause seems to have a strong genetic component; a woman whose mother had a late menopause is more likely to have one herself. The average age at menopause has probably remained unchanged for thousands of years. However, other factors do affect it; smokers, for example, are likely to go through the menopause earlier than non-smokers.

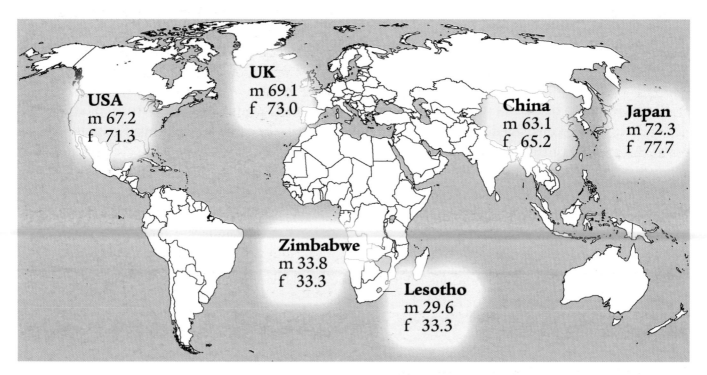

Fig 12.1 Life expectancy at birth in years for males (m) and females (f).

Leading up to the menopause, most women experience a few years in which their menstrual cycle becomes irregular. This is often referred to as the 'menopause', but a doctor will call this the peri-menopause.

The causes of the menopause

The cause of the menopause is the lack of ovarian follicles. You may remember (see page 112) that a baby girl is born with hundreds of thousands of primary oocytes in follicles in her ovaries. From the age of around 12, one of these follicles ruptures and releases an oocyte each month. Many of the follicles never do this, instead just gradually disappearing. Eventually, there are no follicles or oocytes left.

The follicles secrete oestrogen, so with no follicles the woman no longer has this hormone circulating in her body. Nearly all of the features of the post-menopausal stage of life described below are caused by the lack of oestrogen.

As oestrogen secretion declines, the secretion of FSH and LH increases, reaching a peak at around one to three years after the last menstrual cycle. However, the secretion of these hormones gradually ceases over time.

The media like to talk about the 'male menopause', but men do not experience anything like the female menopause. They do not have a sudden drop-off in sex hormones. There may well be changes in their physiology as they age, but this cannot be linked to hormonal changes such as are seen in women.

Why does the menopause happen?

The gradual death of oocytes and follicle cells is pre-programmed and is a built-in part of the life cycle of a woman. It seems strange that women should experience menopause while men don't. We cannot be certain why this is so, but it is arguable that the female menopause may have some evolutionary advantage.

Producing a baby is not an easy thing for a female body to do. The demands on the body during pregnancy and birth are considerable, and it is probable that, at least in times or places where no medical care was available, an older mother and her baby would stand a significantly smaller chance of survival than a younger woman. So perhaps the menopause is a 'safety measure' helping older women to live longer. This could explain why men continue to make sperm all their lives; fathering a child is much less demanding physiologically than being a mother.

But this answer still begs the question of why a woman should live so far beyond the age at which she can reproduce. Once she has finished reproducing there is no reason, according to natural selection, why she should go on living at all. She is not going to pass on her genes to any more children.

Some research, however, indicates that a post-menopausal woman may still be able to increase the chance of her genes surviving in future generations. In non-industrial societies, old people are greatly valued as contributors to their community. They may have memories of previous events that they can use to advise the younger generation. For example, in a serious drought of a kind that has not happened for 50 years, it is the old people who may remember what their community did on that occasion in order to survive. Giving their advice can help their descendants to cope with the situation this time around. They may also make a contribution on a day-to-day basis, perhaps by caring for their grand-children while the parents are working.

In early societies, as in a number of countries today, such as Zimbabwe and Lesotho (Fig 12.1), most women did not live long enough to reach the menopause. It may be that the menopause did not really 'evolve' at all, but is simply an accident of the fact that now women can live longer, beyond the age at which their ovaries continue to produce viable oocytes.

Changes in physiology

Leading up to and following the menopause, women may experience a number of changes in their physiology.

Some of these changes affect the reproductive system itself. The ovaries gradually decrease in size, and all the follicles within them disappear, so the woman becomes **infertile**. She may also experience dryness of the vagina, which may decrease enjoyment of sexual activity.

Many women experience **hot flushes**. A hot flush is a feeling of suddenly increasing warmth, especially in the upper body. For some women they cause great discomfort. They may happen during the night, disrupting sleep patterns and therefore indirectly causing tiredness. They are often accompanied by sweating. Hot flushes are most likely to happen in the first few years after the menopause, and are caused by the effective 'withdrawal' of oestrogen.

In almost all women, there is an increased rate of loss of bone density after the menopause. Bone is a living tissue, and is constantly being re-made throughout life. Cells called **osteoclasts** break down bone tissue, while **osteoblasts** build it up. As we age, there is an increase in the activity of osteoclasts and a decrease in the activity of osteoblasts, so that the density of bone tissue slowly decreases throughout life. For most of us, this loss begins around the age of 30.

As bone becomes less dense, it is increasingly easy for it to fracture. Once density drops below about $830 \, mg \, cm^{-3}$, the person is said to have **osteoporosis** (Fig 12.2). Even a sudden movement can cause a bone to fracture. It is estimated that half of all women over 75 years of age have fractures in their vertebrae, and this is responsible for the 'hunched' posture of some older women. A fall may break the pelvic girdle (hip bones), which in an elderly person may cause permanent disability or even death.

Both women and men may develop osteoporosis, but it is commoner in women, perhaps at least partly because their bone mass tends to be less than that of men to start with.

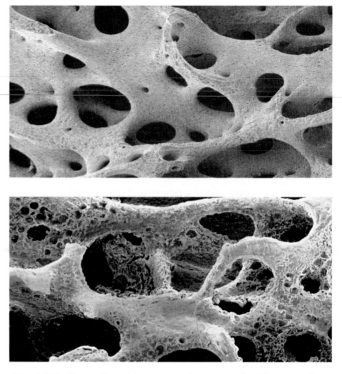

Fig 12.2 Scanning electronmicrograph of normal bone (top) and bone from a person with osteoporosis (bottom).

Oestrogen protects against loss of bone mass, which is why this loss increases after the menopause. Other risk factors (besides being female and post-menopausal) include smoking and the use of steroid hormones on a regular basis.

Another aspect of physiology that changes after the menopause is the risk of **cardiovascular disease**. Oestrogen appears to help arterioles to dilate, and also reduces blood cholesterol levels, so once oestrogen is no longer produced the risk of cardiovascular disease rises.

HRT

HRT stands for **hormone replacement therapy**. It is a therapy used by many women to combat the unpleasant symptoms and risks associated with the menopause.

HRT consists of regular doses of **oestrogen**, which reverses all of the physiological effects described above. Because oestrogen alone has been shown to increase the risk of uterine cancer, it is taken in combination with progestin, a progesterone-like hormone.

Types of HRT

There are many different kinds of HRT that a woman may try.

Unopposed oestrogen therapy involves providing the body with oestrogen each day, but not with progesterone. This kind of therapy is prescribed to women who have undergone 'early menopause' because they have had a hysterectomy (removal of the uterus).

Because oestrogen alone is known to increase the risk of **endometrial** (uterine) cancer, women whose uterus is still in place will also be prescribed progestin, as this reduces this risk. This is called **combined HRT**. In some cases, the progestin is taken on all the days that oestrogen is taken, whereas in others it is only taken for part of the time.

Some women take the same hormones all the time, on every day of the month. This is known as a **continuous schedule**. A woman may take the HRT hormones orally (in tablet form), or they can be administered through a skin patch (Fig 12.3) or as an under-skin implant, which lasts for three months. The skin patch is popular because, once in place, it can be forgotten about. It also has the advantage that it can deliver the hormones steadily, whereas tablets provide surges just after they are taken. Because the skin patch delivers the hormones straight into the blood stream, lower doses are needed than with tablets and so side effects tend to be less of a problem. The patch usually needs to be replaced once or twice a week. It can be kept on while swimming or in the bath.

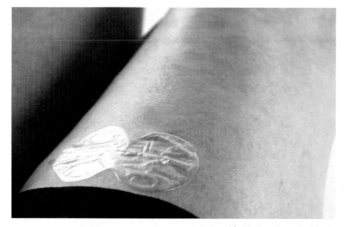

Fig 12.3 HRT skin patch.

Another possibility is a **cyclic** regime. In one kind of cyclic therapy, oestrogen and progestin are taken for three weeks, and then stopped for the next week, during which the woman will have a 'period'. Alternatively, oestrogen may be taken continuously while progestin is taken for 10 to 14 days each month, following which a 'period' takes place, known as withdrawal bleeding. This does not happen if a continuous schedule is used.

Benefits of HRT

There is no question that a woman taking HRT can expect a number of benefits.

Regular doses of oestrogen and progestin can prevent hot flushes, reduce the risk of developing osteoporosis, and prevent vaginal dryness.

HRT greatly reduces the incidence of osteoporosis. The presence of oestrogen in the body protects bones from the increasing rate of loss of mass that is seen after the menopause.

Undesirable effects of HRT

Many women who begin HRT don't continue with it, because of unpleasant side effects that they experience. These side effects include mood changes, discomfort in the breasts and worries that they might develop problems in the circulatory system or get breast cancer. Overall, only about one in three women stick with HRT for more than one year. It is likely that this will increase as new ways of taking HRT reduce the side effects. A woman may need to try several different HRT regimes until she finds one that really suits her.

HRT, especially that which includes both oestrogen and progestin, does increase the risk of breast cancer. A large British study published in 2003 showed that women who take combined HRT for five years or more are twice as likely to develop breast cancer as if they did not take HRT, while for those taking oestrogen only the risk was three times greater than normal. The longer HRT was taken, the greater the risk of breast cancer. However, it is important to realise that these risks are still fairly small. For example, in a group of 1000 women taking combined HRT between the ages of 50 and 55, six developed breast cancer by the age of 65. In a similar group taking HRT until they were 60, 19 developed breast cancer. Other studies, especially a large one undertaken in the USA, have also indicated an increased risk although not as high as was found in the British study.

There is also some evidence that HRT may slightly increase the likelihood of developing Alzheimer's disease (see page 261).

Other studies suggest that HRT can increase the risk of cardiovascular disease. A very large study undertaken in the USA, which stopped in 2002, followed 8506 women taking HRT and another 8102 who took a placebo instead. They found that, if there were 10 000 HRT users, seven more would have heart attacks than in 10 000 non-HRT users, eight more would have strokes and eight more would suffer a pulmonary embolism.

JUST FOR INTEREST

Misunderstandings

The way that data are reported can have a large effect on their perception by most members of the public.

For example, in the large study in the USA mentioned above, in five years 166 members of the HRT group had developed breast cancer, compared with 124 in the placebo group. To be able to make a fair comparison, a calculation needs to be made that takes into account the different numbers of participants in each group. The researchers worked out the number of women out of 10 000 who would be expected to get breast cancer. They also calculated the number per year, rather than the total numbers over five years. As there were 8506 in the HRT group and 8102 in the non-HRT group, this works out as:

HRT group breast cancer incidence per 10 000 per year $= \dfrac{10\,000 \times 166}{8506 \times 5}$

$= 39$

non-HRT group breast cancer incidence per 10 000 per year $= \dfrac{10\,000 \times 124}{8102 \times 5}$

$= 31$

This means that out of 10 000 women, you would expect eight more women per year to get breast cancer if they took HRT than if they did not. This is a tiny increase.

Another way of showing this risk is to convert it to a percentage. 39 per 10 000 is 0.39%. 31 per 10 000 is 0.31%. So we can say that the percentage risk of getting breast cancer is 0.08% greater if you take HRT than if you don't. That doesn't sound too scary. But it can also be expressed another way. If 39 per 10 000 get breast cancer with HRT and 31 per 10 000 get breast cancer without HRT, we can say that the percentage increase is:

$$\dfrac{(39 - 31) \times 100}{31}$$

$$= 25.8\%$$

It is perfectly correct that the risk of getting breast cancer is 25.8% greater if you are on HRT than if you are not. But many women don't understand this. They see that figure and think that they have a 25.8% chance of getting breast cancer if they take HRT. The media picked up on this (probably the journalists did not understand the figures) and published scare stories. Not surprisingly, many women have made the decision that this risk is too great for them to take, and have stopped taking HRT.

Alternatives to HRT

Many women who have tried HRT and didn't feel well on it, or who don't want to try it at all, look for alternative remedies to relieve unpleasant symptoms and to reduce the risk of developing heart disease or osteoporosis.

A popular alternative remedy involves **phytoestrogens**. These are chemicals, found in plants, that have a similar molecular structure to oestrogen, and can act at the same receptor sites on cell surface membranes, so they can mimic some of the effects of oestrogen. However, these effects are much smaller than those produced with HRT. Phytoestrogens include:

- isoflavones, found in beans, especially soya
- coumestans, found in germinating seeds, such as alfalfa
- lignans, found in cereal grains, most vegetables and fruits.

Several studies have been carried out on the effectiveness of a diet rich in phytoestrogens, and some studies suggest that they do produce a significant decrease in post-menopausal symptoms for some women. However, in the

SAQ

12.1 The graph shows the results of the large study in the USA into the health of women taking HRT compared with those not taking HRT. The study involved 8506 women taking HRT and 8102 who did not take it.

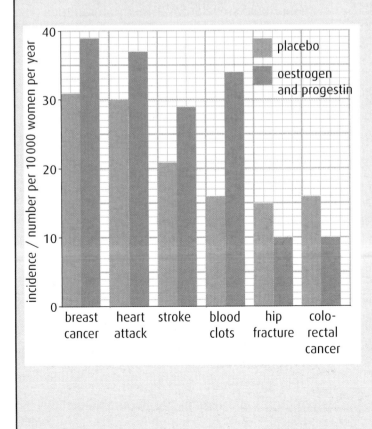

a Summarise the broad findings of this study in relation to the beneficial and harmful effects of taking HRT.

bi Use the graph to calculate the difference in the number of women per 10 000 per year on HRT who suffered a stroke, compared with those not on HRT.

ii Use your answer to i to determine how many more women in 100 would be expected to suffer a stroke when on HRT and when not on HRT.

iii Calculate the percentage increase in the risk of a stroke if a woman takes HRT. (See the Just for Interest on page 256 if you are not sure how to do this.)

iv Explain why the value you have calculated could mislead many women.

v What do you think would be the best way to present these data so that most women could understand what they mean?

c This study had been intended to run until 2005, but when the set of results shown in the graph emerged, indicating the increased risk of breast cancer, it was decided to stop the study. Discuss the merits of this decision.

year 2000 a double blind trial (that is, one in which neither the subjects nor the researchers knew whether a woman was taking phytoestrogens or a placebo) involving 94 post-menopausal women found that soy products had no effect on menopausal symptoms. And many studies indicate that they do not have any effect on osteoporosis.

A similar product that is on sale in health food shops is wild yam cream. It is advertised as containing oestrogen- and progesterone-precursors. It does contain a substance called diosgenin, and this can be converted into oestrogen and progesterone in a laboratory. But this does not happen in the body because we don't have enzymes that can do it. Wild yam cream has not been shown to have any benefits.

Many women also take **antioxidant** supplements to relieve menopausal symptoms.

These include **vitamin A** and **beta-carotene**, **vitamin C** and **vitamin E**. Antioxidants can combine with free radicals produced within the body, preventing them from causing damage to cells. However, there is little evidence that taking these as supplements does any good; it does in fact seem that taking beta-carotene supplements if you smoke can increase the risk of lung cancer. But eating a diet with plenty of foods containg antioxidants is good for you. For example, a diet rich in vitamin E may protect against cataracts, cancer and Alzheimer's disease. The best advice is therefore to eat a good diet rather than taking antioxidants as supplements. Foods containing high quantities of antioxidants include all red, yellow and dark green fruits and vegetables, and citrus fruits.

Summary

1. Women usually stop ovulating at the age of around 50 to 54. This is known as the menopause.

2. After the menopause, oestrogen is no longer secreted from the ovaries. There are no oocytes produced, so the woman is now infertile. The lack of oestrogen may cause hot flushes, vaginal dryness and a loss of bone density that can lead to osteoporosis. It also increases the risk of heart disease.

3. Post-menopausal women may benefit from hormone replacement therapy, HRT. This involves providing the body with oestrogen. Oestrogen alone increases the risk of endometrial cancer, and so – unless the woman has had her uterus removed – it is normally given alongside progestin.

4. Some HRT programmes involve continuous administration of the hormones, either through a skin patch, an implant under the skin or by taking tablets every day. Other programmes are cyclic, in which there is a change in the hormones in a four-week cycle.

5. HRT can have unwanted side effects. It does slightly increase the risk of breast cancer, Alzheimer's disease and cardiovascular disease. However, these effects are all small, and may be outweighed by the beneficial effects.

6. Phytoestrogens are an alternative treatment for post-menopausal symptoms. Some women can benefit from these, but trials do not show consistent effects. Trials of antioxidant supplements have failed to find any beneficial effect of these in post-menopausal women. However, eating foods rich in antioxidants does appear to reduce symptoms and risks of developing some illnesses.

Other effects of ageing

Would you like to live forever? Each year, the life expectancy of a child born in the UK increases. A male baby born in 1910 could expect to live to the age of 55, whereas a male baby born in 2000 has a life expectancy of 74. Women have done even better. A female baby born in 1910 had a life expectancy of 58, but if she were born in 2000 it would have been 82.

Unfortunately, the news is not all good for the latter stages of our lives. Although we may live longer, we are likely to spend a longer period of our lives with some form of health problem that may reduce our ability to enjoy life. Although life expectancy has greatly increased, the age at which we begin to experience ill health related to ageing has not increased as much. In the future, each of us is likely to spend many more years suffering from ill health than if we had been born 100 years ago. Between 1981 and 2001, a man's life expectancy increased by 6.8% (from 70.9 to 75.7) while the amount of time he could expect to have poor health increased by 34% (from 6.5 years to 8.7 years).

These statistics have implications for society and the economy. With more elderly people in the population, many of them in ill health, more money will be needed to care for them. Pensions will need to be paid for longer. To meet this expense, taxes may need to be increased. Retirement ages may also be increased, so that everyone keeps working longer and has fewer years during which they receive a pension.

Prostate cancer

Prostate cancer is the most common cancer in men. The **prostate gland** is situated close to the bladder, where it secretes fluid into the urethra. This fluid contains substances that help sperm to swim actively (see page 117).

A healthy prostate gland is about the size of a walnut. In many men, it enlarges as they age and can constrict the urethra so that it becomes difficult for urine to pass. This condition is known as benign prostate hyperplasia. It is not a cancer. It is usually treated, if necessary, by surgically removing some of the prostate gland to give more room for urine to flow through the urethra.

About one in 14 men in the UK will get prostate cancer. This occurs when cells in the prostate gland divide uncontrollably, forming a tumour. This makes the prostate gland bigger, so the symptoms – difficulty in urinating – are the same as those for benign prostate hyperplasia.

The good news is that prostate cancer usually grows very slowly, and many men who have early prostate cancer will have died of something else before the cancer begins to threaten their life. There is disagreement over whether screening men for prostate cancer is a good thing to do. The cancer may be diagnosed before there are any symptoms, so it can cause worry in a man who is otherwise living a normal life. At the moment, it isn't possible to tell the difference between a normal, slow-growing and non-threatening prostate cancer and one which will grow fast, spread to other parts of the body and endanger life. If the cancer is an aggressive, threatening one, it may be treated with radiotherapy or surgery. Unfortunately, radiotherapy can damage the cells involved in spermatogenesis and cause sterility. Surgery runs a risk of damaging the ureter or rectum. There have been some promising trials of a technique using ultrasound focussed precisely onto the cancer, which avoids these side effects.

We don't know what causes prostate cancer. Age is the biggest risk factor (Fig 12.4). Half of all prostate cancers diagnosed each year are in men

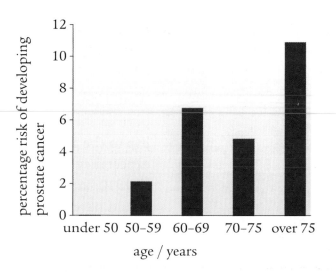

Fig 12.4 The risk of developing prostate cancer. (Data from Canada and including all races.)

JUST FOR INTEREST

Venerable worms

Much of the research into the ageing process in the last 40 years has involved a transparent, 1 mm long nematode worm that normally lives in the soil.

Caenorhabditis elegans was chosen for this role because it can be cultured as easily as a microbe, feeding on bacteria growing on agar jelly in a petri dish. Its life cycle is only two weeks long, so it is easy to breed large numbers of worms. This short life cycle also makes it good for studying ageing, as its ageing process happens very quickly. What's more, the worm is completely transparent so you can see what is happening inside it, and it is always made up of exactly the same number of cells – 959 of them – which develop in exactly the same way and take up exactly the same place and role in every adult worm. Despite its simplicity, it has a fully functional nervous system, and shares some important biochemistry with humans – for example, the way in which its cells respond to insulin.

C. elegans has been used to study the molecular basis of cell death and what happens during ageing. It is clear that the worm's genes affect the rate at which it ages. Mutations in one particular gene can double both the mean age of the worms and also the maximum age that an individual can reach, as shown in the graph. These mutations also involve an age-specific increase in the activity of some enzymes, including catalase. Catalase catalyses the conversion of hydrogen peroxide, a powerful oxidising agent, to water and oxygen, so these results suggest that perhaps the ability to protect cells from oxidising free radicals may help to prolong life.

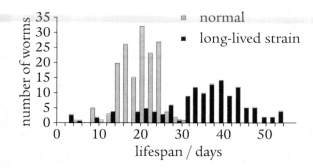

over 75. Three quarters are in men over 65.

There is some evidence that diet may affect the risk of prostate cancer. A diet rich in animal fats may increase the risk, while one containing antioxidants (see page 258) may help to protect against it.

Genetics also play a role. Two genes that increase the risk of breast cancer, BRCA1 and BRCA2, also increase the risk of prostate cancer.

Ageing and the nervous system

All parts of the nervous system, both central and peripheral, undergo deterioration as we age. It was thought for a long time that neurones in the brain began to die from the age of about 18, and they were not replaced. There is now some evidence that at least partial replacement may occur but, nevertheless, some older people do not have the faculties that they had when they were younger. But this is by no means the norm, and many people retain a sharp mind into their eighties and beyond.

Alzheimer's disease

The loss of mental abilities such as memory, logical thinking and language is known as **dementia**. Around 750 000 people in the UK suffer from dementia. About half of them have the form of dementia known as **Alzheimer's disease.** In this disease, tissue of some parts of the cerebral cortex, especially the hippocampus (see pages 79–80) becomes very abnormal. Some of the neurones have bundles of fibres in them, called 'tangles', whilst in between the neurones are dark-staining deposits not present in a normal brain. These deposits are called 'plaques' (Fig 12.5).

Neither tangles nor plaques show up on any of the types of brain scan that are currently available. It is therefore not possible to make a definite diagnosis of Alzheimer's disease in a person until after death, when the structure of their cerebral cortex can be investigated. CAT or MRI scans do, however, show a reduction in size of the brain in patients with Alzheimer's disease. Normally, though, the diagnosis is done purely by looking at the changing pattern of behaviour of the patient, and it is not always possible to be certain whether this is due to Alzheimer's disease or some other form of dementia.

The symptoms usually begin with an increasing loss of memory. The person becomes more and more forgetful, especially for recent events. So, for example, they may say the same thing or ask the same question repeatedly during a conversation. It becomes more and more difficult for them to concentrate on anything. Anxiety increases, and there may be considerable personality changes – for example, the person may become aggressive or depressed. They may have hallucinations, or imagine that they are being persecuted by someone. Eventually they may lose the ability to identify people, even their close family. These personality changes put a great strain on family members who are attempting to care for them. Speech and language deteriorate and there is general loss of cognitive function. Voluntary muscle control decreases and the patient becomes incontinent.

The causes of Alzheimer's disease

We still do not know what causes Alzheimer's disease. We do not know exactly what makes the tangles and plaques form in the brain, nor even if these are causing the symptoms or are just a result of some other change in the brain that causes both the symptoms of Alzheimer's disease and the development of tangles and

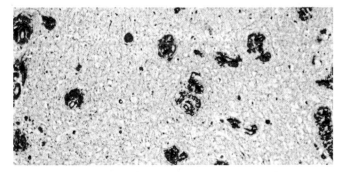

Fig 12.5 Brain tissue from a person with Alzheimer's disease. Normal tissue is shown blue and abnormal tangles red. Dendrites are lost from neurones in the tangles, so they do not work.

plaques. We do know that the tangles in the neurones are made of a protein called **tau**, and that as tau builds up in the neurones they die, and we know that the plaques contain a peptide known as **beta amyloid**.

Beta amyloid is made from a larger protein molecule called beta amyloid precursor protein, or APP. APP is a protein found in the cell surface membranes of all mammalian cells, but its function is not known. Some APP is converted into beta amyloid by an enzyme that cuts off the part of the APP molecule that protrudes from the outer surface of the membrane. This is a normal event. But in Alzheimer's disease there is either much more beta amyloid than normal, or the beta amyloid is a chain of 42 amino acids rather than the usual 40. So, is abnormal metabolism of APP the root cause of Alzheimer's disease?

A clue can be found by looking at the tiny proportion of people with Alzheimer's disease who have what is called 'familial' Alzheimer's disease, in which the disease is inherited. People with inherited Alzheimer's disease tend to develop it relatively early in life, between the ages of 35 and 50. Some forms of familial Alzheimer's disease are caused by different alleles of the gene that codes for APP, while others are caused by different alleles for the enzymes that act on APP to form beta amyloid. People suffering from inherited Alzheimer's disease have increased levels of beta amyloid 42. So it does look as though the cause of inherited Alzheimer's disease is something to do with the metabolism of APP.

However, in the vast majority of people with Alzheimer's disease, there is no evidence of a purely genetic cause. Some other environmental factors must also be influencing it. Ageing is one of these factors. Less than one person in 1000 under the age of 65 has Alzheimer's disease, whilst one in 20 over the age of 65 have it, showing the risk of getting it increases with age. However, these figures also show that nine out of ten people over 65 do not get Alzheimer's disease, so obviously ageing alone is not the cause. Other possible environmental factors include the use that is made of the brain throughout life. For example, some studies suggest that people who lead varied and active lives are less likely to get Alzheimer's disease. Severe blows to the head, especially if this happens to someone over the age of 50, may increase the risk of getting Alzheimer's disease. There is also evidence that risk factors for coronary heart disease, such as smoking and high cholesterol levels, may also be risk factors for Alzheimer's disease. However, the results from all of these studies are inconclusive, and the importance of all of these possible risk factors is controversial.

We do not know how the visible changes in the brain cause the symptoms of Alzheimer's disease. Certainly the cells in the regions of the brain that are affected by the plaques and tangles are known to secrete less of the neurotransmitter acetylcholine (see page 72). Clearly, as the changes are in the cerebral cortex, the part of the brain that is responsible for all higher-order processes (see page 79), it is not surprising that the symptoms involve memory, language and emotions.

Preventing and treating Alzheimer's disease

Currently, we can neither prevent nor treat Alzheimer's disease. There are drugs that can temporarily reduce some of the symptoms, but nothing that can genuinely halt the progress of the disease. For example, drugs that inhibit acetylcholinesterase (the enzyme that breaks down acetylcholine at synapses) can help for a while, by slowing down the rate at which levels of acetylcholine decline in the affected parts of the brain. This has a short-term beneficial effect on memory, but does nothing to stop the development of the disease in the long term.

Much research is being carried out to try to find drugs that could be used to treat the disease. This is really difficult to do, however, when we do not fully understand what is causing it. For example, some pharmaceutical companies are trying to develop inhibitors of the enzymes that cleave APP to produce beta amyloid, but as these enzymes have not yet been identified this is a very difficult task. Stem cells might eventually help to provide at least a partial cure, if they could be persuaded to produce new neurones to replace those which have been damaged or destroyed.

In the meantime, the best that we can do to reduce the chances of developing Alzheimer's disease is to make sure that we use our brains regularly for a variety of different things, avoid blows to the head and follow the same rules as those for avoiding heart disease – a good diet and plenty of exercise.

Caring for people with dementia

A person with dementia finds it difficult to remember and communicate. As the changes progress, it becomes more and more difficult for them to look after themselves. Very often, the burden of care falls on relatives. It is made doubly difficult because the mental changes in the person can make them aggressive, suspicious and ungrateful. Eventually they may cease to recognise the person who is looking after them. For a husband, wife, son or daughter who loves their relative, this can be extremely stressful and upsetting.

In the UK, there are many sources of advice about how to care for a person with dementia. A carer can get help, support and guidance from their GP, health visitors and social workers. There may be voluntary agencies that can help, such as the Alzheimer's Society or the Dementia Relief Trust.

Initially, in the early stages, the elderly person may still be able to do a lot for themselves, given guidance. The simple steps described for helping a person to recover from a stroke (see pages 88–89) will also help in this situation. In general, it is usually best for them to remain in their own home as long as possible, with the help of family or other carers.

As the dementia progresses, it may become necessary to have a carer in attendance 24 hours a day. The person may need to be fed, taken to the toilet, washed and dressed. They are likely to be unable to deal with money matters, and it may be necessary for other members of the family to be given legal control over their finances. Eventually, it may become necessary for the person to move into a residential care home.

This can be a stressful time for both the person with dementia and the carers. However, in a well-run care home the person's life can become much fuller than if they remain at home. They have the opportunity to interact with others and to partake in activities such as trips and visits. At home, possibly alone, they could become isolated and lonely. In a care home they may be much happier than when at home on their own or with an exhausted carer.

But here another problem arises – who will pay for this residential care? There are allowances that can be paid to help a person who is in a private care home, such as the disability allowance, but this will not pay for all the fees. A person without any financial means of support will have a publicly funded place provided for them in a home. There is, however, a shortage of residential homes in most areas.

Ageing and the peripheral nervous system

As we age, there are changes in both the somatic and autonomic systems (see page 75). Although some neurones do die, overall the systems continue to work well in most people. Indeed, the activity of the sympathetic nervous system appears to increase, especially those parts of it which innervate the muscles, heart and the alimentary canal.

The most noticeable changes in the peripheral nervous system are in our senses, especially hearing and sight. These steadily deteriorate in most people as they enter their 70s or 80s. Most people begin to lose ability to hear high-pitched sounds even in their 20s, and hearing loss in later years can make it difficult to hear and understand speech. Most of this loss can be explained by the death of hair cells in the cochlea and of neurones in the auditory nerve.

In the eye, cells in the retina may be lost. This happens because, throughout life, rhodopsin and iodopsins (see page 53) are constantly being broken down by lysosomes and replaced. Over time, some insoluble fragments generated by this process may accumulate in lysosomes in the epithelium that lies next to the rods and cones. These may cause macular degeneration (see page 49) which can cause blindness.

The lens in the eye also undergoes changes as it ages. It is made of stacks of cells containing proteins. These cells are normally transparent and elastic, but with age the proteins begin to denature. This causes the lens to lose its elasticity, so it is more difficult to focus on objects at different distances. For most people, this means that they need glasses both for close and distant vision.

The denaturation of the proteins in the lens can also cause them to clump together and form a cloudy area through which light cannot pass. Most of us suffer from some clouding of the lens as we age, but in some people the opacity of the lens becomes so bad that they can scarcely see at all. This is known as a **cataract** (Fig 12.6).

Treatment for a cataract may involve complete replacement of the lens, usually under local anaesthetic. It is then replaced with an artificial lens, the most sophisticated of which can change shape and therefore provide at least some accommodation for near and distant vision.

The treatment can be done as daycase surgery (not requiring staying in hospital overnight). A local anaesthetic is used and drops dilate the pupil. A tiny incision is made in the eye, which can be as small as 3 mm. A probe is passed through and into the lens. This probe vibrates at very high frequency (an ultrasonic frequency), which breaks the lens into fragments. These fragments are sucked out by the same probe. An artificial lens can now be inserted through the hole.

Vision is greatly improved for the patient, but they may not be able to deal as effectively when accommodating to near and distant vision, so glasses may need to be worn.

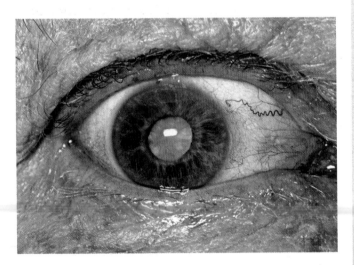

Fig 12.6 With a normal lens, the pupil of the eye appears dark. When there is a cataract in the lens, you can see the lens through the pupil and it has a characteristic 'milky' appearance.

ACTIVITY 12.1

The care of the elderly and those suffering dementia

Divide into groups. Discuss and produce a list of 'issues'. Recombine into the whole class and produce one collective list of the issues.

1 Choose one issue from the list. Using the internet and any other appropriate sources prepare:

- a concise description of the issue;
- a description of the impact of the issue on (i) other family members (ii) society as a whole;
- an outline of ways in which the issue is handled at the present time.

2 Discuss improvements that could be made to the ways in which the issue is currently handled.

Ageing and the skeletal system

Some of the changes that take place in our bodies as we age involve bones, joints and muscles.

Osteoarthritis

Arthritis is a general term for a disease that affects the joints, causing pain and loss of movement.

There are several different types of arthritis. One of these is rheumatoid arthritis, in which the body's own immune system treats the cartilage at the joint surfaces as if it were an invading organism; it is an autoimmune disease (see *Human Biology for AS,* page 233). Rheumatoid arthritis is most common in people with the histocompatibility allele HLA-DR4, and it is probable that other genes are also linked with a person's likelihood of suffering from this disease.

Osteoarthritis, on the other hand, does not appear to have any genetic link, nor is it an autoimmune disease. In a person with osteoarthritis, the normally very smooth surface of the cartilage at joints becomes rougher, making joint movement less easy and sometimes very painful (Fig 12.7). Some degeneration of the cartilage at joints happens in everyone as they age, so that almost anyone

Fig 12.7 These finger joints are badly affected by osteoarthritis and are making life difficult for this elderly lady. In addition to the damage to the joint cartilage, extra cartilage grows around the joint.

over the age of 60 has some degree of roughening of the cartilage in their joints. In most people, though, this is not enough to produce any more than very mild symptoms. The term 'osteoarthritis' is normally only used when the degeneration gets so bad that there is significant pain and loss of mobility.

In osteoarthritis, changes occur in the collagen and glycoproteins that help to give cartilage its resilience, so that these gradually break down. At the same time, the normal balance between the gradual breakdown and replacement of cartilage is disrupted, so that breakdown happens faster than replacement. The result is a loss of cartilage from the surface of bones at joints, and also a reduction in the flexibility and resilience of the cartilage that remains. The bone ends become roughened by friction, and there is a reduction in the amount of synovial fluid. It becomes increasingly painful to move the joint, and eventually movement at some joints may be completely lost. The joints that are most frequently affected are those in the hands, knees and hips.

Despite much research, it is still not at all clear why some people develop osteoarthritis while others do not. There is some evidence that the way joints are used early in life may affect this. For example, people who play sports or dance professionally, where there is repeated and vigorous bending of the knees, seem to be more likely to suffer from osteoarthritis in the knee joints later in life. This is also true if the joints suffered an injury, particularly twisting injuries in the knee. Overweight people are also more likely to develop osteoarthritis, especially in the load-bearing joints at knees and hips.

The pain and inflammation at arthritic joints can be partly relieved by non-steroidal anti-inflammatory drugs, such as aspirin. These reduce pain, stiffness and swelling. However, for long-term relief the only option is joint replacement. Such surgery is now very successful, and people with joint replacements can often return to the degree of mobility they had before osteoarthritis set in.

Osteoporosis

We have seen (pages 254 to 257) that post-menopausal women run an increasing risk of losing bone mass as they age, a condition known as osteoporosis, and how HRT can greatly help to prevent this from happening. But it is not only post-menopausal women who can suffer from osteoporosis. It can happen to all of us as we age. It is estimated that one in two women and one in five men over the age of 65 will suffer a broken bone due to osteoporosis.

It seems that we can help our chances of avoiding this disease by taking care over our lifestyles while we are younger. Having a high bone density helps. To achieve this, regular exercise is needed which applies forces to the bones. Bones respond to this by growing denser and stronger.

Diet is also important. Bones contain calcium, so a good supply of calcium in the diet will help to maintain bone density. Good sources of calcium include dairy products, but many people avoid these because they are thought to be 'fattening' and because they have a high fat content. Calcium is not absorbed and used effectively without the presence of vitamin D, so this too needs to be present in the diet. People who diet and keep their weight artificially low may be more likely to suffer from osteoporosis in old age. Cigarette smoking also appears to increase the risk of osteoporosis.

PROCEDURE 12.1

Bone density measurement

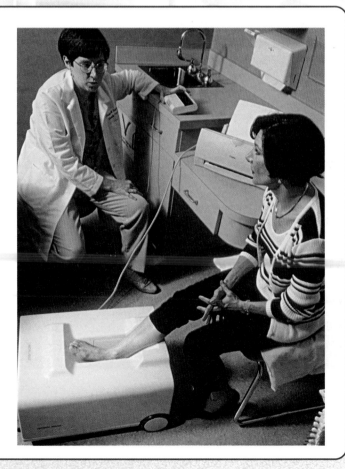

Bone density or bone mineral density is a measure of the amount of calcium in bone.

Dual X-ray absorptiometry (DXA) (or dual energy X-ray absorptiometry – DEXA) relies on the absorption of X-rays by the mineral matter of bone. The greater the bone density, the more absorption of X-rays. In this procedure, the patient may lie on a padded table and an X-ray scanner passes over one or more areas, especially the lower spine or the hip. However, other areas can be scanned, such as the heel, as shown in this photograph. This takes just a few minutes. The X-ray dose is less than that from a chest X-ray.

The results from the scan are then compared against an international standard. This standard is the bone density normal for women in their thirties, which is when bone density is at its maximum. Low density indicates osteoporosis.

Ageing and the cardiovascular and respiratory systems

As we age, many of the problems that can arise in the heart and blood vessels, and in the respiratory system, become more common. Some of this is probably inevitable and can be considered to be part of the normal ageing process, but some is affected by lifestyle and could be slowed down by avoiding risk factors such as smoking and obesity (see *Human Biology for AS*, Chapter 6).

The cardiovascular system

In the heart, the thickness of the wall of the left ventricle increases, and the valves become less efficient at preventing backflow of blood. There is an increased heart rate at rest, and a loss in the ability of the heart to beat very quickly, which reduces the ability of the person to exercise strenuously.

The sino-atrial node beats more slowly than in a young person, and it becomes less able to alter its rate. This means that the person's heart cannot respond well to changes in demand, such as during exercise.

The walls of the arteries become less elastic, so they are less able to accommodate the surge in pressure during systole (the stage of the heart beat when the ventricle walls contract).

Cardiovascular disease is the cause of death of 70% of people over the age of 65. 40 to 50% of people of this age probably have high blood pressure, although not all of them will be aware of it. Over the age of 70, around 15% of men and 9% of women have coronary arteries that are partially blocked and may need to have heart bypass operations.

All of these processes are seen to some extent in everyone as they age. However, it seems that regular exercise and a good diet, which keeps the HDL : LDL ratio low (see *Human Biology for AS*, page 112), can help to slow them down.

The respiratory system

Various changes take place in the lungs as a person ages, some of which lead to symptoms very like emphysema. Supporting tissue in the walls of the alveoli slowly disappears, resulting in the air spaces enlarging and the surface area available for gas exchange decreasing. The elasticity of the alveoli decreases. Nevertheless, for most people gas exchange is still perfectly adequate to supply body cells with oxygen and remove carbon dioxide as fast as is required. Problems are more likely to arise, however, when infection sets in, because there is less spare capacity in the gas exchange system to cope with this. Forced expiratory volume (FEV) drops with age (see *Human Biology for AS*, page 124).

Infections of the respiratory system become more frequent with age. 30% of notifications of TB in the UK are in people over 65. This is probably because many of them were infected with *Mycobacterium tuberculosis* earlier in their lives, and the bacterium is still there in their cells. Because the immune system tends to become less effective with age, the disease reactivates.

In fact, almost all kinds of respiratory infections are more common in older people. They can also be more dangerous. For example, an older person is more likely to catch 'flu than a younger one, and considerably more likely to die from it. This is why elderly people are encouraged to have a 'flu vaccination before winter.

Many cancers are most likely to strike in old age, probably because there has been more time for defects in genes to accumulate. Bronchial cancer is very strongly age-linked, and half of all cases are in people over 70.

Old people with asthma have particular problems to face. It can become increasingly difficult for them to use an inhaler properly, either because of loss of precision in finger and hand movements, or because of a decline in mental ability.

The social consequences of ageing

In the United Kingdom, as in Europe as a whole, we have an ageing population. As we have seen, life expectancy is rising; people are living longer. At the same time, fertility – the number of children born to each woman in her lifetime – has decreased as women have become more independent, are more likely to follow a career and delay having children until later in life. So, with birth rate decreasing and people living longer, the proportion of elderly people in the population is steadily increasing. In 2004, around 20% of the population of Europe was over 60, and it is predicted that by 2050 it will be 33%.

This increase in the proportion of elderly people in the population has numerous consequences for society. We have already seen (in this chapter) that many elderly people suffer from some kind of ill health and will be reliant on others to at least some extent to help them to enjoy their lives. If this help is given by family carers, it can affect the lifestyles of these younger members of the family, reducing their freedom to work or to enjoy leisure time. If the help is provided by government-funded or local authority-funded organisations, then the money to pay for this has to come from that which is generated by taxing the working population.

When most people stop working, they rely on their pension to provide them with a regular income. The money for this comes from contributions made by working people. As the number of elderly people increases, there is an increase in the dependency ratio – that is, the ratio of pensioners to the working population who provide money (through taxes) for their support. In 2004, the retirement age for men was 65. So, if a man began work when he was 20, he will have paid into a pension scheme for 45 years. If he lives to be 100, he will be taking his pension for 35 years. It is difficult to make these figures add up to provide a large enough pension for an old person to live above the poverty line.

One possible solution to this is to make people work for longer – for example, by raising the retirement age to 70. But we know that most people are already living with a significant health problem by the time they reach their mid-50s, and not many 70-year-olds will be able to work as hard or for such long hours as in their younger days. It may be possible for employment to be made more flexible for them – for example, by allowing them to work shorter hours or in kinds of tasks that they are still able to do really well. All the same, many people will die before they reach the age of 70, or very soon afterwards, so they would never enjoy retirement. Perhaps the retirement age needs to be more flexible, making it possible for those who want to retire early, and have sufficient finance available, to do so, whilst the large number of people who want to carry on working can work on past the age of 70.

The ageing population puts different demands on healthcare systems. As we have seen, many diseases become more common in elderly people. As medical and technical advances occur, it becomes more possible for people to live to an extreme age, but often only with medical support. It is inevitable that increasing demands will be put onto health services. Chronic diseases such as cardiovascular disease, arthritis, osteoporosis, dementia and visual impairment will need treatment for many years. It will be important to find ways of reducing the impact of these diseases, which will have the advantage of helping old people to enjoy their lives as well as reducing the tax burden on the working population who are effectively paying for their health care.

COLEG LLANDRILLO COLLEGE
LIBRARY RESOURCE CENTRE
CANOLFAN ADNODDAU LLYFRGELL

Summary

1 The incidence of prostate cancer increases with age. In many cases, it does not grow quickly enough to need treatment. However, some prostate cancers are aggressive and require treatment with ionising radiation or surgery.

2 Ageing processes in the central nervous system can lead to a reduction in mental abilities, and sometimes to dementia. Alzheimer's disease is a form of dementia in which cells in parts of the cerebral cortex die. The cause is not known, and so far no successful treatments have been found. The care of an elderly person with dementia can put great strains on their family.

3 The peripheral nervous system may also deteriorate with age. For example, the central part of the lens in the eye may become cloudy, a condition known as a cataract. This can be treated surgically by removing the lens and replacing it with an artificial one.

4 Ageing also affects the skeletal system. Osteoarthritis affects the cartilage that normally protects bones at joints. It makes movement at these joints painful and difficult. Osteoporosis involves a loss of bone density, which can eventually lead to fractures of vertebrae and other bones. Tests of bone density can help to predict a person's risk of suffering from osteoporosis, so that diet and exercise can be used to help to slow down its development.

5 Diseases of the circulatory system become more prevalent with age. The ability of the heart to change its rate of activity lessens, as does the elasticity of blood vessel walls.

6 Changes in the lungs similar to those seen in emphysema occur as a person ages. Elderly people are also more likely to suffer from respiratory infections.

7 We have an ageing population, in which the proportion of the community made up of elderly people is increasing. This puts considerable demands on health services and the working members of society, who directly or indirectly have to pay for care of the elderly, many of whom suffer from chronic illnesses that need regular treatment.

Answers to self-assessment questions

Note – answers to open-ended questions are not provided.

Chapter 1

1.1a DNA is a polynucleotide and ATP is a nucleotide. The nucleotides that make up DNA, and ATP, are made up of a pentose sugar, a nitrogenous base and inorganic phosphate.

  b ATP has three phosphate groups rather than one. The nitrogenous base in ATP is adenine, while the nucleotides in DNA may contain adenine, thymine, cytosine or guanine. The pentose sugar in ATP is ribose, while in DNA it is deoxyribose.

1.2a Sodium ions and potassium ions are moved up their concentration gradients, by active transport.

  b These are anabolic reactions. Energy is needed to form the bonds between the monomers in these polymers.

  c There are many different possibilities, for example: moving organelles around inside the cell; active transport of substances other than sodium, potassium and calcium; synthesis of other molecules such as glycogen; contraction (in muscle cells); movement of cilia.

1.3 A muscle fibre is about 80 μm wide and can be several centimetres long. A lymphocyte is about 12 μm in diameter. The volume of a muscle fibre is huge compared with that of a lymphocyte. The nucleus of a cell contains DNA, from which mRNA is transcribed; the mRNA then moves out of the nucleus and is used in translation of the DNA code into a protein molecule. Muscle fibres need many nuclei so that no part of the cell is too far away from the DNA.

1.4a A = I band, B = A band, C = Z line, D = myosin

  b The H band is very narrow.

  c $51 \times 1000 \div 27\,000 = 1.9\,\mu m$

1.5a P = myosin or thick filament, Q = actin or thin filament, R = Z line

  b The muscle is relaxed. The troponin and tropomyosin molecules are covering the sites on the actin to which the myosin heads can bind.

  c Diagrams C or D, because there is the greatest overlap of the myosin and actin filaments, so the maximum number of cross-bridges and therefore the greatest force applied by the movement of the myosin heads.

  d The sarcomere cannot shorten any more, without crumpling the actin and myosin filaments.

  ei The myosin heads can only tilt in one direction. They are arranged so that when they do this they pull on the actin in such a way that the sarcomere is shortened. They can't pull the actin the other way. When the muscle relaxes, the relative positions of the actin and myosin fibres will stay exactly as they are unless something else pulls them back again.

  ii In the human body, most muscles are arranged in antagonistic pairs. For example, when the biceps muscle in the upper arm contracts (shortens), it can be pulled back into its longer state by contraction of the triceps muscle. You can also make this happen just using the weight of your lower arm, or by placing a heavy weight on the hand.

1.6 Triose phosphate.

1.7 The carbon dioxide diffuses into the blood, and is transported to the lungs where it diffuses into the alveoli and is removed from the body during expiration.

1.8 Approximately 32 molecules of ATP are made from one glucose molecule in aerobic respiration, while only 2 are made in anaerobic respiration. Therefore, aerobic respiration results in the formation of 30 more ATP molecules than anaerobic respiration.

Chapter 2

2.1 Increase in heart rate increases the rate at which oxygen is delivered to the respiring muscles so they can respire faster and make more ATP. The secretion of adrenaline helps to increase the heart rate. The secretion of nitric oxide, which dilates the arterioles, helps to increase blood flow back to the heart. This stimulates the heart to beat faster and harder, which also increases the delivery of oxygen to muscles.

  Dilation of arterioles delivering blood to the muscles again increases oxygen supply to them. Dilation of arterioles delivering blood to the skin increases the rate of heat loss, which prevents the heat produced during muscle activity from increasing the core body temperature.

  The increase of tidal volume and breathing rate helps to maintain a large concentration gradient, for both oxygen and carbon dioxide, between the air in the alveoli and the blood in the lung capillaries. This increases the rate at which oxygen is taken up by the blood and at which carbon dioxide is lost from it. This in turn increases the rate at which oxygen is supplied to the respiring muscles and carbon dioxide is removed from them.

  Detection of high acidity (low pH) by chemoreceptors increases the rate and extent of contractions of the diaphragm and intercostal muscles. This increases tidal volume and breathing rate, as described above. It is important to remove carbon dioxide rapidly, as otherwise it would lower the pH of the blood plasma and reduce the activity of enzymes.

2.2 The muscle fibres that tend to be used during exercise are slow-twitch fibres, which respire aerobically. The increased cross-sectional area of these fibres increases the quantity of muscle that is used during aerobic exercise.

  The increased number of capillaries in the muscles

increases the blood flow to them, which brings more oxygen and takes away carbon dioxide more effectively.

The increased concentration of myoglobin increases the quantity of oxygen stored in the muscles, which they are able to use for aerobic respiration when their oxygen concentration is very low.

Mitochondria are the sites of the link reaction, the Krebs cycle and the electron transfer chain. The increase in number and size of mitochondria, and hence the quantity of respiratory enzymes that they contain, therefore results in an increase in the amount of aerobic respiration that can take place at the same time.

An increase in VO_2 max means that muscles can respire aerobically for longer. This is achieved by having more red blood cells, which can bring more oxygen to the muscles. The rate at which oxygen is supplied to the muscles is also increased by the development of more heart muscle and the increase in stroke volume. Resting heart rate is lower. Increases in maximum breathing rate, tidal volume and vital capacity also help oxygen to be supplied more rapidly to the muscles.

2.3a VO_2 max is the maximum rate at which the body can use oxygen before it has to switch to anaerobic respiration.

b During the first seven weeks of the training, VO_2 max rose steadily from $3.2\,dm^3\,min^{-1}$ to $3.5\,dm^3\,min^{-1}$. This is an overall increase of $0.3\,dm^3\,min^{-1}$. The rate of increase is $0.04\,dm^3\,min^{-1}$ per week. There was little change from seven weeks onwards.

c The increase in VO_2 max is brought about by the changes described in the answer to SAQ 2.2.

2.4a i As power output increases, so does the concentration of lactate in the blood. The relationship is directly proportional. However, the increase in lactate concentration is slight, only rising from about $1.8\,mmol\,dm^{-3}$ to $2.1\,mmol\,dm^{-3}$ as power output increases from $50\,W$ to $175\,W$. This is an approximate increase of $0.002\,mmol\,dm^{-3}$ for a $1\,W$ increase in power.

ii The muscles are able to respire mostly aerobically up to a power output of $175\,W$. However, some anaerobic respiration does occur and this is the source of the lactate in the blood. As power increases, anaerobic respiration also increases, but only slightly.

b i The liver.

ii Before training: $175\,W$
After training: $225\,W$

iii Any long-term changes that bring more oxygen to the muscles more swiftly, or allow muscle fibres to carry out more aerobic respiration, can help to explain these figures. They are listed and explained in the answer to SAQ 2.2.

c An increase in lactate threshold means that an athlete can go on using aerobic respiration in their muscles even when they are working hard. This allows trained endurance athletes to work faster or harder for a longer period of time than an untrained person.

2.5 The large numbers of mitochondria in slow-twitch fibres mean that more aerobic respiration can take place. The mitochondria contain the enzymes required for the link reaction and Krebs cycle, and also the carriers of the electron transfer chain.

The large concentration of myoglobin in slow-twitch fibres provides an oxygen store that they can use when oxygen concentration is very low, thus allowing them to carry on using aerobic respiration for a little while when oxygen supply runs short. Fast-twitch fibres do not need much myoglobin, because they respire anaerobically.

The relatively small diameter of slow-twitch fibres increases their surface-area-to-volume ratio. This helps oxygen to diffuse to the mitochondria more quickly. Fast-twitch fibres can be larger because they do not rely on a supply of oxygen.

The large numbers of capillaries supplying slow-twitch fibres ensures that plenty of oxygenated blood can reach them quickly, and also means that no fibre is very far away from a capillary, thus reducing the diffusion distance for oxygen and carbon dioxide.

2.6 Amino acids and fatty acids can only be used when oxygen is available, because they enter the link reaction and the Krebs cycle which will only take place when oxygen is available to take up electrons at the end of the electron transfer chain. Glucose and glycerol can be broken down in glycolysis, which can continue even without the presence of oxygen.

2.7 Andrea's muscles could not carry out glycolysis, because she was lacking phosphofructokinase, which catalyses one of the steps in glycolysis. However, her muscles could still obtain some ATP using substrates that could be fed into the link reaction or the Krebs cycle.

2.8a A high RQ suggests that carbohydrate and/or protein are being metabolised.

b The obese people with a low RQ were using fats as their respiratory substrate. If they continued to do this after dieting, then their bodies would use fat for respiration rather than storing it away. The obese people with a high RQ were using carbohydrate and protein, so more fat could be stored away.

c This suggests that heredity may play a part in the type of substrate that a person tends to use for respiration. This in turn indicates that there is a gene which influences this, and that some people have genes that result in a tendency to metabolise fat, while others do not.

2.9a The percentage saturation with oxygen is the amount of oxygen that the Hb is carrying, as a percentage of the total amount that it is capable of carrying. Thus a percentage saturation of 50% means that the Hb is carrying half of the total quantity that it is able to carry.

   b   You can read this value off the graph; it is 97%.

   c   You can read this from the graph also; it is 23%.

   d   In the lungs, haemoglobin loads up with oxygen until it is carrying 97% of its possible load. In the tissues, the oxygen concentration around the Hb molecules is lower, and they drop most of the oxygen they are carrying, so that in total they continue to hold less than one quarter of their possible load.

2.10   In the muscles, where the concentration of carbon dioxide is high, the haemoglobin saturation is shown by the curve on the right in Fig 2.10. The curve shows that, at every concentration of oxygen, the haemoglobin is less saturated with oxygen than when carbon dioxide concentration is low (curve on the left). This means that it will unload more oxygen in conditions of high carbon dioxide concentration, such as are found in respiring muscles.

2.11a You could sort the results in several different ways, but the categories that you produce should keep all 'explosive' events (100 m, 200 m, 400 m, high jump and long jump) together, and the endurance events (500 m, 10 000 m and marathon) together. You could choose to keep the women's and men's events separate, or place them together.

      You should then show in some way the difference in performance in 1968 compared with 1964. You could perhaps draw a bar chart, in which the y axis has a negative scale below the origin and a positive scale above it; you could then draw bars to represent the percentage increase or decrease in performance. You will need to remember that in some events a larger number means improvement, while in others it means exactly the opposite.

   b   In general, performances in explosive events increased. In the examples shown, six out of nine performances in these events produced a new world record. In contrast, times for the three long-distance races all increased.

   c   At high altitude, the thin air makes it easier for athletes to run fast, jump high and throw long. They will use anaerobic respiration for the short time their activity lasts. However, endurance events rely on aerobic respiration, and the low oxygen concentration at high altitude reduces the rate at which oxygen can be supplied to muscles, and therefore reduces the rate at which they can produce ATP.

2.12a i The times of the low-low group improved up to six weeks, and then worsened (got longer) for the next five weeks, which is completely unexpected – you would expect their times to get shorter as they trained. They then improved a

little, but still had not returned to their baseline level at the end of the experiment.

   ii 5000 m is a long race, and the body heat generated by muscle contraction is considerable. In hot, humid conditions, sweat does not evaporate from the skin. This is the major way of keeping the core temperature normal. So these athletes had difficulties in keeping their body temperatures from rising very high, and this may have reduced their performances.

   b i Both the high-high and high-low groups' performances improved during the 13-week experiment. The high-high group showed a small improvement (about 0.5%) in their performance compared with the baseline time, while the high-low group showed a much bigger improvement (3%).

     ii Both of these groups had the benefit of high-altitude training, which increases the ability of muscles to obtain and use oxygen (see pages 41–42). However, it may have been more difficult for the high-high group to train really hard, because of the lack of oxygen. The high-low group obtained all the benefits of high-altitude living, but were able to train harder because they returned to sea level to do this.

   c   If these results are reliable, then you would advise athletes to live at high altitude for as long as possible before competing. They should return to low altitude for training.

Chapter 3

3.1a Pigment B – about 400 nm to just over 500 nm
      Rhodopsin – just over 400 nm to about 580 nm
      Pigment G – about 450 nm (with a very small degree of sensitivity down to 400 nm) to just over 600 nm
      Pigment R – about 460 nm to about 680 nm

   b   The only pigment that is sensitive to dim light is rhodopsin. Colour vision depends on the relative degree of stimulation of the three different iodopsins. As the brain receives information from only one pigment in dim light, there is not enough information for it to interpret the colour of the light.

3.2   If cells from other parts of the retina were transplanted into the region of the macula, they should continue to respond to light. It would probably be necessary to transplant all the retinal cells together – that is rods, bipolar cells and ganglion cells – keeping their connections to the optic nerve intact. (This is because it is unlikely that, if rod cells were transplanted alone, they would be able to grow new connections to bipolar cells.) So your brain would interpret the stimulation of this transplanted retina to mean that light is falling on the part of the retina that the transplant came from, rather than from its new position. With time, it might be possible for the brain to relearn this.

      Moreover, as most cone cells are near the macula,

it is likely that the retinal transplant would contain only rods. Therefore colour vision would be lost, as would the high degree of resolution that is possible with the densely packed cone cells in the macula and their one-to-one connection to ganglion cells.

3.3 A mirror could be used. If the chart were placed level with the person and the mirror 3 m in front of them, they would see an image of the chart as though it were 6 m away. (The image you see in a plane mirror is the same distance behind it as the object is in front of it.)

Chapter 4

4.1 There is no answer to this question.

4.2a The line should be drawn at about −65 mV – that is, a horizontal line drawn across starting at the point (0, −65).

b The inside of the axon has a charge of −65 mV compared with the outside.

c By active transport using ATP to power the sodium–potassium pump in the membrane of the axon. Both sodium and potassium ions are positively charged. Three sodium ions are pumped out for every two potassium ions pumped in, so this builds up a positive charge outside compared with inside the axon.

d i It is called depolarisation because the axon was polarised so that it had a negative charge inside and a positive charge outside. Now this is altered and there is a negative charge outside and a positive charge inside.

ii Sodium channels in the membrane open and allow sodium ions to flow in down their electrochemical gradient. As they enter the axon, their positive charge causes the negative charge inside the axon to be brought to zero and then continue to become more positive until it reaches about 30 mV.

e Between 1 ms and 2 ms the axon is repolarised. The sodium channels close again, and potassium channels open. Potassium ions flood out of the axon and therefore make the outside more positive than the inside. The potential overshoots the resting potential, temporarily becoming even more negative inside than it was before. Then the sodium–potassium pump kicks in again and the resting potential is restored.

f About 4.0 s.

4.3 During the refractory period, the resting potential is being brought back to normal by the action of the sodium–potassium pump. While this is happening no action potential can happen. So an action potential can't be started in the part of the axon from which an action potential has just come, as it will be in its refractory period.

Chapter 5

5.1a In both women and men, the chance of having a stroke increases with age. Below the age of 45, stroke is very rare in both sexes.

In men, the incidence of a first stroke increases more rapidly as they age from 55 to 65, and the risk increases even more sharply between the ages of 65 and 85. This rate of increase slows after the age of 85.

This pattern of rate of increase is also shown in women. However, at all ages between 55 and 90, women have a lower risk than men. Only beyond the age of 90 do women have a greater risk of a stroke than men.

b As a person ages, the degree of damage to their arteries through atherosclerosis increases. As time goes on, the damage may become so great that it becomes more and more likely that a blood clot in the brain or a burst blood vessel will happen. There are a number of possible reasons for the lower risk of stroke in women than men, including a protective effect from oestrogen or lower stress levels.

5.2a More than 360 000 men were admitted to hospital in 2000 as a direct result of alcohol abuse. The majority of these (more than 140 000) were over the age of 40. The next most frequent age group was the 30–39 year olds, followed by 20–39 year olds and then men below 20 years of age. So the number of admissions increased with age.

b Less than 100 000 admissions were due to cannabis use, so there were 3.6 times as many admissions due to alcohol than due to cannabis. Here, the number of admissions decreased with age, in contrast to the increase with age seen for alcohol abuse. By the age of 40, only a very few admissions occurred.

c The pattern of increase in admissions due to alcohol abuse with age in women is similar to that seen in men, but here there are 2.9 times fewer overall – 125 000 instead of 360 000. The difference is shown throughout all four age ranges, but is greatest in the 20–29 and the 40+ age range.

d For every person admitted to hospital following abuse of a drug, there will be many more who are using the drug but do not need hospital admission. This number will differ for different drugs. For example, it is likely that the percentage of cocaine users who are admitted to hospital is greater than the percentage of alcohol users.

Chapter 6

6.1 The term 'reduction division' can be applied to the first division of meiosis. This is when the 46 chromosomes in a normal cell, made up of two complete sets (diploid) are reduced to 23 chromosomes, made up of one complete set (haploid).

6.2a During interphase.

b During prophase I or metaphase I of meiosis. (It cannot be mitosis, because in mitosis homologous chromosomes don't pair up like this.)

c As the caption says, this is at the end of meiosis – in telophase II.

6.3

Feature	Mitosis	Meiosis
number of divisions that take place	one	two
appearance of chromosomes in prophase	chromosomes are made up of two chromatids joined by a centromere; homologous chromosomes do not pair up	in meiosis I homologous chromosomes pair up to form bivalents; each chromosome is made up of two chromatids as in mitosis, but there are now four chromatids lying side by side
formation of chiasmata	does not happen	crossing over takes place between the chromatids of homologous chromosomes in prophase I
metaphase	chromosomes line up on the equator, each behaving independently of all the rest	in metaphase I chromosomes line up in their homologous pairs at the equator, each homologous pair behaving independently of all the rest
anaphase	the centromere splits and individual chromatids are pulled to opposite poles	at anaphase I the centromeres do not split, and the chromosomes of each homologous pair are pulled to opposite poles
end result	two daughter cells are formed, genetically identical with each other and with the parent cell	at the end of meiosis II, four daughter cells are formed, each with half the number of chromosomes as the parent cell, and genetically different from each other and from the parent cell

NB: meiosis II is essentially the same as mitosis.

6.4a Yes. Two genetically identical haploid cells would be formed.

b No. Meiosis can only take place in cells with two complete sets of chromosomes.

6.5 The long tail provides propulsion, allowing the sperm to swim from the vagina to the oviduct. Numerous mitochondria provide ATP for this, which is produced by aerobic respiration. The nucleus is haploid (it contains one set of chromosomes) so that when fertilisation occurs the nucleus of the zygote will be diploid. On contact with the egg, the acrosome releases its hydrolytic enzymes which digest a way into the cytoplasm so that the male nucleus can enter.

6.6 The relatively large size provides space to store food reserves (as lipid) that will be needed to fuel mitosis if fertilisation takes place. The nucleus is haploid (it contains one set of chromosomes) so that when fertilisation occurs the nucleus of the zygote will be diploid. There are microvilli to absorb nutrients, lysosomes to dispose of unwanted organelles and cortical granules in the cytoplasm.

6.7 In spermatogenesis, diploid cells divide by mitosis to form spermatogonia. This is identical to the first events in oogenesis, in which diploid cells divide by mitosis to form oogonia. The spermatogonia and oogonia then divide by mitosis to form primary spermatocytes and primary oocytes, respectively. However, in males this does not happen until a boy is about 11 years old, whereas in females this stage happens before a girl is born.

In both processes, meiosis then takes place. In males, this happens straight away, whilst in females the primary oocytes do not continue dividing until the girl reaches puberty. The first meiotic division produces haploid secondary spermatocytes and haploid secondary oocytes. In males, meiosis I produces two secondary spermatocytes of equal size, whilst in females it produces one large secondary oocyte and one small polar body. In males, thousands of secondary spermatocytes are formed all at the same time, whilst in females only one secondary oocyte is formed at one time.

In males, meiosis I continues straight on into the second meiotic division, forming four spermatids, each of which develops into a sperm. However, in females it stops here. The secondary oocyte does not complete meiosis II until it is fertilised. Once again, the division is unequal and one large ovum is produced and one tiny polar body.

6.8a 23 days.

b Each day, steroid levels rise to a peak and then fall. They rise just after a pill is taken and then fall. During the seven days when no pills are taken, days 21 to 28, the steroid concentrations remain very low.

c Follicular activity remains low and relatively constant throughout the days when a pill is taken. During days 21 to 28, when no pill is taken, follicular activity gradually increases. The progesterone and oestrogen in the pill inhibit the secretion of LH and FSH from the anterior pituitary gland. Their disappearance allows these hormones to be secreted, and they stimulate the development of a follicle in the ovary.

d From the appearance of the graph, the 'follicular activity' does seem to rise rapidly throughout the pill-free seven days, but we cannot tell how great this 'activity' is compared with the normal activity that would be associated with ovulation. Certainly in the normal menstrual cycle, the presence of FSH and LH first cause a follicle to develop and then a surge in LH causes ovulation to take place. This follicle development takes place over roughly days 5 to 12 of the cycle, but in the pill-taking woman it won't begin until she stops taking her pills on day 21. So it is possibly not a long enough time to allow a follicle to develop and be ready for ovulation to take place.

e Most women like to be reassured that they are still fertile, and they mistakenly associate this with having a period (menstruating). They also like to be sure that they are not pregnant, and once again having a period confirms to them that this is so.

6.9a

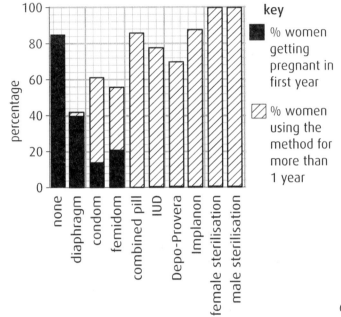

b i The diaphragm was much less successful than condoms in preventing pregnancy. A diaphragm is less easy to put into place than a condom, and it may be that some women did not do this effectively. Some may also have taken the diaphragm out too soon after intercourse. It is also very important to use spermicidal cream with a diaphragm, but many women find this messy and may not always have used it.

ii Implanon was extremely successful in preventing pregnancy, even better than condoms. Implanon provides a continuous stream of anti-ovulation hormones into a woman's blood, so there is never an oocyte available to be fertilised. A condom, however, needs to be thought about and used carefully, and it is always possible that it is not put on correctly or soon enough, and that some semen is not trapped in it and does manage to reach an oviduct where an oocyte is present.

c i Fewer than half (42%) of women continued using a diaphragm after the first year. They probably did not like the fuss of having to put it into place before intercourse, nor the rather messy procedure of using spermicidal cream with it or leaving in place for 6 hours after intercourse. In contrast, 86%

continued with the contraceptive pill, which is simply taken each day.

ii Implanon was more likely to be continued into a second year than Depo-Provera®. Once Implanon is implanted, it can just be forgotten about. Depo-Provera®, on the other hand, requires injections which some women probably did not like.

6.10a The number of oocytes increases rapidly during the first six months of development in the uterus, reaching a peak of almost 7 million. It drops rapidly between 6 and 7 months, and then continues to fall until at birth there are just over 2 million present. The number of oocytes continues to fall until the age of 8 years, and then again at a slower rate until 22 years of age. It remains constant at about 0.1 million and then drops to 0 around the age of 50.

b The very large number of oocytes present at 6 months after conception could not be sustained for any length of time. Only a few are needed to allow successful reproduction; a woman normally only produces one secondary oocyte per month during the years from puberty to menopause.

c Fecundity is the likelihood that a woman will conceive during one cycle. The number of oocytes present in her ovaries drops between puberty and the menopause, and this might make it less likely that a healthy secondary oocyte is released at ovulation each month. (However, there are other factors that also contribute to the drop in fecundity, not only the number of oocytes present.)

6.11a ICSI requires specialised equipment and a very well-trained person to use great skill in injecting a sperm into an egg, whereas in IVF rather less skill is needed to add sperm to an egg and allow one of them to fertilise it.

b Semen will be assessed to make sure that there are plenty of sperm present, and that they appear to be healthy and are fully motile. For some methods of fertility treatment, the sperm will be separated from other components of the semen to reduce the likelihood of viruses or bacteria being transferred along with the sperm.

c i It is most unlikely that a woman under the age of 23 would be given fertility treatment. Even if she had tried and failed to get pregnant at that age, she would be advised to continue trying for several more years before fertility treatment would be considered necessary.

ii The chance of success of fertility treatment in a woman over the age of 40 is only 6%. It is difficult to justify expenditure by the National Health Service in such a situation, when each attempt would cost around £1000 or more.

6.12a The gold is used to make the anti-hCG antibodies visible when large numbers of them accumulate in one place.

b A goat could be injected with mouse serum. Its B

lymphocytes would produce antibodies against antigens in the mouse serum, and these could be used to produce monoclonal anti-mouse goat antibodies.

c This region should always go pink when the dipstick is dipped into urine, because the anti-mouse goat antibodies will trap and hold the antibody–gold complexes that should have been carried up the stick. So this region tells you if the test has been done correctly or not, and if the stick is working. If so, then you know that a negative result (the Patient Test Region does not show a pink line) really does mean that the woman is not pregnant, not just that the test hasn't worked.

6.13a

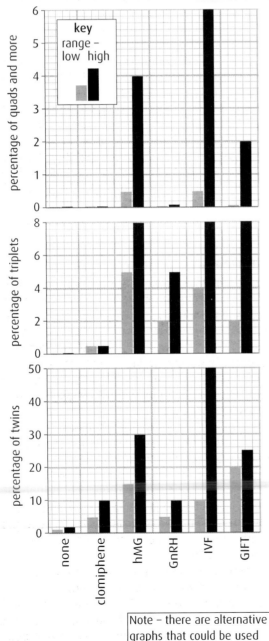

Note – there are alternative graphs that could be used

b More than one oocyte could be released from the ovaries at once, and two or more of these could be fertilised by different sperm. Or one zygote might split into two, each of which would develop into an embryo.

c i Between 10 and 25 times more likely.
  ii In IVF treatment, two embryos are usually placed in the uterus.

d Using two embryos increases the chance that at least one of them will implant. However, more than two runs the risk of triplets, quadruplets or higher numbers of embryos, and this greatly increases the chance that the pregnancy will not go to term.

e GIFT involves placing sperm and oocytes into the oviducts, and there is no way of controlling how many zygotes are formed. As sperm are placed with the oocytes, there is a very high chance that all the oocytes will be fertilised. In other methods, sperm may have to swim through the uterus to the oviducts, a process in which many fail.

Chapter 7

7.1 Stock such as cattle egest faeces, which contain material that forms humus. On mixed farms, this may be spread on the fields to use as fertiliser. On purely arable farms, fertilisers have to be bought in and most farmers will choose inorganic fertilisers as they are less bulky and unpleasant to handle.

7.2a These include: initial soil nutrient level, use of pesticides, use of herbicides, aspect of fields, mass of fertiliser applied, time of fertilisation application, time of sowing and harvesting, geographical location, cultivar of wheat or barley in each plot.

 b 48%, 110%, 130%

 c For wheat, farmyard manure provides the highest increase in yield, while for barley inorganic fertiliser is best.

 d Factors to be considered might be: availability and cost of the fertilisers, ease of application, acceptability to people living close to the field, the effect on the humus content of the soil. It is not easy to suggest how the choice might affect wildlife in the field, but it is possible that the use of manure might support a greater population of earthworms, and therefore other organisms that feed on them. Whichever the farmer uses, there is potential to cause harm to other habitats nearby, including streams and ponds, if the fertiliser is allowed to contaminate them.

7.3a The wheat yield on this plot fell from $1.1\,t\,ha^{-1}$ to $0.4\,t\,ha^{-1}$. Overall, there was a drop in yield of $0.7\,t\,ha^{-1}$ between 1854 and 1925.

 b New varieties were being introduced every few years, and perhaps those used from 1940 onwards gave higher yields than the older varieties. Also, from 1957, herbicides began to be used. These could reduce competition between the crop and weeds, allowing the wheat to grow faster and produce greater yields of grain, but in fact there does not seem to be benefit from these in terms of yield.

c The results for these two plots are almost identical.

d i Nitrate ions may enter watercourses, where they can increase the growth of green algae. These block light from reaching other plants in deeper areas of the water. When the algae die, they are fed upon by aerobic bacteria, whose populations therefore increase. These bacteria take oxygen from the water, lowering its oxygen content and making it difficult for other aerobic organisms, such as fish and many invertebrates, to live there. Anaerobic decomposition may then occur (see pages 152–153).

d ii These results suggest that manure can cause just as much or even more leaching of nitrate ions as inorganic fertilisers. These results do not support the view that organic fertiliser is better for the environment in respect of leaching. However, there may be other beneficial effects of adding humus to the soil and therefore increasing biodiversity in it. The table provides data for only one aspect of the possible effects of the use of these two types of fertiliser.

7.4a Breed of pigs; age of pigs; quantity and quality of food provided; availability of water; air temperature; number of pigs per unit area of housing.

b In general ammonia emissions were lower in autumn, winter and spring than in summer.

c Higher temperatures in summer might cause ammonia to be released from the dung more easily. Pigs might drink more in summer and might produce greater volumes of urine from which ammonia could be emitted. Higher temperatures might increase the rate of metabolism of bacteria and other decomposers breaking down pig dung, releasing ammonia from it more rapidly.

7.5a Of the 2500 kJ y^{-1} taken in by cattle, 120 kJ y^{-1} are passed to humans.
Efficiency = $(120 \div 2500) \times 100 = 4.8\%$.

b We are fussier about what we eat compared with other secondary consumers. While a lion, for example, will eat all the parts of the body of its prey, we reject most of its internal organs, its head and its hide.

7.6a It would be best to show these data as a line graph.

b The graph in Fig 7.22 shows the population size over time. The graph drawn from the data here shows by how much the population size is increasing each year. The data in this graph indicate that the rate of growth of population increased from 1900 to 1990, and then began to fall. However, the population itself was still increasing every year. Not until we see negative numbers in the second graph would it indicate that the population size was actually falling.

7.7a Birth rate fell until 1950, then rose slowly until 1970 and then fell.

b i 0.3 births per thousand per year
ii 0.1 births per thousand per year

c We have no information about any other factors during these periods, so almost any suggestion would be acceptable. Remember, though, that this birth rate is per thousand people, so suggestions relating to there being more people in the country are not relevant.

d We do not know about death rates, immigration rates or emigration rates, all of which have an effect on change in population size.

Chapter 8

8.1 The gametes from the father are F and f. The genotypes of the offspring are FF and Ff, in equal proportions (you could write this as 1:1). Therefore the chance of a child with cystic fibrosis is zero.

8.2 Follow the complete format at the top of page 174 for your answer; do not take any short cuts, as there are often marks for showing all of the steps in the problem, not just for the answer.
Your symbols should be a capital letter for the Huntington's allele (for example, H) and a small one (for example, h) for the normal allele. The parents' genotypes are Hh and hh. The gametes of the man will be H and h in equal proportions, while all of the woman's eggs will be h. The offspring will be Hh and hh in equal proportions. Therefore the chance of having a child with Huntington's disease is 50%.

8.3 $q^2 = 1 \div 15\,000$
$= 0.000067$
$q = 0.0082$

8.4 The Huntington's disease allele is dominant. Any zygotes with the genotype HH never develop, so there are no homozygous dominant people in a population. Each person with the disease has one copy of the Huntington's disease allele. So if we count these people we know that half of their alleles are the Huntington's allele. So the frequency of the allele is the frequency of people with this disease divided by two.

8.5 Make sure that you use the proper symbols, that is, an I with the appropriate superscript. Do not be tempted to take a short cut and just write down A, B and so on, because these stand for the blood group a person has, not the alleles.
You should find that one in four children born to this couple would be expected to have blood group O. This can also be expressed as a probability of 0.25, or as 25%.

8.6 It is almost always best to work from the bottom up when dealing with a pedigree like this.
We know that persons 2 and 3 had a child with blood group AB, so person 2 must have the allele for blood group A. They also had a child with blood group O, so both of them must have the allele for blood group O.

So person 2 has the genotype $I^A I^o$ and person 3 has the genotype $I^B I^o$.

The blood group of 2 is therefore A.

Both person 1 and his wife must have an I^o allele, as they have a child with blood group O. Person 1 must therefore have the genotype $I^A I^o$.

8.7 A son is conceived when a sperm carrying a Y chromosome fuses with an egg (all eggs carry an X chromosome). Therefore none of the genes on a man's X chromosome, including the haemophilia gene, can be passed on to his son.

8.8 The woman's uncle was $X^h Y$, so he received X^h from his mother. Her genotype was therefore $X^h X^H$. The woman could therefore be $X^h X^H$ or $X^H X^H$.

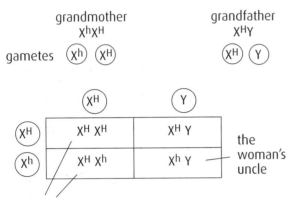

grandmother $X^h X^H$

grandfather $X^H Y$

the woman's uncle

the two possible genotypes of her mother

If her mother is $X^h X^H$, then the woman could be either $X^h X^H$ or $X^H X^H$, as shown in the genetic diagram above.

If the woman is a carrier, then there is a 25% chance that she could have a son who is $X^h Y$, as shown in the genetic diagram.

8.9 i 0.25
ii 3 normal : 1 with haemophilia

8.10a The condition appears to be dominant, as it seems to appear in the sons and daughters of everyone who has it. It would be possible for this pedigree to arise if the allele was recessive, but this is unlikely.

b Equal numbers of males and females have brachydactyly, so it does not appear to be sex-linked. However, as it is a dominant allele it could possibly produce most of this pattern even if it was on the X chromosome. (Try it out on one or two parts of the pedigree.) The piece of evidence against this possibility is that a man in the middle row has a son who has the condition, even though the man's wife did not have it. As we have seen, it is not possible for a man to pass on an allele on his X chromosome to his son.

8.11a i Person 3 and his wife have two children with

PKU, even though neither of them had it. This could happen if the allele was recessive, and if they were both heterozygous.

ii Both a son and a daughter of this man and his wife have the disease. As we have seen, it is not possible for a man to pass on an allele on his X chromosome to his son.

b First state your symbols. Here we will use P for the normal allele and p for the one causing PKU. Work backwards.

Person 4 has the disease, so must be pp.

Her brother does not. He could be either PP or Pp.

Person 3 does not have the disease but does have allele p (because he has passed it on to a son and a daughter) so he is Pp.

His wife is also Pp. So one of her parents must be Pp, but we can't tell if this is person 1 or 2. The other is probably PP, but could be Pp.

c There is a 50% chance that person 5 is a carrier for PKU, with genotype Pp. If she is, and if she marries another person who is also a carrier, there is a 25% (one in four) chance that a child born to them will have genotype pp and have PKU. If she isn't, or if she marries someone who is not a carrier, then there is no chance that her child will have PKU.

8.12 Each cell should be shown with two chromosomes (each will be a single thread, not with two chromatids), one long with one of the A/a alleles and one short with one of the B/b alleles.

8.13 They are all Ab.

8.14 They will be AB or Ab, in equal proportions.

8.15a She is $ff I^A I^o$. He is $FF I^o I^o$.

b Make sure that your genetic diagram is truly complete.

The woman's gametes will have genotypes $f I^A$ and $f I^o$, in equal proportions.

The man's gametes will all have genotypes $F I^o$.

The possible genotypes of the children are therefore $Ff I^A I^o$ and $Ff I^o I^o$, with an equal chance of each combination arising.

The phenotypes corresponding to these two genotypes are no cystic fibrosis with blood group A, and no cystic fibrosis with blood group O.

8.16a Begin with what you can tell immediately from the information in the question.

The man's genotype for sickle cell must be $Hb^S Hb^S$, because he has sickle cell disease.

His wife must be $I^A I^B$ but we do not know her Hb alleles – they could be $Hb^A Hb^A$ or $Hb^A Hb^S$.

We cannot tell the father's blood group. However, as one child has blood group AB we know that he must have either an I^A or an I^B allele. So he could be $Hb^S Hb^S I^A I^A$, or $Hb^S Hb^S I^A I^B$, or $Hb^S Hb^S I^B I^B$ or $Hb^S Hb^S I^A I^o$ or $Hb^S Hb^S I^B I^o$.

b As this child has sickle cell disease, the mother must also have the sickle cell allele. Her Hb genotype is $Hb^A Hb^S$. She has sickle cell trait, but –

like many people with this condition – has shown no symptoms.

8.17a The possible genotypes of the father's gametes are YG, Yg, yG and yg. All the mother's gametes are yg.

The possible genotypes and phenotypes of their children are YyGg (yellow, grey), Yygg (yellow, orange), yyGg (blue, grey) and yygg (blue, orange) in equal proportions.

b As the mother is yygg, we should assume that the y and g allele are on the same chromosome.

Therefore the father's gametes have two possible genotypes, YG and yg.

The possible genotypes and phenotypes of their children are now YyGg (yellow, grey) and yygg (blue, orange) in equal proportions.

8.18 If crossing over took place during meiosis to form the man's sperm, then a few of his sperm cells could end up with a different combination of alleles – that is, Yg and yG. Therefore there would be a small possibility that children with genotypes Yygg (yellow, orange) and yyGg (blue, grey) could be born.

Chapter 9

9.1 a Each cell is likely to have only two copies of a gene – one on each of two homologous chromosomes. If, however, that cell is expressing a gene, then it will have many copies of the mRNA made from it. Because each cell only expresses a particular selection of genes, that mRNA will make a significant proportion of the mRNA in the cell.

b Each type of restriction enzyme cuts DNA at a particular base sequence, different from those cut by other restriction enzymes. Therefore the sticky ends that a particular restriction enzyme leaves are always the same. This will allow the sticky ends from the human DNA and the plasmid to pair up, as the exposed bases will be complementary to one another.

c The sticky ends allow hydrogen bonds to form between the exposed bases of the two different DNA molecules, holding them in place so that DNA ligase can link their sugar-phosphate backbones together.

d This is to allow the bacteria that have successfully taken up the required gene to be identified. You cannot easily 'see' if the plasmid has got into the bacteria or not. However, you can easily find out if they are resistant to an antibiotic, simply by trying to grow them on agar with the antibiotic in it. Any bacteria that are resistant must have taken up the plasmid with the resistance gene on it, and so you know they will also have taken up the hGH gene.

9.2 a i A retrovirus contains RNA, rather than DNA. HIV is a retrovirus.

ii In this context, a vector is a means by which a gene is transferred from one organism to another.

b Retroviruses contain an enzyme called reverse transcriptase, which makes a DNA copy of their RNA when they enter the cell. In many cases, this DNA is then inserted into the host cell's DNA and becomes part of its chromosomes. Viruses that contain DNA do not do this.

9.3a i The frequency of ebony-bodied flies is shown by the lower curve. At the beginning of the experiment, they had a frequency of 0.25, meaning that one quarter of the flies had ebony bodies. However, after two generations this had already dropped to 0.2, and by the 18th generation it was practically zero. 80% selection appears to make the ebony-bodied flies almost extinct.

ii The ebony body allele is present in the flies with genotype Ee, as well as those with genotype ee. Although the ee flies became extinct, this does not happen to the Ee flies even after 20 generations, so the ebony body allele remains in the population. You can work out the actual frequency of this allele – q – in any one generation by reading off the value for q^2 and finding its square root. In later generations, when you cannot read off q^2 because it is so small, you could read off p^2, find its square root and then find q from the equation $p + q = 1$.

b This is difficult to predict. After many generations, the curves are all flattening out, but we cannot be certain what they will do in future generations. If the population was a large one, then there would probably always be enough heterozygous flies surviving to ensure that the allele did remain in the population. However, if the population was small, then just by chance the few heterozygous flies might not breed and the allele could be lost quite quickly.

c Although humans and their breeding patterns are very different from those of fruitflies, nevertheless these data do give food for thought. Are we in any way exerting selection pressures against particular alleles in our populations? Or is just the reverse the case – are we allowing alleles to survive that would, in a 'wild' population, disappear due to selection? Try to discuss both sides of the argument, and to give particular examples to illustrate the points you make.

9.4a Restriction endonucleases are enzymes that are made by bacteria to defend themselves against viruses. They cut DNA molecules. They are used in genetic engineering to cut DNA strands at particular points, so that a gene can be cut out of a long DNA molecule, or a plasmid can be cut open. For example, EcoR1, from the bacterium Escherichia coli, cuts DNA at places where the base pair sequence GC, AT, AT, TA, TA, CG is found.

A reverse transcriptase is an enzyme found in retroviruses. It makes DNA copies of their RNA when inside a host cell.

b Gene therapy is a particular application of genetic

engineering. Genetic engineering is a very general term used to describe almost any method by which the genetic make-up of an organism is altered. Gene therapy involves inserting a correct copy of a gene into the cells of an organism that has a faulty allele of that gene.

c   Somatic cells are 'body' cells, all the cells in an organism's body apart from the ones that will form gametes. Germ cells are those from which gametes will be formed. Their DNA may be passed on to the next generation. The DNA from somatic cells is not passed on.

d   Blood group is determined by the type of ABO, or Rhesus, antigen found in the cell surface membranes of the red blood cells. Tissue type is determined by the different types of antigen found in the cell surface membranes of all other cells. The most important of these are the HLA antigens, encoded by a group of linked genes known as the MHC complex.

e   *Homo sapiens* is our own species. *Homo erectus* belongs to the same genus (*Homo*) as us but to a different species. *H. erectus* became extinct about 200 000 years ago. They walked upright like us, and might have been our ancestors. They used tools and fire, making them very human-like.

Chapter 10

10.1a Water is a better heat conductor than air. It is therefore easier for heat to leave the body than in air, so the core temperature drops more quickly.

Water also has a higher thermal capacity. This means that it absorbs a lot of heat before its temperature rises. So even the water next to the body does not warm up easily. This maintains a high temperature gradient between the body and the water, maintaining a high rate of heat loss.

When the water close to the body does heat up, convection currents cause the low-density warm water to move upwards and away from the body, and cooler water moves in to take its place. (This, of course, is also true of air.)

b   Water in the wet clothes evaporates into the air. Water has a high latent heat of evaporation, so heat is taken from the skin as the liquid water changes to water vapour.

c   Air is trapped inside the bag, around the person's body. Air is a poor conductor of heat, so it takes a while for heat from the body to be lost into the trapped air.

As the air cannot escape from the bag, there are no convection currents that can remove the warm air and replace it with cold air. The warm air is trapped inside the bag.

The silvery surface of the bag is a poor emitter of radiation, so this also reduces heat loss from the bag to the air outside it. The inside of the bag is also silver, so that much of the heat radiated from the person's body is reflected back inside the bag.

d   A woollen blanket contains millions of tiny pockets of air which are trapped inside it. Air is also trapped between the blanket and the body. As explained in c, air is a poor conductor of heat and this slows down the rate of heat loss from the body to the air. Convection currents are also reduced.

10.2 If the food is hot, its heat will help to warm the body.

The digestion of food in the alimentary canal involves hydrolysis reactions. These are exothermic and so generate heat that helps to warm the body.

After the food has been absorbed, it can be used by body cells in respiration or in other metabolic reactions. Many of these are exothermic, and will release heat that can increase the temperature of the cells.

10.3a While they were sitting beside the pool, the body temperature of both people remained relatively stable between 37.4 and 37.6 °C. As they entered the pool, the temperature of both dropped slightly. During the rest of the investigation, the temperature of person A dropped to 34.2, whereas that of person B dropped only to 36.8 °C. If normal core temperature for these two people is taken to be 37.5 °C, this represents a fall of 3.3 °C for person A but only 0.7 °C for person B – a difference of 2.6 °C.

b   Person A is using energy for muscle contraction, and this will be generating heat within the body. However, this extra heat production in person A is more than outweighed by the greater heat loss he is experiencing because of his swimming movements. These continually bring his body into contact with colder water, so he rapidly loses heat by conduction from his skin. In contrast, person B remains still. He initially loses heat from his skin to the water next to him, but then this water remains in position so that the heat gradient from his body to the water becomes very small and he loses less heat by conduction.

10.4a At first the temperature rose. The rate of increase was greater during the first 16 minutes, then slowed between 16 and 56 minutes, then slowed even more until 72 minutes. It then remained approximately constant at 38.8 °C up until 120 minutes.

b   The activity of the muscles produces heat, which is absorbed by the blood and carried around the body. This is why the core temperature rises as an athlete runs.

As the athletes are running at a steady pace, the rate of heat production by the muscles will remain approximately the same throughout the 120 minute period. However, as blood temperature rises, the hypothalamus detects this and nerve impulses are sent via the autonomic nervous system to effectors which respond to increase the rate of heat loss. Sweating will increase, and vasodilation will take place. These actions slow the rate of temperature increase, and eventually a balance is achieved between heat generation and heat loss resulting in an approximately constant core temperature.

c The mean core temperature of the runners who did not drink rose much faster than in those who did drink. By 120 minutes, their mean temperature was 40.2 °C, which is 1.4 °C higher than that of the drinking group. Whereas, in the drinking group, the rate of temperature increase decreased with time, this rate was always much higher and did not decrease anywhere near as much as in the drinking group. By 120 minutes their mean core temperature was still rising.

d The non-drinking group was unable to sweat as much as the drinking group, because their blood contained less water. Sweating cools the body because, as water changes from liquid to vapour, it absorbs heat from the skin.

e i A 5000 metre race takes around 10 minutes. In this time, there is only a relatively small gain to be had by drinking fluids. After 10 minutes, the mean core temperature of the non-drinking group was 37.6 °C while that of the drinking group was only one tenth of a degree lower at 37.5 °C. The 5000 m athlete should not drink during the race as the time lost by drinking would far outweigh any small benefit.

ii A marathon lasts longer than 2 hours. By this time, the mean core temperature of the non-drinking group was 1.6 °C higher than that of the drinkers, and this could adversely affect performance. A marathon runner would gain an advantage by drinking during the race.

10.5a Exocrine glands secrete many different substances, including enzymes. Endocrine glands secrete hormones. An exocrine gland secretes its product into a duct, whereas an endocrine gland secretes its product directly into the blood. The salivary glands are exocrine glands, and the thyroid gland is an endocrine gland.

b A beta cell is found in the islets of Langerhans in the pancreas, and it secretes insulin when it detects a high blood glucose level. A B lymphocyte is a type of white blood cell that secretes antibodies that act against pathogens.

c Glycogen is a polysaccharide whose molecules contain many glucose molecules linked by α 1–4 and α 1–6 glycosidic bonds. It is stored in muscle and liver cells, where it can be broken down to provide glucose as a substrate for respiration.

Glucagon is a polypeptide, whose molecules are made of amino acids linked by peptide bonds. It is secreted by alpha cells in the pancreas when blood glucose levels are too low.

d Both facilitated diffusion and active transport involve the movement of a non-lipid soluble substance through a protein channel (transporter) in a cell membrane. In facilitated diffusion, there is no energy input by the cell because the substance moves down its concentration gradient. In active transport, the substance is moved up its concentration gradient, which requires ATP provided by the cell.

10.6a i The glucose in the drink travels swiftly through the alimentary canal and is absorbed through the walls of the small intestine. It takes about 10 minutes for the glucose to be detected in a blood sample.

ii As the blood glucose level begins to rise, this is detected by beta cells in the pancreas, and they respond by secreting insulin.

iii The blood glucose level falls because insulin increases the rate at which glucose is taken from the blood by cells in the liver, muscles and adipose tissue. Another reason for the fall is that cells use the glucose in respiration.

iv There is a time lag between the fall of glucose concentration in the blood, its detection by the beta cells and their response of secreting less insulin.

b i In the second graph, blood glucose levels continue rising until 60 minutes, in contrast to the first graph where they level out at 20 minutes. In the person with diabetes, the blood glucose level reached a maximum value of 190 mg 100 cm^{-3}, almost twice as great as the value of 110 mg 100 cm^{-3} seen in the person without diabetes. It also fell more slowly, and had reached 110 mg 100 cm^{-3} by the end of the experiment, in contrast with the person without diabetes where it fell to 65 mg 100 cm^{-3} by this time.

ii The pattern of blood insulin concentration in the person without diabetes closely follows that for blood glucose. It rises higher in the person with diabetes, and then plateaus at its highest value (200 μU cm^{-3}) at 90 minutes, 30 minutes later than in the person without diabetes. By the end of the experiment at 240 minutes, the blood insulin concentration in the person with diabetes has only fallen to 90 μU cm^{-3}, whilst in the person without diabetes it is only just above its starting value by this time.

iii In the person with diabetes, it appears that the pancreas is secreting insulin normally – that is, more insulin is secreted as the blood glucose concentration increases. However, this rise in insulin does not appear to be affecting the blood glucose concentration at all. In the person without diabetes, the graph shows that as insulin concentration rises the glucose concentration falls. Because the insulin secreted by the person with diabetes does not reduce blood glucose concentration, insulin continues to be secreted at high levels, until something else brings the blood glucose concentration down.

10.7a Bread contains starch, which is made up of thousands of α glucose units linked together. When the bread is eaten, amylase in the saliva begins to hydrolyse the starch to maltose. When it reaches the small intestine, amylase from pancreatic juice continues the conversion of starch to maltose, and then the maltose itself is hydrolysed to glucose by maltase present in the brush border of the epithelium of the villi. Only then can the glucose be absorbed. This explains the fact that a peak in blood glucose concentration does not occur until 30 minutes after the bread has been ingested.

The fall from 30 minutes up until 120 minutes will have been brought about by increased secretion of insulin by the beta cells in the islets of Langerhans in the pancreas. This takes a short while to happen, which is why the blood glucose does not begin to fall until 30 minutes after ingestion.

b All three foods produced a maximum level of blood glucose after 30 minutes. This maximum level was much lower in the lentils and soya, at +13 and +05 mg 100 cm^{-3} respectively, compared with a value of +52 mg 100 cm^{-3} after bread was eaten. The blood glucose level then fell very rapidly for bread, but much less so for lentils and soya, and these continued to provide a relatively steady blood glucose level throughout the rest of the 120 minutes. At the end of this time, the blood glucose levels for bread and soya were identical at −2 mg 100 cm^{-3}, while that for lentils was still relatively high at +11 mg 100 cm^{-3}.

c It appears that the carbohydrate in the lentils and soya is less easy to digest, so it takes longer for glucose to be produced and for it to be absorbed into the blood. This would explain the fact that the blood glucose level did not rise as quickly, and, for lentils, stayed at a relatively high value throughout the rest of the experiment; we can guess that it might have continued at this level for some time afterwards.

Another possibility is that some of the carbohydrate in the lentils and soya could be cellulose, which we are not able to digest at all.

Another possibility is that some of the carbohydrate in the lentils and soya was made up of monosaccharides other than glucose – for example, fructose.

Chapter 11

11.1 Most (around 80%) of the water is reabsorbed from the filtrate in the proximal convoluted tubule. This means that solutes such as urea are now dissolved in less water, so their concentrations are higher.

11.2a The y axis is shown as 'number of times greater'

because the actual concentrations of each substance are very different from each other, so each would need a separate scale. It is also a logarithmic scale, so that it can accommodate a very wide range of values. It has no 0, because a value of ×1 means 'no change'. Values above 1 represent an increase in concentration, and values below 1 represent a decrease.

b Amino acids and glucose are completely reabsorbed into the blood in the proximal convoluted tubule.

A small amount of urea is reabsorbed in the proximal convoluted tubule, but its concentration increases because there is now less water present. As more water is reabsorbed throughout the loop of Henlé, the concentration continues to increase.

Although both potassium ions and sodium ions are reabsorbed in the proximal convoluted tubule, their concentration does not change because water is also reabsorbed at the same time. The concentrations of both increase as they go down the descending limb of the loop of Henlé, because water is lost from here by osmosis into the tissue fluid around it, as this has a relatively low water potential. As it passes up the ascending limb, sodium ions are actively pumped out, so their concentration decreases. More water is lost in the distal convoluted tubule and collecting duct, so the concentrations of both ions increase. (Potassium ions are actively transported into the distal convoluted tubule, which explains why their concentration rises more than that of sodium ions.)

Chapter 12

12.1a The results suggests that HRT reduces incidences of hip fracture and colo-rectal cancer, and increases incidences of breast cancer, heart attack, strokes and blood clots.

b i 29 − 21 = 8 more

ii 8 × (100 ÷ 10 000) = 0.08

iii From bi, 8 more out of 10 000 have a stroke. Number having stroke without HRT is 21 per 10 000. So percentage increase = (8 ÷ 21) × 100 = 38%

iv They might think that they will have a 38% chance of having a stroke.

v The data need to show the actual percentages of women having a stroke with and without HRT, not the percentage increase.

c This is a difficult judgment to make, and valid arguments can be put forward for stopping or continuing the study. Your answer should include arguments on both sides of the debate, backed up by figures wherever relevant.

Glossary

abuse – the use of drugs in such a way that damage is done to the user's health or to the well-being of their family and friends

acclimatisation – adapting to new environmental conditions

acetyl coenzyme A (acetyl CoA) – the product of the link reaction in a mitochondrion, which enters the Krebs cycle

acetylcholine – a neurotransmitter involved, for example, in transmitting a nerve impulse from a motor neurone to a muscle and also in the parasympathetic nervous system

acetylcholinesterase – an enzyme that breaks down acetylcholine at a synapse

acrosome – a lysosome at the tip of a sperm, containing hydrolytic enzymes that enable the sperm to fertilise a secondary oocyte

actin – a globular protein which polymerises to form the thin filaments in a myofibril

action potential – a fleeting change in the potential difference across the cell surface membrane of a nerve cell, that sweeps along the cell; a nerve impulse

adenosine deaminase – an enzyme whose absence leads to SCID

adenosine triphosphate – an energy-containing molecule made in respiration and in the light-dependent reaction of photosynthesis; it is the immediate energy source for all cells

ADH – anti-diuretic hormone; a peptide hormone released from the posterior pituitary gland, which increases the reabsorption of water from urine

adrenaline – a hormone produced by the adrenal glands that affects many body organs; for example, it speeds heart rate

aerobic exercise – exercise for which the energy is provided by aerobic respiration; for example, long-distance running, dancing

aerobic respiration – a metabolic pathway in which a substrate such as glucose is oxidised with the release of energy that can be used for ATP synthesis; it involves glycolysis, the link reaction, Krebs cycle and oxidative phosphorylation and can only take place when oxygen is available

afferent – taking towards, e.g. the afferent arteriole delivers blood to a glomerulus

alcohol dehydrogenase – an enzyme in liver cells that catalyses the conversion of ethanal to ethanol, and also the reverse reaction

alleles – alternative forms of a gene

allosteric – involving a change in shape; for example, the allosteric effect of combination with oxygen on the shape of a haemoglobin molecule

Alzheimer's disease – a form of dementia

amygdala – part of the limbic system involved in emotions

anabolic – an anabolic reaction is one in which large molecules are built up from small ones

anaerobic respiration – a metabolic pathway in which glucose is oxidised to pyruvate, which is then converted to lactate (in humans) or alcohol (in plants and fungi); it involves glycolysis and the lactate pathway (or ethanol pathway) and takes place when oxygen is not available

anaphase – the stage in cell division in which homologous chromosomes (in meiosis I) or chromatids (meiosis II and mitosis) separate and go to opposite poles

anti-diuretic hormone – see ADH

antioestrogen – a substance that interferes with the action of oestrogen, used to stimulate ovulation

antioxidant – a substance that helps to prevent free radicals damaging cells

aquaporins – groups of proteins in cell surface membranes that increase permeability to water

aqueous humour – the watery fluid in the front of the eye

association area – a part of the cerebrum in which impulses from different sensory areas are integrated

ATP – adenosine triphosphate; an energy-containing molecule made in respiration and in the light-dependent reaction of photosynthesis; it is the immediate energy source for all cells

ATPase – an enzyme that catalyses the breakdown of ATP into ADP and P_i, or the formation of ATP from ADP and P_i

autonomic nervous system – the part of the nervous system including all the motor neurones carrying impulses from the central nervous system to internal organs

autosomal linkage – the inheritance of two genes together, because their loci are on the same chromosome

autosomes – chromosomes other than sex chromosomes

axial filament – the group of microtubules in the middle piece and tail of a spermatozoon, which produce movement

axon – a cytoplasmic process that transmits action potentials away from the cell body of a neurone

beta amyloid – a peptide found in the brain; its build-up is associated with the development of Alzheimer's disease

biodiversity – the number of different species in a habitat

bipolar neurone – a nerve cell in which there are two long cytoplasmic processes emerging from the cell body

bladder (urinary) – an organ in which urine is stored

283

blastocyst – a small, hollow ball of cells formed by repeated mitotic divisions of a zygote

blink reflex – rapid closing of the eyelid when something approaches the eye

blood doping – an illegal procedure in which athletes increase the concentration of red blood cells in their bodies by removing, storing and replacing blood before their event

blood–brain barrier – a barrier, consisting of relatively impermeable capillary walls, that prevents easy exchange of many materials between the blood and the brain

Bohr effect – the decrease in the affinity of haemoglobin for oxygen in the presence of carbon dioxide

Bowman's capsule – the cup-shaped part at the beginning of a nephron

Broca's area – part of an association area in the left cerebral hemisphere responsible for the production of language

Calvin cycle – the light-independent reactions of photosynthesis, which take place in the stroma of a chloroplast

cannabis – a preparation from the hemp plant, *Cannabis sativa*, used as a drug (usually recreationally)

cap (contraceptive) – *see* diaphragm (contraceptive)

capacitation – the process by which sperm, following ejaculation, become able to fertilise an egg

carbohydrate loading – eating carbohydrate to increase glycogen stores in muscles before a race

carbon cycle – the pathways by which carbon passes between living organisms and the environment

catabolic – a catabolic reaction is one in which large molecules are broken down to small ones

cataract – a cloudy area in the lens

cDNA (copy DNA) – DNA produced by reverse transcription from RNA

central nervous system – the brain and spinal cord

centromere – the part of a chromosome at which the two chromatids are held together

cerebral cortex – the outer layers of the cerebrum

cerebral hemisphere – one of the two sides of the cerebrum

cerebrospinal fluid – a fluid that fills the ventricles of the brain and the central canal of the spinal cord

cerebrum – the largest and most anterior area of the brain, highly folded, responsible for functions including conscious thought, emotions, language

cervix – the neck of the womb where the uterus meets the vagina

CFTR – a protein that forms calcium ion channels in cell surface membranes, defects in which may cause cystic fibrosis

chemical thermogenesis – production of heat by chemical reactions

chemoreceptors – sensory cells that respond to pH or the concentration of a chemical such as oxygen

chiasma (plural – chiasmata) – a point at which the chromatids of homologous chromosomes are held together during meiosis I

chlorophyll – a green, photosynthetic pigment found in chloroplasts

chloroplast – an organelle found in plant cells, in which photosynthesis takes place

cholinergic synapse – a synapse at which the neurotransmitter is acetylcholine

chondroitinase – an enzyme that is used to digest scar tissue that has formed in nerve tissue

choroid – a layer of cells containing melanin, behind the retina in the eye

chromatids – two identical strands of DNA attached to one another by a centromere, making up a chromosome

chromosome mutation – a random and unpredictable change in the structure or number of chromosomes

ciliary muscle – a muscle attached to the suspensory ligaments that contracts and relaxes to adjust the tension on them, and therefore the shape of the lens

cirrhosis – a disease in which liver tissue is damaged

citrate – a 6-carbon compound that is an intermediary in the Krebs cycle

climatic climax community – the final community that develops in a habitat as a result of the prevailing climate

climax community – the final community that develops in a habitat as a result of succession

clomiphene – an antioestrogen

clone – a group of genetically identical organisms

codominance – the existence of two alleles which both have an effect on the phenotype in a heterozygous organism

coenzyme – a molecule that must be present in order for a reaction catalysed by an enzyme to take place; NAD and FAD act as coenzymes in glycolysis and the Krebs cycle

coenzyme A – a coenzyme that enables the transfer of an acetyl group from one molecule to another

collecting duct – the final part of a nephron, leading into the ureter

colourblindness – the inability to distinguish between two or more colours

combined oral contraceptive – pills containing oestrogen and progesterone, which suppress ovulation

competition – the need of organisms for a resource which is in insufficient supply for all of them

condom – a flexible, impermeable sheath that can be placed on the erect penis, preventing semen from passing into the vagina during sexual intercourse

conduction – the transfer of heat via direct contact between two materials; also the transfer of an electrical signal

cone – a receptor cell in the retina which responds to higher intensity light than rods; cones are responsible for colour vision

consumers – organisms that depend on producers for their source of organic nutrients

contraception – preventing fertilisation from happening during sexual intercourse

convection – the transfer of heat as warm air or liquid rises and cold air or liquid falls

core temperature – the temperature deep inside the body

corpus callosum – a band of tissue connecting the left and right sides of the cerebrum

corpus luteum – 'yellow body'; a structure formed from granulosa cells in a follicle after ovulation, which secretes progesterone

cortex – outer layers; for example, of the kidney or the cerebral hemispheres

cortical reaction – the release of hydrolytic enzymes from lysosomes in an oocyte, into the space around it, at fertilisation

co-transport – a form of active transport in which the movement of one substance down its concentration gradient enables the movement of another substance up its concentration gradient

cranium – the part of the skull that protects the brain

creatine phosphate – a substance found in muscle that acts as an energy store

crossing over – the exchange of alleles between chromatids of homologous chromosomes

CT scan – computer-assisted tomography scan: X-rays are used to build up a 3D image of the body, using computers

cytokinesis – the stage in cell division in which the cytoplasm splits to form two cells

deamination – the removal of the $-NH_2$ group from an amino acid

decarboxylation – the removal of carbon dioxide; for example, when pyruvate is converted to acetyl CoA in the link reaction

decomposers – organisms that break down dead bodies, faeces and urine

deflected succession – succession whose direction is affected by farming or other human activities

deforestation – the loss of forests

dehydrogenase – an enzyme that catalyses reactions involving the removal of hydrogen from a compound

dementia – the loss of mental abilities

dendrite – one of many short cytoplasmic processes extending from the cell body of a neurone

density-dependent factor – an environmental factor whose influence increases as population density increases

depolarisation – a decrease in the resting potential across the cell surface membrane of a neurone; it may become less negative or even be reversed

Depo-Provera – a contraceptive that is injected into a woman's body, which prevents ovulation

depressant – a drug that reduces the activity of the brain

diabetes insipidus – a condition in which too much dilute urine is excreted

diabetes mellitus – a disease in which blood glucose levels are not properly controlled

dialysis – use of a partially permeable membrane to mimic the role of the kidneys in ultrafiltration

diamorphine – the name given to heroin when it is used medicinally, for pain relief

diaphragm (contraceptive) – a flexible device that fits over the cervix, preventing the entry of sperm to the uterus during and after sexual intercourse

dihybrid inheritance – the inheritance of two genes

diploid – containing two complete sets of chromosomes

dissociation curve – *see* haemoglobin dissociation curve

distal convoluted tubule – the part of a nephron between the loop of Henlé and the collecting duct

dizygotic twins – twins developed from two eggs; they are as genetically different as any two siblings

DNA ligase – an enzyme that catalyses the formation of covalent bonds between phosphate and deoxyribose molecules, forming the backbone of a DNA molecule

dominant allele – an allele which affects phenotype whether or not a recessive allele is present

donor profile – a collection of information about a sperm donor, which may be provided to a woman or a couple considering using donated sperm to fertilise her eggs

dopamine – a neurotransmitter found in the brain

dorsal root – the branch of a spinal nerve that enters the dorsal region of the spinal cord

dorsal root ganglion – an area in the dorsal root of a spinal nerve in which the cell bodies of sensory neurones are found

Douglas bag – an expandable, gas-tight bag that is used to collect expired air for analysis

Down's syndrome – a genetic disease in which body cells have three copies of chromosome 21, as a result of non-disjunction

drug – a substance that alters the body's physiology

drug dependency – the inability to manage without the drug

Duchenne muscular dystrophy – a sex-linked genetic disease caused by a faulty recessive allele of the dystrophin gene

dystrophin – a protein found in the Z lines in muscle tissue

effector – a cell, tissue or organ that carries out an action in response to a stimulus

efferent – taking away from; for example, the efferent arteriole carries blood away from a glomerulus

efficiency – useful energy output divided by energy input, multiplied by 100

egestion – the removal of faeces from the body

electrochemical gradient – a difference in concentration and charge; for example, the difference in the concentration of positively charged hydrogen ions across the inner membrane of a mitochondrion

electron carriers – a series of molecules along which electrons are passed; they are found in the inner membrane of mitochondria and in the membranes within chloroplasts, and are closely involved with the formation of ATP as a result of respiration and the light-dependent reactions of photosynthesis

electron transfer chain – *see* electron carriers

endocrine gland – an organ that secretes hormones into the blood

endometriosis – a condition in which endometrial tissue develops in other areas of the body

endometrium – the inner wall of the uterus

endorphins – neurotransmitters in the brain, involved in reduction of pain sensations

endothermic – able to produce heat inside the body to help to maintain body temperature

enkephalins – neurotransmitters in the brain, involved in reduction of pain sensations

epididymis – part of the testis in which sperm mature and are stored

Epo – *see* erythropoetin (Epo)

EPOC – excessive post-exercise oxygen consumption; the total oxygen consumed after exercise in excess of the pre-exercise level (*see also* oxygen debt)

erector muscle – a muscle attached to the base of a hair

follicle that raises the hair when it contracts

erythropoetin (Epo) – a hormone produced by the kidneys that stimulates the production of red blood cells

ethanol – the correct chemical name for the type of alcohol found in alcoholic drinks

eutrophication – the addition of extra nutrients to lakes, rivers or the sea; this can cause an increase in oxygen-demanding bacteria which deplete oxygen levels

excretion – the removal of unwanted, sometimes toxic, products of metabolism from the body

exocrine gland – a gland which secretes its products into a duct

extensive farming – using low inputs and stocking densities

factor VIII – one of several factors necessary for blood clotting

FAD – flavin adenine dinucleotide; a co-enzyme that picks up hydrogen during the Krebs cycle and other metabolic reactions

family planning – controlling when to have children

fast-twitch fibre – a muscle fibre adapted for short bursts of intense activity

fertilisation membrane – an impenetrable barrier that forms around the oocyte, immediately following fertilisation

filament – *see* thick filament, thin filament

follicle – a small, fluid-filled space within an organ; for example, in an ovary, or in the thyroid gland

follicle stimulating hormone – *see* FSH

food chain – a diagram showing how energy flows from one organism to another

food web – several interconnecting food chains

fovea – the part of the retina where cone cells are packed most tightly; also known as the macula

fructose bisphosphate – a phosphorylated hexose sugar, an intermediary in glycolysis

fructose phosphate – a phosphorylated hexose sugar, an intermediary in glycolysis

FSH – follicle stimulating hormone; a peptide hormone secreted by the anterior pituitary gland

GABA – a neurotransmitter in the brain

gamete intrafallopian transfer – *see* GIFT

gametogenesis – the production of gametes

ganglion – an area containing cell bodies of many neurones

ganglion cell – a neurone which receives nerve impulses from bipolar cells in the retina and transmits them to the brain

gene mutation – a random and unpredictable change in the base sequence of a gene

gene therapy – treating a disease by adding 'correct' copies of a faulty gene

genetic diagram – a conventional lay-out, sometimes including a Punnett square, showing the possible genotypes of offspring from two parents

genetic isolation – the inability of two populations of a species to breed successfully together, because of differences in their genomes

genetic screening – testing an organism to find out if a particular allele is present

genome – the genes possessed by an individual, or by a species

genotype – the alleles of a gene or genes possessed by an organism

genus – a group of similar species

geographical isolation – separation by a geographical barrier; for example, a mountain range

germ cells – cells from which gametes may be formed

germinal epithelium – a layer of cells near the outer edge of a testis or ovary, from which gametes are derived

GIFT – gamete intrafallopian transfer; the insertion of semen and oocytes into an oviduct, used as part of fertility treatment

glial cells – cells found in nervous tissue other than neurones; for example, Schwann cells, astrocytes

global warming – an increase in mean global temperature

glomerular filtrate – the liquid that filters from the blood into a Bowman's capsule

glomerulus – a knot of capillaries lying inside the cup of a Bowman's capsule

glucagon – a peptide hormone secreted by the alpha cells in the islets of Langerhans in the pancreas, which increases blood glucose levels

glutamate – an excitatory neurotransmitter in the brain

glycerate 3-phosphate (GP) – a 3-carbon molecule that is an intermediary in the light-independent stages of photosynthesis and in glycolysis

glycolysis – the first stage of respiration, in which glucose is converted to pyruvate in a series of small steps, producing a small amount of ATP and reduced NAD; it takes place in the cytoplasm

GnRH – gonadotrophin releasing hormone; a hormone secreted by the hypothalamus that causes the secretion of LH and FSH from the anterior pituitary gland

gonadotrophin releasing hormone – see GnRH

granulosa cells – cells that surround a follicle in the ovary, and also a secondary oocyte after ovulation; some also remain in the ovary where they form the corpus luteum

greenhouse effect – the reduction in loss of heat from the atmosphere caused by carbon dioxide and other gases, keeping the Earth warmer than it would otherwise be

greenhouse gas – a gas which contributes to the greenhouse effect; for example, carbon dioxide, methane

H band – part of a sarcomere where only myosin filaments are present

haematocrit – the percentage of blood volume that is taken up by cells

haemodialysis – a form of dialysis in which blood is passed through a machine where it is separated from dialysis fluid by a partially permeable membrane

haemoglobin dissociation curve – a graph showing how the degree to which haemoglobin is combined with oxygen varies with increasing oxygen concentration

haemoglobinic acid – a compound formed by the combination of haemoglobin with hydrogen ions

haploid – containing one set of chromosomes

Hardy-Weinberg equations – a pair of equations linking the frequencies of two alleles and of the three associated genotypes in a population

heat stroke – a condition in which the body is overheated and unable to lower its temperature

heroin – an opiate drug

heterozygous – having two different alleles of a gene

hippocampus – part of the limbic system involved in memory

histology – the study of tissues

HLA – human leucocyte antigen system; a group of antigens found in the cell surface membranes of most body cells

homeostasis – the maintenance of a constant internal environment

homologous chromosomes – two chromosomes carrying the same genes at the same loci

homozygous – having two identical alleles of a gene

hormone replacement therapy – see HRT

hot flush – a feeling of heat, often accompanied by sweating, associated with the loss of oestrogen during the menopause

HRT – hormone replacement therapy; the use of oestrogen, with or without progesterone, to alleviate symptoms of the menopause

human chorionic gonadotrophin – a glycoprotein hormone secreted by an early embryo

human growth hormone – a protein hormone secreted from the anterior pituitary gland which stimulates growth and strength of bones and muscles

human leucocyte antigen system – see HLA

human placental lactogen – a peptide hormone secreted from the placenta, which may enable oestrogen and progesterone to stimulate the growth of breast tissue

huntingtin – a protein of unknown function, defects in which may cause Huntington's disease

hyperglycaemia – having too high a level of blood glucose

hyperthermia – a body temperature significantly above normal

hypoglycaemia – having too low a level of blood glucose

hypothalamus – part of the brain that regulates the autonomic nervous system and is involved in homeostasis

hypothermia – a body temperature lower than 35 °C

I band – part of a sarcomere where only actin filaments are present

ICSI – intracytoplasmic sperm injection; the injection of a sperm into an oocyte, used as part of fertility treatment

Implanon – a contraceptive that is implanted under a woman's skin, which inhibits ovulation

in vitro fertilisation – see IVF

independent assortment – the ability of either allele of one gene to end up in the same gamete as either allele of another gene, following meiosis in a heterozygous cell; it results from the independent arrangement of maternal and paternal chromosomes in their homologous pairs during metaphase I

infertility – the inability to conceive a child after trying for 12 months

inhibin – a hormone released by Sertoli cells which inhibits FSH secretion

insulin – a peptide hormone secreted by the beta cells in the islets of Langerhans in the pancreas, which reduces blood glucose levels

intensive farming – using high inputs and high stocking densities to achieve high outputs of crops or other products from a relatively small area of land

interleukin – a cytokine secreted by T lymphocytes

intermediate neurone – a neurone in the spinal cord or brain, which has synapses with both a sensory neurone and a motor neurone

intracytoplasmic sperm injection – see ICSI

intra-uterine insemination – the insertion of semen into the uterus, used as part of fertility treatment

iodopsin – the light-sensitive pigment in cones

iris – coloured tissue containing circular and longitudinal muscles that can alter the size of the pupil in response to different intensities of light

iris reflex – the alteration of the size of the pupil in response to a change in light intensity; also known as the pupil reflex

IUD – intra-uterine device; a small piece of coiled copper that is placed inside the uterus, and inhibits fertilisation and implantation

IVF – in vitro fertilisation; the addition of sperm to oocytes outside the body in a Petri dish, for example

ketoacidosis – a condition associated with a high level of ketone bodies in the blood

ketone bodies – substances produced from the metabolism of fatty acids in the liver

Krebs cycle – a series of reactions that take place in the matrix of a mitochondrion when oxygen is available, in which acetyl CoA is combined with oxaloacetate and then re-converted to oxaloacetate; it is part of aerobic respiration

lactate pathway – the conversion of pyruvate to lactate, in which reduced NAD is converted to NAD; it takes place when oxygen is not available and is part of anaerobic respiration

lactate threshold – the point at which oxygen begins to run out and muscles respire anaerobically, producing lactate

lens – a structure made of transparent cells that determines the fine focussing of light rays to form a clear image on the retina

levodopa – a drug used to treat Parkinson's disease

Leydig cell – a cell in the tissue between the seminiferous tubules in a testis, which secretes testosterone; also known as interstitial cell

LH – luteinising hormone; a peptide hormone secreted by the anterior pituitary gland; sometimes known as interstitial cell stimulating hormone in men

ligase – see DNA ligase

limbic system – an association area in the cerebrum responsible for emotions and memory

link reaction – a reaction that takes place in the matrix of a mitochondrion, in which pyruvate is converted to acetyl CoA

linkage – see autosomal linkage, sex linkage

locus – the position of a gene on a chromosome

loop of Henlé – the part of a nephron which forms a hairpin loop dipping down into the medulla of a kidney

luteinising hormone – see LH

M line – a darkly staining line in a myofibril, to which the myosin filaments are attached

macula – the part of the retina where cone cells are packed most tightly; also known as the fovea

major histocompatibility complex – see MHC

medulla (kidney) – the inner layers of a kidney

medulla oblongata – the part of the brain next to the spinal cord, which controls involuntary movements; sometimes simply called the medulla

meiosis – a type of cell division in which one diploid cell forms four haploid cells

meninges – the membranes that surround the brain and spinal cord

menopause – the cessation of the menstrual cycle

menstrual cycle – an approximately 28-day cycle of hormonal secretion and activity in the ovaries and uterus

menstruation – the breakdown and loss of the lining of the endometrium

metabolic pathway – a series of enzyme-controlled reactions; for example, glycolysis

metaphase – the stage in cell division in which chromosomes are lined up on the equator

MHC – major histocompatibility complex; a group of genes on chromosome 6, which code for the human leucocyte antigens

monoclonal antibodies – a group of identical antibodies

monohybrid inheritance – the inheritance of one gene

monozygotic twins – twins developed from a single egg; they are genetically identical

morphine – an opiate drug

motor area – a part of the cerebrum from which action potentials are sent to effectors

motor neurone – a neurone that transmits action potentials from the central nervous system to an effector

motor unit – a group of muscle fibres all supplied by the same neurone

MRI scan – magnetic resonance imaging; images of the inside of the body are built up using differences in magnetic field strength

muscle fibre – a long, cylindrical syncitium (a 'cell' containing many nuclei), in skeletal muscle

muscular dystrophy – *see* Duchenne muscular dystrophy

mutation – a random and unpredictable change in the base sequence of a gene or in the structure or number of chromosomes

myelin sheath – a material made of many cell surface membranes packed tightly together, which acts as an electric insulator around the axon of a neurone

myofibril – a long, thin cylinder containing actin and myosin filaments, one of many that lie side by side within a muscle fibre

myoglobin – a globular protein; a respiratory pigment present in muscle cells, which acts as a store for oxygen

myometrium – the muscular outer wall of the uterus

myosin – a fibrous protein that makes up the thick filaments in a myofibril

NAD – nicotinamide adenine dinucleotide; a co-enzyme that picks up hydrogen during glycolysis and other metabolic reactions

NADP – a coenzyme that accepts hydrogen ions during the light-dependent reaction of photosynthesis

nail patella syndrome – a genetic condition in which fingernails and kneecaps may develop abnormally

nandrolone – a breakdown product of anabolic steroids, that can be detected in urine

natural selection – the differential survival of individuals with different characteristics; those with features that provide better adaptation to their environment are more likely to survive and reproduce

negative feedback – a mechanism for keeping a parameter relatively constant; a shift away from the norm brings about actions that reverse the shift

nephron – a kidney tubule; one of many thousands in which urine is produced in the kidneys

nerve – a bundle of processes (axons) of neurones

nerve conduction velocity test – a test done to determine the speed at which neurones are conducting impulses

nerve growth factors – chemicals that help damaged neurones to regrow

nerve impulse – an action potential

neuromuscular junction – a synapse between a motor neurone and a muscle fibre

neurone – a nerve cell; a cell that is adapted for the rapid transmission of action potentials

nitric oxide – a gaseous hormone produced by blood vessel walls in conditions of low oxygen concentration, and which causes the smooth muscle in arteriole walls to relax

nitrogenous excretory product – an unwanted nitrogen-containing product of metabolism that is excreted; in humans the main one is urea

node of Ranvier – a gap in the myelin sheath around the axon of a neurone

non-disjunction – the failure of homologous chromosomes to separate during meiosis I

noradrenaline – a neurotransmitter involved, for example, in the sympathetic nervous system

nurse cell – *see* Sertoli cell

oestrogen – a steroid hormone secreted by the ovaries

oogonium – a diploid cell derived from the germinal epithelium of an ovary, which can divide to form a primary oocyte

opiates – a class of drug derived from opium poppies, including heroin, opium, pethidine, morphine

opium – an opiate drug

optic nerve – the nerve that carries impulses between the eye and the brain

optometry – the testing and measurement of eye function

osmoreceptors – cells that detect changes in water potential

osmoregulation – the control of water balance

osteoarthritis – a disease in which the surfaces of bones at joints become rough, making movement difficult and painful

oestoblast – a cell that builds up bone tissue

osteoclast – a cell that breaks down bone tissue

osteoporosis – a serious drop in bone density

ovarian follicle – a follicle within an ovary containing a secondary oocyte

ovary – the organ in which oogenesis takes place

overgrazing – allowing so many animals to graze on an area of land that the soil and vegetation is damaged

oviduct – a tube linking an ovary to the uterus; also called Fallopian tube

ovulation induction – the stimulation of ovulation in a woman in whom it does not naturally happen

oxaloacetate – a 4-carbon compound that is an intermediary in the Krebs cycle

oxidation – the addition of oxygen, loss of hydrogen or loss of electrons

oxidative phosphorylation – the formation of ATP in a process which involves the acceptance of electrons and hydrogen ions by oxygen

oxidoreductase – an enzyme that catalyses oxidation and reduction reactions

oxygen affinity – the ease with which a respiratory pigment picks up oxygen

oxygen debt – the extra oxygen that is required by the body after exercise has taken place, in order to convert lactate (formed in anaerobic respiration) to pyruvate; *see also* EPOC

oxygen deficit – the shortfall in the oxygen that is required by muscles

oxyhaemoglobin – haemoglobin that is combined with oxygen

oxytocin – a peptide hormone secreted by the posterior pituitary gland, which stimulates contraction of the myometrium at birth, and of milk ducts during lactation which enables milk to flow from the breast into the nipple

parasympathetic nervous system – the part of the autonomic nervous system in which the motor neurones have cell bodies inside the spinal cord or the brain, and which uses acetylcholine as a neurotransmitter

pedigree analysis – using information about the phenotypes of individuals in different generations of a family to determine their genotypes

peripheral – near the outside or edge

peripheral nervous sytem – the nerves and sense organs

peritoneal dialysis – a form of dialysis in which dialysis fluid is passed into the peritoneal cavity in the abdomen

PET scan – positron emission tomography; images of the inside of the body are built up by picking up differences in the metabolic activity in the tissues

phenotype – the visible or measurable characteristics of an organism

phosphorylated nucleotide – a nucleotide to which phosphate groups are attached; for example, ATP

phosphorylation – the addition of phosphate to a molecule

physical dependency – a type of drug dependency in which the drug becomes part of metabolism and withdrawal symptoms are experienced if the drug is not taken

phytoestrogens – substances produced by plants that are similar to oestrogens

phytoplankton – microscopic photosynthetic organisms that float in the sea or fresh water

pioneer plant – a plant that is able to colonise land where no, or few, other plants are already growing

pituitary gland – an endocrine gland attached to the hypothalamus which releases a number of hormones that control the activities of other endocrine glands

plagioclimax – a climax community whose composition is affected by human activities; for example, farming

plasmid – a small circular molecule of DNA found in bacteria

podocyte – a cell with many projecting fingers, making up the inner wall of a Bowman's capsule

polar body – a very small cell formed after meiosis I and meiosis II in oogenesis

polycystic ovarian syndrome – a condition in which follicles within the ovary do not develop properly, leading to infertility

postsynaptic neurone – the neurone along which an impulse travels from a synapse

presynaptic neurone – the neurone along which an impulse arrives at a synapse

primary consumers – herbivores

primary oocyte – a diploid cell formed by growth of an oogonium

primary sensory area – a part of the cerebrum that receives impulses from sense organs

primary spermatocyte – a diploid cell formed by growth of a spermatogonium

primary succession – succession that begins on bare ground

producers – the organisms that first make organic nutrients in a food chain, normally by photosynthesis

progesterone – a steroid hormone secreted by the ovaries, especially the corpus luteum, and also by the placenta

progestin – a synthetic form of progesterone

prolactin – a steroid hormone secreted from the anterior pituitary gland, which stimulates the secretion of milk by the breasts

prophase – the first stage in cell division, in which chromosomes appear and the nuclear membrane and nucleolus disappear

prostate gland – a gland found where the vasa deferentia join the urethra, which secretes components of semen

proton – a positively charged particle found in the nucleus of an atom; a hydrogen ion

proximal convoluted tubule – the first part of a nephron, in which most reabsorption occurs

psychological dependency – a type of drug dependency in which a person craves the drug if it is not taken

pupil – the gap in the centre of the iris

pupil reflex – the alteration of the size of the pupil in response to a change in light intensity; also known as the iris reflex

pyruvate – a 3-carbon molecule that is the end product of glycolysis

radiation – a method of energy transfer; for example, the transfer of heat as infrared rays

RAPD – relative afferent pupillary defect; the inability of one or both eyes to show a pupil response reflex, which can indicate damage to the optic nerve

receptor – a cell or organ that detects a change in the external or internal environment

recessive allele – an allele which only affects phenotype when no dominant allele is present

recombinant – an organism possessing DNA from another organism

recombination – the appearance of new combinations of characteristics in offspring, as a result of crossing over during gamete formation

recreational – a way of using drugs in which the person takes them occasionally and does not suffer health problems or behavioural problems as a result

reduction – the loss of oxygen, gain of hydrogen or gain of electrons

reduction division – a term used to describe the first division of meiosis, in which the diploid number is reduced to the haploid number of chromosomes

reflex action – a rapid and automatic response to a stimulus, not involving conscious thought

reflex – a stereotyped, fast response to a stimulus

reflex arc – a pathway taken by a nerve impulse from receptor to effector, without involving areas of the brain responsible for conscious thought

refraction – the bending of light rays as they pass from one substance and into another

refractory period – a period following an action potential, during which another action potential cannot be produced

renal artery – an artery supplying oxygenated blood to the kidneys

renal capsule – a structure in the kidney cortex consisting of a Bowman's capsule and glomerulus

renal dialysis – *see* dialysis

renal vein – a vein removing deoxygenated blood from the kidneys

repolarisation – the re-establishment of the resting potential across the cell surface membrane of a neurone, following depolarisation

reproductive isolation – the inability of two populations of a species to breed together

respiration – the oxidation of glucose within a cell, releasing energy which can be used to make ATP

respiratory pigment – a molecule such as haemoglobin which combines reversibly with oxygen

respiratory quotient – *see* RQ

respiratory substrate – a substance, such as glucose, that can be metabolised to produce ATP by respiration

resting potential – a difference in charge across the cell surface membrane of a resting neurone, usually about 65 mV more negative inside than outside

restriction endonuclease – an enzyme made by bacteria that cuts DNA

retina – the part of the eye in which the receptors (rods and cones) are present

reverse transcriptase – an enzyme made by viruses that catalyses the production of DNA from RNA

Rhesus antigen (factor) – an antigen found on red blood cells; also known as Rhesus factor

rhodopsin – the light-sensitive pigment in rods

ribulose bisphosphate – *see* RuBP

ribulose bisphosphate carboxylase – *see* Rubisco

rod – a receptor cell in the retina which responds to low intensity light

RQ – respiratory quotient; the volume of carbon dioxide given out divided by the volume of oxygen taken in; its value indicates the type of substrate that is being respired

Rubisco – ribulose bisphosphate carboxylase; an enzyme that catalyses the combination of carbon dioxide with ribulose bisphosphate in the matrix of a chloroplast

RuBP – ribulose bisphosphate; a 5-carbon sugar that combines with carbon dioxide in the light-independent stage of photosynthesis

saltatory conduction – the transmission of an action potential along an axon, in which the action potential jumps from one node of Ranvier to the next

sarcolemma – the cell surface membrane of a muscle fibre

sarcomere – part of a muscle fibril between two Z lines

sarcoplasm – the cytoplasm of a muscle fibre

sarcoplasmic reticulum – the endoplasmic reticulum within a muscle fibre

Schwann cell – a glial cell that forms the myelin sheath around neurone axons

SCID – severe combined immunodeficiency disease; a rare inherited disease in which the immune system does not function

sclera – the tough, outer coat around the eye

secondary consumers – carnivores that eat herbivores

secondary oocyte – a haploid cell formed when a primary oocyte completes the first division of meiosis

secondary spermatocyte – a haploid cell formed when a primary spermatocyte completes the first division of meiosis

secondary succession – succession that begins when a community is already present in the habitat

selective reabsorption – taking substances back into the blood from the glomerular filtrate

semen – a fluid containing sperm, formed by the addition of secretions from the prostate gland and seminal vesicles

seminal vesicle – a gland found where the vasa deferentia join the urethra, which secretes components of semen

seminiferous tubule – one of the small tubes within a testis in which spermatogenesis takes place

senescence – deterioration of the body with age

sensory neurone – a neurone that transmits action potentials from a receptor to the central nervous system

sere – a stage in ecological succession

Sertoli cell – a large cell present in the seminiferous tubules, which assists the development of spermatids to spermatozoa

sex linkage – the appearance of a phenotype in one sex (usually men) more than in the other; it is a result of a gene locus being present on the non-homologous part of the X chromosome

sickle cell anaemia – a genetic disease caused by a faulty gene for haemoglobin; also known as sickle cell disease

sickle cell trait – a condition in which a person has one allele for normal haemoglobin and one for sickle cell haemoglobin

skeletal muscle – muscle tissue that is attached to the skeleton

sliding filament theory – the method by which muscle contraction is believed to occur, in which myosin and actin filaments slide between each other

slow-twitch fibre – a muscle fibre adapted for sustained activity

slurry – semi-liquid waste containing urine and faeces from farmed animals

Snellen chart – a standardised chart used to measure visual acuity

somatic cells – cells that are not involved in producing gametes

somatic nervous system – all the sensory neurones, and also all the motor neurones that innervate striated muscle

speciation – the production of a new species

species – a group of organisms that can interbreed amongst themselves, but cannot breed successfully with other species

sperm bank – a store of frozen sperm that can be used in fertility treatments

spermatid – a haploid cell formed when a secondary spermatocyte completes the second division of meiosis

spermatogonium – a diploid cell derived from the germinal epithelium of a testis, which can divide to form primary spermatocytes

spermatozoon – (sperm) a male gamete

spermicidal cream – a cream containing chemicals that kill sperm, used as a contraceptive

spinal nerve – a nerve from the spinal cord, containing processes from both sensory and motor neurones

sporadic case – a case of a genetic disease appearing for the first time in a family

sterilisation (contraceptive) – surgery which blocks the vasa deferentia or oviducts, so preventing fertilisation

steroid – a type of substance whose molecules are similar in structure to cholesterol; progesterone, oestrogen and testosterone are examples of steroids

sticky ends – unpaired regions at the ends of a DNA molecule

striated muscle – muscle tissue which appears striped when stained and seen under the microscope, because of the arrangement of myosin and actin within it; skeletal muscle and cardiac muscle are striated

stroke – damage to the brain caused by a blockage of blood flow or a burst blood vessel

substantia nigra – a part of the brain damage to which causes Parkinson's disease

succession – the directional change over time in a community in a habitat, leading to a climax community

suspensory ligament – a circular band of ligaments that supports the lens in the eye

sustainable – able to be maintained for many years

sweat gland – a gland in the dermis of the skin that secretes sweat

sympathetic nervous system – the part of the autonomic nervous system in which the motor neurones have their cell bodies in ganglia close to the spinal cord, and which uses noradrenaline as a neurotransmitter

synapse – an area where two neurones meet

synaptic cleft – a 20 nm wide cleft between two neurones at a synapse

syncitium – a 'cell' containing many nuclei; for example, a muscle fibre

target cells – cells which possess receptors for a hormone, and so can be affected by it

tau – a protein that forms 'tangles' in neurones in the brain, in Alzheimer's disease

taxonomy – the study of classification

telophase – the stage in cell division in which chromosomes decondense and nuclear membranes re-form

testis – the organ in which spermatogenesis takes place

testosterone – a steroid hormone secreted by the testes and ovaries

theca – a layer of cells surrounding a follicle in an ovary

therapeutic – beneficial to health

thick filament – a group of myosin molecules within a myofibril

thin filament – a filament made from many actin molecules, found within a myofibril

thyroid gland – an endocrine gland in the neck, which secretes thyroxine

thyroid stimulating hormone – *see* TSH

thyrotrophin releasing hormone – *see* TRH

thyroxine – a hormone containing iodine, secreted by the thyroid gland, that increases metabolic rate

tissue – a group of similar cells that work together to carry out a particular function

tissue typing – checking the antigens in cell membranes

tolerance (to drugs) – the need for increasing quantities of a drug to maintain the same effect

translocation – the transfer of a piece of one chromosome to another

transmitter substance – a chemical that is made and stored in the presynaptic neurone, and that diffuses across the synaptic cleft and affects the polarisation of the membrane of the postsynaptic neurone

traumatic brain injury – physical damage to the brain caused by a blow to the head

TRH – thyrotrophin releasing hormone; a hormone produced by the hypothalamus which stimulates production of thyroid stimulating hormone by the anterior pituitary gland

triose phosphate – a 3-carbon phosphorylated sugar that is an intermediary in the light-independent stages of photosynthesis and in glycolysis

trisomy 21 – the possession of three chromosome 21s, causing Down's syndrome

trophic level – a stage in a food chain

tropomyosin – a fibrous protein which twists around the actin filaments in a myofibril

troponin – a protein that is closely associated with actin and tropomyosin filaments in a myofibril

TSH – thyroid stimulating hormone; a hormone secreted from the anterior pituitary gland which stimulates the release of thyroxine from the thyroid gland

T-tubule – an infolding from the sarcolemma that runs deep into the muscle fibre

tubal ligation – surgery which blocks the oviducts

tympanic membrane – the ear drum

type I diabetes – a form of diabetes mellitus which develops at a very young age, associated with an inability of beta cells to secrete insulin

type II diabetes – a form of diabetes mellitus which normally develops in later life, associated with a lack of response of target cells to insulin

ultrafiltration – filtration on a molecular scale

urea – the main nitrogenous excretory product of humans

ureter – a tube that carries urine from a kidney to the bladder

urethra – the tube that carries urine from the bladder to the outside of the body; in men, it also carries semen

urinogenital system – the urinary and reproductive systems

uterus – the organ in which a foetus develops

vagina – the passage from the uterus to the outside of the body

vagus nerve – part of the parasympathetic nervous system, containing motor neurones that carry impulses from the brain to the viscera

vas deferens – the tube linking the testis and urethra

vasectomy – surgery which blocks the vasa deferentia

vasoconstriction – the narrowing of arterioles

vasodilation – the widening of arterioles

vector – an organism that transmits DNA (or a disease such as malaria) from one organism to another

ventral root – the branch of a spinal nerve that enters the ventral region of the spinal cord

ventricle (of brain) – a space within the brain that contains cerebrospinal fluid

viscera – the internal organs; for example, the alimentary canal, heart, lungs

visual acuity – the ability of the eye to perceive sharply focussed images

vitreous humour – the viscous fluid that fills the eye behind the lens

VO$_2$max – the maximum rate at which oxygen can be used before muscles have to switch to anaerobic respiration

Wernicke's area – part of an association area in the left cerebral hemisphere responsible for understanding language

wind chill – a perceived lowering of temperature because of wind movement

xenotransplant – a transplant from an organism of a different species

Z line – a darkly staining line in a myofibril, to which the actin filaments are attached

zona pellucida – a protective layer of glycoproteins surrounding a secondary oocyte

zygote – a diploid cell formed by the fusion of two haploid cells

Index

physical dependency 94
phytoestrogens 257
phytoplankton 157
pigments 53
pituitary gland 78, 243
placenta 118, 119
plagioclimax 151
plasmid 196–199
Plasmodium 179
podocytes 238
polar body 112–113
pollution, of water 152–153
polycystic ovarian syndrome 133
population 166–170
potassium ion channels 54, 68
pregnancy testing 139
primary consumers 159
primary sensory area 80
primary succession 150
progesterone 46, 114–116, 118–119, 133
progestin 254–255
prolactin 119, 120
prophase 105–106
prostate cancer 259–261
prostate gland 102, 259
proton leak 16
proximal convoluted tubule 239–240, 242
psychological dependency 94
pupil response test 60–61
pyruvate 11–12, 19–20

radiation 218
RAPD (relative afferent pupillary defect) 60
receptor cells 50
receptors 65, 215–216, 219
recessive allele 173
recombinant plasmid 196–199
recombination 190–191
recreational drug use 93
rectal temperature 219, 222
reflex action 60–61, 65
reflex arc 65
refraction 51–52
refractory period 68
rehabilitation therapy 88, 90
renal artery 237
renal capsule 237–238
renal dialysis 248–249
renal vein 237
replica plating 198
repolarisation 67
respiration 10–21, 30, 267
respiratory disease 267
respiratory pigments 36–40

respiratory quotient 31–32
respiratory substrates 29–30
resting potential 54, 66
restriction enzyme 196–197
retina 51, 53–55, 57, 264
retinal 55
retrovirus 200
reverse transcriptase 196
rheumatoid arthritis 265
rhodopsin 53–55
ribulose bisphosphate 158–159
ribulose bisphosphate carboxylase 158
rod cell 51, 53–55
RQ 31–32
Rubisco 158
RuBP 158–159

saltatory conduction 68–69
sarcolemma 4–5
sarcoplasmic reticulum 4–5
Schwann cell 63–64
SCID 200
sclera 51
secondary consumers 159
selection 179
selective reabsorption 239–240
semen 117
seminal vesicle 102
seminiferous tubules 110–111
sensory neurone 64
sere 150
Sertoli cells 110–111, 114
sex linkage 179–180, 201
sickle cell anaemia 178–179
single gene inheritance 172–184
sino-atrial node 76
skeletal muscle 3–9
sliding filament theory 6–7
slow-twitch muscle 25, 28
slurry 152
Snellen chart 59
sodium ion channels 54, 68, 72
sodium–potassium pump 66
somatic cell 204
somatic nervous system 75
speciation 211–212
species 209–212
sperm bank 136
spermatids 110–111
spermatocytes 110–111
spermatogenesis 110–111, 114
spermatogonia 110–111
spermatozoa 110–111
spermicidal cream 124
spinal cord 65, 78–79
spinal cord injury 85–88

spinal reflex 65
spindle 105–106
spirometer 33
sporadic cases 177
stem cells 88, 263
sterilisation 126
steroid hormones 114
steroids 46–47
sticky ends 196–197
striated muscle 3–9
striatum 95
stroke 84–85, 88–90
substantia nigra 94–95
succession 150–151
suspensory ligament 51–52
sustainable farming 146
sweat glands 220
sympathetic nervous system 23, 75–76, 220
synapses 71–75
synaptic cleft 72
syncitium 4

T lymphocytes 200
target cells 228
tau 262
taxonomy 210–211
TBI 84
telophase 105–106
temperature regulation 217–227
temporal lobe 80
tertiary consumers 159
testis 102
testosterone 114
thalamus 78
THC 97
thecal cells 113
therapeutic drugs 92
thermogenesis 220–221
thyroid gland 221
thyroxine 221–222
tissue typing 208–209
training 23–27
transgenic organisms 195–199
translocation 193
transmitter substance 63, 72
transplants 207–209, 212–213, 249
transporter proteins 172
traumatic brain injury 84
TRH 221
triose phosphate 158–159
trisomy 193
trophic factors 87
trophic levels 159–160
tropomyosin 6–7
troponin 6–7
TSH 221